Democracy and Socialism in Republican China

The Politics of Zhang Junmai (Carsun Chang), 1906–1941

Roger B. Jeans, Jr.

ROWMAN & LITTLEFIELD PUBLISHERS, INC.
Lanham • Boulder • New York • Oxford

ROWMAN & LITTLEFIELD PUBLISHERS, INC.

Published in the United States of America
by Rowman & Littlefield Publishers, Inc.
4720 Boston Way, Lanham, Maryland 20706

12 Hid's Copse Road
Cummor Hill, Oxford OX2 9JJ, England

British Library Cataloguing in Publication Information Available

Library of Congress Cataloging-in-Publication Data

Jeans, Roger B.
Democracy and socialism in Republican China : the politics of Zhang Junmai (Carsun Chang), 1906-1941 / Roger B. Jeans.
p. cm.
Includes bibliographical references and index.
ISBN 0-8476-8706 (cloth : alk. paper). – ISBN 0-8476-8707-4 (pbk. : alk. paper)
1. Chang, Chün-mai, 1886-1969–Political and social views.
I. Title.
DS778.C4919D46 1997 97-183347
CIP

ISBN 0-8476-8706-6 (cloth : alk. paper)
ISBN 0-8476-8707-4 (pbk. : alk. paper)

Printed in the United States of America

™ The paper used in this publication meets the minimum requirements of American National Standard for Information Sciences—Permanence of Paper for Printed Library Materials, ANSI Z39.48–1984.

Democracy and Socialism in Republican China

For Sylvia

and Our Parents:

Joe (1918-1997) and Belle

Roger Sr. and Shirley

Contents

Illustrations

Maps
Following Page xv

Photographs
Following Page 147

Acknowledgments

Despite popular belief, the making of a book is not a solitary occupation. I have accumulated many debts during the years of work, and it is a pleasure, at long last, to have the opportunity to thank the many who lent a helping hand. For financial support, I am grateful to Washington and Lee University, which has supported my summer and sabbatical research and writing with grants from the John M. Glenn Fund, the Andrew W. Mellon Foundation, the Class of '62 Fellowship, the Class of '39 International Studies Fund, and the Emory Kimbrough Fund. The Elizabeth Lewis Otey Professorship in East Asian History, established through the kindness of Elizabeth Lewis Otey Watson, has also provided support for this work. I am indebted to William T. Murphy and his son, Thomas H. Murphy ('77), for generous aid over the years.

The staffs of many libraries and archives have helped with this project: the Library of Congress's Chinese Section, the National Archives, Hoover Institution's East Asian Collection and Archives, University of Washington's East Asian Library, Columbia University's East Asian Library and East Asian Institute's Chinese Oral History Project, Dwight D. Eisenhower Library, Herbert Hoover Library, George C. Marshall Research Library, Rockefeller Archive Center, Franklin D. Roosevelt Library, Harry S. Truman Library, Second Historical Archives, Nanjing Library, Nanjing University Library, Beijing University Library, Beijing Library, Chinese Academy of Social Sciences' Institute of Modern History, Central China Teachers College Library, Hubei Provincial Library, Wuhan Municipal Library, Southwest Teachers College Library, Yunnan University Library, Yunnan Provincial Library, Shanghai Academy of Social Sciences' Institute of History Library, Shanghai Library, Universities Service Centre, University of Hong Kong Library, Academia Sinica's Institute of Modern History and Fu Ssu-nien Library, Kuomintang Party Archives, Academia Historica (Guoshiguan), Yangmingshan Library, Taiwan University Library, Toyo Bunko, Kyoto University's Institute for Research in the Humanities, British Library, Public Record Office, and School of Oriental and African Studies Library.

Librarians, archivists, and colleagues who have been especially helpful include Joy Pui-fun Au-yeung, W. G. Beasley, Terry Bishop, Robert J. C. Butow, Chang P'eng-yuan, Chen Qinghua, Ch'eng Wen-hsi, Ping-feng Chi, James H. Cole, Anthony R. Crawford, Dai Xugong, John Dolfin, Glen Dudbridge, Feng Yurong, Hisako Honjo, Huang Chi-lu, Robert L. Irick, Jiang Shaozhen, Maria Keipert, Edward Krebs, Li Yun-han, Mao Jiaqi, Sharon Nolte, Kazuko Ono, David Pong, Kenneth W. Rose, Lawrence N. Shyu, Robert Scalapino, Philip Shen, Tilman Spengler, Mark Tam, Yasuko Tanaka, Tang Zhijun, John E. Taylor, Phyliss Waldman, C. Martin Wilbur, Hellmut Wilhelm, Wu Guilong, Wu Qiandui, Xie Benshu, Tatsuo Yamada, Sung L. Yao, Zhang Xianwen, and Zhang Zhongli. I am deeply grateful to Zhang Kaiyuan, who made possible my research trip to China in 1981-82. Finally, it was my teacher, the late Franz H. Michael, who inspired—and continues to inspire—me, for which I am eternally grateful.

At a crucial moment in the life of this book, Lamar Cecil, Joanne Sandstrom, and Frederic Wakeman encouraged me. My colleagues at Washington and Lee have been ever ready to offer assistance. Especially helpful have been John Elrod, Richard Grefe, Marshall Jarrett, Barry Machado, Robert McAhren, Henry Porter, Ken White, John Wilson, Mary Woodson and the late Minor Rogers.

For indispensable assistance with Chinese, German, and Japanese language problems, I am grateful to Jing Bennett, James Chang, Luke L. Chang, Winnie Chow, David F. Connor, Clara K. S. Yue Dean, Goetz B. Eaton, Tomoko Hisano, Stephen A. Jones, Regin Keung, Isabella W. P. Lam, Betty Siu-man Lee, Cindy Lin, Alice Wai-ping Lo, Ione Lo, Kathleen A. Morrison, Ann Rogers, William B. Sherwin, and Robert Youngblood. Harold Hill rendered valuable assistance in preparation of the glossary. I am grateful to I-hsiung Ju, who prepared the beautiful calligraphy for the cover of the paperback edition. Thanks also to Pat Hinely, who reproduced the photographs.

Any acknowledgments would be incomplete without thanking the Chang and Wang families. Diana Tun-hua Chang has patiently answered my questions about her father for twenty-five years. Zhang Junmai's siblings, Chang Kia-ngau, C. C. Chang (Zhang Jiazhu), and Chang Yu-i (Zhang Youyi) kindly allowed me to interview them and conscientiously answered my letters. Zhang Junmai's son, Chang Kuo-liu, and daughter, June Tun-fu Tung, generously lent me precious photographs, as did Pang-Mei Natasha Chang, who allowed me to reproduce pictures from the Hsu Chi-kai family album.

Three people in particular helped make this book a reality. Betsy Brittigan has been more of a research assistant than an interlibrary loan librarian, ever cheerful and eager to help. Jennifer Ashworth worked long hours to ensure the manuscript was error-free and properly formatted. Susan McEachern, executive editor at Rowman and Littlefield, made clear once again why her name appears in the acknowledgments of so many books by proving to be the ideal editor.

This book is dedicated to my wife, Sylvia, and our parents, especially Sylvia's father, who did not live to see this book. He was a second father, as well as friend, for thirty years.

It goes without saying that none of the people cited above bear any responsibility for this book. Its shortcomings are mine alone.

A Note on Romanization

Since the pinyin system is used in most scholarly and popular writings about China at present and is the official romanization system in the People's Republic of China, I have used it in place of the older Wade-Giles for most names and terms in this book.

Our subject almost always signed his Chinese-language books and articles with the characters for "Zhang Junmai," while he invariably used "Carsun Chang" when publishing or writing in English. Since he also is known by other names or romanizations (Chang Chia-sen, Chang Chün-mai), I have included these in the book's index with cross-references to the form used throughout this work, Zhang Junmai.

In cases where a person is universally known in the West by a particular romanized form, such as Chiang Kai-shek, or has published books in English under a certain name, such as Chang Kia-ngau (Zhang Jiaao, Chang Chia-ao, Zhang Gongquan, Chang Kung-ch'uan), the decision has been made to leave the name in the older and more familiar historical form. In any event, the Chinese characters for names (and various terms) are listed in the glossary.

Abbreviations Used in the Notes

(Full details on these sources may be found in the bibliography.)

BDRC	Boorman and Howard, *Biographical Dictionary of Republican China*
GBFO	Great Britain Foreign Office
GS	Li Dasheng, "Guoshi: Zhang Junmai xiansheng"
LHWLX	Wu Xiangxiang, "Zhang Junmai laohe wanlixin"
NA	National Archives (U.S.)
NBCB	Cheng Wenxi, "Junmai xiansheng nianbiao changbian"
NP	Ding Wenjiang, *Liang Rengong xiansheng nianpu.*
SEPL	Zhang Junmai, *SuE pinglun*
STLZX	Zhang Junmai, *Shitailin zhixia zhi SuE*
USDS	United States Department of State
WCSH	Zhang Junmai, "Wo cong shehui kexue tiaodao zhexue zhi jingguo"
XDG	Zhang Junmai, *Xin Deguo shehui minzhu zhengxiang ji*
YX	Cheng Wenxi, "Junmai xiansheng zhi yanxing"

CONTEMPORARY CHINA

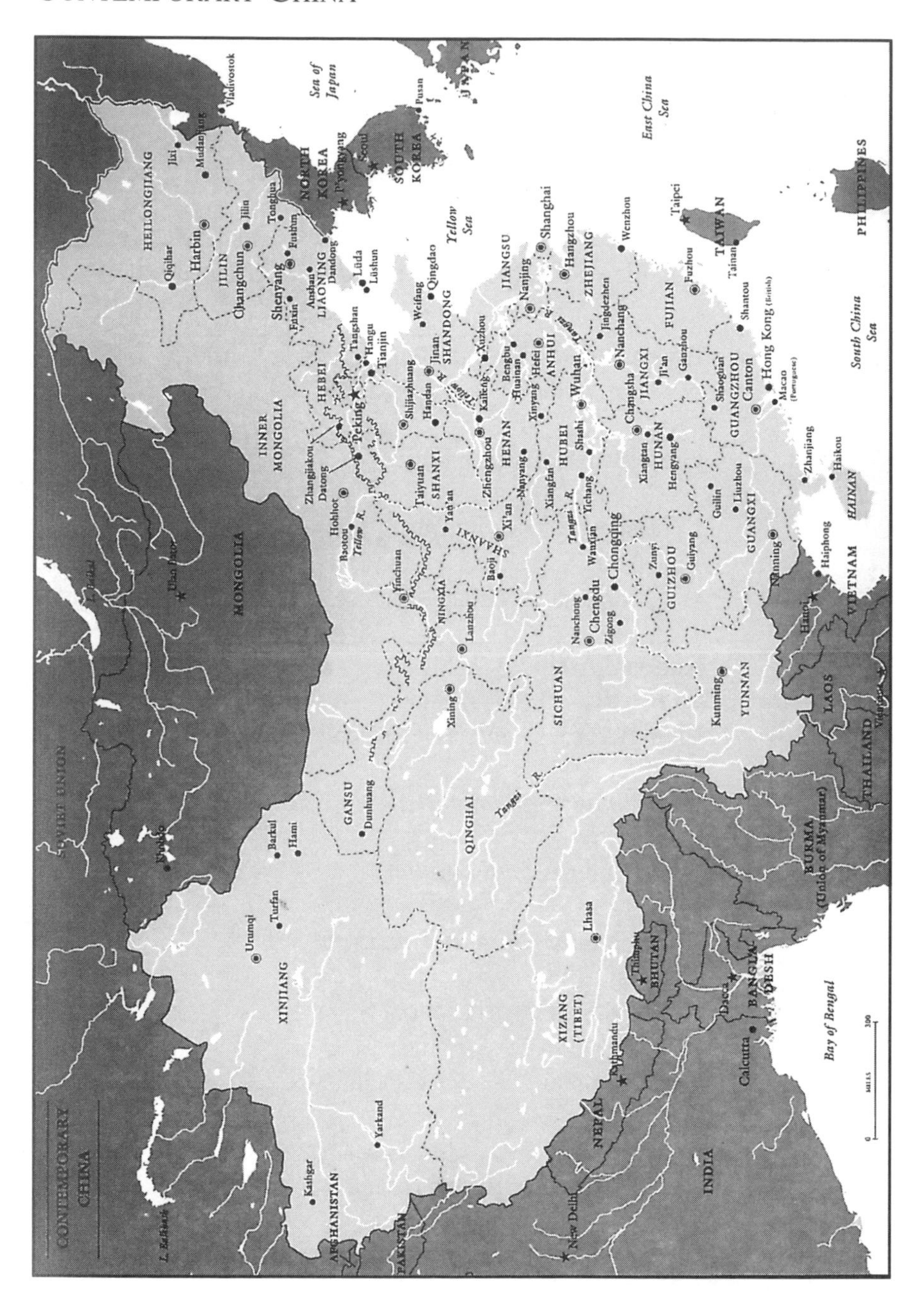

SOUTHWEST CHINA

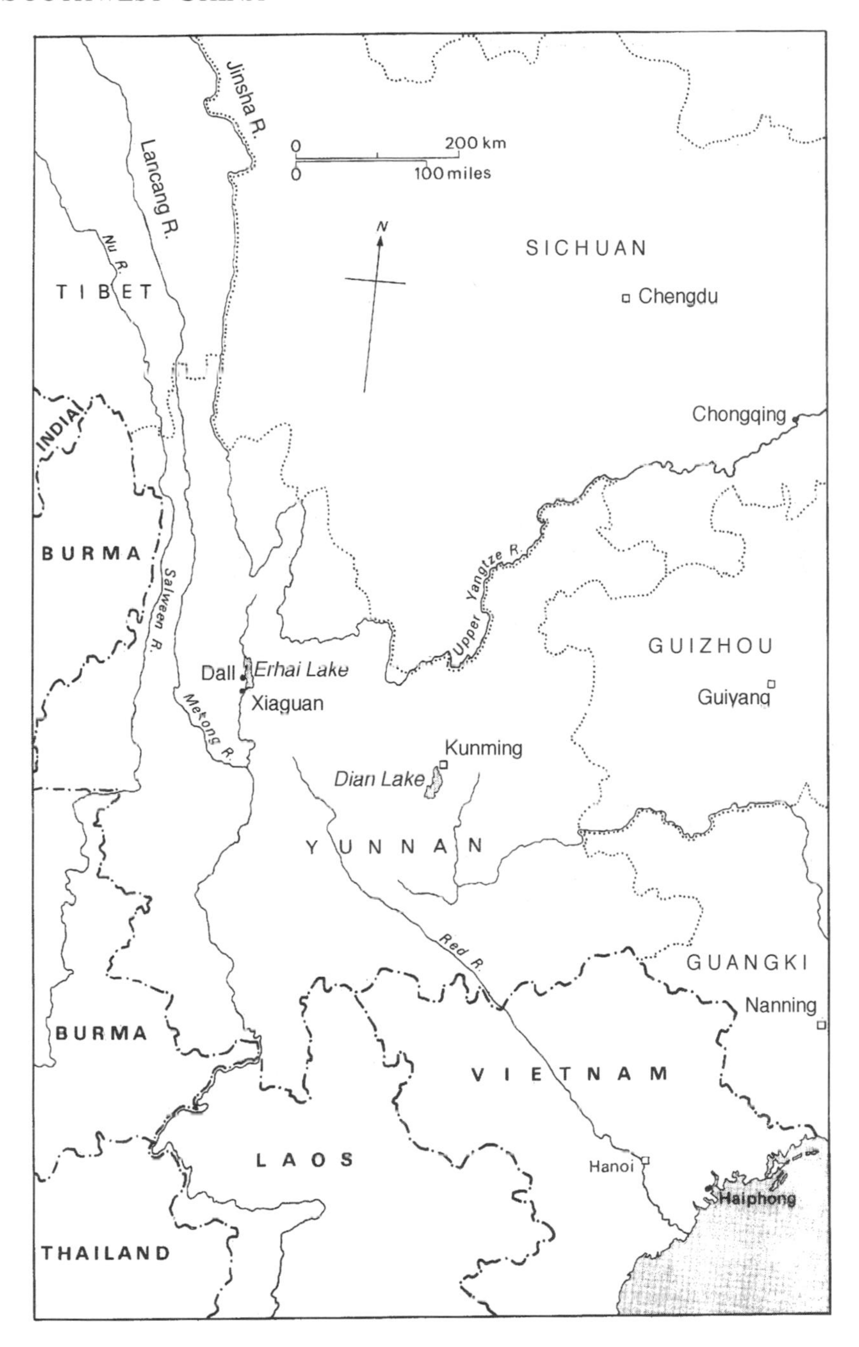

Reprinted, with permission and minor changes, from Charles Backus, *The Nanchao Kingdom and T'ang China's Southwestern Frontier* (Cambridge University Press, 1981).

Shanghai City

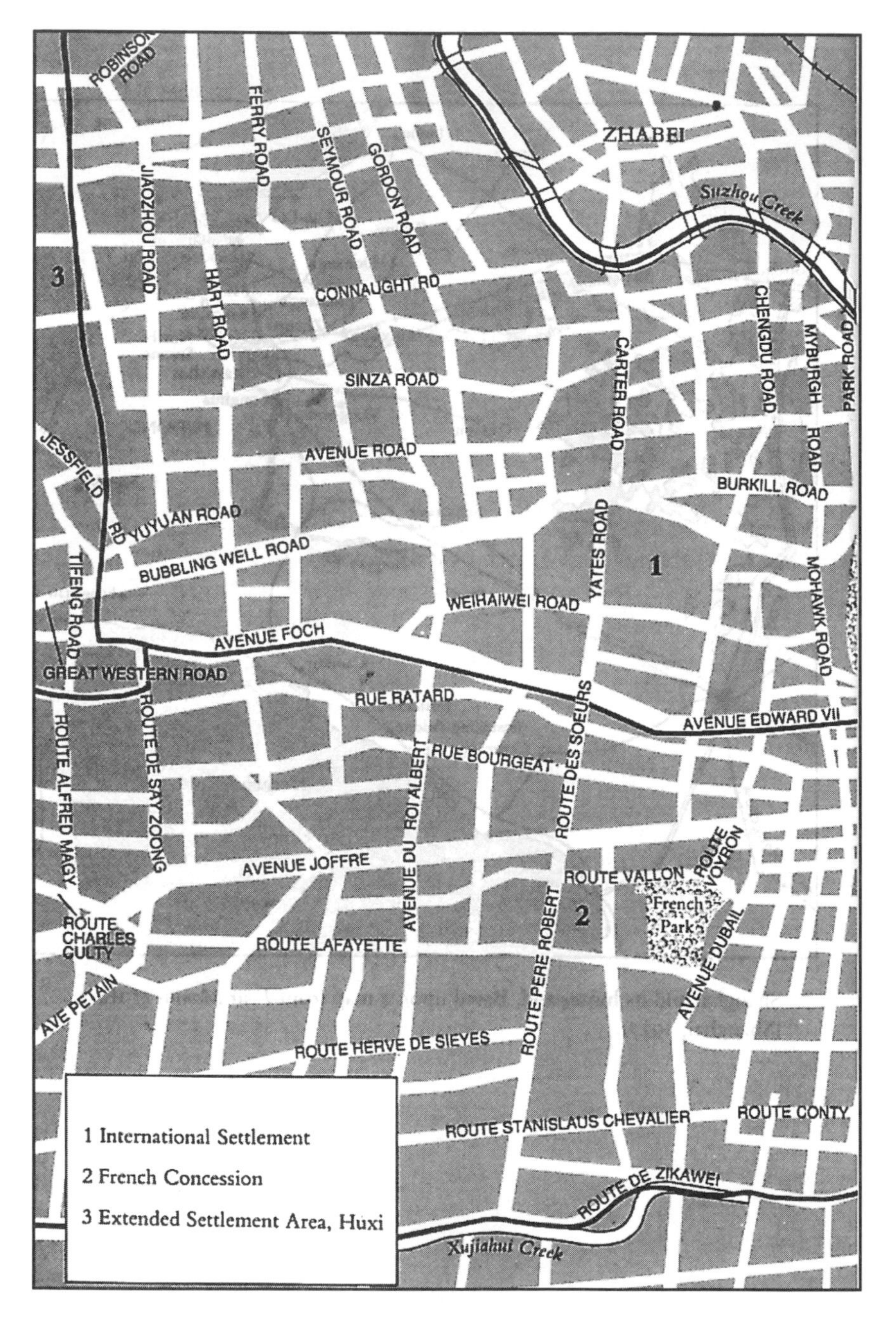

SHANGHAI CITY

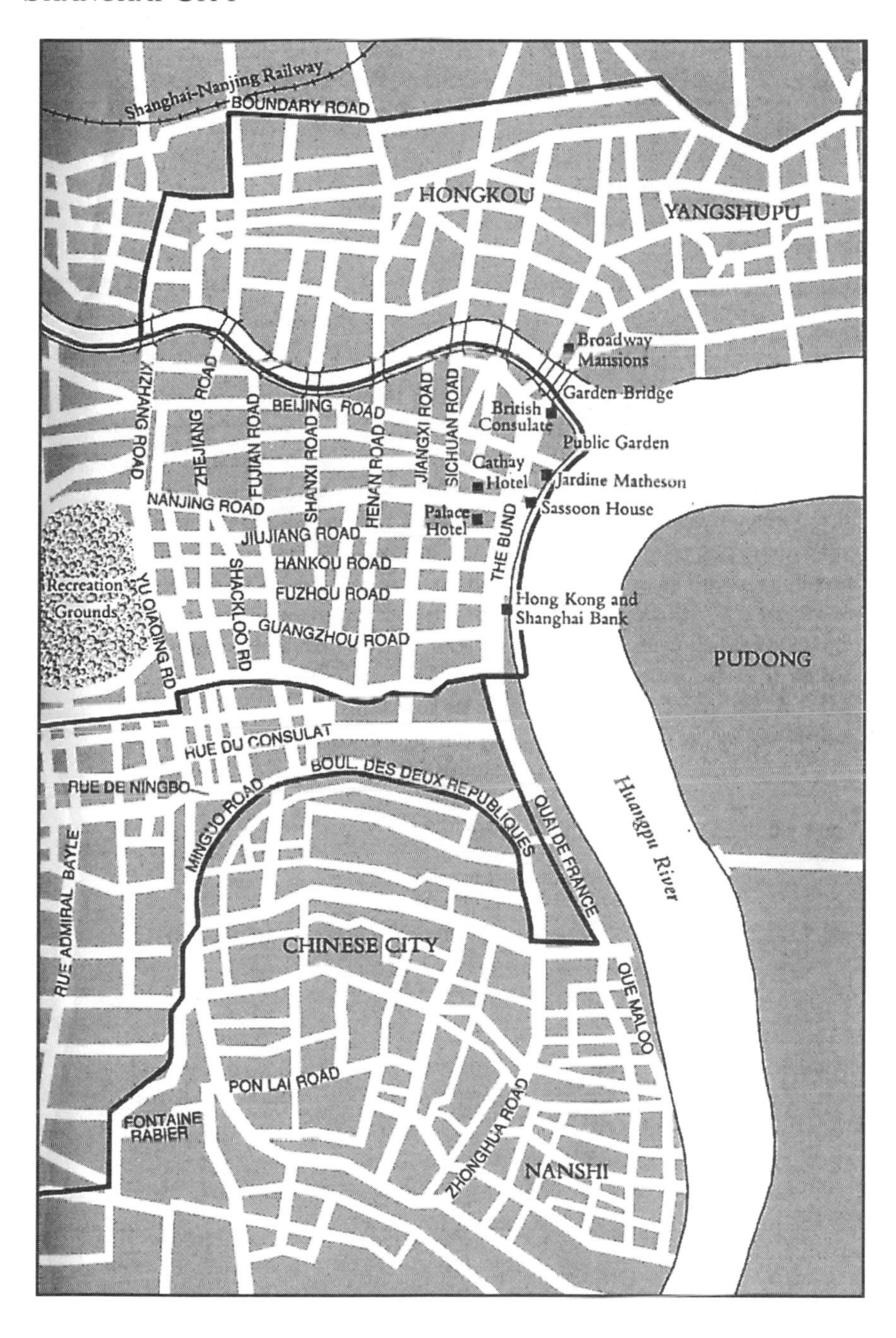

THE SHANGHAI AREA

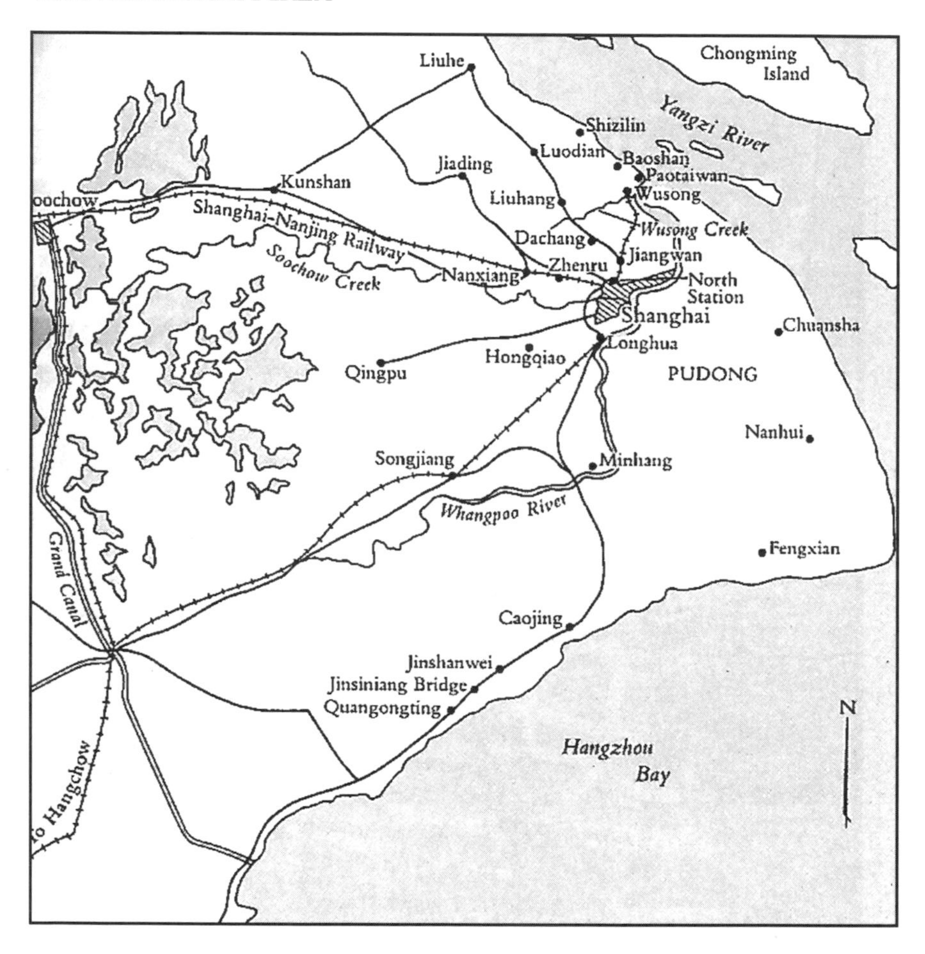

Reprinted from *Passivity, Resistance, and Collaboration* by Poshek Fu, with the permission of the publishers, Stanford University Press. © 1993 by the Board of Trustees of the Leland Stanford Junior University.

Introduction

The period between the fall of the last of the Chinese dynasties in 1912 and the triumph of a strong central government in 1949 was not a happy one for most Chinese. Many of them tend to view all of modern Chinese history as a "dark period" (*heian shidai*), with the Republican interregnum between the Qing and the People's Republic of China the blackest age. During those years, the old Chinese nightmare of "internal and external troubles" (*neiyou waihuan*) occurring simultaneously came to pass. Warlords carved up the land, opium addiction was widespread, and Westerners and Japanese held privileged positions in the social and economic life of the "Republic." Constant warfare and struggles for power became the dreary daily fare of the people, who yearned for peace and order. During the early 1930s, China's troubles were vastly intensified by civil war with the resurgent Chinese Communists, while at the same time the Japanese occupied one part of China after the other. Ultimately, the Japanese invasion led to a horrifying eight-year war in which millions of Chinese perished. That conflict was followed in short order by four years of civil war, intermittent in the beginning but full-scale by 1947. The monumental struggle between two ruthless political organizations, the Chinese Communist Party (CCP) and the Nationalist Party (Guomindang; GMD), ran like a thread through most of this period (from the 1920s through the 1940s).

A quarter of a century ago, while a graduate student combing the stacks for a likely Ph.D. dissertation topic, I ran across a quasi-memoir by Carsun Chang (Zhang Junmai) entitled *Third Force in China.*[1] I had already noticed that it frequently appeared in the bibliography of books having to do with the history of Republican China, in particular the period of the civil war (1945-1949). At that time, I was not interested in doing a dissertation on the CCP or GMD. Instead, I wondered whether there had been any democratic alternatives in Republican China to the authoritarian—in the case of the Chinese Communists, totalitarian—states proposed by the two major political parties. Hence, the words "Third Force" in the title of Zhang's book intrigued and excited me.

As the late John K. Fairbank pointed out, however, historians often seem to drift backward in time, looking for the source of events.[2] The same thing happened to me. I began a study of Zhang and his political parties in the 1930s and 1940s and ended up preparing a dissertation on the formative years from his birth in 1887 to 1923, when his participation in the debate over science and metaphysics marked a turning point in both his and Republican China's intellectual and political courses.

During the summer vacations following the beginning of my teaching career in 1974, I began to collect materials on Zhang in archives and libraries around the world, while simultaneously publishing articles and presenting conference papers on various aspects of his political career during the 1920s, 1930s, and early 1940s. In the course of these labors, it became clear that Zhang was well known to Chinese who reached maturity in the 1930s and 1940s, when his name was often in the newspapers as one of China's leading intellectuals, as well as the head of two small political groups, the National Socialist Party of China (*Zhongguo guojia shehui dang*; NSP) and later, the Chinese Democratic Socialist Party (*Zhongguo minzhu shehui dang*; DSP). Although he was spurned in both Taiwan and China for some years after 1949, in the early 1970s the former published a collection of his writings (albeit a censored version), while in the 1980s the mainland also began to notice him, first placing him in the category of "negative examples" and later mentioning him as part of the publishing boom on "democratic parties and groups" (*minzhu dangpai*). Hence, nowadays there are numerous Chinese-language materials by and about Zhang.[3]

Very little has been published about Zhang in the English language,[4] however, with the result that—in contrast to his fellow intellectuals, such as Hu Shi and Ding Wenjiang, who have both been subjects of book-length studies in English[5]—Zhang is not well known in the West. Hence, I offer this collection of twelve essays on key themes and experiences in his life through 1941 (especially democracy and socialism) as a first step toward making him better known to readers of modern Chinese history. It is my hope that this will be a pioneering work on an important intellectual leader and minority-party leader, with the full biography to come later. In preparing this study, I have freely quoted and paraphrased his writings, to help the reader get the measure of the man through his own words.

Certainly, his story deserves to be known, for Zhang was an intellectual and politician of some note in the elite circles of Republican China, and thanks to his industry and curiosity (he seems never to have passed up a debate) a study of him invariably takes on the form of a study of the period. In addition, he came by his credentials as a "third-force" (*disan shili*) figure honestly and early. In 1907, he participated in Liang Qichao's Political Information Society (*Zhengwen she*), a "third-force" organization caught in the cross fire between the conservatives at the Qing court and the Revolutionary Alliance (*Tongmeng hui*). From then until Liang's death in 1929, he participated in every one of his "mentor's" various political organizations, including the Progressive Party (*Jinbu dang*) and the Research Clique (*Yanjiu hui*). At the same time, Zhang was scouring the world, looking for models China could usefully emulate. As a result of his study and travel in Japan (1906-10), Germany and England (1913-16), France and Germany (1919-21), and, finally, Germany once again (1929-31), he fixed upon democracy and socialism as the twin means to "save China." In doing so, he opposed the foe of those two isms, communism. However, he was not blinded by his anticommunism to whatever "merits" communist systems might offer; hence, he praised the Soviet New Economic Policy and Five-Year Plan, including the collective and state farms (chapters 6 and 7).

As a good disciple of Wang Yangming's advocacy of the unity of thought and action, Zhang tried to implement his ideas for national salvation. First, he founded institutions of higher education, in an attempt to convey his vision of a new China (chapter 4). The first of these schools was the Institute of Political Science in Shanghai (*Guoli zhengzhi daxue*; 1923-27). It was followed by the Xuehai Institute (*shuyuan*), which Zhang helped the warlord of Guangdong province, Chen Jitang (1890-1954), set up. Finally, while Japanese bombs rained down on Chongqing in 1939, Zhang established the Institute of National Culture (*Minzu wenhua shuyuan*) in Southwest China. As he was to discover over and over again, though, it was impossible to separate education from politics, and all three schools were closed by the Guomindang regime.

It was no use trying to carry out reform through writing, teaching, and education, in an environment dominated by dictatorships and guns. Hence, unlike Hu Shi, Zhang ended up joining with other intellectuals to found a political party, the NSP. This was even more dangerous than opposing the regime by intellectual and educational means, however, and Zhang spent much of the 1930s leading a semiunderground existence. His party was not officially tolerated until the outbreak of the Sino-Japanese War in 1937 forced a united front upon the GMD regime. That united front lasted only until the outbreak of the Pacific War in late 1941, when Chiang Kai-shek discovered he could do without the assistance of a small party like the NSP, now that he was allied with the United States against the Japanese invaders. As a result, Zhang's school was closed, and he was placed under "city arrest" in Chongqing.

The chapters that follow deal first with the origins of his lifelong attachment to democracy, as a result of his studies at Waseda University in Tokyo (chapter 1). Chapter 2 focuses on the critical period following World War I, when the battle between communism and socialism raged in Western Europe. As this section shows, Zhang chose to side with German social democracy and repudiated the communist model some of his fellow Chinese intellectuals decided held out the promise of a brighter future for China. Following his return home from this three-year sojourn in a Europe menaced by social revolution, Zhang fervently opposed his twin foes, the GMD and the CCP, and their alliance with the Soviet Russia whose politics he repudiated (chapter 3). For his troubles, he was attacked in print by the CCP, while as soon as the Northern Expedition reached Shanghai in 1927, the GMD closed his school and issued a warrant for his arrest. This forced him, like numerous Chinese dissidents before and after, to take refuge in the foreign concessions, where he occupied himself with a full-length study of Soviet Russia (chapters 5 and 6). Dwelling in the concessions did not help him in a lawless society, though, and in mid-1929 he was kidnapped for ransom. Following his release, he wisely concluded that China was not a safe place for an opponent of the GMD and journeyed to Germany to take up an appointment teaching philosophy at the University of Jena.

While in Germany, he heard much about the Soviet "experiment," especially the Five-Year Plan, and hence was determined to return home via Moscow so he could see the changes for himself (chapter 7). Following his return to Peking, he and other former disciples of Liang Qichao (who had died in 1929) decided to create their own political party as a means of pushing their vision of China's future (chapter 8). In doing so, the NSP leaders were quite aware they were exposed to GMD retaliation; hence, much like Sun Yat-sen earlier, they launched a China-wide search for a "good warlord"—a search that, like Sun's quest, was doomed to failure.

By the early 1930s, then, there was ample evidence of the failure of the Republic of China and its latest incarnation, the GMD. This spurred a debate during the 1930s over whether democracy or dictatorship was the best model for China. To his credit, in a decade in which this question was being asked throughout the world, not just in China, Zhang defended democracy (chapter 9).

The coming of the Sino-Japanese War in the summer of 1937 put an end to such "pen wars" in favor of real wars. In response to the Japanese invasion, the GMD included minor political parties like the NSP and the Chinese Youth Party (*Zhongguo qingnian dang*; CYP) in their United Front, as well as the CCP (chapter 10). The first year, 1937-1938, represented a halcyon period—referred to as the "Hankou spirit"[6]—before tensions recurred, not only between the two major parties but also between the NSP and the CCP and GMD. The explosion between the NSP and the Communists came with publication of an open letter in late 1938, in which party leader Zhang criticized the CCP's retention of its own territory and army in the midst of foreign invasion (chapter 11). The clash with the GMD was to come later, with its closing of Zhang's school and confinement of him to the wartime capital (chapter 12).

As I hope the essays that follow show, then, it was not easy to maintain a position of a "plague on both your houses" during the Republican period, especially when your party was composed mostly of unarmed intellectuals. Hence, by late 1941, it appeared that Zhang and the NSP had reached the end of their ropes. As made clear in the epilogue, though, news of the demise of the two proved premature, for they rallied during the postwar struggle between the CCP and GMD and carved out a small space within which to maneuver. In doing so, however, Zhang and his party were forced to take sides, and that led to a destructive split in the DSP. Hence, by the time the party ended up on Taiwan following the CCP victory of 1949, it was a shattered entity, and the GMD had no trouble confining it to a "window-dressing" role during the decades that followed. As for Zhang, he was true to his "third-force" stance and declined to remain in GMD (Taiwan) or Communist (the People's Republic of China) China. Instead, he resigned himself to a lonely exile in the United States, a sojourn that lasted until his death in 1969 during the height of America's war in Vietnam.

Notes

1. New York: Bookman, 1952.

2. In his opinion, wrote Fairbank, "regression in time is typical of Ph.D. thesis research. . . . Historical research progresses backwards, not forward." John K. Fairbank, *Trade and Diplomacy on the China Coast: The Opening of the Treaty Ports, 1842-1854* (Cambridge: Harvard University Press, 1953; Stanford: Stanford University Press, 1969), ix.

3. Recently, two studies of Zhang have been published in Taiwan: Xue Huayuan, *Minzhu xianzheng yu minzuzhuyi de bianzheng fazhan: Zhang Junmai sixiang yanjiu* (The Dialectical Development of Constitutional Democracy and Nationalism: A Study of Zhang Junmai's Thought) (Taipei: Daohe chubanshe, 1993); Yang Yongqian, *Zhonghua minguo xianfa zhi fu: Zhang Junmai zhuan* (The Father of the Republic of China's Constitution: A Biography of Zhang Junmai) (Taipei: Tangshan chubanshe, 1993). In addition, some time ago Hung Mao-hsiung, a Taiwan scholar studying in Germany, published his dissertation, entitled "Carsun Chang (1887-1969) und Seine Vorstellungen vom Sozialismus in China" (Inaugural-Dissertation zur Erlangung des Doktorgrades des Fachbereichs 12 an der Ludwig-Maximilians-Universität München, 1980). For other writings on Zhang in Chinese, see the

bibliography at the end of this work.

4. For a detailed account of Zhang's formative years, see Jeans, "Syncretism in Defense of Confucianism: An Intellectual and Political Biography of the Early Years of Chang Chun-mai, 1887-1923" (Ph.D. diss., George Washington University, 1974). There is a short biographic sketch (albeit one containing a number of minor errors) in Howard L. Boorman and Richard C. Howard, eds., *Biographical Dictionary of Republican China*, 5 vols. (New York: Columbia University Press, 1967-79), 1: 30-35 (hereafter, BDRC). See also Chester C. Tan, *Chinese Political Thought in the Twentieth Century* (New York: Doubleday, 1971; Anchor Books, 1971), 253-66; Wen-shun Chi, *Ideological Conflicts in Modern China: Democracy and Authoritarianism* (New Brunswick, NJ: Transaction Books, 1986), 135-55.

5. On Hu Shi, see Jerome B. Grieder, *Hu Shih and the Chinese Renaissance: Liberalism in the Chinese Revolution, 1917-1937* (Cambridge: Harvard University Press, 1970); Chou Min-chih, *Hu Shih and Intellectual Choice in Modern China* (Ann Arbor: University of Michigan Press, 1984). On Ding, see Charlotte Furth, *Ting Wen-chiang: Science and China's New Culture* (Cambridge: Harvard University Press, 1970).

6. For an example of usage of the term, see Theodore H. White and Annalee Jacoby, *Thunder Out of China* (New York: Da Capo, 1980), 53.

PART ONE

The Making of a Constitutionalist and Socialist

1

Chinese Constitutionalist in Late-Meiji Japan, 1906-1910

Republican China went to school in Japan.
—John K. Fairbank[1]

In November 1946, Chiang Kai-shek and the Guomindang (GMD), tiring of the protracted negotiations with the Chinese Communists, announced their intention to convene the long-awaited National Assembly. When the Communists and the China Democratic League flatly refused to participate, the GMD was faced with the embarassing possibility, in the eyes of the world, of a one-party parliament. Hence, it began to woo the two strongest minority parties then on the scene, the Chinese Youth Party (CYP) and the Chinese Democratic Socialist Party (DSP).

The leader of the latter was Zhang Junmai, more commonly known to Western readers as Carsun Chang. He made headlines in newspapers ranging from right to left in political orientation with his insistence that Chiang and his party promise to work toward constitutional democracy in a series of steps.[2] In brief, Zhang relinquished a decades-long, on-and-off animus against the GMD, because of its promise to carry out constitutionalism. What was the source of such abiding faith in an imported ism?

As in the case of so many Republican-era Chinese, the origins of Zhang's faith in constitutionalism can be found in his years of study and political activism in Meiji Japan (1868-1912). Thereafter, he never wavered in the beliefs acquired during those years. At the end of his life, he was still chastizing both Chinas for their failures to put into effect constitutional governments. Here, we shall trace the origins and early development of his political thought, first taking a brief look at the years prior to his journeying to Japan and then devoting the greater part of this chapter to his experiences in that rapidly modernizing nation.

Early Political Influences

There are several salient features of Zhang's early life that should be emphasized. First, he was born in the Shanghai area (Jiading *xian*), which in 1887, the year of his birth, meant he took root and flourished in the shadow of the Western presence.[3] Second, although it is difficult to say with exactitude just what the Zhang family financial standing was in those waning years of the nineteenth century, at the very least they were well enough off (Zhang's grandfather was an official and his father, a doctor) to give their children good educations. Hence, Zhang attended the Jiangnan Arsenal's Guang fangyan guan (literally, the School for the Study of Many Dialects), where he added a prolonged exposure to the new Western learning to his foundation (in the family school) in the Classics.[4] Here, for example, he began his lifelong study of English, which he also used in his studies in Japan. Since the civil service examinations had not yet been abolished (an imperial decree of 1905 dictated their abolition in 1906), Zhang also took and passed the exam for the first level in the system, the *xiucai* (flowering talent) decree, in 1902.[5] Following that, he resumed his modern education, studying at the Aurora Academy (*Zhendan xueyuan*) in Shanghai and the Jiangnan Higher School (*Gaodeng xuexiao*) in Nanjing.[6] In short, like so many of his fellow students during that period, Zhang had one foot in traditional China and the other in the new, Western-influenced world.

The third characteristic of his life prior to going to Japan is perhaps the most relevant for a consideration of his constitutionalism. In part, it involves a question (questions constantly confront the biographer in any attempt to reconstruct a life): Was Zhang politically active, in those turbulent years at the end of the Qing Dynasty, and, if so, what was his political bent—toward the revolutionaries, led by Sun Yat-sen and others and active in uprisings against the Qing authorities since 1895, or toward the constitutionalists, led by Kang Youwei and, more and more as time went by, by Kang's student, Liang Qichao? The evidence is thin on this basic question. We have, though, three incidents, reported either by Zhang himself in his rare and scattered reminiscences, or by his biographers.

The first is one that obviously made a deep impression on the young Zhang. As he recalled it again and again throughout his long life (1887-1969), while he was studying at the Guang fangyan guan in 1898 he saw a wanted poster calling for the arrests of Kang and Liang hanging outside the school's gate. According to Zhang's memoirs, this was the first time he had heard of the two reformers.[7] Moreover, it is also clear that, like many of his schoolmates, he was reading Liang Qichao's journal, *Xinmin congbao* (The New People's

Journal), at this time. The year after he attained the *xiucai* degree, he later recalled, he read an article in *Xinmin congbao* by Liang entitled, "Best Wishes for the Future of the Aurora Academy." These words, Zhang later wrote, "aroused him tremendously" and made him want to enter the Shanghai school.[8] In the absence of a diary or other self-revealing writings from that period, however, it is difficult to go much further than this: he was aware of Kang and Liang and was, in at least one instance, influenced in his life's course by Liang's journal.

The second incident constituted at least a fringe involvement with the revolutionaries on Zhang's part. It was also evidence of his early nationalism. In 1903, while he was studying in Nanjing, the Russians—having occupied part of Manchuria during the Boxer Rebellion—presented the Chinese with a list of seven demands to be met before they would withdraw. This led to what one historian has called "China's first modern student protest."[9] Although the heart of the opposition was in Tokyo, meetings were also held in China. One of the Tokyo leaders, Niu Yongjian, returned to China to organize a volunteer corps to fight the Russians, and it was this group Zhang is said to have joined. Since Niu was a revolutionary,[10] this may be viewed as a passing flirtation with revolution on Zhang's part. In any event, this outburst of youthful nationalism did not last. As a result of his actions, he was expelled from the Jiangnan Higher School, when the government cracked down on the volunteer corps in late June 1903.[11]

Finally, there is an intriguing puzzle connected with Zhang's teaching experience in Hunan, following his expulsion from the Nanjing school. Thwarted by family opposition in his hopes to study in Japan (would he have become a revolutionary if he had gone in 1903, immediately after participating in Niu's volunteer corps?), he spent two years as an English teacher in Changsha, Changde, and Lizhou. Although very little is known about his experiences in Hunan, the first school at which he taught, the Mingde School (*xuetang*) in Changsha, was a hotbed of revolutionary activity, thanks to the presence on the faculty of revolutionaries such as Huang Xing, Zhang Ji, and Wu Luzhen.[12] According to Huang's son, the school had a close relationship with the Society for the Revival of China (*Huaxing hui*). Since Zhang left the school after only two months, it is tempting to speculate that he left because he was not pleased with what he saw and heard. That would be too simple, though, for the school also had connections with the constitutionalists. Tan Yankai contributed funds, and a number of important constitutionalists taught there at one time or another.[13]

In the absence of Zhang's own testimony, then, the biographer is reduced to constructing the most probable scenario. In view of his short tenure at the school, reports that—despite the connections with the constitutionalists—it was really dominated by the revolutionaries (according to one source, students who did not support revolution were condemned by their classmates),[14] and the assistance he received from well-known constitutionalists (Xiong Xiling and the prefect of Changde, Zhu Qiyi) in obtaining a teaching position at Changde Middle School,[15] it seems likely that Zhang did not feel at home at the Mingde School and hence sought escape. Since he later became a constitutionalist, this smacks of reading later events into earlier history. In sum, although there is no evidence to suggest that Zhang became a member of the constitutionalist party prior to going to Japan in 1906, there are grounds to conclude he was probably closer to the constitutionalist side of the political equation than the revolutionist.

In any event, he had not abandoned his desire to study in Japan, during his time in Hunan. He later wrote that he saved four hundred silver dollars while teaching, which enabled him to undertake the journey to Japan. Following a demonstration of the tugs of old and new on Chinese of his generation—an arranged marriage followed by the removal of his queue—he left for Japan in 1906.[16]

Origins of a Constitutionalist in Japan, 1906-1910

Armed with a government stipend from his family's native *xian* (Baoshan),[17] in 1906 Zhang joined the flood of Chinese students who went to Japan during the last years of the Qing. It was no coincidence that this year also marked the end of the ancient civil service examination system; study abroad would thenceforth be the new path to success for Chinese youth. There were other reasons drawing Chinese youth to Japan: it was closer to home and less expensive; the Japanese language used numerous Chinese characters (*kanji*), making it easier to learn; and Japan did not seem as alien as the West to Chinese students, and, in fact, offered them what it had already distilled from Western learning, making their task easier.[18]

As in the case of many of these students, Zhang was supported by his *xian* government on condition that he study science. His instructions were to enter a department of physics and chemistry in a Japanese higher normal school (*gaoshi*),[19] which meant he was destined for a career in education, for these institutions were designed exclusively (in the Japanese track system) for producing teachers. Their academic standards were not high; according to one study, their goal was to turn "lower-class achievers" into "reliable martinets in the primary school classroom."[20] After six months at such a school (his fragmentary reminiscences do not tell us which one), Zhang withdrew and entered the Higher Preparatory School of Waseda University to pursue his first loves, law and political science. After one academic year, in September 1907 (midyear in the Japanese school-year calendar) he entered Waseda's School of Political Science and Economics to continue his studies.[21] There was no doubt he had achieved entry into one of Japan's finest and least regimented schools; Waseda was a "pioneer institution for the spreading of modern, liberal ideas," and many later-to-be-famous Chinese iconoclasts of one political persuasion or another studied there before and after Zhang.[22]

His studies at this "liberal" school were to be of pivotal importance for his subsequent political career and thought. It was at this time that he studied the classics of Western political thought and thus laid the foundations for his lifelong attachment to constitutional democracy. He read, for example, John Locke's *Two Treatises of Government*, John Stuart Mill's *Considerations on Representative Government* (around the same time, he published a selective translation of several chapters of this work), William R. Anson's *The Law and Custom of the Constitution*, Woodrow Wilson's *The State: Elements of Historical and Practical Politics*, and John W. Burgess's *Political Science and Comparative Constitutional Law*. While drafting the new Republic of China constitution many years later (1946), Zhang acknowledged his debt to these and other works he had first studied in Japan.[23]

In the course of his studies, he also fell under the influence of two Waseda professors in particular. One was Ukita Kazutami, with whom he studied political philosophy, focusing on Locke's *Two Treatises on Government*. Nearly thirty years later, he remembered Ukita as a "kind and wonderful teacher."[24] The other was Ariga Nagao, a professor of constitutional law. After completing his studies and returning to China, he often cited Ariga's views in his writings on provincial government systems in China.[25]

His life in Japan, however, was not entirely devoted to school matters. Like most of his fellow students in Japan, he became intensely involved in politics. As he later recalled, the Chinese students in Japan "knew about only politics and national salvation" and considered their studies a means to those ends.[26] It may indeed have been the need to earn funds for his and his brother's support that led him to contribute articles to *Xinmin congbao* (XMCB),[27] but more importantly this was the means by which he first met Liang Qichao (the answer to the question of *why* he offered to write for the constitutionalist journal, rather than—like the majority of his fellow students in Japan—a revolutionary publication, may lie, as we argued earlier, in his life before Japan). He later wrote that at the age of twenty-one *sui* (1906 or the same year he began to write for XMCB), he joined Liang's Constitutional Party.[28] From that time on, he "followed Rengong [Liang Qichao] . . . and advocated constitutional government."[29] The personal relationship was a close one, too. The two men often talked and exchanged books, with Zhang later recalling that their relationship had been "one of teacher and friend (*shi you zhijian*)."[30] Moreover, it was important for Zhang's budding faith in constitutionalism that by the time they met, Liang had turned away from an earlier flirtation with revolution and the revolutionaries. As Zhang explained, "after 1904 he [Liang] came back to the fold of his teacher Kang [Youwei], and maintained that a constitutional monarchy was all that was needed." Liang detested revolution, he added, viewing it as likely to be followed by tyranny and terrorism.[31] Instead, Liang urged like-minded people to join with him to found an organization to work toward a speedy and peaceful transition toward constitutional government.

The organization, dubbed the Political Information Society (PIS), was founded on 17 October 1907 in Tokyo. It was to work in the open, and thus Liang hoped to attract the support of such powerful figures as Yuan Shikai, Zhang Zhidong, and Zhang Jian. Since it would be active in China, it could not be formally led by Kang Youwei and Liang Qichao, who were "wanted" by the Qing. Hence, they stayed in the background, leaving the top offices of the organization to Zhang's old teacher, Ma Liang (Ma Xiangbo; 1840-1939), and Xu Junmian (Xu Qin; d. 1945) (destined to become a key figure in the future NSP).[32]

The PIS's membership was said to number 1,500 largely "moderate" Chinese in Japan.[33] One of these was Zhang Junmai, who is credited with being one of the founders of the society as well as one of its most energetic members.[34] Liang, for example, sent him on at least one (abortive) mission to China on behalf of the society.[35]

For a short while, the society flourished. Subsequently, it shifted its headquarters to Shanghai, where its journal, *Zhenglun* (Political Discussion), had been publishing since October 1907. In addition to the Shanghai and Tokyo offices, branches cropped up everywhere, even in Beijing. Some sources even mention, in vague terms, the establishment of newspapers and schools, as well as the launching of a boycott.

The main goals of the society, however, remained the winning over of high officials of the court and the launching of a movement petitioning for the early convention of a parliament. At first, both approaches seemed successful. Contact was made with Prince Su (Shanqi; 1863-1921), minister of the interior from 1907 to 1911, in an attempt to get Yuan Shikai (1859-1916)—who threatened to have the society dissolved—dismissed from office. This proved a futile gesture, since Prince Su was under the protection of Yuan.[36] To further the petition movement, cadre were dispatched to China. Zhang himself headed the drive, and at the end of March 1908 reported to Liang Qichao that over three thousand signatures had been collected, adding that he had hoped for ten to twelve thousand "to remove the disgrace of our society's inability to act." Nor was this the only example of his involvement in the PIS. He also suggested, in a letter to Liang in the spring of that year (endorsing a suggestion by one Hou Xuefang), that members of the PIS operate manufacturing enterprises and enter officialdom to broaden the society's power.[37] In short, he proposed an infiltration of the "establishment."

These activities of the PIS, mild as they may seem in comparison with those of the revolutionaries, aroused the hostility of the Qing authorities. Officials sympathetic to the PIS were dismissed and, in August 1908, an imperial edict was issued banning the society and ordering the arrest of the membership. Following this blow, the society simply collapsed, for as one scholar has written, "its very rationale was legitimacy; it could not long survive the decision that it was illegitimate by those very people on whom it had gambled."[38]

Viewing its demise in a broader perspective, it resembled the fate of the later "third-force" movement Zhang was involved in during the late 1940s and early 1950s. The PIS was caught in the crossfire between the court on the right and the revolutionaries (the Revolutionary Alliance) on the left. Attacked from both sides, it was not surprising that it did not last long (less than a year). And yet, although the government administered the coup de grace, it was the revolutionaries' hostility that was to prove most enduring, lasting until the late-1980s liberalization in Taiwan, where the PIS's lineal descendant, the DSP, still existed.

We have examined Zhang's education and his involvement with Liang Qichao's political organization. What about Zhang's own views on the problems facing China during the last days of the Qing? Fortunately, he had already begun that prodigious writing that continued until the end of his life. Thus, it is possible to trace some of his ideas, which not surprisingly resembled those of his "mentor," Liang.

In a series of articles published during his first two years in Japan (1907-1908), he took the constitutionalists' side in the ideological dispute with the revolutionaries. Like Liang, he preferred political evolution to revolution, or what he called the British approach to the French. The revolutionaries, he wrote, were guiding the Chinese people in accordance with the bad precedent set by the French Revolution. Why were they doing this? Because the scholars of the East were indiscriminate in their borrowings from Western precedents (this from a man who was steeping himself in Anglo-American writings).[39] Like Liang, he saw revolution breeding disorder and disaster in its wake, not peace and order.[40]

Again like Liang, Zhang opposed the revolutionaries' anti-Manchu racialism. To justify their revolution, he wrote, they cited the "differences in racial interests," arguing revolution was necessary to overthrow the alien Manchus. Zhang's counterargument focused on the revolutionaries' assertion that Han Chinese and Manchus could not live together. In a manner that was to be characteristic of his approach to politics thoroughout his life, he wrote that he would try to "study this problem with you gentlemen." Contrary to the Revolutionary Alliance's argument that the two races could not coexist, he asserted, the Manchus had already been assimilated. He urged the revolutionaries to think about this calmly, for it was not an issue that could be solved by emotionalism. Instead of attacking the entire Manchu race, he tried to direct his readers' anger against "evil" authorities, whether Manchu or Han. In surprisingly violent language for one who fervently opposed revolution, he called for "the point of the people's sword" to be directed against "this despotic and corrupt government."

In sum, then, he was calling for political reform in which Han and Manchu would cooperate and declaring his opposition to racial revolution.[41] Insisting on a "true national movement" and quoting Theodore Roosevelt and Western proverbs on the need for deeds as well as words, he wrote, "We who advocate political reform believe that at present the urgent task is to quickly establish a constitutional government." Why? Because as soon as a country followed the constitutional path, there was advancement in every respect. Thus, he asserted that faith in the magic power of constitutionalism he was never to abandon, even in the darkest days of the history of the Republic of China.

In proposing the Han work with "good" Manchus for political reform and constitutionalism, he realized he was opening himself up to charges by the revolutionaries that the constitutionalists had sold out to the government. Attempting to counter these charges, he wrote that he and his colleagues did not support constitutionalism and oppose revolution to please the government or for their own advantage but to resist the revolutionaries' insurrections. "If this rottenness [the insurrections] lasts for a long time," he concluded, "there will never be a day when our people achieve a positive result."[42]

All of this, of course, left unanswered the crucial question: how could constitutionalism be implemented? It was easy enough to write about it, but realizing it was more of a challenge in the Chinese context. Zhang tackled the issue head-on. The way to attain constitutional government in "this time of troubles," he wrote, was simply to adopt a constitution and launch preparations for the implementation of a parliamentary system. In envisioning a long period of such preparations, he was clearly influenced by the Meiji experience. It took more than ten years to prepare for the convening of a parliament in Meiji Japan, he wrote, adding, "Now we should know what our urgent task is today."[43] Moreover, in urging a protracted period of laying the foundations for a parliament, he was right in step with the Qing government's plans, which (like the Meiji) projected a nine-year lead time before achievement of a constitutional regime. However, he broke with both Meiji and Qing when he argued for the Anglo-American system, rather than the Prussian.[44] The Prussian and Japanese systems, he wrote, were well known for concentrating power in the hands of the monarch; therefore, their constitutionalism was inferior to that of England and America.

His admiration for the Anglo-American model was yet another manifestation of his respect for things from that quarter of the globe. In this, as in so much else, he resembled Liang Qichao. The Chinese, Zhang wrote, should emulate the Anglo-Saxons' virtues: their actions were based on customs and habits; they possessed common sense and a sense of history (these first two points could just as well apply to the Chinese as to the Anglo-Saxons!); their individual freedom was highly developed; and they fought to attain self-government. In contrast, Zhang—reminding one of Taiwan writer Bo Yang's "Ugly Chinaman" writings of many years later[45]—identified as Chinese characteristics emotionalism, trouble-making, bragging, borrowing from abroad, passive reactions to despotism, and reliance on the leadership of the powerful rather than self-government.[46] It was clearly Zhang's hope that these "Chinese traits" could be replaced by those he ascribed to Anglo-Saxons.

Finally, three other points were raised in his writings at the time that had implications for his constitutionalism. First, he strongly believed it would be necessary to rely on an elite to implement that ism.[47] A four-thousand-year-old nation, he declared, could not be reconstructed in a few months or years by relying on an empty piece of paper (a constitution), nor could the people help, for they were hopeless. In expressing this sentiment, he perhaps revealed the influence of Liang's "enlightened despotism," which the latter first publicized the year Zhang arrived in Japan and joined Liang's movement. "When a country has long been under barbaric absolutism," wrote Liang, "with political freedom extremely restricted . . . the tutelage of an enlightened despotism is required."[48]

Zhang's faith in an elite seemed to go beyond this, however. Even universal education, he argued, would not be able to produce members of parliament. The politics of the nation would still depend on an elite, whom Zhang labeled "dedicated patriots," "the one or two heroes," "the few people with vision," "the one or two scholars," "a few people," and "the extraordinary people." As usual, he drew his intellectual support from the West. Look at the examples of nineteenth-century Germany and Italy, he wrote. Their successes resulted from the advocacy of one or two scholars or the actions of one or two heroes. Difficult things, he concluded, could not be achieved by a few hundred educators but, when opportunity beckoned, by one or two heroes.[49]

Second, Zhang supported the idea that "the end justifies the means," a position that is startling in light of his later political views (e.g., in 1920). In 1907, he did not shrink from violence or bloodshed so long as it was for a good cause, leading one to wonder whether it was only the revolution advocated by the Revolutionary Alliance he opposed and not its violence, only the disorder it created and not the bloodshed. Sounding suspiciously like the later Mao Zedong, he declared that in political movements it was inevitable that there would be killings. "We absolutely must shoulder this agony," he insisted. "Supposing we sacrifice several tens, hundreds, thousands, or ten thousands of lives, but the happiness of four-hundred-million compatriots is promoted—then our happiness and hopes will be increased."[50] In these sentiments, it is difficult to see any difference between Zhang and bomb-throwing revolutionists and anarchists (at least in thought).

Finally, Zhang seemed to have a premonition (like Liang) of the political horrors to come in China. What worried him, he wrote in an apparent reference to the conflict between the revolutionaries and constitutionalists at the time, was not that the level of the majority of the people was so low but that the minority could not unite to supervise the government.[51] Revealing another influence of the Meiji environment, he seemed to foresee the party struggles following the founding of the Republic in 1912: "My hope is that party sentiment will not get the better of the great unity (*Datong*), so that we will not repeat the bad examples of Japan's Progressive (*Kaishintō*) and Liberal (*Jiyutō*) parties, for that would be unfortunate for both the nation and the race."[52]

Zhang's involvement in the PIS and the publication of his ideas in Liang's journal, along with his studies at Waseda, consumed the first half of his stay in Japan. Events in China from mid-1908 to mid-1909 marked the beginning of a second stage in his Japanese experience. First came the August 1908 dissolution of the PIS. Then in the same month, the Qing issued an edict outlining a nine-year (clearly copying the Meiji) period of preparation for constitutionalism. In November came the death of the Guangxu Emperor, an event that pulled the rug from beneath the reformers' plans for a constitutional monarchy.[53] It had been bad enough in an age of rising Han nationalism that the monarch was a Manchu; the new Manchu ruler, the Xuantong Emperor, was a mere infant as well. Finally, in early 1909, a special order was issued by the government directing the provinces to establish provincial assemblies within the year. In local elections held between February and June, those provincial assemblies—the first elected representative bodies in China—were duly chosen.

All these changes redirected the energies of the constitutionalists. Since there no longer seemed any hope on the national level, they devoted themselves to efforts on the provincial level. Zhang later wrote that Liang and his comrades busied themselves preparing for the establishment of provincial assemblies "in order to establish a model for constitutional government."[54] Zhang also took part in these activities. In June 1909, he joined with several other former members of the PIS's Tokyo branch to establish the Association for Investigation of Provincial Assemblies' Affairs (*Ziyiju shiwu diaocha hui*) in Tokyo. Its purpose was to investigate the powers and limitations, as well as the administrations, of those provinces under the direct control of the central government. This work, it was hoped, would establish the powers and limitations of the provincial assemblies, and hence those provinces could be reformed. In August 1909, Zhang and his colleagues founded a journal, *Xianzheng xinzhi* (New Annals of Constitutionalism), to convey the results of their studies to the provinces.[55] This, we might add, was Zhang's initial experience with the founding and running of a journal, an activity that consumed much of his energy in the following decades.

In 1910, the constitutional movement in China moved into high gear, with constitutionalists in the provincial assemblies leading a nationwide petition drive for the early convening of a national parliament. By October, three large petitions had been presented to the court, which was "the first time that large numbers of Chinese under the leadership of the constitutionalists had spoken out." "In 1910," wrote one scholar, "the attention of the whole nation seemed to be attracted by the petitioners." The petitions themselves expressed the view that only a national parliament could save China from revolution and partition by the foreign powers. Growing progressively stronger in tone, they ended by accusing the Qing of being a corrupt and dying regime and threatening revolution if a parliament was not immediately convened. The court's reply was a small concession: the period of preparation for constitutionalism was reduced by three years. However, this was followed in November by an order directing the petitioners to dissolve their organization.[56]

Both at the time and in later years, Zhang defended the actions of the constitutionalists. In 1907, he argued that "the initial losers but ultimate victors will be those who demand constitutionalism. The first winner but final loser will be the government that opposes constitutionalism."[57] His prediction that the government would lose was to be fulfilled, of course. It was not the constitutionalists, however, who were to be the "ultimate victors" but the revolutionaries. Reminiscing in later years about the the latters' hostility toward the constitutionalists, he compared them with Mazzini and the constitutionalists with Cavour, during Italy's era of national reconstruction.[58] Puzzled, he wrote that the constitutionalists' position had been the same as that of the monarchists in Europe, but whereas such a position was not considered strange there, in China it was castigated as protection of the emperor and loyalty to the Manchus.[59]

In later years, Zhang often reflected on the role of the constitutionalists in the years preceding the 1911 Revolution. At that time, he explained, they had two main motives for their advocacy of political reform rather than revolution. The first and most important was the fear that "even if revolution was successful, Manchuria and Mongolia would certainly be lost."[60] The second was their concern that the people's level was too low. The latter anxiety prodded Liang Qichao, he explained, to advocate enlightened despotism, a proposal that was attacked by the revolutionary newspaper, *Minbao* (People's Journal). Yet, he concluded, Liang's proposal was eventually adopted by Sun Yat-sen, as could be seen in the latter's theories of military government and political tutelage.[61]

Zhang's assessment of the constitutionalists' role combined a sense of accomplishment with an admission of tragedy. If it had not been for the reformers' introduction of constitutional thought into China, he wrote defiantly, where would China have obtained the concepts of constitutionalism and self-government? If it had not been for the establishment of the provincial assemblies, where would China have gotten the practice of election of military and civil governors of the provinces?[62] On the other hand, he admitted, the constitutionalists (referring to Kang Youwei, Liang Qichao, and their followers) were exiled abroad. As a result, they had no reliable political power, which along with the stupidity of the Qing spelled their doom.[63]

It could be argued that the failure of the constitutionalists benefited Zhang in the long run, though, for if they had been a roaring success, it is quite possible he never would have completed his studies at Waseda. As it turned out, his studies of the new provincial assemblies and involvement with *Xianzheng xinzhi* did not prevent him from graduating from Waseda in July 1910 with a B.A. in political science.[64] This was no mean feat, for studies have shown that only a small percentage of the thousands of Chinese students in Japan before the 1911 Revolution ever completed their studies; in the year Zhang received his degree, for example, only 682 Chinese graduated from reputable Japanese universities.[65] Thus, it was with degree in hand that the young constitutionalist returned home in the summer of 1910.

Conclusion: Influences of the Japanese Experience

It is quite clear that Zhang's years in Japan had a tremendous influence on his political thought. It was at Waseda that he perused the books that made him a fervent, lifelong proponent of constitutionalism, although it was not the Japanese (and Prussian) model but the Anglo-American one he found most appealing. That was natural, for those were the books the Japanese were studying in their classrooms, too (for example, Zhang's reading of Locke's *Two Treatises of Government* with Professor Ukita). Moreover, most of the reference books used in Japanese schools at that time were in English, which Zhang had studied since his days at the Guang fangyan guan in Shanghai. On the other hand, the German influence was also very much in evidence at Waseda. His professors, Zhang recalled, frequently mentioned famous German scholars, and he himself took three years of German.[66] Although he preferred the Anglo-American constitutional model, throughout his subsequent career he also would exhibit a healthy interest in German politics, and both of those influences can be traced to his sojourn in Japan.

In addition, it was in Japan that Zhang met Liang Qichao and joined his political movement, participating first in the short-lived PIS and later the Association for Investigation of Provincial Assemblies' Affairs. It was the constitutionalist journals that gave Zhang his first chance to publish his emerging views on Chinese politics. Although his subsequent writings show that he did not consider Liang above criticism, Zhang was to remain his follower and admirer up to and beyond Liang's death in 1929. Since the latter was in exile in Japan during the years prior to the 1911 Revolution, if Zhang had not studied there, it is possible he would not have fallen under Liang's sway. Hence, the establishment of the connection (*guanxi*) with Liang must be reckoned a crucial influence of the Japan years on Zhang's subsequent political thought and career.

Zhang was also influenced by late-Meiji Japanese politics. He agreed with the cautious, prolonged period of preparation for constitutionalism the Japanese government pursued in the 1880s, which had succeeded in implementing the constitution of 1889 and parliamentary government. There were signs, though (in his worry that China would experience the rivalry seen in Japan between the Progressive and Liberal parties), that he was not enamored of the political party strife he witnessed while in Japan.

It is also to the Japan years that we can trace his earliest use of the term that has pervaded so much of Chinese political discourse in the twentieth century, *imperialism* (*diguozhuyi*). In an article published in the fall of 1907, Zhang showed that he was as bitter about the Powers' encroachments on China as the revolutionary students. Look at the agreements foreign powers have imposed on China since the Sino-Japanese War (1894-95), he lamented, and try to imagine how many hundred-thousand-square *li* (roughly a third of an English mile) of China's territory they have secretly taken away. He revealed his awareness of Japanese imperialism, too, by describing the protectorate they had established over Korea, although he hastened to make clear his first priority by adding that "we do not even have time to pity ourselves; how can we have time to sympathize with the Koreans."[67]

One is driven to wonder, when discussing imperialism, whether Zhang was aware of the stance of one of his favorite teachers, Ukita Kazutami, concerning overseas expansion. Ukita argued in writings published as early as 1895 that Japan should copy Britain and practice a "natural" expansion fostered by economic interests and develop colonies and provide them with good government. In short, he was opposed to aggressive imperialism led by militarists.[68] Was Zhang aware of Ukita's position while the two of them sat side by side in the classroom and read John Locke together? No evidence in Zhang's writings indicates he was cognizant of this side of Ukita.

It also was in Japan that he continued and deepened his knowledge of the modern world in general. His studies at Waseda were exclusively devoted to Western subjects (as his transcript reveals). Moreover, at Waseda he found mentors whose influence on him was profound. On the other hand, there is a paucity of references, in his various autobiographical statements, to Japanese friends. A half-century later, he confessed that while studying at Waseda, he "did not have one Japanese friend, except for the teachers who instructed me."[69] One may speculate that, busy with his studies, trying to support himself by writing for various journals, and intensely involved in politics, he had no time to pursue friendships with Japanese students. Perhaps, like many of his fellow Chinese students in Japan during that period of ferment and turmoil, he also wore "China" around him like a shield, making him impervious to his Japanese classmates (although such major figures as Liang Qichao and Sun Yat-sen had a large number of Japanese friends and contacts).

These, then, were some of the influences of the "Japanese experience" on the young Zhang, impressions that he was to carry with him throughout his subsequent political career in Republican China.

Notes

1. John K. Fairbank, Edwin O. Reischauer, and Albert M. Craig, *A History of East Asian Civilization*, vol. 2, *East Asia: The Modern Transformation* (Boston: Houghton Mifflin, 1965), 631.

2. For the exchange of letters between Zhang and Chiang Kai-shek in which the latter agreed to Zhang's proposals, see Chang, *Third Force*, chap. 11.

3. Although he was born in Jiading, his native *xian* (district) was considered to be Baoshan, where successive generations of his family had lived. Both places were within a twenty-mile radius of Shanghai proper. Li Dasheng, "Guoshi: Zhang Junmai xiansheng" (National Scholar: Mr. Zhang Junmai), *Mingbao yuekan* 4, no. 4 (1969): 33 (hereafter, GS).

4. For a detailed history of this school, see Knight Biggerstaff, *The Earliest Modern Government Schools in China* (Ithaca: Cornell University Press, 1961), 154-99. For Zhang's recollections of his studies there, see "Wode xuesheng shidai" (My Student Era), *Zaisheng*, no. 239 (1948): 7.

5. GS, 4, no. 4, 33.

6. Cheng Wenxi, "Junmai xiansheng zhi yanxing" (The Words and Deeds of Mr. [Zhang] Junmai), in Wang Yun-wu, *Zhang Junmai xiansheng qishi shouqing jinian lunwen ji* (A Collection of Essays Commemorating Mr. Zhang Junmai's Seventieth Birthday) (Taipei: Editorial Committee for the above work, 1956), appendix, 11 (hereafter, YX).

7. Chang, *Third Force*, 23; Zhang Junmai, "Chongyin *Wuxu zhengbian ji* xu" (An Introduction to the Reprint of *A Record of the 1898 Coup d'Etat*), in Liang Qichao, *Wuxu zhengbian ji* (Taipei: Wenhai chubanshe, 1957), 9.

8. Zhang, "Wode xuesheng shidai," 6-7.

9. Charlotte Furth, "May Fourth in History," in *Reflections on the May Fourth Movement: A Symposium*, ed. Benjamin I. Schwartz (Cambridge: Harvard University Press, 1972), 60.

10. See his biography in BDRC, 3: 44-46.

11. YX, 11.

12. Ibid. For an account of Huang Xing's connection with the school, see Chun-tu Hsueh, *Huang Hsing and the Chinese Revolution* (Stanford: Stanford University Press, 1961), 16-21. Wu Luzhen was a physical education teacher. Chien-nung Li, *The Political History of China, 1840-1928* (Princeton: Van Nostrand, 1956), 202. There are biographies of Zhang Ji, as well as the school's founder, Hu Yuantan, in BDRC, 1: 15-20; 2: 182-83.

13. Huang Yizhou, "Huang Xing yu Mingde xuetang" (Huang Xing and the Mingde School), in Zuo Shunsheng, *Huang Xing pingzhuan* (A Critical Biography of Huang Xing) (Taipei: Zhuanji wenxue chubanshe, 1968), 171-72. For a short biography of Tan, see BDRC, 3: 220-23.

14. Y. C. Wang, *Chinese Intellectuals and the West* (Chapel Hill: University of North Carolina Press, 1966), 246.

15. YX, 11.
16. Zhang, "Wode xuesheng shidai," 8; YX, 11-12.
17. Ibid.
18. Philip C. Huang, *Liang Ch'i-ch'ao and Modern Chinese Liberalism* (Seattle: University of Washington Press, 1972), 42.
19. Zhang, "Wode xuesheng shidai," 8.
20. Donald Roden, *Schooldays in Imperial Japan: A Study in the Culture of a Student Elite* (Berkeley: University of California Press, 1980), 52.
21. Zhang, "Wode xuesheng shidai," 8; Chang, *Third Force*, 23; Nishikatsu Rihei, Head of the Office of Academic Records, Waseda University, Tokyo, letter to the author, 6 October 1972.
22. Harold Z. Schiffrin, *Sun Yat-sen and the Origins of the Chinese Revolution* (Berkeley: University of California Press, 1968), 259.
23. Zhang Junmai, "Wo cong shehui kexue tiaodao zhexue zhi jingguo" (My Leap from the Social Sciences to Philosophy), *Yuzhou xunkan* 3, no. 11 (1935): 9 (hereafter, WCSH); Zhang Junmai, *Zhonghua minguo minzhu xianfa shijiang* (Ten Lectures on the Democratic Constitution of the Republic of China) (Shanghai: Shangwu yinshuguan, 1947), introduction, 1.
24. WCSH, 9.
25. Ibid., 9; Zhang Junmai, *Shengzhi tiao yi* (A Discussion of Provincial System Regulations), 2d ed. (Shanghai: Shangwu yinshuguan, 1916), 12, 15, 24.
26. WCSH, 10-11.
27. Ibid., 8.
28. Chang, *Third Force*, 23.
29. Zhang Junmai, "Women tuiju Xu Fulin xiansheng jingxuan fuzongtong" (We Nominate Mr. Xu Fulin to Run for Vice-President), *Zaisheng*, nos. 210/211 (1948): 4.
30. Wang Yanjin, "Xiang qianbei Zhang Junmai xiansheng yishi" (Anecdotes about a Member of the Previous Generation from My Native Place, Mr. Zhang Junmai), *Minzhu shehui* 5, no. 3 (1969): 7; Zhang Junmai, "Ping Liang Rengong xiansheng *Qingdai xueshu gailun* qizhong guanyu Ouzhou wenyi fuxing Song-Ming lixue Dai Dongyuan zhexue san dian" (A Critique of Mr. Liang Qichao's [Treatment of] the European Renaissance, Sung-Ming Neo-Confucianism, and the Philosophy of Dai Zhen in [His Book], *Intellectual Trends in the Qing Period*), *Minzhu pinglun* 15, no. 2 (1964): 26.
31. Chang, *Third Force*, 44-45.
32. Huang, *Liang Ch'i-ch'ao*, 103-04; Lo Jung-pang, *K'ang Yu-wei: A Biography and a Symposium* (Tucson: University of Arizona Press, 1967), 208; Cheng Wenxi, "Junmai xiansheng nianbiao changbian" (A Chronological Biography of Mr. [Zhang] Junmai) 21, no. 2 (1970): 13 (hereafter, NBCB); YX, 23.
33. Huang, *Liang Ch'i-ch'ao*, 104.
34. Wu Xiangxiang, "Zhang Junmai laohe wanlixin" (Zhang Junmai: Old Crane with the Ten-Thousand *li* Heart), in Wu Xiangxiang, *Minguo bai ren zhuan* (Biographies of One Hundred Men of the Republic), 4 vols. (Taipei: Zhuanji wenxue chubanshe, 1971), 3: 4 (hereafter, LHWLX); Ding Wenjiang, ed., *Liang Rengong*

xiansheng changbian nianpu chugao (First Draft of a Chronological Biography of Liang Qichao), 2 vols. (Taipei: Shijie shuju, 1958), 1: 249 (hereafter, NB); Wu Xianzi, *Zhongguo minzhu xianzheng dang dangshi* (A Party History of the Chinese Democratic Constitutionalist Party) (San Francisco: Shijie ribao, 1952), 55.

35. YX, 11-12; NBCB 21, no. 2 (1971): 13; LHWLX, 4; GS, 4, no. 4, 34.

36. Joseph R. Levenson, *Liang Ch'i-ch'ao and the Mind of Modern China* (Cambridge: Harvard University Press, 1953), 79; Lo, *K'ang Yu-wei*, 209, 274(n. 42); BDRC, 2: 472. On Prince Su, see Arthur W. Hummel, ed., *Eminent Chinese of the Ch'ing Period (1644-1912)* (Taipei: Cheng-wen, 1970), 281.

37. NB, 1: 273-74, 283.

38. Huang, *Liang Ch'i-ch'ao*, 106-07.

39. Zhang Junmai, "Mule Yuehan yiyuan zhengzhi lun" (John [Stuart] Mill's *Considerations on Representative Government*), *Xinmin congbao*, no. 90 (1906): 35-36.

40. Zhang Junmai, "Lun jinhou mindang zhi jinxing" (On the Advancement of the People's Party Henceforth), *Xinmin congbao*, no. 95 (1907): 9.

41. Zhang, "Mule Yuehan," 36, 56-59.

42. Zhang, "Lun jinhou mindang," 1-2, 14.

43. Ibid., 2, 5-13. In 1881, the Japanese oligarchs had the Meiji Emperor announce that a national assembly would be convened in 1890.

44. One wonders what, if any, influence Okuma Shigenobu had on Zhang's thinking. Chancellor of Waseda University from 1907-14, in 1881 Okuma shocked his colleagues in the Meiji oligarchy, who supported the Prussian model of constitutional development, by advocating the immediate adoption of the British parliamentary system.

45. Bo Yang, "The Ugly Chinaman," in *Seeds of Fire: Chinese Voices of Conscience*, ed. Geremie Barme and John Minford (New York: Farrar, Straus and Giroux, 1988), 168-88.

46. Zhang, "Lun jinhou mindang," 2, 5-13, 15-16.

47. Zhang, "Mule Yuehan," 36, 38-39; NB, 1: 283; Zhang, "Lun jinhou mindang," 11, 16-17.

48. Robert A. Scalapino and George T. Yu, *Modern China and Its Revolutionary Process: Recurrent Challenges to the Traditional Order, 1850-1920* (Berkeley: University of California, 1985), 137.

49. Zhang, "Lun jinhou mindang," 10, 14-16; Zhang, "Mule Yuehan," 35-36.

50. Zhang, "Lun jinhou mindang," 2-3.

51. Ibid., 17.

52. Zhang, "Mule Yuehan," 59. Following their establishment in the early 1880s, the Liberal and Progressive parties "attacked each other with great bitterness, thus making it all the easier for the government to deal with them." Richard Storry, *A History of Modern Japan* (Harmondsworth, Middlesex: Penguin, 1972), 114.

53. If the portrait of the Guangxu Emperor in Marina Warner's *The Dragon Empress: Life and Times of Tz'u-hsi, 1835-1908, Empress Dowager of China* (New York: Atheneum, 1986) is accurate, he was a weak crutch for the constitutionalists to

lean on.

54. Zhang Junmai, "Liang Rengong zhuan xu" (An Introduction to a Biography of Liang Qichao), in Mao Yiheng, *Liang Qichao* (Hong Kong: Yazhou chubanshe, 1957), 2.

55. NB, 1: 303; NBCB 21, no. 2 (1971): 14.

56. Chang P'eng-yuan, "The Constitutionalists," in *China in Revolution: The First Phase, 1900-1913*, ed. Mary C. Wright (New Haven: Yale University Press, 1968), 160-65.

57. Zhang, "Lun jinhou mindang," 2-3.

58. Zhang Junmai, "Guomin zhengzhi pinge zhi tigao" (The Elevation of the Character of National Politics), *Gaizao* 4, no. 2 (1921): 5.

59. Zhang, "Liang Rengong zhuan xu," 2.

60. Zhang Junmai, "Wu guo zhengdang fazhan zhi huigu yu wu dang zhi jianglai" (Retrospect on the Development of Our Nation's Political Parties and the Future of Our Party), *Zaisheng*, no. 109 (1946): 3.

61. Zhang, "Liang Rengong zhuan xu," 2.

62. Ibid.

63. Zhang, "Guomin zhengzhi pinge," 5. Zhang's analysis reminds one of the analogous position of those who opposed Deng Xiaoping's regime from overseas exile following the 1989 Tiananmen massacre. See, e.g., Carl Goldstein, "Innocents Abroad," *Far Eastern Economic Review*, 15 September 1994, 22-27.

64. Nishikatsu Rihei, letter to author, 6 October 1972.

65. Fairbank, Reischauer, and Craig, *East Asia: The Modern Transformation*, 618.

66. WCSH, 9.

67. Zhang Junmai, "Waiguo bannian jishi" (A Record of Events Abroad [During the Past] Six Months), *Zhenglun* 1, no. 1 (1907): 7-8, 19-20, 24-25, 28.

68. Schiffrin, *Sun Yat-sen*, 283-84.

69. Zhang Junmai, "Zhang Junmai xiansheng fangRi jiangyan jiyao" (Extracts from Mr. Zhang Junmai's Lectures While Visiting Japan), *Minguo Zhongguo* 2, no. 5 (1959): 6.

2

Western Model for China?

Sojourn in Weimar Germany, 1919-1921

German Influences on China before the Weimar Republic

Beginning in the mid-nineteenth century, when the tottering Qing dynasty proved unable to hold off the expanding Western powers, China slowly accepted the need to learn first from the modern West and then Meiji Japan. It was a painful process for a civilization accustomed to being the teacher to become the student. At first, it was thought that all China needed to learn was modern science and technology, especially that with military applications. Hence, the Self-Strengthening Movement dominated the scene from 1861 to 1895. During this period, the British and French were the primary models for military modernization. Following the catastrophic defeat in the Sino-Japanese War of 1894-1895, however, it became clear to most that this approach was not enough. Therefore, Kang Youwei and others advocated institutional change (*bianfa*) and began to speak of constitutional monarchy, chambers of commerce, and the like. Reform turned into revolution, with the toppling of the dynasty in 1911-1912, followed by the attack on Chinese tradition in the May Fourth movement of the late 1910s and early 1920s. During the period from 1898 to 1915, Japan became the dominant model. Moreover, during the course of this ever-deepening transformation, the Chinese begrudgingly and belatedly searched for other models for the reform effort.

The German impact on China is not as well known as that of the British, Japanese, Americans, and Russians. The pre-Weimar (1919-33) German impact on China was dominated by two isms: militarism and imperialism.[1] Although Germany signed a trade treaty with China as early as 1861 and the German minister participated in drawing up the regulations governing the International Settlement in Shanghai in 1869, Germany's practical influence (as in Meiji Japan) really began in the 1870s, barely a few years after its unification in 1871. Despite the fact that Germany had joined the other Western powers in 1873 in demanding an audience with the emperor, in 1876 the grand secretary and superintendent of trade for the North, Li Hongzhang (1823-1901),[2] arranged for seven Chinese officers to enter a military academy in Germany, the first Chinese to study in that country. When Li and the governor-general of Guangdong and Guangxi, Zhang Zhidong (1837-1909),[3] established military academies in the 1880s to train a new officer corps, they engaged German instructors. In 1895, Zhang set up a three-thousand-man Self-Strengthening Army in Nanjing,[4] based on the German model. In the same year, Yuan Shikai was selected by the Qing to train a new imperial army with German instructors.[5] With support from the Board of Finance, he soon had a force in Tianjin, called the Beiyang Army, of seven thousand men. In the last decade of the Qing, however, Japanese instructors began to replace the Germans. Not only had Japan demonstrated its military efficiency in defeating first China and then Russia, their advisers were less expensive than the Germans. Hence, the Japanese military model replaced the German.

Imperial Germany was also an imperialist power. During the Sino-Japanese War, the Qing court had appealed to Germany, among other powers, for mediation.[6] Any illusions that Germany was going to help China stave off Japanese aggression, however, were dissipated shortly thereafter, when Germany joined the scramble for spheres of influence that followed the Chinese defeat. In August 1895, they secured a concession in Hankou, through a treaty with China. In March 1896, a German bank joined a British counterpart in lending China funds to pay the indemnity to Japan. When two German missionaries were killed by bandits in Shandong, a German fleet steamed into the harbor of Qingdao in Jiaozhou Bay in November 1897, and the following month Kaiser Wilhelm II declared his intention to seize Chinese territory. In seeking a sphere of influence in China, the Germans were newcomers, just as a unified Germany was a recent phenomenon in Europe. They made up for lost time, however, and swiftly created a quasi-colonial area in Shandong, with a ninety-nine-year lease on Jiaozhou Bay and all land within fifty kilometers, a railway from Jiaozhou Bay to Ji'nan (and later from Ji'nan to Tianjin), and mining rights for thirty *li* on either side of the railway. This process was not slowed by German acceptance of the Open Door notes in 1899, which merely committed the powers to preserve equality of trade in China, not the Chinese state. Following the Boxer Rebellion, in which the German minister to China was assassinated, the Kaiser demanded the right to designate the commander in chief of the occupying allied forces. Count Alfred von Waldersee set up his headquarters in the Imperial Palace, upon his arrival in Beijing in October

1900, and even though the siege of the Beijing legations had been lifted in mid-August, insisted on carrying out punitive expeditions to many North China cities during the following six months.[7] Subsequently (1910), Germany joined other Western powers in establishing the Four-Power Consortium to lend money to China, as well as to divide the railroads of Huguang (Hubei and Hunan) among its members.

World War I (WWI) brought an end to Germany's career as an imperialist, though not to its usefulness as a military model for China. When China declared neutrality in August 1914, Japan—bound to Britain by the Anglo-Japanese Naval Alliance of 1902—declared war on Germany, seized the latter's holdings in Shandong, and interned the German prisoners in Japan, thus securing revenge for Germany's role in forcing Japan to return the Liaodong Peninsula to China in 1895.[8] After a bitter and prolonged debate, in August 1917 the Beijing warlord government declared war on Germany, having already terminated payments on indemnities and loans in March.[9] Like many other countries that were late comers to the war, China hoped that participation would give it a voice in the peace conference and hence help it recover Shandong from the Japanese. In fact, the Paris Conference permitted the Japanese to retain their new holdings in Shandong, and the Chinese had to wait until the Washington Conference of 1921-1922, when Japan signed a treaty promising to return the former German leases in Jiaozhou to China.

German militarism was to have one more period of influence, which spanned the Weimar and Nazi eras, in China. In 1927, Chiang Kai-shek expelled the Soviet advisers to the Northern Expedition (1926-28) and switched to the German military model, utilizing German advisers and weapons (produced by Chinese arsenals). During the Nanjing Decade (1927-37), Nazi Germany also served as an economic model for China. However, this later period of German influence is beyond the scope of this chapter.

Zhang Junmai's First German Experience, 1913-1915

There was another side to the German influence on China, besides militarism and imperialism, and that was the political and cultural impact. Although there were more powerful recipients of this influence—such as Sun Yat-sen and Chiang Kai-shek—Zhang Junmai was also deeply affected. Politically, he was under both the Anglo-American and German influences, but in the realms of philosophy and socialism, it was the German model that attracted him. The origins of that interest may be traced to his studies at Waseda University, where he studied German and his professors often referred to German scholars. As a result, his admiration for German learning was aroused, and, while still in Japan, he already "intended to go to Germany to study."[10] In 1913, he got his chance and in May entered the Department of Political Science at the University of Berlin.[11]

It is clear that during this first sojourn, he did *not* see Germany as a model for China. This was Imperial Germany, dominated by the personality of Kaiser Wilhelm II and at the height of its power and arrogance. While still in Japan, Zhang had made clear his dislike for the German monarch, accusing him of abusing his constitutional powers and of standing for imperialism, colonialism, and overseas expansion.[12]

This is not to say he was unmoved by this first visit to Germany. The result, in fact, was to deepen the German influence on his mind. He later recalled that, despite some initial difficulty with the language and the flexible German system of higher education, he studied under several of the "great professors" he had heard about in Japan. He took finance from Adolf Wagner (1835-1917), economics from Gustav von Schmoller (1838-1917), and international law from Franz Von Liszt (1851-1919). In addition, he attended lectures on civil and criminal law.[13]

He seems to have lived a rather narrow life, however. Although he acquired a taste for German beer,[14] his writings yield no mention of German friends (just as he had no Japanese friends during his four years in Japan). In other words, he failed to escape the tendency he had succumbed to in Japan; instead of the pursuit of learning for its own sake, like many of his fellow students abroad he viewed his studies as "a means to attain the end of saving the nation." Politics continued to be his first concern, and hence his studies suffered. He later confessed that although he studied in Germany for two to three years, he "did not benefit very much from it."[15]

When WWI broke out in August 1914, Zhang immediately abandoned his studies. "My thoughts," he recalled, "turned to studying the various nations' successes and failures in the war, as well as what the future held. Economics, international law, and the like were unable to arouse my interest, for the political science in books ultimately was not as interesting as politics in real life."[16] "Politics in real life" meant witnessing the German mobilization, participating in the rationing system, and living with the danger of being mistaken for a Japanese and hence beaten by the Germans.

Like his later nemesis, Chiang Kai-shek, Zhang admired German efficiency. Within seven days, he recalled, an army of one million men was at the Western front. Moreover, he praised the efficiency of the rationing system. If tried in Shanghai, he complained, the rich would hoard, rationing would be considered an opportunity for dishonesty, and no one would plan for the entire city.[17]

When the Japanese seized Qingdao from the Germans, life for Chinese in Germany became hazardous, and some of Zhang's fellow students asked the embassy to send them home. Zhang, however, thought that this was "an excellent opportunity that occurred only once in a thousand years. [Hence,] I should stay in Europe to observe the development of the war."[18] And observe it he did. He bought maps and books and followed the course of the war in German newspapers. Not content with secondhand information, he also was granted permission to tour the Belgian battle front. He may have had China in mind when he wrote that the fate of the Belgians was a true example of "a nation defeated and a home lost" (*guopo jiawang*) and of being ruled by others.[19]

If he was aware of it, there was a revealing expression of modern nationalism in the Belgian story as well. His teachers, Franz von Liszt and Gustav von Schmoller, joined ninety-one other distinguished German intellectuals in issuing a manifesto denying Germany had violated Belgian neutrality and initiated the war. "It would have been suicide on our part," argued the manifesto, "not to have been beforehand in Belgium." The signatories denied their troops had committed atrocities or violated international law and defiantly declared that "the German army and German people are one."[20]

Zhang admired the fact that, even though Germany was at war, it retained a degree of freedom. This was driven home by one experience in particular. His interest in the war convinced his landlady he was a spy. As a result, he was placed under house arrest. However, the police did not search his room. When Zhang asked why not, the landlady replied that "freedom of the domicile" was involved, and thus the police "could not search it at will." This, he groused, was "vastly different from our country, where policemen go in and out of people's homes at will."[21]

As far away from China as he was, he could not escape the impact of Chinese domestic politics. In August 1915, Yuan Shikai launched his bid to become emperor. Zhang's reaction was to abandon his studies in Germany and travel to England in late September, where he hoped to contribute to the fight against Yuan by influencing British policy.[22] There he remained, observing English democracy in action, until March 1916 when he set out for China.[23] In retrospect, this first stay in Europe did not convince him to advocate Germany as the model for China, nor did he make much progress in his studies of German scholarship. Rather, the lessons he brought home were derived from the Great War he had witnessed and hence were dominated by a Social-Darwinist outlook.[24]

Zhang Junmai and the Weimar Model, 1919-1921

Following his return to China, Zhang participated in the movement to overthrow Yuan. When that finally succeeded with Yuan's death in June 1916, he turned to the world of journalism and accepted the post of editor in chief of *Shishi xinbao* (The China Times).[25] He went on to play an instrumental role, through his association with Liang Qichao and Premier Duan Qirui, in convincing the Chinese government to declare war on Germany in 1917.[26] This was followed by participation in Duan's warlord regime, an involvement that did not last long (August-November 1917) and ended—as was perhaps inevitable—in disillusionment. Following a stint teaching at Beijing University in 1918, he was invited by Liang to accompany him to the Paris Peace Conference, to be held at Versailles. Hence, in early 1919, he found himself back in Europe, a continent nearly destroyed by the years of savage, mechanized warfare.[27]

At first, he had hopes that China's interests would be served by participation in the conference. However, the powers and China were bound by wartime treaties with Japan that committed them to supporting the latter's claims in Shandong. Thus, in April 1919, the Council of Five confirmed Japan's hold over the former German sphere. Zhang was in a dark mood when he traveled with Liang and his small group to Germany, where, on New Year's Day in 1920, he met and instantly became a disciple of the German philosopher and Nobel laureate (1908), Rudolf Eucken (1846-1926). His studies with the latter, as well as his abiding interest in the thought of Immanuel Kant and Georg W. F. Hegel, constituted, in Zhang's mind, a German "philosophical model" for China.[28] The remainder of this chapter, however, will focus on his profound admiration for more practical models for China, the Weimar constitution and German Social Democracy.

The Constitutional Model

According to a prominent historian of the period of intellectual and nationalist ferment known as the May Fourth era, the urgent question then facing Chinese intellectuals was what kind of a political, economic, and cultural system China should adopt to replace that which had collapsed during the first two decades of the twentieth century.[29] Hence, like many Chinese studying abroad following WWI, Zhang was interested in finding a Western model. As he put it, he was searching for a "most fundamental strength that [our] people could use to establish a [modern] state."[30]

He was not impressed by either the French or English governments at that time.[31] Instead, he found his political and constitutional model in Weimar

Germany. This new Germany had arisen from the ashes of defeat in WWI and struggled to survive during the civil war that followed. After toppling the monarchy, in January 1919 a new National Assembly was elected and convened at Weimar on 6 February. In May, it moved to Berlin, where in the following month it was compelled to accept the humiliating peace imposed by the Allies at Versailles. On 31 July, it approved the Weimar Constitution, which came into effect on 14 August. Its main drafter was Hugo Preuss (1860-1925), a liberal academic lawyer. Imbued with elements from the American, British, French, and Swiss democratic models, it was amended and supplemented during the Assembly's debates.

The constitution established a centralized and unified republic, based on the sovereignty of the people. The new central government possessed more power than the old, for it controlled the army and its own independent finance. The constitution also provided for a bicameral system. A weak federal council (*Reichsrat*) represented the states, while the Reichstag—based on secret, universal suffrage and proportional representation—was the sovereign legislative power. Although the states retained a large degree of control over local government, they were obligated by the constitution to practice universal suffrage and proportional representation. There was a president, but governing power resided with the chancellor, who was appointed by the president but esponsible to the Reichstag. The supreme court was modeled after that of the United States, while the practice of referendum was borrowed from the Swiss. Finally, the constitution guaranteed the basic rights of citizens.[32]

It is not surprising that Zhang, the fervent constitutionalist, was attracted by the Weimar Constitution, for it has been described as "one of the most completely democratic paper constitutions ever written."[33] Moreover, there was an obvious parallel between China and Germany, in that both had overthrown their monarchies and founded republics. In Zhang's view in the early 1920s, however, the similarities ended there, for Germany had succeeded while China's attempt had been an abject failure. China had not been able to establish a stable government or adopt a constitution during the years since the 1911 Revolution, he lamented, but the Germans had accomplished both in six or seven months. Hence, he called on his countrymen to "study ten thousand times" the history of Germany's establishment of a republic.

Why had Germany been successful in such a short time? For Zhang, the simple answer was the Germans' adoption of a constitution. He was still nagged, however, by the question of how they were able to succeed in that task, whereas China had failed. At first, he thought the secret merely lay in the way in which the Germans approached the drafting of the document. In the National Assembly, he pointed out, there had been a spirit of working together for a common cause (*hezhong gongji*). German successes also had been due to the great courage of the assembly, in contrast to China's assemblies under Yuan Shikai and the military governors (*dujun*) in the provinces. In Germany, political parties had yielded to each other and striven for unanimity. Would China ever be able to attain that? Zhang wondered. In addition, the completion of the German constitution had demonstrated support for the polity (*guoti*) on the part of the German people and the special forces outside the assembly, such as the military. Perhaps with China in mind, Zhang complained that if a nation resorted to armed force to resolve matters like those, it was "not a nation, and it was useless to discuss a constitution." Would China ever see the day when everyone would support the polity and obey the law? he lamented.

Upon further reflection, though, he thought the characteristics that enabled the Germans to behave so sensibly in enacting their constitution and maintaining the essential institutions of a republic (cabinet, parliament, etc.) lay even deeper. Because China had been unable to accomplish these two tasks, he wrote, it had suffered from disorder right up to the present. "Why can they achieve these," he agonized, "but we cannot?" The answer, he proclaimed, lay in the "strength . . . of . . . [their] citizens' knowledge and morality" and their "observance of discipline and love for order."[34] Conversely, China's failure was due to its lack of those qualities. Hence, his proposals for political reform in China were dominated by the question of how to cultivate those qualities in the Chinese people.

Thus, Zhang advocated that China use the new German constitutional system as a model. First, he wrote, China should imitate the fact that the Germans *had* a constitution and not stop to worry about how *good* it was. A constitution, he declared, was an expression of the unity of the people's thought, something that was lacking in a China in which there were splits and factions everywhere. If China desired a constitution, he continued, it should also imitate the spirit of mutual concession (*jiaorang*), assistance, and harmony of the German constitution. Germany's constitution, he marveled, simultaneously satisfied everyone with its compromises. It contained both the cabinet and presidential systems, legislation by parliament and provision for referendums, and the separation of powers as well as centralization. "Capitalist and worker, soviet and non-soviet, private enterprise and socialization, esteem for religion and rejection of religion—each obtained what he desired, but it was limited to the proper scope."

There is no doubt that his search for a parliamentary and constitutional model in postwar Europe ended here: "Alas! When the talent of legislators reaches this level, I can only sigh and look no further." As a result, he urged China to imitate "the magnanimity (*duliang*) and knowledge (*zhishi*) of its

[Germany's] legislators."

He also urged his compatriots to be prepared to imitate the long, bitter struggle the Germans had endured to enact a democratic constitution. "The proverb has it," he wrote, "[if you] approach the sea and covet fish, the best thing to do is to withdraw and make a net." The German constitution was the "fish" and the struggle of the German Social Democratic Party, the "net." "If we only admire the ease with which they obtained the fish," he wrote, "and forget their hardship in making the net, this is not sufficient to speak of imitating Germany."

This struggle of a handful of German Social Democrats and the achievements of the German legislators in drafting a constitution also strengthened Zhang's faith in an elite. In a state of exhilaration, he wrote, "All of the world's political and social reforms start from the minds of one or two men who are unbending." "In the past, there was Trotsky, and today there is Lenin. In the past, there was Marx, and today there is [Chancellor Friedrich] Ebert."[35] The tone of these words suggests that Zhang was determined to become one of those heroes, a supposition that is supported by his adherence at that time to a philosophy of free will, activism, and belief in people's power to mold their world. Furthermore, there were suggestions in Zhang's earlier writings of the traditional responsibility of the Confucianist (an ideal that was especially apparent in the activism of Wang Yangming).

In addition, his faith in gradualism was reinforced by how long it took the German Social Democrats to come in from the wilderness. Sounding suspiciously like his mentor, Liang Qichao, before the 1911 Revolution, Zhang wrote: "I do not seek fast results and do not ask about the future harvest. [Let us] wait for ten, twenty, thirty, forty, [or] fifty years. Then we can compare the advantages and disadvantages [of the new] with this old society and old system of government and consider such-and-such to be worthless."[36]

One of the practices in the Weimar constitution that most impressed him was its addition of direct democracy to the representative system. England and France, he explained, practiced "absolute parliamentary government"; that is, their policies were decided by their parliaments, and there was no power superior to those representative bodies to which to appeal. His views are especially interesting in view of the fact that he became a political party leader a scant decade later. Obviously, he was thinking of the dismal record of Chinese parliaments and political parties since the 1911 Revolution. A parliament, he complained, meant political parties, and they followed mere routine, were fond of their own selfish desires, and blocked the public's interests. Because of the reaction against parliamentary and political party government, he concluded, "the general trend in nations is clearly toward direct democracy." Germany was the first large nation to combine parliamentary government with direct democracy, he pointed out, and that was good, for "no longer could a minority of political-party representatives and delegates in parliament usurp authority under a false name and regard themselves as the masters." In other words, no longer could the *representatives* of the people's will consider themselves *to be* the people's will, for that led to dictatorship. Instead, in Germany the people were able to exercise the right of referendum, which Zhang considered the essence of direct democracy, making the people the ultimate masters. Thus, he concluded, the spirit of the German constitution was "people's parliamentarism" (*Volkparlamentarismus*).

China was in great disorder, in his view, precisely because its constitution had embraced the theory of absolute parliamentary sovereignty and lacked the slightest trace of direct democracy. It had provided for no appeal to the people in the event a stalemate arose between parliament and government. Thus, the latter two quarreled, while "the citizens, who are the masters, 'watch the fire from the other bank' and behave like people with their hands in their sleeves." Not only were they indifferent, both government and parliament ignored them. "It is called a republic," he wrote, "but . . . [it is] almost without any expression of the sovereignty of the popular will. Can this be called a true democracy and a true republic?" He felt that if a way had been provided in the Provisional Constitution of 1912 for appeal to the people in the event of a deadlock between parliament and government, the issue of declaring war in 1917 and the ongoing problem of enacting a constitution would not have gone to the extremes they did. "Why," he lamented, "was it necessary to take up arms and rebel?" Worst of all were the continuous wars fought between rival warlords. Nine of ten people in China, he wrote, wanted peace. However, they could not obtain it, for "except for parliament, the whole body of citizens has no right to speak out."

The solution to the people's lack of power, in his view, was "to follow the German constitution and implement direct democracy." If China implemented the referendum, then it would be able to harness the unanimous opposition of four hundred million people to continued fighting in China. What could the parliament or the soldiers do then? he asked. He felt it imperative to broaden representation of the popular will beyond a few hundred members of parliament, but he was aware that China's huge population would make it difficult to carry out a referendum. His solution was to propose that certain provincial organizations stand in for the people in referendums. Those organizations—chambers of commerce, peasants' associations, learned societies, and local assemblies—were the only ones he thought were expressing popular sovereignty (e.g., by sending telegrams and convening meetings).

He proposed that they be combined to create provincial electoral commissions. Their representation of the popular will, he wrote, would "naturally be truer than that of several hundred members of parliament." Thus, even though absolute direct democracy was impossible due to China's size, he conceded, "is not relative [direct] democracy much better than the so-called popular will of several hundred members of parliament?"[37]

The Germans' combination of direct democracy with representative government also offered him a way to reconcile his disgust concerning the way parliamentary government had operated in China since 1912 with his stubborn conviction that parliamentary government was still the best form of government. In the case of a bad parliament, one could by pass it and appeal directly to the electoral commissions by holding a referendum. He also hoped to use this higher power of referendum to stop the incessant civil wars in China and, at the same time, broaden the people's participation in politics. It was only through such political participation, he felt, that the Chinese people would acquire the skills necessary to operate a democracy.

Finally, he was impressed by the administration of the German elections he observed. He admired their lack of corruption, which contrasted so sharply with China's elections, and hence proposed that China take them as its model.[38]

He was not happy with everything about the new German government and constitution, though. His greatest disappointment was the constitution's lack of provisions placing the military on a democratic footing. However, in his view, this was not the Germans' fault. The reason, he explained, was that the Allies had not let Germany solve its own military problem but had decided it for that nation in the peace treaty. "In other words," he wrote, "it was not a constitutional problem but a treaty problem." He believed that disarmament would be more enduring if carried out by the German people themselves rather than by international treaty. In support of his argument, he pointed to the Americans and English as examples of people controlling their military. In response to charges that Germany was based on militarism and thus outside restrictions were necessary, he pointed to the German Social Democratic Party's long history of opposition to militarism. He noted in particular that its Erfurt program of 1891 had advocated replacement of Germany's standing army with a "citizens' army" (*guomin jun*) like that of the Swiss. In addition, he wrote, a member of the Germans' postwar committee to draft the constitution had insisted that the Social Democrats had planned to put their military administration on a democratic basis and had complained, "Why do the Allies not let us do it ourselves but [instead] use a treaty to force us?"

Zhang agreed that the Social Democrats should be allowed to take care of their own military problem for their own sake: "If they change their slave army into a citizens' army, their militarist government into a national government, their militarist diplomacy into a national diplomacy, then their democracy and social revolution can be maintained for a long time."

In wishing that the new German constitution contained a military system based on a democratic spirit, he also was thinking of his own country. The world's warlord governments, he lamented, could use Germany's failure as a defense behind which to hide. "How could this only be the Germans' regret?" he concluded. "It is also the common regret of the world's people."[39]

The Socialist Model

Following WWI, socialism and communism were both on the upswing in Europe. As a result, it was not surprising that Zhang took an avid interest in them. During his sojourn from 1919 to 1921, he rejected communism and capitalism, while adopting a lifelong belief in social democracy. He had been aware of socialism since his years of study in Japan prior to the 1911 Revolution.[40] However, his conviction that it was worthy of adoption by China became apparent only during the last months of 1919, in his writings in the journal of Liang Qichao's Research Clique,[41] *Jiefang yu gaizao* (Emancipation and Reconstruction). In short, Zhang was yet another illustration of the groundswell of interest in socialism during the May Fourth era in China.

In mid-1919, the journal's editor, Zhang Dongsun (1886-1972), wrote Zhang that "the world's general trend is already in the direction of moderate (*wenjian*) socialism" and asked him to investigate the situation.[42] In response, Zhang Junmai studied the socialism of the Labour Party and the radical wing of the Liberal Party in Britain and reported that socialism was on the rise in England, while being repudiated in France.

It is clear that his interest in socialism was largely motivated by intense concern with "social revolution" and the "social question." How, he asked, could France avoid social revolution? His answer was to advise it to go with the socialist tide. Moreover, it was not only in France that he glimpsed the specter of social revolution. The whole situation in postwar Europe seemed to point in that direction. Immediately upon his arrival in February 1919, he was struck by the lack of food, the crowded housing, and the hardships caused by numerous strikes (which he also experienced).[43] He was deeply alarmed and later wrote that he "heard about these kinds of things daily and felt that if European life was this restless, then its present social organization definitely could not be maintained."[44]

Although he spoke of Europe, he worried that the threat of upheaval was worldwide. Late in 1920, he voiced his fear that China also would be engulfed. "The world today is one of social revolution," he wrote. "Business and industry are developing daily, while the gap between the poor and the rich is widening daily. If we do not solve this problem, then before we succeed in our political revolution, we might be overtaken by a social revolution."[45] How was China to prevent such an disaster? It had to "go with the world's tide" and implement socialism. Offering a gradualist—and perhaps even Confucianist—solution, he wrote that this could be accomplished by emphasizing the principles of socialism in political education. That, he hoped, would "take some of the wind out of the sails of those who preach class warfare."[46]

Although he was confronted with more than one kind of socialist model in postwar Europe, one could guess from his temperament, his middle-of-the-road constitutional politics, and the moderate brand of socialism that had been advocated by Liang Qichao and the constitutionalists in Japan prior to the 1911 Revolution—social democracy was the dominant form of Japanese socialism in 1906, the year Zhang arrived in that country—that he would embrace social democracy.[47] In addition, since his stay in Europe coincided with the rise to power of the Social Democrats in Germany, where he had studied and whose language he knew, it was that version that captured his attention.

The German Social Democrats had been the most successful in Europe. Established in 1875, their party was the first to be based on the doctrines of social democracy. During the 1880s, the latter became the general pattern of socialism in Europe. Social democracy was even more successful in Germany than elsewhere, though, and after 1890 the German Social Democratic Party became the largest of the parliamentary socialist parties in Europe. By 1912, it was the largest single party in the Reichstag, and by 1914, its membership had reached one million.[48]

Zhang's first contact with German Social Democrats occurred during his trip to Germany in December 1919 and January 1920. He visited the co-founder of the Independent Social Democratic Party, Karl Kautsky (1854-1936), described as "one of the first European Marxists whose interpretation was familiar to the Chinese; his writings on the economy and ethics were the most complete works by a European Marxist available in the early May Fourth period, and his *Class Struggle* was published shortly thereafter [1921]."[49] Two different translations of Kautsky's *Oekonomische Lehren* were published in 1919. This work, an explication of the first volume of Marx's *Capital*, was popular in China and served for several decades after its publication as (in the words of Leszek Kolakowski) "a handbook of Marxist economic theory for beginners."[50] It is doubtful that Zhang was attracted to Kautsky, however, for the latter stressed the deterministic side of Marxism while Zhang was then a strong voluntarist, thanks to his philosophical studies. Hence, he merely recalled of his visit that from his sickbed Kautsky railed against the Russian dictatorship.

Zhang also met German socialists who were far less well known in China—if at all—in 1919-1920.[51] He was introduced to radical Independent Socialists, such as Rudolf Hilferding (1877-1941)—a theoretician—and Rudolf Breitscheid (1874-1944)—a foreign affairs specialist and member of the Reichstag. Their doctrines did not appeal to him either, and later he was often critical of the Independent Socialists.[52] He also met the leader of the revisionist school of Marxism, Eduard Bernstein (1850-1932). Beginning in the 1890s, Bernstein had pointed out that events were not confirming Marxist predictions: the number of people who owned property was increasing, workers were freer and better off, and the capitalist system was becoming stronger and more successful. Hence, he argued, socialism should abide by the "inevitability of gradualness" and concentrate on reforming society through parliamentary democracy and the improvement of workers' lives. He and his supporters pointed to the achievements of parliamentary and democratic social legislation in Britain and the United States, which were in stark contrast to the legislative failures of the German Social Democrats, despite their strength in the Reichstag.[53] Yet, Bernstein must have startled Zhang when he told him in their meeting that there was no hope of implementing European socialism.[54]

Of all the German socialists Zhang met, it was Philip Scheidemann (1865-1939), whom he met in January 1920, who made the deepest impression on him. A leader of the Majority Socialists, Scheidemann had served as chancellor of the new Weimar regime during the first half of 1919. The two men discussed socialization, and Zhang welcomed Scheidemann's idea of a "mixed economy" (*Gemischtwirschaft*). "He used simple language to tell me," wrote Zhang, "[that] pure socialization definitely could not be implemented, [but] the method of joint public-private administration could."[55] This approach would avoid the disaster that had resulted from the Russians' sudden and complete socialization, which had appalled Zhang.[56] It also had the advantage, in his eyes, of resembling a traditional Chinese institution. The method of joint public-private administration, he wrote, was "similar to our country's so-called official-merchant partnership (*guanshang hegu*) or official supervision-merchant management [system] (*guandu shangban*)."[57] This perceived similarity with a native Chinese system may have facilitated his acceptance of the "mixed economy."

Just as important as his meetings with socialists were his conversations in December 1919 with Dr. Hugo Preuss (1860-1925), the drafter of the new

German consitution.[58] A lifelong admirer of the German scholar, Zhang praised Preuss and compared his constitutional achievements with those of Ito Hirobumi (who died in 1909, the year before Zhang graduated from Waseda University) in Meiji Japan, as well as Thomas Jefferson and Alexander Hamilton. When he returned to France in January 1920, Zhang took with him both Preuss's original draft of the German constitution and the final version passed by the Constituent Assembly.[59] In April, his translation of the latter was published in *Jiefang yu gaizao*.[60] Preuss, as well as German political party leaders, also aided Zhang in writing the articles on German social democracy that he published in *Jiefang yu gaizao* during 1920-1921.[61]

Clearly, Zhang was excited by the German constitution. Preuss's draft, he exclaimed, "was able to combine the ideological trends of the nineteenth and twentieth centuries." This "launched a new era in the world of public law," he continued, "[and] I continuously pondered and could not dismiss this [from my mind]."[62] To Zhang, this constitution represented a compromise between the representative and soviet forms of governments, between individual freedom and socialism, and between the laboring and capitalist classes. But most important, he wrote, it represented the tide of social revolution in the twentieth century and hence was the model for all nations. "In the past," he declared, "France was considered the forerunner of political revolution, and all of Europe . . . imitated her. But henceforth the various nations will select Germany, the forerunner of social revolution, as the standard."

By mid-1920, then, he was proclaiming to his countrymen that German social democracy was the model for China and that he was a social democrat. "I want to follow my countrymen," he wrote enthusiastically, "and devote myself to this revolutionary current of twentieth-century social democracy."[63]

However, just as there were Chinese who opposed socialism, there were Chinese who endorsed "socialism" but favored the Soviet, rather than the German, model. Zhang later recalled that when he was in Europe following WWI, the Chinese moderates favored English Fabianism and German social democracy, while the radicals sided with the Soviets' communism.[64] In the spring and summer of 1920, Zhang found himself defending the German model against his old friend and colleague in the Research Clique, Zhang Dongsun. The exchange began after Zhang read an editorial by Dongsun in the 27 February 1920 *Shishi xinbao*, which led off with the following statement: "Yesterday, *Guomin ribao* (National Daily) carried an article on revolution which was rather critical of Zhang Junmai's advocacy of a pro-German and anti-Russian [policy]."[65] Zhang chose to reply to Dongsun, rather than the GMD organ, in a letter dated 17 April 1920.[66] He first made it clear, perhaps to deflect charges that he was a conservative, that he approved of revolution.

Describing it as a way of attaining "our goal of transforming the people and molding our customs," he wrote: "Today we live in China and are bound by a history of four-thousand years of doing everything according to the old patterns. Therefore, we should welcome and introduce all kinds of revolution, regardless of whether they are ideological, political, or social. Why? Because this is the way to reform the old age and enter into the new age." However, he continued, there were two kinds of revolution. In one type, a leader was worshipped as divine, as the founder of a religion. In the other, revolution was regarded as temporary rather than permanent, as something in which, without going to extremes, the people could be shown which path to take.

The important thing for Zhang was to find that path for China. Lenin, he wrote, was an example of the first type of revolution. His exploits had been so amazing that it would be impossible to imitate him. However, the German Revolution was a different story. Supported by the citizens, he wrote, it had succeeded in forming a government and passing a constitution. He conceded that "the ideal of social revolution had not been entirely realized." However, he continued, "the pattern is there. Following this track, the will of the people will naturally mature, after much labor."

He also admitted that the Germans' moderate course had yielded no "glorious achievements." Thus, he added, "it is not admired and applauded by [my] contemporaries." However, that did not matter to him. What did matter was that the German example, unlike the Soviet, could be emulated. "There are none who cannot imitate it," he asserted, "and, having imitated it, there are none who cannot attain it." Hence, although he admired the "nobility of Lenin's principles," his "bravery in action," and felt him to be "the forerunner of social revolution,"[67] when it came to "depth and genuineness of foundation as well as earnestness and sincerity in action," he "esteemed only Germany's Socialist Party."

In his own editorial, Zhang Dongsun proposed that revolutions be evaluated according to whether they corresponded to the popular will and humankind's welfare. Zhang Junmai gave his own appraisal of these two concepts. The popular will, he wrote, had to arise from universal suffrage and equality and could not be thwarted by the use of force. It should reflect the wishes of all the people and not be contrary to law. The popular will, he declared, could not be forged by "one or two heroes." He opposed "one or two men" in Russia deciding the well-being of their people and doubted the Russian people considered those decisions constituted their welfare. He insisted that the Russian leaders should have waited for the ripening of public opinion and then acted. If it was a question of the people's well-being, he concluded, he was pro-German and anti-Russian.

Zhang Dongsun also proposed that revolutionaries be judged by their willingness to suffer for their principles. There was no doubt, replied Zhang Junmai, that the "German Socialist Party was not as brave and aggressive as Russia." However, it "far surpassed Russia in planting its feet on solid ground." Even if Lenin restored the Russian people's freedom, he added, it was not certain that his accomplishments could match Germany's. In sum, Zhang selected German social democracy as China's model because it could be imitated, it valued public opinion and the welfare of its people, and its leaders "had their feet planted on solid ground."

Perhaps most important, however, were the "means" the two revolutions had employed to attain their ends. "My pro and con [attitude] toward the German and Russian revolutions," he declared, "is not based upon their implementation of socialism but upon the means they adopted. I am one of those who hopes to use legal means to decide the social revolution. Therefore, I do not dare lightly agree to a Leninist revolution." The socialist articles of the new German constitution, he acknowledged, had definitely not satisfied the wishes of the German socialists. Yet, he approved of them because they used "legal means."[68]

He went on to explain what he meant. While he believed that respect for labor on the part of those who supported "industrial democracy or democracy in a productive sense" (his English) was right, overrespect to the point that others were excluded from participation in politics was a great inequality. That legal inequality, he added, was one reason he did not praise Leninist revolution. Instead, he was for a Chinese nation based on law. "A nation must rely upon law for its establishment," he argued. "If there is no law, the nation cannot exist. The establishment of law requires a definite organ and a definite order. If it is illicitly changed by the power of a minority, then the law is not law and the nation will be in disorder."

The underpinnings of his faith in law as the basis for the establishment of the nation—a belief that contrasted with his disgust with international law following the Versailles Conference—derived partly from his legal, especially constitutional, training at Waseda and Berlin universities. But even more fundamentally, such a position rested on his strong belief in reason and rejection of emotionalism, a position he had first revealed in 1907 in response to the Revolutionary Alliance's call for a racial revolution.[69]

He had yet another reason for preferring the German model. The proposals of the German socialists, like those of Eucken and the other antipositivists to whom he was attracted, fit his Confucian beliefs. China should emulate the German socialists, he wrote, because their program corresponded to the "golden mean" or "middle way" (*zhongyong*):

> Our Sage [Confucius] . . . said that what should be taught to others lies in showing them the way of the golden mean (*zhongyong zhi dao*). What exceeds the golden mean, the Sage does not wish to use to lead the world. If we truly accept these words, then what our countrymen should imitate is the German Social Democratic Party's planting their feet on solid ground (*jiaota shidi*) and not Lenin's immediate achievements and quick results.[70]

He realized that the German model, like the Russian, had involved revolution. He tried to come to grips with the discrepancy between that revolution and his advocacy of legal means, reason, and the golden mean by stressing the difference between socialist parties' parliamentary and revolutionary approaches. "Germany, because it leans toward the parliamentary strategy," he wrote, "loses in socialism but gains in legality. Russia, because it leans toward revolutionary methods, gains in socialism but loses in legality." While recognizing the difficulty, he tried to reconcile the two strategies and his simultaneous calls for revolution, reason, and legal means: "We should use revolutionary means to elimate the warlords, but we should adopt the parliamentary strategy for the advancement of the laborers' position and the transfer of political power."[71] But was it possible to apply revolutionary means selectively? Could the revolutionary genie, once unleashed on the warlords, be confined to that arena and not affect the transfer of power and the laborers' position? The experience of the revolutionary 1920s, still on the horizon in 1920-1921, suggests that his compromise was academic rather than practical.

In the course of arguing for German socialism rather than Russian communism as China's model, in April 1920 Zhang offered his own economic program. Although this was the first such program he proposed, it was not the last. It is quite interesting, for it was a point-by-point prescription for what he perceived to be China's economic and social ills. It was, in fact, his plan for avoiding the social revolution he feared was coming to China.

First, China's economic organization should not repeat the history of European capitalism's failure.[72] Hence, he rejected Western capitalism as a model for China and advocated instead German-style social democracy.

Second, socialization of enterprises had to begin with railroads and mines and be administered by a joint organization of government, technicians, and consumers. This administration, he warned, could not be entrusted to bureaucrats. Here, he was obviously influenced by the "mixed economy" advocated by Scheidemann and the German Social Democrats, which appealed to Zhang as a middle course between two evils. On the one hand was the capitalism he thought made the rich richer and the poor poverty stricken. On the other hand, while socialism's nationalization of land and the means of production "made the rich unable to obtain their selfish desires and the poor able to enjoy equality of human happiness,"[73] if complete socialization was carried out it would result in bureaucracy managing all industry. Then, he wrote, "the evils that arose would certainly be more numerous than [those that arise from] private ownership and capitalism."[74] The "mixed economy," he argued, would avoid those two extremes by clearly recognizing the great principles of individual freedom and private property, while socializing the important means of production, that is, those related to the public interest.[75]

It was clear from his other writings that this socialization was to be carried out by legal means, unlike Russia's expropriation measures. This meant there would be compensation for nationalized properties, and nationalization would be according to law. The implementation of socialism, he argued, should "take democracy as its foundation."[76]

Third, banks and large industries should be heavily taxed and prevented from using their wealth to influence politics.

Fourth, newly developed commercial ports and land should be municipalized, and the nation's uncleared land should not be administered and developed by individuals. In fact, the latter point may have represented a compromise for him. Although he supported nationalization of land in theory—writing that if it was not implemented, it would be "absolutely impossible to pretend to the name of communism or socialism"—he avoided discussion of concrete measures. However, he did come out against distribution of the land of great landlords to the peasants. That, he argued, was not socialism but merely changing large private property into small private property.[77] In the final analysis, he failed to offer a solution to China's land problem. It is unclear whether that had anything to do with his standing as a member of the gentry class or whether he had land holdings to protect.

Fifth, it was necessary to explain in detail how much harm accompanied the foreign banking consortium's interference in China's finances, reduction of its sovereignty, and disturbance of world peace. China, he continued, should request the support of the League of Nations or the public opinion of other nations in devising a way to abolish it. Such opposition to foreign control over China's finances was a familiar theme in his writings. Even though he opposed much of what Lenin and the Russian Revolution had done, for example, he endorsed Lenin's cancellation of Russia's foreign debts. That action, he wrote, had "imperishable merit" as a warning to the "international capitalists."[78] Nevertheless, just a few months after publication of his economic program, Britain, France, Japan, and the United States established a new International Consortium to lend money to China.[79]

Sixth, China should gradually establish workers' councils (*gongren huiyi*) in the factories. With a note of urgency, he argued that "it is impossible to wait until after they [the workers] and the capitalists are mutually opposed and then implement a remedy." In advocating this measure, he was clearly influenced by Article 165 of the Weimar constitution, which called for the establishment of local, district, and national workers' councils, to look after the workers' social and economic interests.[80] He thought this provision preserved the benefits of the soviet system ("I absolutely approve of . . . the soviet system that removes the distinction between factory owner and worker"), while restricting it to the economic sphere. Although the "form" of Russia's soviets could not be transplanted to Western Europe, he admitted, the "spirit" already had been. As evidence, he cited the workers' councils and the National Economic Council in Germany, as well as the Industrial Parliament convened in England at the time of the 1919 railroad strike.[81]

He was not blind to the defects of the workers' councils. He criticized their workings in Germany and called them merely an aid to the factory owner, "an organ that neglects the workers," and "very far removed from the ideal of socialism." They did not represent socialism, for they were administrative and had nothing to do with the abolition of private property.[82] However, he declared, they were "the beginning of the German socialist revolution, not the end." They would enable the workers to participate in factory administration and thus "train and gain experience in order to prepare for the later nationalization of industry and abolition of the factory-owner class."[83]

Along the same lines, he was impressed by the schools for workers established by the German Social Democratic Party educators following passage of the Workers' Council Law. Those schools, he explained, were to advance the ability of the workers to administer the affairs of the factory. If they were successful, he argued, then worker self-government would be possible. Hence, he observed the operation of one such institution in Jena.[84]

His lifelong "addiction" to constitutionalism was never far beneath the surface. The establishment of the workers' councils, he noted, would "almost" create a "constitutional organization of the factory." "The workers' and factory owners' negotiation of conditions from positions of opposition," he wrote, "is like the constitutional form of government in which the monarch and the people jointly rule." In the same spirit, however, the ultimate goal was the "republican form of government" within the factory: "The removal of the factory owner, nationalization of the factory, and its administration by the worker is the republican form of government." The Russians, he asserted, had already attained the "republican form of government" in their factory organization, but the Germans were still in the era of "joint rule by monarch and people."[85] Certainly, this was a vivid demonstration of the hold constitutionalism exerted on his view of the world.

By the time of his return to China in late 1921, then, he was convinced that German-style social democracy—not capitalism, communism, or guild socialism—was absolutely necessary for China. To objections that socialism was not suitable for China, he replied that, thanks to the foreign capital that concentrated China's industry just when it was just beginning to develop, "no country is more suitable for the implementation of socialism than China." He continued optimistically: "The awakening of our country's workers has occurred simultaneously with the development of capitalism; therefore, the socialist movement certainly will ripen earlier than in other countries."[86] In fact, he hoped China could bypass capitalism and move straight into socialism.[87]

He still thought it too early to organize a socialist party, though. In 1920, he advised Liang Qichao, who evidently had ideas about establishing such an organization, that it could not be done.[88] Yet, if a socialist party was impossible, exactly how did Zhang propose to implement socialism in China? Certainly not through the warlord governments. Part of the answer lay in his new activist and voluntarist philosophy. If a few men with true beliefs would enthusiastically rise up, he believed, a new society and history could be created. The other part of the answer was the gradualist one of socialist education and his hope to "reap our harvest in a decade or a century."

Conclusion

Before WWI, the German impact on China was dominated by militarism and imperialism. This was natural, for those two isms characterized the post-unification Germany of the Kaisers. Following the war, German influence changed (at least temporarily, for the military model was to be imported again during the Nanjing Decade) and presented China with political and economic choices.

A returned student from Germany, Zhang was a strong proponent of the German model, specifically the Weimar Constitution and German social democracy. In propounding the former, he was actually supporting *Western* constitutionalism, for the Weimar constitution was an amalgam of several countries' practices. Moreover, although he had been a firm believer in constitutionalism since his student days in Japan, that faith was undoubtedly reinforced by the postwar feeling that democracy had triumphed over despotism in WWI (a perception that also had a positive impact on Japan). As one European historian explained, "In democracy, it seemed, lay the secret of success in the modern world. Democracy came into vogue."[89]

In addition, there was much about postwar Germany that must have struck Zhang as familiar. Germany had been humiliated in war, much as China had been since the Opium War of the nineteenth century. The Weimar regime, like China, had to contend with a barely controllable military. Following WWI, extremists were abroad in both lands as well. Both nations had toppled their monarchies and replaced them with republics. Although Zhang could not have known it at the time, the Weimar republic was to fail within a few years (1933), just as had the Chinese republic. The German Social Democrats he so admired would be destroyed by the rise of a strong man and his personality cult, as democracy in China would be stumped by the likes of Chiang Kai-shek and Mao Zedong. Eventually, both republics had to cope with hyperinflation, although China's did not become full-blown until the late 1940s. Finally, both were severely tried by the World Depression of the 1930s. On the other hand, in contrast to China, Germany—even in defeat (like Japan in 1945)—possessed the prerequisites of an advanced country, with an educated population, skilled managers, and trained workers. It was unfortunate that those modern instruments would be put to use by Hitler before long.

This chapter has traced Zhang's attempts in the late 1910s and early 1920s to convince his country that the German model was worthy of adoption. In advocating social democracy for Republican China, he was not alone. The first leader of the CCP, Chen Duxiu, ended his days supporting a combination of parliamentary democracy and democratic socialism. Yet, in the 1930s and 1940s, other men would arise to support other Western models for China (such as fascism and communism). One can only wonder, in light of the history of the half-century following WWI, what China would be like today if Zhang's arguments had won the day and China had become a constitutional, social-democratic country in the early 1920s.

Notes

1. The following survey of German influence on China is based on Colin MacKerras and Robert Chan, comps., *Modern China: A Chronology from 1842 to the Present* (London: Thames & Hudson, 1982); John K. Fairbank and Edwin O. Reischauer, *China: Tradition and Transformation*, rev. ed. (Boston: Houghton Mifflin, 1989).

2. For a succinct biography of Li, see Hummel, *Eminent Chinese of the Ch'ing Period*, 464-71.

3. For a short biography, see ibid., 27-32.

4. During the Sino-Japanese War, Zhang—then residing in Wuchang as governor-general of Hubei and Hunan—was appointed acting governor-general in Nanjing (1894-96). Ibid., 29.

5. For a brief biography of Yuan, see ibid., 950-54. For detailed studies of his life, see Jerome Ch'en, *Yuan Shih-k'ai*, 2d ed. (Stanford: Stanford University Press, 1972); Ernest P. Young, *The Presidency of Yuan Shih-k'ai: Liberalism and Dictatorship in Early Republican China* (Ann Arbor: University of Michigan Press, 1977).

6. In the early stages of the Second Sino-Japanese War (1937-45), the Germans again were pressed into service as mediators.

7. For the German commander's recollections of his experiences in China, see *A Field-Marshal's Memoirs* (London: Hutchinson, 1924).

8. In fact, in 1911 Germany had already signed a convention with Shandong province agreeing to return the railway and mining rights there. MacKerras and Chan, *Modern China*, 235-36.

9. In June 1924, China and Germany reached agreement resolving those Chinese debts to Germany. Ibid., 295.

10. WCSH, 9.

11. YX, 14.

12. Zhang, "Waiguo bannian jishi," 7-8.

13. WCSH, 9-10. For the possible influence of Schmoller and Wagner on Zhang and the NSP's economic platform in the early 1930s, see infra, chap. 8.

14. Xie Fuya, "Zhang Junmai xiansheng er san shi" (Two or Three Matters about Mr. Zhang Junmai), *Minzhu shehui* 5, no. 2 (1969): 23.

15. WCSH, 10.

16. Ibid.

17. Zhang Junmai, *Guo xian yi* (Discussion of the National Constitution) (Taipei: Taiwan shangwu yinshuguan, 1970), 65; Zhang Junmai, "Yizhe xu" (Translator's Introduction), in Erich Ludendorff, *Quan minzu zhanzheng lun* (*Der Total Krieg*), trans. Zhang Junmai (Chongqing: Shangwu yinshuguan, 1943), 15. All the powers, not only Germany, were tied to their railway timetables for the swift and efficient mobilization necessary to rush their armies to the front. In their mobilization, e.g., the French used 4,278 trains, with only nineteen running late. Alistair Horne, review of *War by Time-Table: How the First World War Began*, by A. J. P. Taylor, in *The Washington Post Book World*, 30 November 1969.

18. Zhang, "Wode xuesheng shidai," 8; Zhang, "Yizhe xu," in *Quan minzu zhanzheng*, 14.

19. Zhang, *Zhonghua minguo minzhu xianfa*, 36; Zhang Junmai, "Oudong xin zhanqu zhi waijiao chaoliu" (Diplomatic Currents in the New War Zone in Eastern Europe), *Dongfang zazhi* 13, no. 2 (1916): 33; Zhang, "Yizhe xu," in *Quan minzu zhanzheng*, 16.

20. Koppel S. Pinson, *Modern Germany: Its History and Civilization* (New York: Macmillan, 1954), 315-16. Liszt's and Schmoller's approval of German aggression reminds one of the approval of Japanese expansion expressed by Zhang's Waseda mentor, Ukita Kazutami.

21. Zhang, *Zhonghua minguo minzhu xianfa*, 36.

22. LHWLX, 7; Zhang, "Wode xuesheng shidai," 8; WCSH, 10.

23. YX, 15.

24. For Zhang's "lessons of the war," see his "Ying junxu dachen Lude Qiaoqi shi zhi junhuo yu zhanzheng guan" (The Views of England's Secretary of War, Lord Kitchener, on Munitions and War), *Dongfang zazhi* 13, no. 4 (1916): 18-23; *Guo xian yi*, 64-66; "Yizhe xu," in *Quan minzu zhanzheng*, 16, 18.

25. WCSH, 10; YX, 15.

26. For a description of that role, see Jeans, "Syncretism in Defense of Confucianism," 152-62.

27. YX, 16.

28. Zhang Junmai, "Xueshu fangfa shang zhi guanjian" (My View of Scholarly Methods), *Gaizao* 4, no. 5 (1922): 1-2. For a detailed discussion of Zhang's studies with Eucken, as well as interest in other European philosophers, see Jeans, "Syncretism in Deense of Confucianism," chap. 7. Eucken, too, was a German nationalist, as seen in his signing of the manifesto on Belgium mentioned earlier in this chapter. Pinson, *Modern Germany*, 316.

29. Chow Tse-tsung, *The May Fourth Movement: Intellectual Revolution in Modern China* (Cambridge: Harvard University Press, 1960), 228.

30. WCSH, 12.

31. Jeans, "Syncretism in Defense of Confucianism," 289-92.

32. David Thomson, *Europe since Napoleon*, 2d ed. (New York: Knopf, 1962), 552-54.

33. Ibid., 552.

34. The previous discussion is based on Zhang Junmai, *Xin Deguo shehui minzhu zhengxiang ji* (Notes on the Political Aspects of the New German Social Democracy) (Shanghai: Shangwu yinshuguan, 1922), 1-2, 5, 61-63 (hereafter, *XDG*).

35. The prior discussion is summarized from ibid., 118-19. On his admiration for the protracted struggle of a handful of German Social Democrats, see also ibid., 6, 53-54.

36. Ibid., 119.

37. The previous discussion is summarized from ibid., 3-5, 80-81, 86-94.

38. Zhang, *Guo xian yi*, 39.

39. The prior discussion is summarized from *XDG*, 112-18.

40. See, e.g., his "Mule Yuehan yiyuan zhengzhi lun," 44; "Waiguo bannian jishi," 7-8.

41. Chow, *The May Fourth Movement*, 243. After the death of Yuan Shikai, the Progressive Party was dissolved. In 1916-17, its former members joined with other moderate politicians to establish the Constitutional Research Society (*Xianfa yanjiu hui*)—popularly known as the Research Clique (*Yanjiu hui*)—as a club in the parliament. Like the Progressive Party, the Research Clique was led by Liang Qichao. Ibid., 76, n. a. For a historical sketch of the organization during the 1910s, see Andrew J. Nathan, "Constitution Research Society," in *Political Parties of Asia and the Pacific: Afghanistan-Korea (ROK)*, ed. Haruhiro Fukui (Westport, CT: Greenwood,

1985), 236-37. Nathan is mistaken when he asserts that members of the Clique "did not constitute an organized party or movement" after 1918, for many of its members (including Zhang Junmai) went on to serve as mainstays of the NSP and its successor, the DSP, in the 1930s and 1940s.

42. NB, 2: 567.

43. Jeans, "Syncretism in Defense of Confucianism," 250-53.

44. Zhang Junmai, "Yijiuyijiu zhi yijiueryi nian lu Ouzhong zhi zhengzhi yinxiang ji wuren suo de zhi jiaoxun" (My Political Impressions during My Stay in Europe, 1919-1921, and the Lessons I Learned), *Xinlu* 1, no. 5 (1928): 19-20.

45. Zhang Junmai, "Zhengzhi huodong guo zuyi jiu Zhongguo ye?" (Are Political Activities Really Sufficient to Save China?), *Gaizao* 3, no. 6 (1921): 6. For a discussion of the desire of many Chinese to avoid social revolution by adopting socialism, see Arif Dirlik, *The Origins of Chinese Comunism* (Oxford: Oxford University Press, 1989).

46. Ibid. In stressing education, Zhang echoed Confucianism's preoccupation with education as the answer to many of humanity's problems.

47. Martin Bernal, "The Triumph of Anarchism over Marxism," in *China in Revolution: The First Phase, 1900-1913*, ed. Mary C. Wright (New Haven: Yale University Press, 1968), 100; Robert A. Scalapino and Harold Schiffrin, "Early Socialist Currents in the Chinese Revolutionary Movement: Sun Yat-sen Versus Liang Ch'i-ch'ao," *Journal of Asian Studies* 18, no. 3 (1959): 338, 341.

48. Thomson, *Europe since Napoleon*, 366-68.

49. Dirlik, *The Origins of Chinese Communism*, 110.

50. Ibid., 98, 105, 107-08. The Kolakowski quotation is from his *Main Currents of Marxism*, 3 vols. (New York: Oxford University Press, 1981), 2: 33.

51. The names Hilferding and Breitscheid do not appear in Dirlik's list of writings on socialism published in China during 1919-1920. Dirlik, *The Origins of Chinese Communism*, 99-103.

52. See Zhang Junmai, "Zhongguo qiantu: Deguo hu, Eguo hu?" (China's Future: Germany or Russia?), *Jiefang yu gaizao* 2, no. 14 (1920): 7; *XDG*, chap. 2. On Hilferding, Breitscheid, and the Independent Social Democrats, see David W. Morgan, *The Socialist Left and the German Revolution: A History of the German Independent Social Democratic Party, 1917-1922* (Ithaca: Cornell University Press, 1975).

53. Thomson, *Europe Since Napoleon*, 369.

54. On Zhang's meetings with Kautsky, Hilferding, Breitscheid, and Bernstein, see his "Xueshu fangfa," 1; "Yijiuyijiu lu Ouzhong," 21.

55. Ibid.; Zhang Junmai, *Liguo zhi dao* (The Way to Establish the State), 5th ed. (Taipei: Central Headquarters, Chinese Democratic Socialist Party, 1969), 193. This work was first published in Guilin in September 1938.

56. See, e.g., Zhang, "Yijiuyijiu lu Ouzhong," 22, where he castigated Russia's expropriation of all heavy industry after the revolution. That was not true public ownership, he wrote, but only destruction of the people's production.

57. Ibid. It is doubtful the systems were "similar." The official in the "mixed economy" probably did not have the power over the private sector his Chinese counterpart had. On the *guandu shangban*, see Albert Feuerwerker, *China's Industrialization: Sheng Hsuan-huai (1844-1916) and Mandarin Enterprise* (Cambridge: Harvard University Press, 1958).

58. See the photograph of Preuss, which the latter gave to Zhang, in *XDG*. In comments written on it, Zhang stated that Preuss had given it to him while Zhang was traveling in Germany with Liang Qichao. The photograph is dated 23 December 1919, Berlin.

59. Zhang, "Yijiuyijiu lu Ouzhong," 20.

60. Zhang Junmai, "Deyizhiguo xianfa quanwen" (The Complete Text of the German Constitution), *Jiefang yu gaizao* 2, no. 8 (1920): 39-84.

61. *XDG*, introduction.

62. Zhang, "Yijiuyijiu lu Ouzhong," 20-21.

63. *XDG*, 2-5, 66, 119.

64. Zhang Junmai, "Zhang Dongsun xiansheng bashi shouxu" (Wishing Mr. Zhang Dongsun Longevity on His Eightieth Birthday), *Ziyou zhong* (Liberty Bell) 1, no. 3 (1965): 22.

65. Zhang, "Zhongguo qiantu," 1.

66. The following discussion is based on ibid., 1-6, 8-9.

67. For further praise of Lenin, see Zhang's "Du *Liu xingqi zhi Eguo*" (On *Six Weeks in Russia*), *Gaizao* 3, no. 1 (1920): 61-71; no. 2 (1920): 51-63.

68. For a further explanation of his assertion that the socialist articles of the German constitution had not satisfied the German Socialist Party, see his "Deguo xin gonghe xianfa ping" (A Critique of the Constitution of the New German Republic), *Jiefang yu gaizao* 2, nos. 9-12 (1920).

69. Zhang, "Mule Yuehan," 36, 56-59.

70. Zhang, "Zhongguo qiantu," 6.

71. Ibid., 9.

72. The six points of Zhang's economic program discussed here are from ibid., 10.

73. *XDG*, 3-4.

74. Zhang, "Du *Liu xingqi zhi Eguo*," 71.

75. *XDG*, 4.

76. Ibid., 4, 96; Zhang, "Du *Liu xingqi zhi Eguo*," 67; Zhang, "Yijiuyijiu lu Ouzhong," 22.

77. Zhang, "Du *Liu xingqi zhi Eguo*," 67; *XDG*, 309-10, 312.

78. Ibid., 391.

79. MacKerras and Chan, *Modern China*, 277.

80. Rene Brunet, *The New German Constitution*, trans. Joseph Gollomb (New York: Knopf, 1922), 335.

81. *XDG*, 241, 256; Zhang, "Du *Liu xingqi zhi Eguo*," 53.

82. *XDG*, 251-52, 256, 309.

83. Ibid., 257.

84. Zhang, "Yijiuyijiu lu Ouzhong," 23; *XDG*, 261.

85. Ibid., 249, 257.

86. Ibid., 324.

87. Zhang Junmai, "Xuanni zhi shehui gaizao tongzhi hui yijianshu," (Presentation of a Proposal by the Association of Comrades for Social Reform), *Gaizao* 4, no. 3 (1921): 9.

88. NB, 2: 586.

89. Thomson, *Europe since Napoleon*, 552.

PART TWO

Politician and Educator in Warlord and Guomindang China

3

The Making of a Third-Force Politician in the 1920s

During the period of Guomindang (GMD) rule in China (1927-49), life was rough for those who did not agree with Chiang Kai-shek and the GMD's ways of governing China. Opponents of the regime were executed, assassinated, jailed, or driven into exile.[1] Since many of these figures were anti-Communists as well, they were denied the option of embracing the Chinese Communist (CCP) movement as an alternative to GMD control of China. One of those dissidents was Zhang Junmai, who spent most of the 1920s, 1930s, and 1940s in opposition to both the GMD and the CCP. In place of their programs for China, he offered his own vision, laid out in his writings and speeches during those decades.

This third-party approach was not something Zhang suddenly discovered in the 1930s. A glance at his prior political career reveals that his opposition to the GMD and the CCP had been long in the coming. This chapter will trace the roots of this independent stance, beginning with a brief review of his political activities in Japan before 1911 (more fully treated in chapter 1) and ending with the maturing of his "third-force" stance in the mid-1920s. The question of his dissidence during the Nanjing Decade (1927-1937) is the focus of chapters 5 and 8.

Origins of Zhang's Opposition to the GMD, 1906-1921

By the mid-1920s, hostility between Zhang and the GMD had a history of nearly twenty years. It all began during the period just before the 1911 Revolution, when Zhang was a student at Waseda University in Tokyo. During his stay in Japan, he sided with the constitutional reform group led by Kang Youwei and Liang Qichao, which was battling the Revolutionary Alliance.

The names of Kang and Liang were not new to Zhang when he arrived in

Japan, for he had heard of them as early as 1898. The failure of the Reform Movement that year had made a deep impression on the eleven-year-old Jiangsu native. Over a half-century later, he recalled, "As a boy I was interested in politics. During my high school days, I saw the pictures of K'ang Yu-wei and Liang Ch'i-ch'ao posted on the school gates, with the notice that they were 'wanted' as a result of the coup d'etat of 1898."[2]

In later years, he also praised the Society for the Study of Self-Strengthening (*Qiangxue hui*), established by Kang in 1895, as "the beginning of the real awakening of the Chinese people" and as marking a shift in the initiative for change from the court to the nation's "intellectual leaders."[3] Prior to traveling to Japan, he also was influenced by Liang Qichao's magazine, *Xinmin congbao*, to which students in Shanghai had easy access.[4] In 1903, after reading an article by Liang entitled, "Best Wishes for the Future of the Aurora Academy," Zhang decided to attend the Shanghai school.[5] In later years, he gave vivid testimony to the deep impression Liang's writings made on Chinese youth such as himself:

> There is perhaps no man in the history of modern China who exerted as great an influence through his pen as Liang. His scholarship was not profound, but his knowledge was so embracing, and the style of his writing so charming and effective that anybody who could read immediately came under the spell of his personality. . . . He was a master of political pamphleteering, and his articles began to be read all over the country with unprecedented enthusiasm.[6]

Although familiar with those writings since at least 1903, it was not until Zhang's arrival in Japan that he met the author. He was much impressed and in 1906 joined Liang's Constitutional Party (*Xianzheng dang*), whose program was to "demand political reform under the Manchu Monarchy."[7] Furthermore, during 1906-1907, he contributed articles to *Xinmin congbao*.

In 1907, Liang founded the Political Information Society, which was designed to ensure, through peaceful and orderly means, a swift transition to constitutional government.[8] Zhang was one of its founding members, as well as a contributor to its journal, *Zhenglun*.[9] The society was opposed by the Revolutionary Alliance, as well as the Manchus. When its founding congress was held in 1907, the revolutionaries disrupted it and physically attacked Liang and other participants.[10]

Zhang made it clear that he supported Liang's opposition to the revolutionaries. In his articles in *Xinmin congbao*, Zhang took issue with the Revolutionary Alliance's call for revolution, as well as its anti-Manchu racialism. Instead, he argued for political reform aimed at the establishment of a constitutional government.[11] After the founding of the republic, he later claimed, the hostility between the constitutionalists and the revolutionaries waned. As soon as the constitutionalists saw that the revolution had been successful and widespread internal disorders and bloodshed avoided, he wrote, they pitched in to make the revolution a success. Zhang himself tried to "carry out work to strengthen the republican form of government." Hence, he argued, the Republic was established by the "cooperation between the constitutionalists . . . and the revolutionary party."[12]

The situation at the time was a bit more complex, however. It is true that in December 1911, Zhang raised the possibility of cooperation with Sun Yat-sen's party.[13] Such a move, however, proved infeasible, due to what has been termed "personal and ideological differences between Liang [Qichao] and the T'ung Meng Hui leaders and their long-standing feuds."[14] Thus, a few months later, Zhang complained that the "opposition of the revolutionary party is just as fierce as in the past."[15] In later years, he blamed this lack of cooperation between the two groups on Sun Yat-sen.[16] For their part, the revolutionaries later accused Liang—justly, it seems—of having collaborated with Yuan Shikai while refusing to cooperate with them.[17]

When Liang's Progressive Party was founded on 29 May 1913, Zhang was appointed one of more than three hundred "counsellors" (*canyi*) in the organization.[18] This party stood in opposition to the GMD, constituted from a merger of the Revolutionary Alliance with several other groups at a congress held in Peking on 25 August 1912,[19] during the brief period before Yuan Shikai dissolved the fledging parliament and took all power into his own hands (10 January 1914). Since he was abroad at the time, Zhang was not an active participant in the Progressive Party.[20] However, his brother, Chang Kia-ngau, was, and later testified to the continuing enmity between Sun's and Liang's groups. The "scheming and conflict between the Chin-pu-tang and Kuo-min-tang," he recalled, "caused me to develop a strong aversion to politics."[21]

Yuan Shikai's attempt to reestablish the monarchy succeeded in bringing about a brief period of cooperation between the former constitutionalists and the revolutionaries during the winter of 1915 and spring of 1916. Following the death of Yuan in June 1916, however, the old hostility between the two groups was rekindled. One of the forms it took was a debate over the wisdom of joining the Allies in the fight against Germany and the other Central Powers. Zhang and Liang Qichao argued for a declaration of war against Germany, while Sun Yat-sen opposed such a move.[22] The victory of the former (on 14 August a presidential mandate was issued declaring war on Germany and Austria-Hungary[23]) could not have improved relations between the rival groups. Hence, by the time Zhang journeyed to Europe in late 1918, the antagonism between him and Sun's followers was firmly rooted.

Zhang Becomes an Anti-Communist, 1919-1921

In November 1917, Zhang turned his back in disgust on domestic (i.e., warlord) politics and the following year journeyed to Europe, where he remained until 1921. During that sojourn, he added opposition to communism to his long-standing antagonism toward the GMD. The origins of this lifelong anticommunism can be found in a general antipathy to Soviet communism, which began at this time,[24] as well as personal experience with Communists during his stay in Germany.

During these years in Europe, he became a socialist (see chapter 2), while rejecting both the capitalist and communist models.[25] His dislike for the latter was partly a result of his contacts with German socialists, from whom he heard a great deal about the activities of the Communist Party.[26] Thanks to members of both the left and right factions of the German Socialist Party, he was even able to hear the reports of those who came from Moscow.[27]

By that time, he also was familiar with the Soviet system. In 1919, he translated the Soviet constitution.[28] In addition, he was not pleased with what he heard about the Soviets' economic approach. A decade later, he criticized as a disaster what he termed their sudden and complete socialization. Their expropriation of all heavy industry after the Russian Revolution, he wrote, was not true public ownership but destruction of the people's production.[29] In the debate with his friend Zhang Dongsun in 1920, he made clear that he rejected the Russian model in favor of the German (see chapter 2).

This opposition to Soviet communism was intensified by his experiences while studying in Germany, in particular his witnessing of (and near involvement in) the abortive communist uprising of March 1921 in Halle and Jena. This attempted coup, the "disaster of March 1921," led to a large drop in the membership of the German Communist Party (from 350,000 to 150,000). It meant, in the view of one scholar, that "for the time being" the Communist mass party in Germany had "practically ceased to exist."[30]

Zhang later recalled that he "personally experienced" the March 1921 insurrections. He had been studying factory laws with Karl Korsch, a professor of trial law at Jena University and leader of the Communist Party in Jena:

> He told me beforehand and [in an] ambiguous [manner] that the day of the next uprising of the European communist parties was not too distant. In less than ten days, the rising occurred as expected. Of three or four hundred members of the Jena Communist Party, only one hundred [responded]. [They] took a locomotive at the railroad station and declared to the people: "We have already occupied Jena." The streetcars in the city struck for half a day, but, outside of

> this, there was no other violent uprising, because the majority of the workers did not agree.[31]

For Zhang, this failure of the communists was made more pathetic by the efforts of Korsch to hide, because of his opposition to the coup. Before the event, Korsch told him that even though he was the leader of the Communist Party in Jena, "I am not for the uprising. If it starts, I shall have to hide in your house." To this, Zhang claimed he replied, "I am a Chinese living here who enjoys no extraterritoriality in Germany, as the Germans used to in China." Korsch's reply was that precisely because Zhang was Chinese, no one would suspect that Korsch was hiding at his place. Despite the outbreak of the uprising, added Zhang, the German failed to appear.[32] Although he seemed to view Korsch's actions as a farce, Zhang was impressed with the opposition to the March uprising of Paul Levi, one of the leaders of the German Communist Party, and knew of his pamphlet, entitled *Our Road*, about the failure.[33]

When Zhang did see Korsch again, the professor told him about the mutual deception practiced by Moscow and the German Communists:

> Korsch told me that when the German Communists went to Moscow, they would report how the membership of the German Communist Party had increased, how the subscriptions to the Communist papers had increased, and how their activities were being successfully carried on. And when the Soviet agents came to Germany, they would say that the Soviet Communist Army was ready on the border to come to the rescue of the German Communists if there was an uprising. "If your uprising took place, the Soviet Army would attack, they say. But," Korsch continued, "I am tired of this kind of information and I don't believe it."[34]

As a result of these experiences and study, by the time Zhang was ready to return to China, lifelong opposition to communism was deeply seated in his mind. In November 1921, just a few months after the founding of the CCP, he pronounced communism unsuitable for China:

> Of a nation's most valuable things, none surpasses the people's free and spontaneous spirit and abilities. The [lack of these] is the reason Asia is inferior to Europe. . . . Today, we forget Asia's shortcomings and praise the spread of Lenin's success, desiring to implement the system of the dictatorship of the proletariat in the East. . . . if it succeeds, one party will monopolize the government, and those who covet private profit will be everywhere in the country. We will not be able to see the least bit of the achievements of the communist system, and I also fear that this smashed and unfit old civilization will be completely swept away. This is why the system of proletarian dictatorship is emphatically not suitable for our country.[35]

Third-Force Politician in Action: Struggles against the GMD and CCP, 1922-1927

Opposition to the GMD

Following his return to warlord-torn China in early 1922, Zhang plunged into numerous causes and debates.[36] While pursuing one of those interests, municipal self-government, he resumed his offensive against the GMD. The occasion was the recovery of Guangdong in October 1920 by the troops of Chen Jiongming, who was then appointed governor of that province by Sun Yat-sen. Chen's first steps were to establish Guangzhou (Canton) as a municipality, organize a municipal council, and appoint the American-educated son of Sun Yat-sen, Sun Fo, as mayor. Chen first entrusted the latter with the drafting of regulations for the Guangzhou municipal council, and not until they were issued on 15 February 1921 did Sun Fo receive his appointment. He then occupied this post from 1921-25, with a hiatus in 1922 due to Chen's revolt against Sun Yat-sen. Sun Fo has been praised for his work as mayor: "Despite many obstructions, he prepared the way for the transformation of the old Chinese city of Canton into the greatest modern metropolis in southern China."[37]

Zhang did not share that rosy view of the younger Sun's accomplishments. In a lecture in March 1922, he criticized the Guangzhou municipal system for a lack of democracy. Guangzhou was the only large Chinese city, he stated, that was governed by Chinese. Under the control of Chen Jiongming and Sun Yat-sen's GMD, he continued, in 1921 it had adopted a municipal system, which was probably the "forerunner of our country's formal municipal systems." He had nothing but criticism, however, for the form that "forerunner" had assumed. The fiction, he wrote, was self-government, but the reality was the mayor was appointed by the governor of the province, and the bureau chiefs, by the mayor. That was pure bureaucracy, he complained, for self-government required popular elections. In another slap at the GMD, he insisted that one could not claim that if Sun Fo was mayor, it was self-government, but if he was not, it was bureaucracy. Finally, the lack of a popular voice in the Guangzhou municipal government clashed with Zhang's belief that the people needed political education. In Guangzhou, he declared, the citizens could not directly exercise administrative authority, since the mayor and bureau chiefs were all appointed, and that was "absolutely incompatible with the cultivation of the practice of self-government."[38]

It was not long before the GMD had its chance to strike back at Zhang. In June 1923, Cao Kun and the Zhili Clique forced Li Yuanhong to resign as president of the republic. In October, Cao bribed the members of the parliament to secure his succession to the presidency. Not surprisingly, Zhang was harshly critical of these events. However, his view of the new constitution that accompanied Cao's election—a document viewed by one political scientist as perhaps the best yet drafted under the republic—[39] was mild. Despite its imperfections, the fact that it was completed by the "piggish" (i.e., bribed) parliament, and its rejection of some of the reforms he advocated, Zhang described it as relatively reasonable, perhaps because it followed in many respects a draft constitution he himself had prepared. Hence, he argued it was the people's duty to carry it out.[40] The GMD thought otherwise, and Shao Lizi, managing editor and publisher of *Guomin ribao*, took issue with Zhang in his newspaper. In addition, the following year the GMD made it crystal clear it considered Zhang and his ilk to be enemies, when the proclamation of the January 1924 First GMD Congress singled out as enemies the "constitutional clique" and the "federal autonomy clique."[41]

Opposition to the CCP and the CCP-GMD United Front

During the early 1920s, Zhang also clashed with the Chinese Communists. Years later, he testified that when he returned to China from Europe in 1922, he already knew that communism could not help Chinese but only harm them.[42] It was unworthy, he declared, of "serving as the good medicine to bring our country back to life."[43] During his European sojourn, he had aimed all his criticism of communism at the Soviet Union. Upon his return to China, however, he found *Chinese* Communists with whom to do battle (the CCP was established in July 1921), although he was to continue to be unrelenting in his criticism of the Soviets. In addition, due to the United Front between the GMD and the CCP during the years 1923-1927, what had been opposition to two separate movements—the GMD and communism—in Zhang's mind merged into opposition to one target, a Soviet-GMD-CCP bloc.

The origins of the GMD's collaboration with the Soviets and the CCP are to be found in a meeting between the Dutch Comintern agent, J. F. M. Sneevliet (pseudonym H. Maring), and Sun Yat-sen in the spring of 1921 in Guangxi. Sneevliet was impressed with Sun, and Sun, with the Soviets' New Economic Policy. Sneevliet was convinced that the GMD was the mainstream of Chinese nationalism and that the tiny CCP should expand its influence by joining the GMD. The leaders of the CCP, Chen Duxiu and Li Dazhao, reluctantly consented, and in August 1922 the CCP Central Committee ordered individual Communists to join Sun's party. On 4 September 1922, a GMD conference in Shanghai approved Sun's new policy of "alliance with

Russia; admission of the Communists" (*lianE rongGong*), and it became the key principle in the reorganization of the GMD.[44]

Zhang could not help but notice this transformation of the party he had opposed since his school days in Japan before the 1911 Revolution. Moreover, he was fresh from Europe, where he had become convinced of the threat posed by Soviet communism. He later recalled that when he returned from Europe in 1922, he saw that the GMD was advocating an alliance with Russia and admission of the Communists to the GMD and had "entrusted to Russia their hopes for treatment of us as equals." He was amazed, he declared, for in his view the Russians used foreign nations to protect themselves. The Third International (Comintern), he added, was that type of organization.[45] "I never expected that from 1921-1922 on," he complained, "those who claimed to be prophets would prostrate themselves before Soviet Russia and utilize [the slogan] 'ally with Russia and admit the Communists' to attract young people."[46]

He blamed Sun Yat-sen for that "worship" of the Soviet Union and for the GMD-CCP alliance, as he had blamed Sun for the lack of cooperation between the constitutionalists and the revolutionaries following the 1911 Revolution. Whereas many Chinese felt that the extremism of the Russian Communist Party was not suitable for China, he declared, Sun Yat-sen "was not afraid of anything and boldly announced [the policy] of cooperation with Russia. Many of us onlookers felt that this was dangerous and just like a boy playing with fire."[47] Following the CCP conquest of China in 1949, he was even harsher in his criticism of Sun. It was Sun's "support and encouragement," he wrote, that enabled the Communists to begin to play an important role in China; indeed, he insisted, the foundation for their success in 1949 was the political status granted them by Sun in the early 1920s.[48]

Following the GMD's adoption, in the fall of 1922, of the alliance with the Soviets and the CCP, the Russians dispatched diplomat Adolf Joffe to work out the terms. In January 1923, the Sun-Joffe Declaration, which laid the basis for large-scale cooperation between the Soviet Union and the GMD, was published. Even though it echoed Zhang's own sentiments when it asserted that communism was unsuitable for China, Zhang later recalled that after he saw the declaration, he "often felt a great disaster was imminent."[49] Explaining why he wrote his 1927 work, *SuE pinglun* (A Critique of Soviet Russia)—and perhaps referring to the GMD's use of large numbers of Soviet advisers (including the famous Michael Borodin) during the years 1923-1927—he later argued:

> [My] countrymen's dependency on Westerners (men with blue eyes; *biyaner*)

> was a long-established habit. Hence, in the great task of reforming the national government, [they] also revered foreigners as teachers. But if we could not stand on our own two feet, how could others help us up? I was keenly aware of our danger and troubled that there was no way to remedy the situation.[50]

In late 1923, his suspicions of communism were reinforced by the mission to China of the deputy commissar for foreign affairs and Soviet ambassador to China, Lev M. Karakhan. On 2 September, the latter reached Peking, where he was warmly welcomed by student groups and government officials. His call for the exchange of ambassadors between China and Russia was contrary to the practice of Western powers accrediting only ministers to China (Karakhan would become the first Soviet ambassador in 1924). Moreover, he vowed that the Soviets would practice open diplomacy (which must have reminded some of Woodrow Wilson's Fourteen Points). After months of negotiations, the Sino-Soviet Treaty was signed on 31 May 1924. Although other foreign powers criticized the agreement, support among Chinese was widespread. "China had at last come of age in the modern world," a Western scholar has written, "negotiating a wholly new treaty with a major power on a basis of equality."[51]

As might be expected, Zhang's view of this Soviet approach to China was less sanguine. At the end of his life, he recalled that he had met Karakhan but was "unable to detect any sincerity, on the part of the Soviet Union, regarding China."[52] He was probably right, for while Karakhan was openly negotiating in Peking, he contacted Sun Yat-sen in Guangzhou and dispatched Michael Borodin to the South to assist the GMD.

Sun Yat-sen, the GMD, and the Soviets were not the only targets of Zhang's wrath then and in the years that followed. He also was opposed to the nascent CCP's close relations with the Soviets. Years later, he wrote that Li Dazhao and Chen Duxiu, the founders of the CCP, "greatly praised Russia."[53] His tone turned acerbic when he recalled his relationship with the latter during the early 1920s: "Chen Duxiu and I were acquainted with each other. However, in the publication he operated in Shanghai [*Xiangdao zhoubao* or *The Guide Weekly*], [he] cursed me as 'Master Zhang' [Zhang *laoye*]. His claim to be [a member of] the 'working class' was really childish and ridiculous."[54] When he returned from Europe, he added, Chen's group had become very powerful. "I did not want to participate in any aspect," he declared, "and determined to oppose Marxism my entire life."[55]

Chen, who was general secretary of the CCP, not only "cursed" Zhang in the pages of his political journal in Shanghai, in November 1923 he also challenged Zhang on ideological grounds. During the course of the "Debate over Science and a Philosophy of Life" that raged during 1923, Chen attacked

Zhang's position.[56] He rebutted, from a Marxist point of view, the nine concerns of a philosophy of life Zhang had put forth in his own contributions to the polemic. Those concerns, Chen asserted, were all determined by different objective causes and effects. Social science can analyze them one by one and offer rational explanations. It is hard to find one that is without an objective cause or rather that has arisen without grounds out of a person's subjective, intuitive free will.[57]

In attacking the other leading participants in the polemic, Ding Wenjiang and Hu Shi, Chen summed up his Marxist faith:

> We believe that only objective material causes can change society, can explain history, and can determine one's philosophy of life. That is the "materialistic interpretation of history." We want to ask Mr. V. K. Ting and Mr. Hu Shih: do they believe the "materialistic interpretation of history" to be the whole truth, or do they believe that, apart from materialism and above science, such things as the idealism advocated by people like Chang Chun-mai can also exist?[58]

In his reply, Zhang criticized Chen's mentor, Karl Marx. Marx, he wrote, had been unable to escape the mid-nineteenth-century belief that social evolution had definite laws and that those laws could be applied through the scientific method. Thus, Marx had called his principles "scientific socialism" and had predicted that, as a result of the operation of dialectical and historical materialism, capitalism would inevitably collapse. However, revolution had occurred in industrially backward Russia and not in England or Germany, where capitalism was "ripe." In addition, Zhang pointed to Russia's New Economic Policy and asked why Russia, after a scant two years, was reverting to private ownership of property. "I do not know," he concluded, "what kind of law in the complete works of scientific socialism this kind of fickle situation follows."

The Marxists also argued, he continued, that the evolution of society was controlled by economic factors and did not need the aid of human efforts. Zhang scoffed at that idea and pointed out that Marx—as shown by his propaganda efforts and deprivation and hardship—had obviously relied on human strength in his attempts to bring about change. Furthermore, it was not economic conditions that had produced the revolution in Russia; on the contrary, he asserted, the "influence of human efforts was far greater."

He then turned on Chen and, in the earliest direct criticism of the CCP in his writings, asked how "those like Chen Duxiu who still observe Marx's theories as if [they were] classics [were] seeking truth? I say that this is [only] a political scheme and Moscow's orders!"[59] The CCP, he added, plagiarized Marx.[60]

During the course of the "Debate over Science and a Philosophy of Life," then, Zhang made clear his enmity toward the CCP. A decade later, he reaffirmed his criticism of Chen's message. Chen, he wrote, had intended to use the 1923 debate to advance the materialist conception of history. His motive in advocating it, however, was not to establish a new kind of theory but only to "promote social revolution."[61]

In early 1924, Zhang founded a school in Shanghai, first called the National Institute of Self-Government (*Guoli zizhi xueyuan*) and then, in 1925, the National Institute of Political Science.[62] In view of his opposition to the CCP and the Soviets, it is not surprising that he used his position at the institute to warn his students about the dangers of communism. He later wrote that each week he taught a class in which he criticized Marxism. In this effort, as in so many others, he was influenced by German scholarship. "I had read so many books written by Germans refuting Marx's historical materialism," he recalled, "and wanted to make them well known." At the end of each year, a large volume of his lectures was compiled and edited. In what was perhaps a recognition of the futility of such criticism, though, he added that his criticism of Marxism was hindered by the fact that the GMD was then cooperating with the Communists.[63]

Conclusion: The Emergence of a Third-Force Politician

By the mid-1920s, then, Zhang had added opposition to the Chinese Communists to his long-standing (since 1906) feud with the GMD. In fact, as we have seen, his opposition to the latter was only intensified by its alliance with the CCP and the Soviets. In reflecting on this period in later years, Zhang characterized it as one in which the question of whether to tolerate or oppose the Communists became the overriding issue in China.[64] From 1923 to 1927, the GMD decided to tolerate the Communists, while Zhang's position was quite different. In 1924, when the United Front between the GMD and the CCP was just beginning, he pleaded for democracy and rule of law, in opposition to "those who support communism in China" and "regard dictatorship . . . as a kind of ideal and pray for its realization." He thought those kinds of people were terribly misled:

> The basis of government must have as its principle the recognition of the personality and freedom of the individual. If their [the Soviets'] political system clearly despises the personalities of others and takes away others' freedom, but [we], on the contrary, look to it as an ideal and do our utmost to promote it, this is nothing less than considering dictatorship the best plan, teaching people to worship heroes, and regarding the people as slaves.[65]

Here, he turned to Immanuel Kant, rather than Confucius, to chastize the Chinese Communists. Kant asserted that it was a moral principle that "mankind should be considered the end, not the means." Not only was that true for morality, Zhang argued, it also was true for politics. Every political act that was contrary to the principles of developing freedom and character, "regardless of how fast the results are," should be rejected.

In a direct slap at the Chinese Communists, who argued for "liberation" during the May Fourth era, he wrote, "How can those who are described as loving freedom not raise the masses and enable them o progress together, but, on the contrary, pray for the appearance of a government by heroes?" In Zhang's view, the Communists' practice was just the opposite of what they preached.[66]

By 1924, then, the third-force politician in opposition to the GMD and the CCP had clearly emerged. The years that followed were to witness his persecution by both of these parties. After 1924, he wrote, he and his colleagues felt isolated. On the left were the Communists; on the right, the dictatorship of the GMD with its policy of cooperation with the CCP. "The projectiles of the Left and the Right came and went, and we stood in the line of fire. That can be regarded as [our] most dangerous period."[67] By the late 1920s, GMD hostility forced him into exile, while twenty years later it was the CCP's turn to drive Zhang from his native land (as Yuan Shikai had done in 1913).

Notes

1. Writing of the assassinations of "enemies of the revolution" carried out by the regime's "Blue Shirts" (the *Lixing she*), one scholar concluded that "the terrorism of the *Lixing she* significantly affected the political climate of Nationalist China." Lloyd E. Eastman, "The Rise and Fall of the 'Blue Shirts': A Review Article," *Republican China* 13, no. 1 (1987): 31-32.

2. Chang, *Third Force*, 23. The order for the two men's arrest was issued on 22 September 1898. Levenson, *Liang Ch'i-ch'ao*, 31.

3. Chang, *Third Force*, 42.

4. Grieder, *Hu Shih*, 21.

5. YX, 11; Zhang, "Wode xuesheng shidai," 7-8.

6. Chang, *Third Force*, 44.

7. Ibid., 23. Formerly known as the Society to Protect the Emperor (*Baohuang hui*), its name was changed to the Constitutional Party following the Empress Dowager's decree on 1 September 1906 calling for preparations for constitutional government. Huang, *Liang Ch'i-ch'ao*, 103, 187 (n. 84).

8. Ibid., 104-7.

9. For a description of Zhang's activities as a member of the Political Information Society, see supra, chap. 1; Jeans, "Syncretism in Defense of Confucianism," 64-69.

10. Li Chien-nung, *The Political History of China*, 217.

11. For further details of Zhang's criticism of the Revolutionary Alliance, see Jeans, "Syncretism in Defense of Confucianism," 70-73.

12. Zhang, "Wu guo zhengdang fazhan," 3. He continued to maintain this position while in exile during the 1950s. Carsun Chang, *China and Gandhian India* (Calcutta: Brahmo, 1956), 47.

13. NB, 1: 372.

14. Huang, *Liang Ch'i-ch'ao*, 119.

15. NB, 1: 373.

16. Chang, *Third Force*, 45.

17. Zhang Junmai, "Zhi Liang Hancao xiansheng lun wushi nianlai zhengzhi wenhua han" (A Letter to Mr. Liang Hancao Discussing the Politics and Culture of the Past Fifty Years), *Minzhu Zhongguo* 5, no. 16 (1962): 3.

18. *Jinbu dang xuanyanshu* (Manifesto of the Progressive Party) (n.p., n.d.), 30.

19. MacKerras and Chan, *Modern China*, 242.

20. When asked later if he had taken part in the establishment of the Progressive Party, Zhang replied that although the members were all good friends of his, at that time he was in Germany and thus did not participate. NBCB 21, no. 3 (1971): 11. Following his return to China in the spring of 1916, however, he served as editor in chief of the Progressive Party organ, *Shishi xinbao*. Ibid. no. 4 (1971): 9.

21. Chang Kia-ngau, "Chang Chia-ao Autobiography" (English translation), ca. 1960, Chinese Oral History Project, Special Collections Library, Butler Library, Columbia University, 28-29.

22. WCSH, 11; YX, 15. On Liang's desire to declare war on the Central Powers, see Huang, *Liang Ch'i-ch'ao*, 135. On Sun's opposition, see Li Chien-nung, *The Political History of China*, 364.

23. MacKerras and Chan, *Modern China*, 264.

24. Zhang was a practical statesman as well, however, for in the fall of 1920 he advocated that China's government establish diplomatic relations with the Soviet Union. He called on the Chinese people, for the sake of "a hundred-year-long national friendship between China and the Soviet Union," to demand that the government negotiate peace and conclude a treaty with Russia. "I do not believe," he wrote, "that the government would dare to oppose the popular will." Zhang, "Du *Liu xingqi zhi Eguo*," 62-63.

25. For his rejection of capitalism, see XDG, 306-9.

26. Chang, *Third Force*, 184-85.

27. Zhang Junmai, *Shitailin zhixia zhi SuE* (Soviet Russia under the Rule of Stalin) (Peiping: Zaisheng zazhi she, 1933), preface no. 1, p. 2 (hereafter, STLZX).

28. Zhang Junmai, "Eluosi suweiai lianbang gongheguo xianfa quanwen" (The Complete Text of the Constitution of the Russian Soviet Federated [Socialist] Republic), *Jiefang yu gaizao* 1, no. 6 (1919): 25-39. For other reports by Zhang on

the Soviet Union, see his 1920 articles, "Du *Liu xingqi zhi Eguo*."

29. Zhang, "Yijiuyijiu lu Ouzhou," 21.

30. Franz Borkenau, *World Communism: A History of the Third International* (Ann Arbor: University of Michigan Press, 1962), 213-20.

31. Zhang, "Yijiuyijiu lu Ouzhong," 24; Chang, *Third Force*, 184. Thirty years later, he claimed to have witnessed the coup d'etats of Bela Kun in Hungary and of the Council Government in Bavaria. Just a few years following those events (1928), however, he admitted that he had "only heard about" the Munich uprising, the Hamburg revolts, and the establishment of a soviet in Hungary and "did not witness them." Chang, *Third Force*, 24, 185; Zhang, "Yijiuyijiu lu Ouzhong," 24.

32. Chang, *Third Force*, 184-85.

33. Zhang, "Yijiuyijiu lu Ouzhong," 24-25.

34. Chang, *Third Force*, 185.

35. Zhang, "Xuanni zhi shehui gaizao tongzhi hui yijianshu," 7.

36. For a detailed description of his activities during 1922-23, see Jeans, "Syncretism in Defense of Confucianism," chaps. 10-14.

37. BDRC, 1: 176-77; 3: 163.

38. Zhang Junmai, "Ying De Mei sanguo shizhi ji Guangzhou shizhi shang zhi guancha" (The Municipal Systems of England, Germany, and the United States and Observations of the Municipal System of Canton), *Gaizao* 4, no. 7 (1922): 12-14.

39. Ch'ien Tuan-sheng, *The Government and Politics of China, 1912-1949* (Cambridge: Harvard University Press, 1950), 70.

40. YX, 18-19.

41. Mary C. Wright, *The Last Stand of Chinese Conservatism: The T'ung-chih Restoration, 1862-1874* (Stanford: Stanford University Press, 1957; New York: Atheneum, 1967), 303. For the text of this proclamation, see Li Chien-nung, *The Political History of China*, 450-58.

42. Zhang Junmai, "Dongnan Ya, Aozhou yu Malai ji Zhongguo zhengju ganxiang dawen" (Answers to Questions on My Impressions of Southeast Asia, Australia, Malaya, and China's Political Situation), *Zaisheng*, no. 314 (1952): 4.

43. STLZX (1933), preface no. 1, p. 2.

44. Immanuel C.Y. Hsu, *The Rise of Modern China*, 5th ed. (New York: Oxford University Press, 1995), 519-20.

45. Zhang Junmai, *Shehuizhuyi sixiang yundong gaiguan* (A General Survey of Socialist Thought and Movements) (Taipei, 1978), 3.

46. STLZX (1933), preface no. 1, p. 2.

47. Zhang, "Wu guo zhengdang fazhan," 3.

48. Chang, *Third Force*, 69.

49. Zhang, "Dongnan Ya," 4. In the words of the statement, "Dr. Sun holds that the communistic order, or even the Soviet system, cannot be introduced into China because there do not exist the conditions for the successful establishment of either communism or Sovietism." Theodore McNelly, ed., *Sources in Modern East Asian History and Politics* (New York: Appleton-Century-Crofts, 1967), 99.

50. STLZX (1933), preface no. 1, p. 2.

51. Allen S. Whiting, *Soviet Policies in China, 1917-1924* (New York: Columbia University Press, 1954; Stanford: Stanford University Press, 1968), 228-29; Robert C. North, *Moscow and [the] Chinese Communists* (Stanford: Stanford University Press, 1953), 49-52. The latter's view (p. 52) of the treaty is more cautious than Whiting's.

52. Zhang, *Shehuizhuyi*, 3.

53. Ibid.

54. Ibid. *Xiangdao zhoubao* was published in Shanghai from September 1922 through July 1927.

55. Zhang, "Zhang Junmai fangRi," 8.

56. The debate was launched by Zhang's speech at Qinghua University in February 1923. In his address, he criticized scientism and positivism and argued that those isms could not solve all the problems of human life. For a survey of the controversy, see D. W. Y. Kwok, *Scientism in Chinese Thought* (New Haven: Yale University Press, 1965; New York: Biblo & Tannen, 1971), chap. 6. For a detailed discussion of Zhang's arguments in the debate, see Jeans, "Syncretism in Defense of Confucianism," chap. 13.

57. Ssu-yu Teng and John K. Fairbank, *China's Response to the West: A Documentary Survey, 1839-1923* (Cambridge: Harvard University Press, 1954; reprint, 1979), 249-50.

58. Ibid., 250-51. Chen's fellow Communist, Qu Qiubai, joined the criticism of Zhang. Qu accused Zhang of stressing the voluntarism of Marxism-Leninism and neglecting its deterministic side. Qu Qiubai, "Xiandai wenming di wenti yu shehuizhuyi" (The Problem of Modern Civilization and Socialism), *Dongfang zazhi* 21, no. 1 (1924): 9. In that criticism, Qu was probably right. See Jeans, "Syncretism in Defense of Confucianism," 489-90.

59. Zhang Junmai, "*Renshengguan zhi lunzhan* xu" (Introduction to *The Polemic over a Philosophy of Life*), in *Renshengguan zhi lunzhan*, ed. Guo Mengliang, 2 vols., 3d ed. (Shanghai: Taidong tushuju, 1928), 1: 5-9.

60. In response to Ding Wenjiang's charge that he was a plagiarist, Zhang retorted that Ding plagiarized Karl Pearson; Hu Shi, John Dewey; and the CCP, Marx. Zhang Junmai, "Zailun renshengguan yu kexue bing da Ding Zaijun" (A Further Discussion of a Philosophy of life, with a Reply to Ding Wenjiang), in *Kexue yu renshengguan* (Science and a Philosophy of Life), 2 vols. (Shanghai: Yadong shuju, 1923), 1: 41.

61. Zhang, "*Renshengguan zhi lunzhan* xu," 1: 9.

62. For discussions of the school, see infra, chaps. 4, 5.

63. Zhang Junmai, "Tan zuijin zhengju" (On the Recent Political Situation), *Zaisheng*, no. 244 (1948): 2; Zhang, "Dongnan Ya," 4. One of Zhang's students at the Institute later recalled that on the first day of classes, and thereafter in the first class of each week, Zhang delivered a critique of Marx's historical materialism. YX, 52.

64. Zhang, "Wu guo zhengdang fazhan," 3.

65. Zhang, "Zhengzhixue," 5-6.

66. Ibid., 6.

67. Zhang Junmai, "Nianyunian lai shijie zhengchao jitang zhong women di lichang" (Our Position in the Turmoil of the World's Political Trends during the Past Twenty-odd Years), *Zaisheng*, no. 108 (1946): 4.

4

Schools and Educational Vision, 1923-1941

This chapter will examine, through Zhang's writings, the three schools with which he was linked between 1923 and 1941, focusing on their educational philosophies (as explicated by Zhang), faculty, students, and organization. The political involvement of these "academies" will be left to later chapters. By describing the educational vision and school-building activities of one educator, perhaps this chapter will contribute something to our knowledge of private higher education in the Republican period. Before taking up his schools and thought, however, it would be well to briefly review the educational background of this university president and professor.

Educational Background to the Early 1920s[1]

Zhang was born in the suburbs of Shanghai, an area in which Chinese and Western influences overlapped. His father was a medical doctor, while his grandfather attained the rank of *juren* (provincial graduate) in the traditional civil service system. The latter was the only member of the family to take a degree until the success in the examinations of his grandson, Junmai; unlike his grandfather, though, Zhang chose not to follow the path of officialdom. In light of the influence exerted by Confucianism on Zhang's educational thought, it is interesting to note that his grandfather was a follower of Song Neo-Confucianism's "moral philosophy of self-cultivation" (*yili zhi xue*).

At the age of four, Zhang began to study in the family school. The focus was completely traditional, with the Four Books and the Five Classics the staple texts. In 1898, he was sent by his parents to study at the Guang fangyan guan in Shanghai. Founded by Li Hongzhang in 1863, this institution combined modern Western studies with traditional learning. Thus, on the one hand, he continued his study of Chinese, history, geography, and classical works, while on the other, he took up the study of English, mathematics, physics, and chemistry. His extracurricular reading, though, was dominated by the traditional side; hence, he read works by Sima Guang (1019-1086), Gu Yanwu (1613-1682), and Zeng Guofan (1811-1872). Above all, he was a fervent admirer of the great Song Neo-Confucianist, Zhu Xi (1130-1200), and especially the latter's anthology of early Song thought, *Jinsi lu* (Reflections on Things at Hand).

The influence of his studies at the Guang fangyan guan was crucial for Zhang's later ideas on education. The Sino-Western education he received at this school clearly foreshadowed the cultural syncretism he later advocated as the guiding principle for the educational institutions he established in the 1920s and 1930s. In other words, he based his later schools on the principle of a simultaneous adoption of the best from both Western and Chinese education. However, his later educational beliefs also reflected the Guang fangyan guan's belief that, in the final analysis, Chinese learning was more important than Western.

In addition, as Zhang later emphasized, he was the product of a transitional era in which education was a blend of the old (Chinese traditional learning) and the new (Western learning). He was late enough to enter the Guang fangyan guan but early enough to receive a thorough education in the Classics. Like many young men at that time, he had one foot on each of the educational ladders created by the late-Qing reforms—the network of modern schools as well as the civil service examination system. In 1902, he added success in the latter to his achievements in the former when he earned the *xiucai* degree, the first rung on the traditional civil service ladder. After this, his education appears to have been increasingly devoted to the modern Western aspect. He studied at the Catholic institution, Aurora Academy, in Shanghai and then at the Jiangnan Higher School in Nanjing. After two years teaching English in Hunan province, like many Chinese students of that period he went to Japan to study.

In Japan, he devoted himself almost exclusively (at least in his formal work) to the study of modern subjects. He focused on law and political science at Waseda University, and many of his texts were American and English works. He also was influenced by German scholarship. Finally, it was during those years that he formed a lifelong impression that the discipline of logic was vital for learning and politics. His interest had been aroused earlier by his teacher and principal at the Aurora Academy, Ma Liang. The latter, Zhang recalled, often cited the writings of the seventeenth-century scholar Li Zhizao (?-1630), among whose works was a translation of a medieval treatise on logic that Li entitled *Ming li tan* (An Investigation of Logic).[2] While studying in Japan, Zhang came to believe there was a paucity of Chinese works on this subject, and hence in 1907-08 he translated William S. Jevons' (1835-1882) *Logic*. In his introduction, he explained that he had translated the latter's work because he believed an understanding of logic vital for Chinese politics and learning.[3] In his subsequent writings on education, he seldom failed to mention the need for study of this branch of learning.

In 1911, a year after his return to China, he passed the examination for the degree of *jinshi* (metropolitan graduate). He also passed the examination for entrance into the Hanlin Academy. Since these new-style (the old civil service tests had been abolished in 1905) examinations included modern subjects (such as science and technology), those scholars who had taken their degrees under the former system derisively referred to people like Zhang as "*Yang Hanlin*," or "foreign Hanlin."

Soon after the 1911 Revolution, Zhang went to Germany and entered the University of Berlin to study politics. Although his goal was a Ph.D., he never finished (although he was called Dr. Zhang by many during his lifetime). His political preoccupation with the situation in China (especially the uproar caused by the 1915 Twenty-one Demands) and his intense interest in the course of World War I distracted him from his studies. He did, however, bring home with him in 1916 a deep appreciation of Western science and technology, especially when applied in wartime.

He spent the years 1916-1918 in China. During the last three or four months of 1918, he taught at Beijing University. At the same time, he began to show a renewed interest, after years of pursuing modern learning, in Confucianism, going so far as to join a traditional-style society, the *Song she* (named after Cai Songpo [Cai E]), in early 1918. This society, he wrote at the time, would be "a group for self-cultivation" (*xiuyang tuanti*).

In late 1918, he accompanied Liang Qichao to the Versailles Peace Conference. His extreme disillusionment with the results of the meeting—which sanctioned Japan's occupation of a portion of Shandong province—when added to his disgust with Chinese politics, led him to search for new values. A chance meeting with the German philosopher, Rudolf Eucken, proved decisive in Zhang's decision to turn to the study of Western philosophy. This interest was intensified by meetings with the famous French thinker, Henri Bergson (1859-1941), and the German Vitalist philosopher, Hans Driesch (1867-1941), who lectured in China during 1922-1923. Following Zhang's return to China in early 1922, these philosophers strongly influenced the ideas he expressed during the "Debate over Science and a Philosophy of Life."

Brief Histories and Descriptions of the Three Schools

The National Institute of Political Science, 1923-1927 [4]

Following the departure from China of Driesch, for whom he had acted as interpreter and host, Zhang established the National Institute of Self-Government in September 1923 in Shanghai. His first sponsor was Han Guojun, the civil governor of Jiangsu, whom Zhang had known since at least 1911. In January 1924, examinations were held for new students, and in February, Governor Han appointed Zhang president. A number of prominent people participated in founding the school. They can generally be described as Zhang's old friends and fellow disciples of Liang Qichao and/or natives of Jiangsu enthusiastic about promoting self-government in their home province. Thanks to funds furnished by Shi Liangcai (1879-1934), the owner and publisher of the Shanghai daily, *Shenbao* (Shun Pao), the school was able to rent a building in the French Concession.

After receiving support from the noted Jiangsu industrialist and educator Zhang Jian (1853-1926), the warlord Sun Chuanfang (1884-1935), and others,[5] in 1925 the institute was able to purchase and move to a new site in Wusong (in the suburbs of Shanghai). In October of that year, Zhang changed the school's name to the National Institute of Political Science, in an attempt to model it after the famous political science institutes of Europe. However, when the Northern Expedition reached Shanghai in early 1927, the GMD closed the institute. To avoid arrest, Zhang took refuge in the foreign concessions.

The majority of the faculty of the institutes had studied abroad in Japan, Europe, or the United States. There was also a handful of cultural conservatives, as well as two foreign professors. Not surprisingly, the school lacked the three types of people with whom Zhang battled during the Republican period: cultural radicals (like Hu Shi) and members of the GMD and CCP.

It is difficult to find data on students who attended the institutes. On the occasion of the first entrance examinations in 1923, only eighty-four of the two thousand students who applied for admission were accepted, which certainly argues for high admission standards. Following this, students were solicited every summer and winter vacation, with the number accepted never exceeding forty. On the other hand, the attrition rate was relatively high; of the first class of eighty-four, only forty remained by the winter of 1926. Hence, the student body remained small; at that time, the school had only 150-160 students. Zhang treated his students well, with the result that several of them later joined his political parties.

The Xuehai Institute, 1934-36

The Xuehai Institute—probably named after Guangzhou's nineteenth-century Xuehai tang, where Liang Qichao had studied in the late 1880s[6]—was sponsored by the Guangdong militarist, Chen Jitang. He had two motives in mind: to train talent for his regime (including soldiers) and to provide ideological support for the movement he launched in the fall of 1934 to "revere Confucius" (*zun Kong*) and "study the Classics" (*dujing*).[7]

According to a former teacher at the institute, Chen founded the school at Zhang Junmai's suggestion.[8] In addition, the latter asserted that Zhang Dongsun and he established the institute.[9] However, it was Dongsun, Zhang's colleague in the NSP, who was appointed director of the school, with the secretary-general of Chen's headquarters, Chen Yukun, serving as deputy director. According to a former member of the institute, the real power was in the hands of the latter. In less than six months, Dongsun and Chen Yukun clashed, and as a result, Dongsun returned to Peiping. As for Zhang, he held the position of dean of studies (*xuezhang*), and also taught the Neo-Confucianism of the Song and Ming periods.[10]

Information on the faculty of the institute is scarce, but according to one account, many of the professors were appointed from the faculties of Zhongshan and Lingnan universities. Both civilians and soldiers studied at the institute; hence, there were two classes, "A" and "B." The students of class A were graduates of universities in China or abroad who were selected after strict examinations. As a result of recruitment efforts in the winter of 1934, forty—of whom about 20 percent were overseas Chinese—were picked. Students in this class received free tuition, room, board, and spending money. Class B students were mostly chosen from among the political staff officers of the corps, divisions, and brigades of Chen Jitang's First Army. Their level was uneven, and there were great differences in age. They continued to receive their military salaries while they studied. Both classes matriculated in the spring of 1935 and were to have graduated in two years.[11] According to one estimate, the institute had a total of about one hundred students,[12] including Zhang's brother-in-law and a student who earlier had studied privately under Zhang.[13]

Like the Institute of Political Science, the Xuehai Institute fell victim to the political and military struggles of Republican China. In the spring of 1936, the armies of the central government attacked Chen Jitang in his lair in Guangdong. One of the casualties of his defeat was the institute, which was forced to close its doors.[14] According to Zhang, a few days later its books began to appear in the flea markets of Guangzhou.[15] The students scattered, and Zhang himself was forced to once again take refuge in the foreign concessions in Shanghai, as he had done when the GMD took that port city in 1927.[16]

The Institute of National Culture, 1939-1941[17]

Preparations for the founding of this institute, one of three *shuyuan* established during the war, began in 1938.[18] There may have been other reasons for its establishment, besides Zhang's persistent ambition to found a school. He later implied that it was a product of goodwill generated during the early days of the wartime united-front policy.[19] A follower and former student of Zhang's at the school suggested that it may have been approved by Chiang Kai-shek and the GMD as another means to meet the challenge posed by the Chinese Communists, whose educational institutions were attracting educated youth to their territories. He also maintained that the institute was a reaction to the GMD's Three People's Principles Youth Corp, which, he believed, increasingly "strait-jacketed and intimidated" the political thinking of the students.[20] In addition, Zhang's December 1938 open letter criticizing the CCP may have changed Chiang Kai-shek's view of him to a more favorable one; as a result, according to this argument, Chiang then ordered the National Military Council to provide funds for the institute.[21] A final account asserts that Xiong Shihui (1894-1974)—governor of Jiangxi province and member of the GMD's Political Science Clique, along with Zhang's brother, Kia-ngau—recommended to Chiang that Zhang be invited to found a school.[22]

Planning for the school began with discussions between Zhang and Zhang Dongsun in besieged Hankou. After they decided to establish a *shuyuan*, Dongsun went to Guilin to search for a site. Nothing came of this, however, and he returned to Peiping.[23] The institute was then established at Beipei near Chongqing. Although it received government support through the National Military Council, the facilities at Beipei were contributed by the Sichuanese shipping magnate, Lu Zuofu (1894-1952), who served as vice minister of communications during the years 1938-1942 under Chang Kia-ngau.

There were other reasons, besides his connection with Zhang's brother, for Lu's support of the institute. Beginning in the late 1920s, he had developed Beipei into a model city, with schools, museums, and the like. He also had a strong interest in education, having instituted educational reforms during his earlier service as chief of the education section of the southern Sichuan *daotai*'s (circuit intendant) office. In short, his reform zeal, wealth, and interest in education also help to account for his largesse.[24]

While on a trip from Yunnan to Burma in the spring of 1940, Zhang was impressed by the beauty, history, and ethnic character of the town of Dali in western Yunnan,[25] and hence later in the same year the institute was moved there.[26] As in the case of his earlier schools, he received aid from a militarist when the governor of Yunnan, Long Yun, provided one hundred *mu* (roughly 13.5 acres) of land for construction of the school.[27]

Since it received funds from the central authorities, the institute had to accept a certain amount of government control, manifested through a board of trustees composed of seven to nine men. In addition, the institute's academic regulations had to be submitted to the Ministry of Education "for the record." According to the institute's regulations, the trustees were appointed for three-year terms by the founder of the institute. Judging from the composition of the board, however, the GMD and government had the final say in who served. Thus, the chairman of the board of trustees was Chen Bulei, a prominent GMD figure and confidant of Chiang Kai-shek. The board also included such important party and government personalities as Zhang Qun, Zhang Daofan, Zhou Zhongyue, and Zhu Jiahua. Non-GMD officials, such as Chang Kia-ngau and Lu Zuofu, also served on the board that elected Zhang Junmai director (*yuanzhang*) of the institute. In addition, the board was charged with examination and approval of (*shenyi*) teaching policy, academic regulations, and the budget, as well as planning endowment and expenditures.[28]

There were about thirty members of the faculty, appointed by the director and divided into the ranks of professor, associate professor, and instructor. This group included scholars famous then or later, such as the former foreign minister, Luo Wengan (1888-1941), a member of the NSP since the 1930s; the philosopher Mou Zongsan; and Vincent Shih (Shi Youzhong), Zhang's brother-in-law and a scholar of literature, history, and philosophy. There also was a handful of foreign teachers.[29] In addition, the director appointed a dean of studies, a dean of students, and a director of general affairs (responsible for records, accounting, and the like). As in the case of universities in the United States, the institute could not function without the ubiquitous committee. Hence, there were committees of institute and academic affairs. The faculty were divided among five departments, each with its own chairman, whose subjects reflected the blend of Chinese and Western education pursued at the school. In addition to modern departments of social sciences and philosophy, there also were departments for the study of history (*shi*), classics (*jingxue*), and philosophers (*zixue*). The names of these departments included three of the four classifications of traditional Chinese learning (*shi, jing, zi*), with the only one missing that of literary works (*ji*).[30]

The Dali institute, like the other wartime *shuyuan*, had few students.[31] Although some accounts speak of "more than one hundred" and "several dozen" students,[32] Zhang himself later wrote that the institute had only thirteen students in the fall of 1941.[33] This was despite the school's advertisements for students throughout unoccupied China and in Hong Kong, with each successful candidate to receive free board, room, and tuition, as well as a monthly stipend (Article 17 of the institute's organizational outline). There was also the possibility of prize money for excellent student research papers (Article 18). Selection standards were high, which probably kept down the size of the student body. Incredibly, out of more than six hundred applicants who took the entrance examination in Chongqing in 1939, only three were accepted.[34]

The Dali institute, however, did not last any longer than the other schools Zhang headed or was associated with. When student demonstrations broke out in Kunming in 1941, Chiang Kai-shek concluded that Zhang, members of his NSP, and students at the institute were responsible. The result was a December order from Chiang closing the institute and confiscating its buildings and library collection. Zhang himself was placed under surveillance and not permitted to leave Chongqing.[35] It was no wonder that, as one of his friends later put it, Zhang was "quite depressed at the time."[36]

An Outline of Zhang's Educational Philosophy

Zhang's answer to the question of what type of private higher education Republican China needed was made clear in his writings about his schools. As in his earlier advocacy of democratic socialism and the mixed economy, he sought a *zhongyong* or middle way between the extremes of emulation or rejection of the Western educational model. As with his cultural thought, he tried to adopt and synthesize what he believed to be the strengths of the educational approaches and systems of China and the West.

The Institute of Political Science

In the case of the Institute of Political Science, Zhang argued in 1926 that there were two outstanding ideas in political philosophy: government by men and government by law. China excelled in the first and the West, in the second. His hopes for the future were clear:

> There remains only one way open for China. Alone and unaided, neither of the two systems can be entrusted with the task of her reorganization. If she desires to erect a new government system that is both expedient and enduring, therefore, she must not be engrossed with either of these, but must seek out a middle path between the two that has not been trodden before.[37]

It was the institute's task to help China find that "middle path." To achieve it, Zhang explained, the school had adopted two fundamental policies, "the cultivation of the ability of organization in its students and a critical and objective study of Western political systems." The former was "to correct the habitual weakness of the Chinese people; the latter to rectify a certain superstitious belief among some radicals in the omnipotence of the western system of Government by Law."[38]

To implement the former, he proposed to grant students a broad degree of autonomy:

> They are given the right of self-government so that they may learn the secret of organization through actual practice. They are allowed to choose some of their own studies so that their interest in their work may be intensified and their initiative power strengthened. In addition, a tutorial system, somewhat after the model of Cambridge and Oxford, is introduced in order to give the students beneficent guidance and enable them to attain their fullest development.[39]

The second fundamental policy would be carried out with the aid of four academic departments: politics, economics, sociology, and international relations. In the study of these social sciences, emphasis would be laid on both the theoretical and practical aspects; that is, "bookish knowledge" would be supported by "actual investigation and experiments." To try to avoid the "prejudice and preconception" that often led to "narrow and unbalanced conclusions such as the one-sided theories about the system of Government by Man or that of Government by Law," the institute undertook to "broaden the students' point of view by presenting to them both systems fairly and squarely side by side." All this was done, he continued, in the belief that "the ideal government of human association can only be attained by a union of the two systems . . . and that the success of this union can only be achieved by the evolution of a new and better political philosophy and the wide-spread [*sic*] of that philosophy through education."

In conclusion, he insisted that the institute's aim was not only to impart knowledge, but also—and he viewed this as more important—"to produce good men and to formulate sound systems and programmes which will be the basis of the future reformation and reconstruction of our country."[40]

The Xuehai Institute

In 1935, Zhang made two speeches outlining the educational goals of the Xuehai Institute, one to an affiliated organization, the Mingde she (Illustrious Virtue Society), and the second at the institute itself. In the first, he compared Chinese and Western education and China's traditional academies (*shuyuan*) and Western universities (*daxue*). The English, he asserted, had a knack of changing the teaching approach and materials of schools such as Oxford and Cambridge, while preserving their old appearances. That was not so in China's case. During the past forty to fifty years, he lamented, not only had the buildings of the ancient academies disappeared but also such useful features as the practice of using rents from school-owned lands to meet the academy's expenses (the so-called "*xuetian zhidu*"). That system, he noted, had enabled the academies to remain free from government control during certain eras.

His main theme, though, was the difference between the "cultural spirits" of China and the West. Western education, he argued, stressed "knowledge" (*zhi*); China's emphasized "will" (*yi*). In German universities, he explained, they regarded knowledge as their sole educational objective. At Oxford and Cambridge, however, they also stressed "how to be an upright man" or "how to conduct oneself in society" (*zuoren*); hence, their educational system and spirit were similar to those of China's ancient academies. Compared with China's Song dynasty academies, however, "character or moral education" (*renge jiaoyu*) at Oxbridge was still "too superficial."

The academies, for instance, had masters (*dashi*) who, besides discussing knowledge and learning, "did not forget to cherish and nurture moral character (*pinxing*) and cultivate personality (*peiyu renge*)." In summary, he wrote:

> Western education everywhere emphasizes knowledge; our country's old education universally stressed subduing and governing the mind and body (*xinshen zhi kezhi*), which belongs to [the realm of] will (*yizhi*). At present, it [China's education] is completely opposed to what was done in the old days and [instead] imitates the West. The emphasis on morality (*dexing*) in our country's education, however, naturally possesses its enduring value.[41]

Disturbed by what he felt was China's complete imitation of Western educational ideas, then, Zhang returned to the subject in a speech to the Xuehai Institute six months later. The goal of the institute, he asserted, absolutely was not to "revive the old" (*fugu*); it was "to reconstruct our national culture." He insisted that was not something China's numerous universities, with their exclusive stress on knowledge, could accomplish. In addition, the academies should be revived because they concerned themselves with self-cultivation. The Xuehai *shuyuan,* however, would be different from the academies of the past; in addition to moral training, it would absorb the best from Western knowledge. These twin goals were set forth in the abridged regulations of the institute:

> 1) The aim of this school is to arouse the national culture and blend it with Western learning methods and viewpoints in hopes of . . . constructing a new

> Chinese cultural base.
> 2) This school's education consists of a simultaneous emphasis on scholastic and moral performance. In the transmission of knowledge, we will mostly use the methods of Western scholarship, but in the cultivation of character we will largely select the traditional practices of our country's former Confucianists. It is essential to be certain that the talent produced has knowledge enough to cope with the trends of the world and moral character sufficient to take responsibility for our national revival.[42]

In short, he argued, "our institute does not cling to the old nor does it chase after the new. It desires to simultaneously develop and enhance the strong points of China and the West in order to make up for the deficiencies of the present [Chinese] universities."[43]

The Institute of National Culture

In an article entitled, "Prospectus of the Institute of National Culture," drafted during the winter of 1939, Zhang returned compulsively to the same theme, arguing that it was necessary for his country's higher education to combine the Chinese emphasis on morality with the Western stress on knowledge and to revive the ancient *shuyuan* as the vehicle to carry this out. The institute's goal, he declared, was the "simultaneous cultivation of knowledge and morality and the simultaneous advance of sincerity and understanding."[44] He praised both Confucianism and Western culture, and—like the earlier May Fourth activists and the later Mao Zedong and his Cultural Revolution—advocated the creation of a "new culture," based on what he viewed as the strengths of each. In founding a *shuyuan* in the isolated reaches of Southwest China, he also demonstrated his belief that China's ancient system of learning was worth reviving. However, in adopting a curriculum that blended the best of Chinese and Western learning, he recognized that the old form required new substance. His ambition, in short, was nothing less than a "cultural revival" (*wenhua fuxing*), a goal reminiscent of his earlier statement that the goal of the Xuehai Institute was to reconstruct China's national culture.

Writing when the Sino-Japanese War was in its second full year, he recognized that China was at a crossroads, with the race's survival at stake. In discussing ways to ensure that China had a future, he sprang to Confucius's defense. The Sage, he declared, had "revealed the two great principles of morality and learning" and showed others the way to study thoroughly and pursue sincerity and uprightness (*gezhi cheng zheng*), thus greatly inspiring the formation of China's culture. In a slap at the May Fourth activists' wholesale assault on Confucianism, he demanded to know "how those who later slandered Confucius could deny this."

Later, he continued, the Neo-Confucian scholars of the Song and Ming revived the ideas of Confucius and Mencius to "restore our race's cultural independence" after centuries of invasions and foreign influences, such as Buddhism. On the one hand, this survey of Chinese culture left him discouraged. "Our nation's culture," he declared, "stresses books and slights nature, esteems impractical ceremony and lacks practical applications, [is] often quiescent and seldom active." On the other hand, the need to defend China against barbarian invasions meant that "the teaching that one should die to preserve one's principles penetrated men's minds." Hence, there were men like Wen Tianxiang (1236-1282) and Lu Xiufu (1236-1279), who tried to fight off the Mongols at the end of the Song, and Gu Yanwu, Wang Fuzhi (1619-1692), and Huang Zongxi (1610-1695), who struggled against the invading Manchus in the last days of the Ming. When disorder and vice were everywhere, Zhang declared, those men died to preserve righteousness in the world rather than abandon their principles. During those dark days of the Sino-Japanese War, when China was bearing the brunt of the Japanese assault, he took consolation from Wen's words, which made him feel that "the noble spirits of four-thousand years of ancestors were looking down on us from above, reprimanding us from the side, [and] not tolerating the waverers and cautious ones among their decendants."

In short, he believed that the theories of Confucianism had not been lost by the Chinese race but were "suitable for the righteous cause of a modern people establishing a nation" (*er you heyu jinshi minzu liguo zhi dayi*). The Confucianists of the Tang and Song, he firmly believed, had restored China's cultural sovereignty and attempted to revive the nation. Hence, for him, they were the model for his times, for although they had failed to restore the nation, the "seeds for the establishment of the Republic were planted then." Far from blocking the creation of a modern China, as the May Fourth activists argued, Confucianists should be credited with maintaining the nation-building (*liguo*) spirit from Confucius and Mencius up to the end of the Ming.

Yet, Zhang was no simple Confucian patriot in the traditional mold. He recognized that the penetration of Western culture had rendered the old world at least partly obsolete. Thus, he admitted that Zhu Xi's Five Relationships, which had dominated Chinese social life for a millennium, "did not completely correspond to modern needs." If one compared Chinese with European modern culture, he confessed, it was "difficult to avoid the jeer that we are found to be inferior." The breadth of the Europeans' knowledge surpassed China's, admitted the scholar who had studied for several years in Europe. As for the political and social aspects of that continent, his admiration seemed to know no bounds, despite his disillusionment with European civilization following the carnage of World War I and in spite of the outbreak of World War II in Poland a few months earlier. It was easy to see, he wrote, that Europeans had sufficient food and warm clothing; were studious and intelligent; had a sense of independence, self-respect, and reponsibility; and possessed intense patriotism. In light of his own strivings over the past several decades, it was no surprise that he praised the fact that "the rulers and the ruled calmly yielded to the constitution" ("fundamental law"; *genben dafa*) and that during wartime their nations were united.

Perhaps having his own travels in mind, he noted that when Chinese scholars went to Europe and the United States, they witnessed those sorts of things and "lamented that the flourishing rule of the Three Dynasties [Xia, Shang, and Zhou] was seen once again today [but in Europe, not China]." Hence, he wrote, "one can imagine their emotions of a grieving heart mixed with admiration." There had been attempts in China to imitate those special strengths of Europe, he noted. However, he considered Zhang Zhidong's nineteenth-century formula, "Chinese learning as the essence, Western learning for utility" (*Zhongxue wei ti, Xixue wei yong*) fallacious. Cultural interchange was normal in human history, he insisted. The Europeans had been influenced by Greek culture and Christianity, while China drank deeply from the springs of Buddhism. In a slap at die-hard conservatives, he declared that it was clear that "no people can avoid the gradual permeation of foreign elements." "Why," he asked, "must we consider the adoption of foreign elements a defect?" His message was the same syncretism he had been insisting on for decades:

> We who live today can only bluntly admit the superiority of European culture and greatly expand our tolerance to welcome it, so that the transplantation of European culture will become a remedy for our race's weakness. Thus, we can use it to promote the rise of our race's new culture. This is the most obvious path in politics and learning, as well as the general trend. Who can go against the current and resist this?[45]

Like a good Confucianist, he viewed education as the means to develop that new Sino-Western culture. However, it was not the modern university but (as in the case of the Xuehai Institute) the *shuyuan* that would teach this new synthesis. After a brief survey of the history of the academy system, in which he praised it as possessing an "inseparable relationship with the past one thousand years of Chinese learning," he set forth the reasons for his decision to revive and utilize that most ancient of educational institutions, instead of the modern university.

It took five or six years following graduation from university to produce a scholar, he asserted. The former academies of China, as well as the research institutes and scholarly societies found outside universities in Europe and America, supported the student during this period. It was because the academies were gone and there were few graduate programs at Chinese universities that he advocated a revival of the *shuyuan*. Through its financial support, it would enable the "capable and virtuous graduates of universities to leisurely engage in learning without having to anxiously seek food and clothing." In the case of his institute, university graduates would be recruited, with the period of study to last three years. It was perhaps a disadvantage for his recruitment efforts that no graduation diplomas would be issued; instead, successful students would receive a "certificate of recommendation."

Second, he pointed out the differences in the student-teacher relationship in the university and *shuyuan*. Universities held classes and focused on the completion of research work but lacked "teaching to benefit the people," as well as "dialogue between students and teachers." He favored a resurrection of the *shuyuan*, due to the mutual respect and love between teachers and students in the old academies, as well as the teachers' vigilance concerning the students' behavior. As a good Confucianist, he placed great faith in the teacher's contribution. The goals of the institute's teaching, he declared in the academic regulations, were to complete the individual's character, encourage wisdom to contribute to world learning, and, based on the skill of merging virtue and knowledge into one, serve the great task of managing affairs for practical purposes.

Third, he explained, Western universities focused on the development of the intellect and the advancement of knowledge and did not include the "cultivation of individual morality" as one of the goals of university education. However, the academies of the Song and Ming, he wrote approvingly, had paid attention to cultivation and self-examination. Moreover, he argued, the *shuyuan* defended the Song Confucianists' emphasis on mind.

Finally, and undoubtedly most important in light of his earlier defense of the Xuehai Institute, he thought China's *shuyuan* system superior to Western universities, for while the latter merely stressed the scholastic attainments of the intellect or knowledge, the former "simultaneously emphasized virtue and knowledge, [while] in fact placing particular emphasis on virtue." If China stressed morality and slighted knowledge, he explained, then science would be undeveloped; if it emphasized knowledge and slighted morality, then "in the end we must sink to using the power of knowledge as a weapon to destroy our countrymen and members of our race." Hence, he advocated "morality in learning."

In conclusion, he admitted that it would be impossible to revive the academies of the Song and Ming without any change. His *shuyuan* had to be different, for events in Europe since the Renaissance had vastly changed the world of learning. Hence, as much as he had admired Zhu Xi since his boyhood in Shanghai, he recognized that his own *shuyuan* would have to be a "new White Deer Grotto Academy" (*Bailudong shuyuan*),[46] embracing not only Confucius and his heroes among the Neo-Confucianists but the great thinkers of Europe as well.

Zhang's references to the Chinese "morality" and Western "knowledge" to be combined in this "new culture" taught by his *shuyuan* look simple at first glance. However, in the institute's prospectus, he "modernized" them for his students.[47] Morality, he explained, would include self-cultivation, understanding others, and (a most un-Confucian sentiment) patriotism. There was little new in his explanation of the first; it meant being sincere and honest, humane and brave, and just and loyal, as well as possessing physical discipline. It was clear that sincerity (*cheng*) was the immortal virtue for him; "nothing," he insisted, "is more important than sincerity." "The first request I have for those who come to this institute to learn," he added, "is to cultivate sincerity and that is all."[48] The second meaning of morality, however, contained a new element; after explaining that it meant being respectful and kind, as well as attentive when transacting business, he added—perhaps having in mind Sun Yat-sen's reference to China as a "loose sheet of sand"—that it also meant organizational discipline (*jituan jilü*).

His inclusion of patriotism, of course, was entirely modern for a country that had stressed culturalism, rather than nationalism, throughout its history. It was also intensely political, in a society torn between the competing claims of two party dictatorships. Patriotism meant, he explained, to love and protect China's history, but it also meant to cultivate the spirit of rule of law (*yangcheng fazhi jingshen*) and constantly carry out the duties of a citizen (*luxing guomin yiwu*). In emphasizing law and the role of citizens, he was again sounding themes that dominated his writings during the the 1920s and 1930s but stood little chance of adoption in a land oppressed by warlords and party dictatorships.

He also attempted to define the modern (read, Western) "knowledge"—or as he termed it, the "new learning"—that would be pursued at the institute. If we compare our achievements in modern knowledge to those of the West, he moaned, "there is nothing we can do but regretfully admit we are not as good." Due in part to the examination system, he explained, "what is called learning in our country has been sought only from books; with the exception of books, there has been almost no learning to speak of." To correct that academic style (*xuefeng*) of the past and establish a "new spirit," he singled out four approaches in particular that scholars seeking knowledge should adopt or avoid.

First, they should combine personal observations with the study of books. "The source of knowledge is this world," he insisted, and "those who are good at study should take the world as their book." Newton and Darwin did this in the sciences, he declared, and the same approach should be followed in regard to social problems, where "it would be better to get it from one's own observations than from books." For books on the Miaos or Tibet and Mongolia, for example, one should live with the Miaos or travel to Tibet and Mongolia. Through observations on the spot and protracted thought, one could "almost avoid the defect of the bookish life (*shuben shenghuo*) and obtain 'firsthand knowledge.'"

Second, in arguing that scholars should also energetically seek accurate knowledge, he stressed a theme he had first sounded when a student in Japan nearly three decades earlier—the importance of logic. "Scholars who engage in study," he insisted, "cannot for an instant forget about the science of logic." It was the reason, he added, that Europeans had made great progress in learning each day. Although China had become aware of the importance of logic, it was still seldom applied. Instead, he wrote, echoing his criticism at earlier times, Chinese were "good at showing off expressions in literary compositions and relying on subjective views and deep-seated habits." "The idea of objectively seeking the truth," he complained, "has not penetrated the writings and hearts of scholars."

His message pointed out things to be avoided, too. Scholars should produce new theories, he insisted, rather than simply indulge in the "sickness" of "following the trend of the times." The conservative writings produced by examination candidates in imperial times were "absolutely not worth mentioning as contributions to learning." Yet, he complained, what most scholars had done in recent years was similar to candidates in the examination halls. On the other hand, they had also "chased foreign and novel theories, and propagandized for them in a servile manner." They had catered to what youth liked, repeated what others had said, and placed their own ideas on a shelf and forgotten about them. "I really do not know," he wrote in an exasperated tone, "what . . . scholars have to be conceited about."

He also fervently warned scholars to refrain from factional biases and personal accusations. And yet—reminding one of his charge that the CCP plagiarized Marx—he saved his full attention for the sin of plagiarism. "To steal the property of others," he wrote, "is thievery; to take the theories of others is exactly the same thing." The most valuable things in the world of learning are one's own ideas. Intellectual honesty meant not stealing others' ideas. If one did use someone else's material, he insisted, it should be footnoted. Unfortunately, in China's literary world "it seems that we still have not been able to observe this rule of conduct." Even great Confucianists stole the theories of others, he groused, pointing to the transgressions of Dai Zhen and Kang Youwei. Neither was willing to footnote sources, and hence "committed the crime of stealing." One should energetically refrain from plagiarism, he argued.

Despite these sharp criticisms of China, though, he remained something of a Han chauvinist. If not for China, he queried, to whom else did the position of "master of East Asia" (*DongYa zhurenweng*) belong? At the time he wrote this, the Japanese would have been quick to reply.

Conclusions

Having examined Zhang's views on education, as well as some features of the schools with which he was associated, it is now possible to draw some conclusions concerning his involvement in private higher education during the Republican period.

One of the most obvious was the necessity of working within his political environment, of compromising with the powers that were. In a China dominated by warlords in the mid-1920s, he had no choice but to seek their protection and support. Thus, he solicited aid from the governor of Jiangsu, Han Guojun, to launch the National Institute of Self-Government and from General Sun Chuanfang to reorganize it into the National Institute of Political Science and move it to a new site. In the 1930s, the Guangdong militarist, Chen Jitang, gave Zhang a teaching position at the Xuehai Institute after he had been dismissed from both Yanjing and Zhongshan universities. Finally, the Yunnan governor, Long Yun, granted Zhang the land in Dali on which to build the Institute of National Culture. It is clear why Zhang accepted the militarists' help, but why did they support him? The simple answers might be that they shared his opposition to the GMD and approved of the traditional side of his educational philosophy.

Whereas the warlords aided him, with one short-lived exception the GMD opposed and repressed him. Following its capture of Shanghai in 1927, and even before the final defeat of Sun Chuanfang, the GMD shut down the National Institute of Political Science. After defeating Chen Jitang's forces in 1936, the GMD dissolved the Xuehai Institute, and Zhang lost his third teaching post in four years. As for the Institute of National Culture, in the beginning it was granted financial support by order of Chiang Kai-shek.

However, in late 1941, Chiang, suspecting NSP involvement in demonstrations in Kunming, ordered the institute closed.

In sum, during the 1920s and 1930s, Zhang accepted the support of four warlords, as well as Chiang Kai-shek and the GMD. On balance, the latter was the more malevolent force. Its closing of all three of the schools with which Zhang was associated showed the difficulties faced by private higher education in a China dominated by party dictatorships. "I deeply believe," wrote a discouraged Zhang in the mid-1940s, "that it is impossible to found schools under a one-party dictatorship."[49] In closing his schools, though, the GMD was lashing out not at his educational philosophy but at his political opposition. They had grounds for believing that his schools were party institutions, for a number of teachers and students at the three schools were—or later became—NSP members.[50]

In addition to the political implications of the schools, there were the educational goals. Clearly, Zhang was alarmed at the encroachments of Western educational approaches, while simultaneously recognizing the futility of clinging to the Chinese education of the past. Instead, he argued for a "middle path," for a syncretism of China's traditional emphases on men, morals, and sincerity with what he perceived as the West's concentration on law and knowledge. The ultimate goal—as in the traditional civil service examination system—was to produce "good men," as well as "sound systems and programmes" (betraying the Western influence), which would carry out national and cultural reconstruction. In this sense, his educational vision was quite different from that described by one Western scholar: "The transformation of China's educational system, in urban areas at least, from a Confucian-based program to a distinctly modern one . . . is one of the major changes in China prior to 1949."[51] While in the 1920s, Zhang favored the European politics institute model, on two separate occasions during the 1930s he made it plain that he favored reviving China's *shuyuan* system, albeit with a curriculum that gave full credit to Western learning. Hence, as we have seen in this chapter, he and his schools did not make a complete transformation from a Confucian program to a modern one but at best went partway toward the modern and Western, while keeping one foot firmly planted in the old Confucian world.

Notes

1. This sketch is based on Jeans, "Syncretism in Defense of Confucianism," chaps. 1-7.

2. Zhang Junmai, "Yu Chen Yuan shi lun Li Zhizao yi *Ming-li tan* zhi yuanben" (A Discussion with Mr. Chen Yuan of the [Western] Original for Li Zhizao's Translation of *An Investigation of Logic*), *Zaisheng* 5, no. 1 (1954): 5-6; Fung Yu-lan, *A Short History of Chinese Philosophy*, ed. Derk Bodde (New York: Macmillan, 1948; New York: Free Press, 1966), 330. For an analysis of the term *mingli*, see ibid., 217-18.

3. "Yefangsi shi *lunlixue*" ([William S.] Jevons' *Logic*), trans. Li Zhai [Zhang Junmai], *Xuebao* 1, no. 1 (1907): 1. For a succinct analysis of Jevons's thought, see Paul Edwards, ed., *The Encyclopedia of Philosophy*, 4 vols. (New York: Macmillan and Free Press, 1967), 3: 260-61.

4. From 1923 to 1925, this school was called the National Institute of Self-Government. The following discussion of the Shanghai institutes is based on Jeans, "Syncretism in Defense of Confucianism," 363-74. For an examination of the political side of the institutes, see infra, chap. 5.

5. For a brief biography of Zhang Jian, see BDRC, 1: 35-38. A fuller treatment of this leading social reformer and scholar-entrepreneur may be found in Samuel C. Chu, *Reformer in Modern China: Chang Chien, 1853-1926* (New York: Columbia University Press, 1965). For a biographical sketch of Sun Chuanfang, see BDRC, 3: 160-62. On Zhang's political relationship with Sun, see infra, chap. 5.

6. Hao Chang, *Liang Ch'i-ch'ao and Intellectual Transition in China, 1890-1907* (Cambridge: Harvard University Press, 1971), 58-59; NBCB 20, no. 13 (1970): 8. The term *Xuehai* (literally, "sea of learning") was undoubtedly borrowed—although it is not clear whether it was Zhang's or Chen's idea—from the famous academy established by Ruan Yuan in Guangzhou in 1820. Hummel, *Eminent Chinese of the Ch'ing Period*, 401, 510. In the late Qing, it was known as a center for Han Learning and also as the locus of a movement to combine Han and Song Learning. Chang, *Liang Ch'i-ch'ao*, 58-59. Because of its connection with Liang, Zhang may have been aware of the Xuehai tang at an early age. However, he did not mention it in his writings until 1939, when he asserted that even scholars of Han Learning depended on it for training and publishing. Zhang Junmai, "Minzu wenhua shuyuan yuanqi" (Prospectus of the Institute of National Culture), *Zaisheng* (Taiwan series), no. 14 (1972): 27.

7. Cheng Bijin, *Chen Bonan xiansheng nianpu* (A Chronological Biography of Chen Jitang) (Taipei: Sili deming xingzheng guanli zhuanke xuexiao, 1972), 15; Chen Jitang, *Chen Jitang zizhuan gao* (Draft Autobiography of Chen Jitang) (Taipei: Zhuanji wenxue chubanshe, 1974), 53; BDRC, 1: 32.

8. Xie Youwei, "Wo yu Zhang Junmai xiansheng" (Mr. Zhang Junmai and I), *Wenyi fuxing*, no. 14 (1971): 10. For a discussion of the institute's connections with the NSP (including faculty, students, and library holdings), see infra, chap. 8.

9. Zhang, "Nianyunian lai," 5. One of Zhang's followers later repeated this assertion. Sun Baoyi, "Junmai xiansheng yu minzhu shehuizhuyi" (Mr. [Zhang] Junmai and Democratic Socialism), *Ziyou zhong* 4, no. 2 (1970): 24.

10. Xie Youwei, "Wo yu Zhang Junmai," 10; Yang Jialuo, *Minguo mingren tujian* (Illustrated Biographies of Famous Men of the Republic), 2 vols. (Nanjing: Zhongguo cidian guan, 1937), 1: Part 5, 38.

11. Shi Yi, "Wo suo zhidao Zhang Junmai xiansheng shengping" (What I Know about Mr. Zhang Junmai's Life), *Zaisheng*, no. 345 (1953): 13.

12. Xie Youwei, "Wo yu Zhang Junmai," 10.

13. Xie Fuya, "Zhang Junmai xiansheng er san shi," 23; Sun Baoyi, "Junmai xiansheng jinhou de zhengzhi dongxiang" (Mr. [Zhang] Junmai's Future Political Course), *Zaisheng*, no. 269 (1950): 24.

14. BDRC, 1: 32-33.

15. Zhang, "Nianyunian lai," 5. According to another former teacher at the institute, the books were turned over to the Zhongyuan Library at Mount Guanyin in Guangzhou. Xie Youwei, "Wo yu Zhang Junmai," 11.

16. BDRC, 1: 32-33; Shi Yi, "Wo suo zhidao Zhang Junmai," 13. According to the 1936 edition (5th) of *Who's Who in China: Biographies of Chinese Leaders* (Shanghai: China Weekly Review, 1936), 3, Zhang's "last known address" was 37 Moulmein Road, Shanghai.

17. Zhang preferred to translate *shuyuan* as "institute" rather than "academy." Chang, *Third Force*, 103. For a discussion of the institute's relationship with Chiang Kai-shek and the GMD, see infra, chap. 12. On its organizational outline and academic regulations, see Zhang, "Minzu wenhua shuyuan," 30-31.

18. The other two were the Mianren Shuyuan, directed by Liang Shuming and located in Chongqing, and the Fuxing Shuyuan, directed by Ma Fu and founded in Leshan, Sichuan. Xiong Fuguang, "Ma Fu xiansheng yu Fuxing shuyuan" (Mr. Ma Fu and the Fuxing Academy), *Zhuanji wenxue* 24, no. 3 (1974): 24.

19. Zhang, "Nianyunian lai," 5.

20. Chou Hsiang-kuang, *Modern History of China* (Delhi: Metropolitan, 1952), 161.

21. GS 4, no. 5, 73.

22. Zhou Xiangguang [Chou Hsiang-kuang], "Ji Minzu wenhua shuyuan zhi chuangli yu fengbi" (Recollections of the Founding and Closing of the Institute of National Culture), *Zaisheng*, no. 346 (1954): 12.

23. Zhang Dongsun, "Shi de shiming yu lixue" (The Mission of Scholars and Song-Ming Neo-Confucianism), *Guancha* 1, no. 13 (1946): 3.

24. Zhou Xiangguang, "Ji Minzu wenhua shuyuan," 12; BDRC, 2: 454-55.

25. Zhang Junmai, "Dian you zagan" (Miscellaneous Impressions of a Trip to Yunnan), *Guojia shehui bao*, 26 July 1940, 3.

26. YX, 31.

27. BDRC, 1: 33; Zhou Xiangguang, "Ji Minzu wenhua shuyuan," 12.

28. Ibid., 12-13; Zhang, "Minzu wenhua shuyuan," 31. Chen Bulei (1890-1948) was appointed director of the second department of Chiang's attendance office in 1935, and in that capacity served as Chiang's confidential assistant until his (Chen's) death in 1948. In 1938, he served as secretary-general Zhang Qun's deputy in the National Military Council in Hankou, and from 1939 on he acted as deputy secretary-

general, again under Zhang Qun, of the Supreme National Defense Council in Chongqing. According to one account, he possessed an "acute perception" of the thoughts and aspirations of his superior, Chiang Kai-shek. BDRC, 1: 223-25. Zhang Qun (1889-1990) was a long-standing member of the GMD and a blood brother of Chiang Kai-shek. During the period 1938-42, he served as secretary-general of the Supreme National Defense Council and, from 1940 to 1945, as governor of Sichuan. Ibid., 47-52. Zhang Daofan (1897-1968), a member of the GMD since 1922 and a close associate of the Chen brothers (Chen Guofu and Chen Lifu), entered the Ministry of Education in January 1938. In late 1938, he was appointed senior member of the cultural movement committee of the GMD central propaganda bureau. In August 1939, he was selected as dean of the highest training school for GMD cadres, the Central Political Institute. In 1941, he was promoted to vice-chancellor and hence de facto director of the school nominally headed by Chiang Kai-shek. Ibid., 112-14. Zhou Zhongyue (1876-1951) served as minister of the interior from 1939 on. The Chinese Ministry of Information, comp., *China Handbook, 1937-1943* (New York: Macmillan, 1943), chap. 25, xviii. Zhang's brother was then serving as minister of communications. BDRC, 1: 29. Zhu Jiahua (1893-1963) was a pillar of the GMD regime. During the 1930s and 1940s, he served as minister of education, minister of communications, and vice president of the Examination Yuan. While he was on the board of trustees of the Institute of National Culture, he was also serving as head of the organization department of the GMD. Ibid., 437.

29. Zhou Xiangguang, "Ji Minzu wenhua shuyuan," 12-13. Luo joined the NSP in 1933. Shi Yi, "Wo suo zhidao Zhang Junmai," 15. For a sketch of his career, see BDRC, 2: 438-41. Mou had earlier served as a teacher at the Xuehai Institute. Xie Fuya, "Zhang Junmai," 23. For Vincent Shih's experiences, see Shi Youzhong, "Wo suo renshi de Zhang Junmai xiansheng" (The Mr. Zhang Junmai I Knew), *Zhuanji wenxue* 28, no. 3 (1976): 20.

30. Zhang, "Minzu wenhua shuyuan," 29-31. For Zhang's explanations of the work of each department—including an interesting discussion of the schools of Han Learning and Song Learning—see ibid. The social science department, e.g., focused on political science, economics, sociology, and anthropology.

31. Xiong Fuguang, "Ma Fu," 24.

32. Shi Yi, "Wo suo zhidao Zhang Junmai," 13; Zhou Xiangguang, "Ji Minzu wenhua shuyuan," 13.

33. Chang, *Third Force*, 103.

34. Zhou Xiangguang, "Ji Minzu wenhua shuyuan," 12-13.

35. Ibid., 14; Chang, *Third Force*, 103-04.

36. Chen Guangfu, "The Reminiscences of Ch'en Kuang-fu," as told to Julie Lien-ying How, 1963, Special Collections Library, Butler Library, Columbia University, 117.

37. Carsun Chang, *Bulletin of the National Institute of Political Science: Its Purpose and Its Work* (Wusong, 1926), 12.

38. Ibid., 13-14.

39. Ibid, 14.

40. Ibid., 14-16.

41. Zhang Junmai, "Yanci" (Speech), *Xinmin yuekan* 1, no. 2 (1935): 11-12.

42. Zhang Junmai, "Shuyuan zhidu zhi jingsheng yu Xuehai shuyuan zhi zongzhi" (The Spirit of the Academy System and the Aims of the Xuehai Institute), *Yuzhou xunkan* 4, no. 7 (1936): 15-17.

43. Ibid., 17.

44. Unless otherwise noted, the following discussion of the institute's educational philosophy, organizational outline, and academic regulations is based upon Zhang, "Minzu wenhua shuyuan," 26-31. This principle of the simultaneous cultivation of knowledge and virtue was even included in the academic regulations of the institute. Ibid., 31.

45. Ibid., 27-28.

46. This Song Dynasty academy was founded and operated near Lushan in Jiangxi province by Zhu Xi. In a later work, Zhang termed it "the prototype of the Neo-Confucianist academy." For his description of the academy and its regulations, see Carsun Chang, *The Development of Neo-Confucian Thought* (New York: Bookman, 1957; paperback, New Haven: College and University Press, 1963), 66-68.

47. He also mentioned these elements of the "new culture" in the academic regulations of the institute. Zhang, "Minzu wenhua shuyuan," 31.

48. For Zhang's detailed analysis of the deeper meaning of "sincerity," see ibid., 28.

49. Zhang, "Nianyunian lai," 5.

50. For a discussion of this aspect of the schools, see infra, chaps. 5, 8, 12.

51. David D. Buck, review of *The Dewey Experiment in China: Educational Reform and Political Power in the Early Republic*, by Barry Keenan, in *The American Historical Review* 83, no. 3 (1978): 784.

PART THREE

Opposition to Communism and the Guomindang during the Nanjing Decade, 1927-1937

5

Trials of a Third-Force Intellectual during the Early Years of the Nanjing Decade

There was no room in Chiang [Kai-shek]'s world for a loyal opposition; if they opposed him they were, ipso facto, disloyal to the nation.
—Lloyd E. Eastman, *The Abortive Revolution*

Individual sacrifice for collective ends is extolled as being part of Asian culture. Adversarial politics is not.
—Ian Buruma, *God's Dust*

In March 1927, the National Revolutionary Army (NRA) entered Shanghai. Less than a month later, the GMD carried out a bloody purge of the Chinese Communists in that city. The fate of the Communists is well known to Western historians. Less frequently mentioned (except in the memoirs of the victims) are the concurrent purges of other opponents of the new GMD regime.

One of those foes was Zhang Junmai, and this chapter is a study of his fate during the early Nanjing Decade. His story was not unique; a number of other liberal intellectuals had experiences similar to his at the beginning of this period. Moreover, like him, some of them were later to become leaders of minor parties, as the Nanjing period wore on. Yet, during this era, for the first time a modern one-party dictatorship claimed to rule China. Hence, the question arises: how did the modern educated elite fare? Many, of course, made their peace with the new regime and served it (including Zhang's own brother, Zhang Jiaao, better known as Chang Kia-ngau). Others, frequently influenced by their admiration for Western democracy and constitutionalism,

---

This chapter, with minor revisions, from *Roads Not Taken: The Struggle of Opposition Parties in Twentieth-Century China*, edited by Roger B. Jeans, pp. 37-59.

opposed it, which almost invariably brought them hardships. It was to this latter group that Zhang belonged.

In this chapter, I have attempted to portray his "third-force" position by describing his clash with the Reorganized GMD in 1927, as well as his strong opposition to both Chinese and Soviet communism. I then examine his struggle for survival from 1927 to 1929, which partly took the form of cooperation with another persecuted group, the Chinese Youth Party (CYP).[1] The essay ends with his mysterious kidnapping, which convinced him that Shanghai was too dangerous, and his second period of exile in Germany during the period 1929-1931.

This chapter is an attempt to restore to the pages of history the story of one politically active scholar during the early Nanjing Decade. Perhaps it will help give flesh and bones to abstractions about "persecuted intellectuals" under GMD rule. Since Zhang's fate was all too common among his generation of scholars, his story serves as a case study of the fate of these men at this pivotal moment in China's modern history.

First Clash with Chiang Kai-shek and the Reorganized GMD, 1926-1927

As we have seen in earlier chapters, Zhang had a long history of opposition to the GMD, as a result of his membership in Liang Qichao's political parties and groups. The mutual hostility between the Liang group and the GMD finally exploded in the spring of 1927, when the Northern Expedition's NRA reached Shanghai.[2]

Believing like a good Confucianist that education was a (if not *the*) fundamental approach to saving the nation, Zhang founded the National Institute of Self-Government in Shanghai in the fall of 1923 (see chapter 4). The school was set up with the approval of the civil governor of Jiangsu, Han Guojun, who also may have contributed to its support.[3]

Initially, the institute was a result of Zhang's involvement in the federalist movement in the early 1920s. When that movement evaporated, he retreated to his native province to pursue self-government on a smaller and more manageable scale.[4] At first set up in the French Concession, in 1925 the school changed its name to the National Institute of Political Science and moved to a new site in Wusong, thanks in part to financial support from the new ruler of Shanghai, warlord Sun Chuanfang.[5] A number of the school's professors and students were to join the NSP during the early 1930s.[6]

When the NRA reached Shanghai in the spring of 1927, it cracked down on Zhang and his school. Not only had he been a thorn in the side of the GMD for years, in November 1926—only four months prior to the arrival of the GMD—he published views in the press critical of the GMD and its Northern Expedition.[7] His observations were based on a clandestine trip to Wuhan to see what the GMD-CCP alliance, advised by Soviet agents, was like. His report was ambiguous—straddling the fence between praise and criticism—which may have been what one of Zhang's followers meant when he referred to tensions between Zhang and his lifelong mentor, Liang Qichao, following this trip.[8]

In his report, he approved of the GMD's successes against the Beiyang warlords (even though one of his sponsors, Sun Chuanfang, was a Beiyang warlord). He also rejected the charge that the Southern Army was out to "communize" property, and instead praised the regime's clear and pervasive ideology, politicized and well-behaved party-army, and skill at obtaining the support of the populace. "The Guomindang's strong points are courage and boldness in action," he wrote, "and it is especially good at arousing the masses." "Our admiration for the party-army (*dang jun*)," he added, "may be called extreme."

There was nothing about these views to arouse the enmity of the GMD. However, he went on to criticize his old rivals for their intolerance of different views and doctrines, reliance on force and one-party dictatorship, "partyization" (*danghua*) of education, and incorporation into their ranks of the former warlords. Fearing that the old-style dictatorship would be replaced by a new-style one, he expressed his belief in natural rights (making him a rare bird indeed in twentieth-century China, according to Andrew Nathan[9]) and issued an impassioned appeal for "true freedom" and "true democracy." Wuhan's leaders, he lamented, considered important only the "propagandizing of party principles" and "rallies." They had "no idea how to open up and channel the underground springs of democracy." In the end, the GMD's advocacy of one-party dictatorship and violent revolution outweighed its merits, in his view.

As a result of his observations in Wuhan, he knew what to expect if the NRA took Shanghai. He cited various GMD regulations that called for banning of private schools and the "partyization" of education. It was quite clear, he wrote, that education under the GMD would be "subordinate to the politics of political parties and groups." At the least, as a British diplomat noted, private schools would be required to register with the government, and the party would have the final say in their curricula.[10] Later on, the teaching of GMD principles was made a part of university curricula as well.[11]

During the winter of 1926-27, Zhang sat in Shanghai and awaited the outcome of the struggle between the revolutionaries and Sun Chuanfang. As it became clear the former were winning, his mood turned desperate. Writing (in German) on 1 March 1927 to his old friend, Sinologist Richard Wilhelm, he reported that all of South China was under the control of the Nationalist Regime, with "Party rule . . . the first principle of all administration." Fearing for the future of his school, on which he had lavished so much attention since 1923, he complained that the Nationalists wanted to "convert all institutes of learning to party purposes. Academic freedom no longer exists." Expressing sentiments quite similar to those he voiced on the eve of the communist takeover of China more than twenty years later, he continued:

> Under these conditions, I cannot cooperate. I am thinking of emigrating. . . . I shall be bringing my wife and baby along and, if possible, staying outside China forever. You can imagine how the situation is in China. Dear Friend, I am being serious about everything I am telling you.[12]

Three weeks later (22 March), the NRA entered Shanghai. Zhang was a former member of the Progressive Party. Moreover, he was an active member of the Research Clique during the years leading up to the Northern Expedition in 1926; in fact, the Institute of Political Science served in part as a training center for that group.[13] Both political organizations were anti-GMD. He was also a longtime associate of Liang Qichao, a leading opponent of the revolutionaries. Hence, when the NRA arrived in Shanghai, there was no way Zhang could avoid being labelled a "reactionary." What was worse, as a leader of the CYP later recalled, to be "nonrevolutionary" (*bugeming*) during the first GMD-CCP United Front (1923-27) was to be "counterevolutionary" (*fangeming*).[14]

According to a former student at Zhang's institute, though, at first the GMD gave him a chance to come around to its point of view. A party official was sent to his school to order him to incorporate Sun Yat-sen's Three People's Principles into the curriculum as a required subject. Perhaps predictably, he refused, and the school was closed.[15] The GMD Municipal Party Headquarters placed its seal on the gate, and its funds and library were confiscated.[16]

Things became worse for Zhang when the Shanghai Municipal Government issued a warrant for his arrest as a "dissident" (*yiji*).[17] In addition to his connections with Liang Qichao's political movements and his refusal to accept Sun Yat-sen's teachings as Holy Writ, his relationship with the enemy of the revolution, Beiyang warlord Sun Chuanfang, did not endear him to the GMD. According to a leader of the CYP, Chiang Kai-shek "refused to tolerate anyone having connections with militarists" and later had Zhang's old friend, Jiang

Baili, arrested for his connections with Sun Chuanfang and Wu Peifu.[18]

With his livelihood gone, a family to support,[19] and facing arrest, Zhang retreated into the world of scholarship. Settling down in his home on Seymour Road in the International Settlement, he devoted himself to translation and writing. His major project was a translation of Harold Laski's *A Grammar of Politics*, for which he received two hundred *yuan* a month from the Commercial Press. Despite a common belief among historians that Chinese opposition politicians were safe in the treaty-port concessions, this proved a myth in Zhang's case; even scholarship carried out in the relative safety of the International Settlement was not free from the long reach of the GMD. He later related what happened after he agreed to write an ABC of political science for the World Bookstore's ABC Collected Works:

> Unexpectedly, after the publication of the advertisement, the bookstore received notification from the Shanghai Municipal Party Headquarters of the Guomindang order to burn the plates. The bookstore, assuming that the [foreign] concessions still existed, ignored it [the order] and did not reply. Several months later, the Chief Justice of the Shanghai Provisional Court, Wu Jingxiong, received an order from Party Headquarters commanding him to close the World Bookstore. Wu was my friend and immediately came to see me and report what had happened. I said: "The book has not yet been written. How [can the bookstore] obey and destroy the plates?" Later, the bookstore came to an agreement with the Party Headquarters, and the affair then ended.[20]

The ramifications of the incident did not stop there, however. Like others who had displeased the GMD, Zhang was forced to shield himself against persecution by adopting a pseudonym:

> The Commercial Press heard of the affair and then asked Mr. Yu Songhua to inform me: you cannot use your real name for the [Laski] book you are translating. At the time, I depended on this [work] for [my] livelihood. [Hence,] I did not even dare to insist on the freedom to use my own name. Therefore, I changed [it] to "Zhang Shilin." I selected the *Shi* from the top of *Jia* and the *lin* from the foot of *sen*, i.e., from my name, Jiasen. This was the pain I suffered because there was no freedom of the press.[21]

Opposition to Communism

As we have seen in chapter 3, by the time of his 1927 clash with the GMD Zhang also was bitterly opposed to the Communists. In view of his opposition to the GMD-CCP United Front, it is doubtful whether he shed any tears over the rupturing of that alliance when, on 12 April 1927, Chiang Kai-shek and the

GMD launched a purge of the Communists in Shanghai. Zhang later recalled that Chiang Kai-shek "won the cooperation of the Chief of the Blue [Green] Gang, Tu Yueh-sen [Du Yuesheng], in his project of disarming the Communists in Shanghai where they were just then making preparations to attack the Shanghai Settlement. . . . [A]fter the Shanghai massacre . . . the Kuomintang and the Communists definitely broke with each other."[22] It is unlikely that Zhang's constantly reiterated beliefs in natural rights, freedom, and democracy extended to the Chinese Communists.

In fact, at the time of this break between the GMD and the CCP, he seemed to see the anti-Communist GMD and the CCP as equally bad.[23] "Although the Nanking Regime declares itself anti-communist," he wrote to Richard Wilhelm, "it nevertheless intends to subject China to a party dictatorship." Hence, instead of cheering the GMD for attacking the Communists, he saw nothing but continued warfare in China. In July 1927, he complained: "The war between Nanking and Hankow has begun, and Chiang Kai-shek has ceased marching north. One no longer hears anything about political reconstruction."[24] Moreover, as we shall see in chapter 6, at the same time he clashed with the GMD, he was working on a book about Soviet Russia, which was published at the end of 1927.

Flirtation with the Chinese Youth Party, 1928-1929

Throughout his life, Zhang was never content to be an "armchair scholar." Hence, he was ready, when the opportunity presented itself in the fall and winter of 1927-1928, to plunge back into the world of political activism. It was Li Huang, a leader of the CYP, who helped to give Zhang new hope in the efficacy of political action, and the close relationship between Zhang and the CYP that began at this time lasted until the end of his days.

Li arrived in Shanghai in October 1927. Earlier that year, he had lost his professorship at the National Sichuan University. Moreover, the GMD had issued a warrant for the arrest of his "counterrevolutionary nationalist group." Hence, he feared for his safety and, like Zhang, ended up in the International Settlement, where he took charge of the CYP as acting chairman. Again, as in Zhang's case, living in the foreign concessions did not guarantee safety. Hence, Li recalled, "I was forced to hide in the daytime and work at night." Thus, he felt "quite isolated and lonely." It is not surprising that when the two dejected scholars met, they took comfort in each other's company.

Zhang had already read some of Li's writings and also knew Zeng Qi, the chairman of the CYP. Moreover, Zhang's and Li's situations and outlooks were similar: both were under heavy pressure from the GMD and both were anticommunist. In addition, the CYP's headquarters was near Zhang's home, making it easy for the two to get together "repeatedly."[25] Zhang also met Zuo Shunsheng, another leader of the CYP, at this time,[26] and it was proposed that a new party be formed with Zeng as chairman and Zhang, vice chairman. However, due to Zeng's "stubborn personal opinions," the project fell through.[27]

Xinlu Magazine

Zhang and Li did successfully cooperate, however, in establishing a new journal, *Xinlu* (New Way), that attacked both the GMD and the CCP and thus adopted a "third-force" position. In fact, Zhang's participation in the journal may be viewed as a "way station" between his earlier involvement in Liang Qichao's various groups and the formation of the NSP in the early 1930s. Some of the proposals in the twelve-point program that appeared in the first issue of the journal, published on 1 February 1928, also had been broached in his 1922 work, *Guo xian yi* (Suggestions for a National Constitution), and some would continue to appear in his writings and various political party programs throughout the remainder of the Republican period.

On the positive side, the journal advocated democracy, civil rights, independence and equality of the nation, unification in accordance with the spirit of self-government, development of production and improvement of the lives of the peasants and workers, advancement of China's national culture and development of the scientific spirit, implementation of a budget and financial unification, education of sound citizens, establishment of a system for the protection of civil servants, complete independence of the judiciary, use of the army for national defense, and an emphasis on peaceful reconstruction in national progress. In addition, it declared its opposition to monarchy and one-class and one-party dictatorships; foreign aggression and all actions that sold out and wronged the nation; the deprivation of human rights in the name of political party or military rule; unification through military subjugation; class struggle and other movements that hindered economic development; completely indiscriminate conservatism, as well as uncritical pursuit of the new; the lack of a budget and the imposition on the people of illegal taxes; church and "partyized" education; the arbitrary appointment and removal of government personnel; the "partyization" of the judiciary and excessive use of military law in trying people; the use of the army in private or political party disputes; and destructive revolution.[28]

According to Li, he and Zhang were the main contributors to the journal.

The latter undertook to raise funds for it, while Li took responsibility for its publication. Zhang concentrated on attacking the GMD's political tutelage, while Li focused his fire on the CCP. In later years, Zhang overlooked Li's role and exaggerated the extent of the GMD's control of China, when he declared, "I published a magazine called *New Way,* which opposed the 'political tutelage' of the Kuomintang, which I knew meant nothing less than totalitarianism."[29]

The magazine seems to have been quite successful; according to Li, circulation rose to three thousand copies, with some read in the concessions while others were smuggled out by "covert dispatches." Just as in the case of his books, though, Zhang was forced to resort to a pseudonym to avoid immediate banning of the journal. Hence, he used "Li Zhai," while Li used "Chun Mu." However, people eventually identified them. Hence, after *Xinlu* had published ten issues, the GMD banned it. The GMD held all the cards, according to Li: "Since it was not easy to mail and the print shop did not dare print it any longer, it was then forced to cease publication."[30]

The CYP's Zhixing Institute

Again confronted with the problem of livelihood (ironically, the third of Sun Yat-sen's Three People's Principles), after publication of the last issue of *Xinlu* on 1 December 1928, Zhang once again became an editor of the Shanghai newspaper, *Shishi xinbao*.[31]

As an indication of his continuing political involvement, in the spring of 1929 he volunteered to teach without pay at the Zhixing Institute, a school affiliated with the CYP and located in the International Settlement. This institute was founded by Li Huang and designed as a training institution for CYP cadre. The students were drawn from the CYP's national membership, and the curriculum included party-training courses.

Significantly, according to Li, the school's name meant "to know is to be able to act."[32] Hence, it echoed the famous Ming Dynasty philosopher, Wang Yangming (1472-1529), who argued that "knowledge is the beginning of action; action is the completion of knowledge."[33] It also was reminiscent of Sun Yat-sen's attempted rebuttal of Wang. Sun blamed Wang's concept for China's failure to implement Sun's program. According to the latter, Wang's doctrine had fostered the idea that "to know is easy and to act is difficult." Sun argued for a reversal of the concept—declaring that "it is easy to act but difficult to know"—in hopes that the Chinese would then act, rather than conclude that "there is nothing that can be done in this world."[34] Hence, at the same time, the name of the school carried overtones of traditionalism, as well as of Sun's attacks on that ism.

More important for Zhang, Li also saw the school as a place for his friends, who were being suppressed by the GMD, to teach. The teaching load was only two hours a week, and they would have more freedom of speech than if they taught in the public or private universities.[35] Zhang recalled on one occasion that he taught political thought at the Zhixing Institute and, on another, that he gave classes in political science;[36] according to Li, Zhang taught the history of European political thought.[37]

As in the case of *Xinlu*, this school embodied cooperation between the CYP and some of the intellectuals who founded the NSP in the early 1930s. Six of the fourteen professors who took up posts at the institute—Zhang Junmai, Zhang Dongsun, Zhu Qinglai, Pan Guangdan, Liang Shiqiu, and Luo Longji—later participated in the establishment of the NSP.[38] Most of the other faculty members seem to have been CYP members.

The Kidnapping, June 1929

Zhang was not present when, due to changed circumstances, the institute closed in the summer of 1930.[39] By that time, he was in exile in Germany, and his path there reveals much about the uncertainties of life in Shanghai in the late 1920s. One of those uncertainties was the threat of kidnapping. In mid-June 1929, he was seized and held for several weeks, before being ransomed.[40] He later recalled the circumstances:

> One afternoon at five o'clock, I gave a lecture [at the Zhixing Institute]. At 7:00 P.M., I [set out] on foot to return home. When I got to the intersection of Jing'ansi Road, two gangsters suddenly forced me into an automobile. They stepped on my back with both feet and prevented me from making a sound. After travelling for twenty to thirty minutes, [I] was imprisoned in a room. Everyday, the so-called chief of staff (*canmouzhangzhe*) came at 10:00 P.M. and made me kneel on a chain of iron rings. Furthermore, he asked: what is your purpose in running a school in Shanghai in opposition to the Guomindang? I replied that I considered this a political problem, and was unable to explain it there. It would be better to escort me to Nanjing, and I myself could explain the reasons. Everyday, four men guarded me in the room, without resting day and night. [They] blindfolded me, [but] every morning I heard the sound of a bugle and realized that I was staying in the vicinity of the Wusong-Shanghai Garrison Command. At that time, Zhang Taiyan [Binglin], Du Yuesheng, and others came to my rescue. My eighth brother [Jiazhu] negotiated with the kidnappers, only then learning that the Shanghai Garrison Command had conspired with the kidnappers to embarass me. The two sides published an advertisement in *Shenbao* offering an antique vase for sale as a

> way of negotiating a ransom. After negotiations, the ransom was set at 3,000 [dollars], and I gained my release. When I emerged, first I was driven by car in several circles and then abandoned by the roadside. I returned home by rickshaw. I asked the puller what place that was, and he replied: Longhua. [That] was the location of the Garrison Command. Several days later, a fortune-teller told me: you have escaped with your life from the bottom of a coffin.[41]

Throughout his life, Zhang clung to the belief that it was the Shanghai Garrison Command that kidnapped him.[42] Zuo Shunsheng agreed that the GMD was responsible, adding that Zhang was "not the Kuomintang's only victim. . . . Our [CYP] comrades were kidnapped too."[43]

In an interview a half-century later, however, Jiazhu, the younger brother who had handled the negotiations for Zhang's release, rejected his brother's belief that the culprit was the GMD. It had been, he asserted, simply a kidnapping for ransom. The kidnappers demanded money; yet, when he repeatedly sent payments, they claimed he had not and threatened to cut off Zhang's ears. Finally, Jiazhu got in touch with some gangsters and paid them, with opium purchased from a hotel, to act as middlemen. Ten days later, Zhang was released, although with a leg injury that left him limping for the remainder of his life.[44]

The exact truth of this tragic episode in Zhang's life may never be known. It is possible, however, that both he and Jiazhu were correct; that is, Zhang was kidnapped by gangsters working for the GMD. It is well documented that Chiang Kai-shek and his party resorted to kidnapping for ransom to raise funds for the regime.[45] Kidnapping of wealthy Chinese, sanctioned by the authorities, was a common occurrence in Shanghai in the late 1920s.[46] The gangsters may have been used because it was difficult for the GMD to operate freely in the International Settlement.[47]

The specific setting for Zhang's kidnapping may have been the clash between GMD headquarters and the business community in Shanghai during the spring of 1929. The target of the GMD attack was the Shanghai General Chamber of Commerce.[48] In May 1929, Zhang's brother, Kia-ngau, then head of the Bank of China and thus an important member of the Shanghai business community, left China for nearly a year.[49] He may have done so to escape being kidnapped, for a number of wealthy Shanghai citizens fled the city in 1928 when the renewed Northern Expedition led to another wave of kidnappings for ransom.[50] The GMD, foiled by Kia-ngau's departure, may have seized Junmai as a way of tapping the resources Kia-ngau commanded as head of the Bank of China.

The final mystery concerns the role of Du Yuesheng, a leader of the Green

Gang (*Qingbang*), whom Zhang credited (along with Zhang Binglin) with his release. The Green Gang was known for its involvement in kidnapping and opium dealing.[51] After money failed to win his brother's release, Jiazhu used opium to purchase the assistance of some gangsters. Since opium was the latter's main source of income, the cash may have gone to the GMD, while the opium went to the Green Gang, thus satisfying Zhang's kidnappers.

Finally, the kidnapping of Zhang may well have had its political edge. It finally allowed the GMD to strike at a man whom they had wanted to arrest for the past two years. Moreover, this was someone who had compounded his earlier sins by becoming a mainstay of the anti-GMD journal, *Xinlu*. Their views on such "counterrevolutionaries" certainly had not changed. In late March 1929, the director of the special GMD headquarters in Shanghai issued an official warning against such activities, defining "counterrevolutionaries" as "all those who oppose the Three Principles of the People."[52]

The Second Exile in Germany, 1929-1931

Escape to Manchuria

Regardless of the truth of his kidnapping, even the International Settlement could not protect Zhang while he lived in Shanghai. Years later, he wrote that it was "too difficult to live in safety in Shanghai."[53] Thus, in the fall of 1929, after his leg wound healed, he traveled to Shenyang, where he stayed with the family of Luo Wengan,[54] a well-known figure who served both the Beijing and Nanjing governments before retiring from government service in 1935. Zhang and Luo had first become acquainted when Zhang visited Luo in jail in Beijing, 1922-1924,[55] and remained friends until the latter's death in 1941 during the War of Resistance. As mentioned earlier (chapter 4), Luo joined the NSP in the early 1930s.[56]

At the time of Zhang's visit to Shenyang, Luo was a councilor in the headquarters of the Northeast Peace Preservation Forces, serving under the Young Marshall, Zhang Xueliang.[57] The famous diplomat, Wellington V. K. Koo, recalled that Luo was one of the "highest advisers to the Young Marshall."[58] Another of Zhang Xueliang's advisers, the Australian William Henry Donald, remembered Luo as "a personal friend of the Young Marshall's."[59] This personal relationship, along with the NSP's call for resistance to Japan following the Shenyang (Mukden) Incident in September 1931, may explain why the Young Marshall later became one of the financial supporters of the NSP.[60]

Zhang may have had another motive for traveling to Manchuria at that time. He had been interested in Russian relations with China since 1912, when he protested its policy concerning Outer Mongolia.[61] The latest manifestation of that concern had been the publication of his book, *SuE pinglun* (A Critique of Soviet Russia), less than two years earlier. Hence, while in Manchuria, he took the opportunity to observe the Sino-Soviet War, which had broken out in 1929 over the issue of control of the Chinese Eastern Railway (CER). On 10 July, the Chinese authorities in Heilongjiang had seized the CER from the Soviets. When a Soviet ultimatum demanding a return to the status quo ante went unsatisfied, war erupted between the Soviets and Zhang Xueliang's troops in August. The fighting lasted until late December, when Chinese and Soviet representatives concluded the Khabarovsk Protocol, restoring the pre-10 July status of the CER. The Soviets then withdrew their troops from Manchuria.[62]

Following his arrival in Manchuria, Zhang traveled to the Suifen River in Manzhouli to observe the course of the war. He must have wondered whether he was any safer there than in Shanghai, though, for on the day following his visit the Soviets bombed the Suifen Railway Station.[63]

In addition to the need to flee the dangerous situation in Shanghai, the presence of his friend Luo Wengan, and the opportunity to observe the clash between China and the Soviet Union, Zhang's friendship with leaders of the CYP may have played a role in his decision to visit Manchuria. The CYP had a connection with Zhang Xueliang and, in fact, in September 1929 held their Fourth Congress in Shenyang, where the group formally adopted the name "Chinese Youth Party."[64] In addition, the party had a sizeable following in the Northeast Army (*Dongbei jun*), as Zhang Xueliang's army was called. It was even said that "the Northeast Army is not the army of the northeast but of the Chinese Youth Party." In 1933, however, the Young Marshall purged his army of members of the CYP and, as a result, more than six hundred middle- and low-grade officers were expelled.[65]

Exile in Germany

Whatever his reasons for going to Manchuria, he did not linger. For over two years, he had been deeply interested in going to Germany, where he had lived on two previous occasions. It was apparently his old friend, Richard Wilhelm, who finally made it possible. In 1925, Wilhelm founded the China-Institut in Frankfurt as a center for academic and cultural exchange. During the Nanjing Decade, it served as one of the vehicles for a close Sino-German relationship.[66]

Anxious about the approach of the Northern Expedition, in March 1927

Zhang had written to Wilhelm that he was thinking of emigrating. "I shall be happy to do research in Germany," he declared. "Would it be possible for me to make my knowledge of China in general and Chinese philosophy in particular useful at any German university?. . . I hope you will be of assistance to me on this question."[67] Evidently, Wilhelm was encouraging, for in July Zhang declared his willingness to "temporarily give up all hopes of becoming politically active in China" if his plan to go to Germany succeeded.[68] After some further exchange of correspondence, in 1929 the trip finally became a reality.

As Zhang later recalled, he was "compelled" to leave China.[69] Not long after his return from Germany, he recalled that he "was not allowed to live peacefully in our country, [so I] fled abroad."[70] Perhaps as a way of getting out, he told Wilhelm that he would be glad to serve as China's representative at the "Conference of the Peace Society."[71] As for funds for the trip, Zhang's banker brother, Kia-ngau, was abroad at the time. Hence, Zhang recalled, "Through Luo Wengan, I borrowed seven hundred yuan from Zhang Xueliang, and purchased a steamer ticket to Germany."[72] In addition, he had one thousand yuan from Liang Qichao, who had died earlier that year.[73] There also may have been aid from the China-Institut, for in an earlier letter to Wilhelm, Zhang begged his friend to tell him whether his "connection with your institute is a financial burden," adding that he was awaiting Wilhelm's "frank answer."[74] In any event, he did not require a great deal of money, for, as he later recalled, at that time the cost of living in Germany was "very low." His monthly rent was five hundred marks, he wrote, which was the equivalent of ten yuan.[75]

Although Zhang began his stay at the China-Institut[76] and also may have lectured on Chinese philosophy in Berlin,[77] he later recalled that he went to Germany to "earn my living as a Professor of Philosophy at the University of Jena,"[78] where he had studied with the philosopher, Rudolf Eucken, during the years 1920-1921.[79] Although he and his family were not well off during their stay in Germany, this period has been termed the happiest and most peaceful part of his life since childhood.[80]

While in Germany, he devoted himself to philosophical studies. Before traveling there, he had written Wilhelm of his desire to publish books on Chinese philosophy and the history of Buddhism.[81] While still in China, he had also expressed interest in German Sinology, as well as his old love, European philosophy.[82]

Although in the end he did not publish any such monographs, he did find time, during his two years in Germany, to write several lengthy articles on the history of Chinese philosophy, in which he praised such Neo-Confucianists as

Zhu Xi, Lu Xiangshan (1139-1193), and Wang Yangming, as well as European thinkers such as Immanuel Kant.[83]

He also published his views of the fate of Chinese tradition in the modern world, approaching the question through a consideration of the current standing of the Confucian Classics.[84] He was in a reflective mood, after his trials of the previous few years. "Does China," he asked, "still have faith in tradition?" China had gone through a lot during the past three decades, he mused: the 1898 Reform Movement, the 1911 Revolution, and the "1927 Communist danger." Now it had begun to turn back to "self-reflection." It was clear that he believed the fate of tradition was directly related to politics. Following constitutional reform in Japan, he noted, Confucianism was studied and highly esteemed. Since the Japanese were content with their political situation, they respected the bearers of their culture. From this, Zhang drew the logical conclusion: "Someday, when China becomes a stable Republic, the attack on Confucianism will . . . cease."[85]

As the preceding discussion demonstrates, despite Zhang's desire to take refuge in quiet academic study, he could not get Chinese politics or the desire to run his own school again out of his mind. According to Li Huang, Zhang often wrote him from Germany. "[He] said," reported Li, "that regardless of whether [we] operated a political party, it was our duty to train youth with genuine knowledge, so they would have the ability to work for the future of the nation."[86]

Zhang also retained his abiding interest in constitutionalism, another of his lifelong pursuits. During the same year that he was worrying about the state of tradition in China, he also was expressing anxiety about what he called "The Constitutional Crisis in the Republic of China."[87]

It was a combination of his interest in education and philosophy that brought him back into the political struggle in China after an absence of two years. In 1931, John Leighton Stuart, the president of Yenching University in Peiping, cabled Zhang and invited him to return and teach the philosophy of Hegel.[88] As a private university, Yenching had been spared much of the political control the GMD had established over institutions of higher learning, such as Qinghua University and Peking University. During the 1920s, Yenching had engaged in a drive to add more Chinese professors to the faculty. Moreover, it had a reputation for excellence.[89]

These reasons, as well as the presence of his old friend, Zhang Dongsun, in the philosophy department, probably contributed to Zhang's decision to accept the post.[90] Hence, in August 1931, Zhang and his family began the long trek home via the Soviet Union and the Trans-Siberian Railroad.[91] Although he had no way of knowing it, the years ahead were to be every bit as taxing as those just past.

Conclusion

At first glance, Zhang's story during the early years of the Nanjing Decade appears to be a straightforward one. He stood for the right—democracy—and was suppressed by the GMD for daring to oppose its political tutelage. This view is true, of course. Upon closer examination, though, things were not quite that simple.

The twin goals of the Northern Expedition were to overthrow the warlords and expel the foreign "imperialists." In light of the former objective, the GMD had grounds for its hostility to Zhang. He had a long record of cooperation with China's warlords. Sun Chuanfang's financial support of Zhang's Institute of Political Science was only the most recent example. In fact, following his visit to Wuhan in October 1926, he stopped in Jiujiang to call on the beleaguered General Sun,[92] a gesture that, if the GMD leadership knew of it, could not help but further doom Zhang, once the NRA took Shanghai, for it is impossible to overlook the fact that Sun was one of the main targets of the Northern Expedition and had been responsible for the deaths of many revolutionaries.[93]

In other ways, too, the GMD's enmity was understandable (from its point of view). Zhang was thoroughly identified as a follower of Liang Qichao, with whom the GMD had fought bitterly since its days of exile in Japan prior to the 1911 Revolution. Although one does not have to admire vindictiveness when it surfaces, as it did in 1927, one can understand (again, from its own viewpoint) the GMD's thirst for revenge against its longtime opponent. Hence, while pursuing the Party Purification Movement against the CCP during 1927-1928, it made time to suppress other opponents as well. Even Zhang's views of the GMD, at least in October 1926, were more complicated than one might have anticipated from an old rival of the Nationalists. There were things he admired about the Reorganized GMD, as we have seen, although they were outweighed by those aspects of GMD rule that troubled him.

In the final analysis, one cannot help but admire Zhang. In a China dominated by militarists, he had no choice but to solicit aid from wealthy generals if he wanted to establish a school. Moreover, the contrast between the granting of such aid and the GMD's repression was all too clear in the fate of his Institute of Political Science. During the 1930s, his quest for a sanctuary from GMD persecution, as well as a way to construct a modern China, led him into the arms of warlord after warlord. Like Sun Yat-sen, he never gave up searching for a "good" warlord.

Moreover, in Zhang's case, there was no question of remaining out of politics, as did some of his fellow liberal intellectuals. As a descendant of the scholar-gentry class of imperial China—nay, a member of that class, since he earned the *shengyuan* degree in 1902, the *jinshi* in 1910, and the Hanlin bachelor (*shujishi*) in 1911[94]—he took the idea of political activism very seriously. When his demand for democracy clashed with the GMD's program of political tutelage, something had to give, and that something was Zhang, since the GMD had all the instruments of force on its side (police and army). In the final analysis, the GMD had no more use for educational freedom than the governments that preceded and followed it.

Hence, following the arrival of the GMD in Shanghai (Zhang's hometown), it suppressed him and other opponents of its rule. Schools and journals were closed, arrest warrants issued, and there is even evidence, in Zhang's case, to suggest kidnapping for ransom. Such repression drove others into the embrace of the Chinese Communists. Yet, throughout his ordeal, Zhang maintained his opposition to the CCP, the only viable alternative to the GMD besides the warlords.

In the end, the harsh political climate proved too much for Zhang, and he fled to Germany, as he had done when he escaped Yuan Shikai's wrath sixteen years earlier.[95] When he returned in the fall of 1931, the Manchurian Incident was to offer him and his colleagues a renewed chance for political action, an opportunity they grasped with the formation of the NSP.

Notes

1. The group was known as the "Nationalist Clique" (*Guojiazhuyi pai*) until 1929, when it adopted the name Chinese Youth Party. Chan Lau Kit-ching, *The Chinese Youth Party, 1923-1945* (Hong Kong: Centre of Asian Studies, University of Hong Kong, 1972), 22-23. For the sake of clarity, the latter name will be used throughout this study.

2. For an account of the progress of the Northern Expedition, as well as the taking of Shanghai, see Donald A. Jordan, *The Northern Expedition: China's National Revolution of 1926-1928* (Honolulu: University Press of Hawaii, 1976).

3. Han Guojun, *Zhisou nianpu* (My Chronological Biography upon Arrival at Old Age) (Taipei: Wenhai chubanshe, 1966), 49-50; YX, 19-20.

4. Jeans, "Syncretism in Defense of Confucianism," 352-63.

5. YX, 19; BDRC, 1: 131.

6. Five professors at the institute—Zhang Dongsun, Luo Wengan, Qu Shiying, Lu Dingkui, and Pan Guangdan—later joined one of the parties (the NSP and DSP) Zhang headed from 1932 until his formal resignation as party leader of the DSP in May 1950. In addition, four of the school's students—Cheng Wenxi, Jiang Yuntian, Yang Yuzi, and Feng Jinbai—later joined one of the parties. Jeans, "Syncretism in Defense of Confucianism," 369, 373.

7. Unless otherwise noted, the following discussion is summarized from Zhang Jiasen [Zhang Junmai], *Wuhan jianwen* (Observations in Wuhan) (Wusong: National Institute of Political Science, 1926).

8. Jiang Yuntian, "Zhang Junmai xiansheng yisheng dashi ji" (A Record of Major Events in Mr. Zhang Junmai's Life), *Minzhu shehui* 5, no. 2 (1969): 26.

9. Andrew J. Nathan, *Chinese Democracy* (New York: Knopf, 1985), chap. 5.

10. Great Britain, Foreign Office (hereafter, GBFO) 371\12499 [F3210\3210\10], dispatch, Acting Consul General Brenan, Canton, to Foreign Office, "Control of Private Schools," 25 February 1927.

11. Franklin L. Ho, "The Reminiscences of Ho Lien (Franklin L. Ho)," as told to Crystal Lorch Seidman, postscript dated July 1966, Chinese Oral History Project, Special Collections Library, Butler Library, Columbia University, 287.

12. Carsun Chang, letter to Richard Wilhelm, 1 March 1927, Richard Wilhelm Papers, privately held by Hellmut Wilhelm, Seattle, Washington.

13. Chang P'eng-yuan, *Liang Qichao yu minguo zhengzhi* (Liang Qichao and Republican Politics) (Taipei: Shihuo chubanshe youxian gongsi, 1978), 175.

14. Li Huang, "Jingdao Zhang Junmai xiansheng" (Solemnly Mourn for Mr. Zhang Junmai), *Minzhu shehui* 5, no. 2 (1969): 18.

15. Cheng Wenxi, interview with author, Taipei, Taiwan, 24 June 1976.

16. Hu Ziping, ed., *Zhongguo zhengzhi renwu* (Chinese Political Personalities) (Fuzhou: Dada tushu gongsi, 1948), 186; Zhang Junmai, *Bianzheng weiwuzhuyi bolun* (A Refutation of Dialectical Materialism) (Hong Kong: Youlian chubanshe, 1958), 191; Zhang Junmai, *Zhonghua minguo duli zizhu yu Yazhou qiantu* (The Republic of China's Independence and the Future of Asia) (Hong Kong: Ziyou chubanshe, 1955), 46.

17. "Shi dangbu chengqing tongji xuefa" (The Municipal Party Headquarter's Petition for the Arrest of the School Lords), *Shenbao*, 17 June 1927; reprinted in Tang Zhijun, ed., *Zhang Taiyan nianpu changbian* (A Full Chronological Biography of Zhang Taiyan), 2 vols. (Beijing: Zhonghua shuju, 1979), 2: 888. See also Shi Yi, "Wo suo zhidao Zhang Junmai," 13; Zhang Junmai, *Shehuizhuyi*, 3. In a letter dated 1 April 1927, Zhang's former brother-in-law, Xu Zhimo, noted that Zhang was "under order of arrest." Xu Zhimo, *Xu Zhimo Yingwen shuxin ji* (English Letters of Xu Zhimo), ed. Liang Xihua (Taipei: Lianjing chuban shiye gongsi, 1979), 62.

18. Zuo Shunsheng, "The Reminiscences of Tso Shun-sheng," as told to Julie Lien-ying How, 1965, Chinese Oral History Project, Special Collections Library, Butler Library, Columbia University, 108, 132.

19. In 1929, Xu Zhimo described Zhang as a "penniless, almost mendicant scholar," adding that he had to "part with all his books, his only property last year in order to keep his family fed at all." Xu Zhimo, *Xu Zhimo Yingwen shuxin*, 100.

20. Zhang, "Nianyu nian lai," 5.

21. Ibid. Zhang's translation of Laski's work was not published until October 1930, while Zhang was in Germany. Harold Laski, *Zhengzhi dianfan* (A Grammar of Politics), trans. Zhang Shilin [Zhang Junmai] (Shanghai: Shangwu yinshuguan, 1930). There must have been a steady demand, for it was reprinted in 1934, 1939, 1965, and 1970.

22. Chang, *Third Force*, 73, 75-76.

23. This was in contrast to his stance on the eve of the Sino-Japanese War, when the evidence indicates that if forced to choose between the GMD and the CCP, he would have chosen the former as the lesser of the two evils (see chap. 8).

24. Carsun Chang, letter to Richard Wilhelm, 14 July 1927, Wilhelm Papers.

25. Li Huang, "Jingdao Zhang Junmai," 17-18; Li Huang, "The Reminiscences of Li Huang," trans. Lillian Chu Chin, Chinese Oral History Project, Special Collections Library, Butler Library, Columbia University, 326-27; BDRC, 2: 303.

26. Zuo Shunsheng, "Zhuidaohui zhici" (Speech at the Memorial Service), *Ziyou Zhong* (H.K. ed.) 1, no. 1 (1970): 30-31.

27. GS 4, no. 5, 72.

28. "Fakanci" (Foreword), *Xinlu* 1, no. 1 (1928): 3-4. Since Zhang was one of the main writers for *Xinlu* (along with Li Huang), and there was no article published in this issue under his name, it is quite possible that he was the author of this piece.

29. Chang, *Third Force*, 24.

30. Li Huang, "Reminiscences," 328; Li Huang, "Jingdao Zhang Junmai," 18.

31. Cheng Cangpo, "Zhuiyi Zhang Junmai xiansheng" (Recollections of Mr. Zhang Junmai), *Zhuanji wenxue* 48, no. 1 (1986): 27-28. Following his return from Germany in 1916, Zhang had served as editor in chief of the then Jinbudang organ from November 1916 to March 1917. Jeans, "Syncretism in Defense of Confucianism," 134, 151-52, 157.

32. Li Huang, "Reminiscences," 331-32; Li Huang, "Jingdao Zhang Junmai," 18.

33. William T. De Bary, Wing-tsit Chan, and Chester Tan, comps., *Sources of Chinese Tradition*, 2 vols. (New York: Columbia University Press, 1960), 1: 515.

34. Ibid., 2: 121-24.

35. Li Huang, "Reminiscences," 331; Li Huang, "Jingdao Zhang Junmai," 18.

36. Zhang Junmai, "Zhuiyi [Zeng] Muhan" (Recollections of Zeng Qi), *Minzhu chao* 2, no. 18 (1961): 3; Zhang, *Bianzheng weiwuzhuyi*, 191.

37. Li Huang, "Reminiscences," 332.

38. Li Huang, "Reminiscences, " 332-33; Li Huang, "Jingdao Zhang Junmai," 18. Although Li did not mention him, another future member of the NSP, Lu Dingkui, also is said to have taught at the school. GS 4, no. 5, 72.

39. Ibid., 334-35.

40. Xu Zhimo, *Xu Zhimo Yingwen shuxin*, 100. Xu wrote that Zhang was kidnapped around June 13-15 and held three weeks. Zhang himself later recalled that he was held "about a month." Chang, *Third Force*, 24.

41. Zhang, *Bianzheng weiwuzhuyi*, 191-92.

42. See, e.g., the account in *Third Force*, 24.

43. Zuo Shunsheng, "Reminiscences," 76.

44. Zhang Jiazhu, interview with author, San Francisco, California, 28 July 1976.

45. Parks M. Coble, Jr. *The Shanghai Capitalists and the Nationalist Government, 1927-1937* (Cambridge: Harvard University Press, 1980), chaps. 2, 3.

46. Ibid., 32, 34-36, 45. A British report stated that for some time there had been a "wave of the abduction of prominent Chinese and their children for ransom." GBFO 371\12446 [F9193\143\10], Clearing Office (Enemy Debts) [Shanghai?], to The Controller, The Clearing House (Enemy Debts) [London?], "Situation in China (Monthly Report for October 1927)," 9 December 1927.

47. Police of the three sections of Shanghai (International Settlement, French Concession, and Chinese City) were not allowed to enter each other's sectors. Hence, it was easier for the GMD to rely on the Green Gang rather than extradition. Coble, *The Shanghai Capitalists*, 37.

48. Ibid., 60-65.

49. Kia-ngau spent ten and one-half months visiting eighteen countries before returning to China in March 1930. Chang Kia-ngau, "Chang Chia-ao Autobiography," 66.

50. Coble, *The Shanghai Capitalists*, 45. According to Xu Zhimo, due to the "alarming news of Carsun Chang's ill-fortune," Xu's "terror-stricken" father considered moving the entire family to "some safer places than Shanghai, such as Tsingtao." Hsu, *Xu Zhimo Yingwen shuxin*, 102.

51. Kidnapping was said to be one of the Green Gang's "trades." Harold R. Isaacs, *The Tragedy of the Chinese Revolution*, 2d ed. (New York: Atheneum, 1966), 142. Opium dealing, however, was their main source of income. Coble, *The Shanghai Capitalists*, 37.

52. Grieder, *Hu Shih*, 240-41.

53. Zhang, *Bianzheng weiwuzhuyi*, 192.

54. GS 4, no. 5, 71; LHWLX, 18.

55. On Luo's jailing, see BDRC, 2: 439-40. For Zhang's visit to Luo in prison, see the preface in Luo Wengan, *Yuzhongren yu* (Words from a Prisoner) (Taipei: Wenhai chubanshe, 1971).

56. According to an official party history, Luo joined the NSP in 1933, as the result of a trip south by Zhang Junmai. "Zhongguo minzhu shehui dang jianyao shigao" (A Brief Draft History of the Chinese Democratic Socialist Party), *Minzhu Zhongguo* 1, no. 10 (1951): 19.

57. BDRC, 2: 440.

58. Wellington V. K. Koo, "The Memoirs of Dr. Wellington V. K. Koo," unpub. ms., n.d., done with Julie Lien-ying How et al., Special Collections, Butler Library, Columbia University, 3: 292-302.

59. Earl Albert Selle, *Donald of China* (New York: Harper & Brothers, 1948), 256.

60. According to an October 1941 interview with Xu Fulin, one of the leaders of the NSP in Hong Kong, the party was originally supported by the Young Marshall. Support from that source, Xu added, had been cut off some years before (following the 1936 Xi'an Incident and Zhang Xueliang's arrest?). NA, Military Archives Division, Military Reference Branch, RG 226, Records of the Office of Strategic Services, no. 7724, Addison E. Southard, Consul General, H.K., to SecState, dispatch no. 1035, "Transmitting a Memorandum of a conversation with the representative in Hong Kong of the 'Chinese National Socialist Party' on the subject of that party and of the 'Federation of Democratic Parties in China,'" 23 October 1941, p. 4 of the memorandum.

61. Jeans, "Syncretism in Defense of Confucianism," 103-5.

62. MacKerras and Chan, *Modern China*, 326, 328.

63. YX, 22; GS 4, no. 5, 71.

64. BDRC, 2: 303; P.K. Yu, *Research Materials on Twentieth-Century China: An Annotated List of CCRM [Center for Chinese Research Materials] Publications* (Washington, D.C.: CCRM, Association of Research Libraries, 1975), 111.

65. Chan Lau Kit-ching, *The Chinese Youth Party*, 31.

66. William C. Kirby, *Germany and Republican China* (Stanford: Stanford University Press, 1984), 70.

67. Carsun Chang to Richard Wilhelm, 1 March 1927, Wilhelm Papers.

68. Carsun Chang to Richard Wilhelm, 14 July 1927, Wilhelm Papers.

69. Chang, *Third Force*, 24.

70. STLZX (1933), preface no. 1, p. 2. This sentence was censored from the 1971 Taiwan reprint.

71. Carsun Chang to Richard Wilhelm, 30 August 1928, Wilhelm Papers. I have been unable to identify this "society" or "conference."

72. Zhang, *Bianzheng weiwuzhuyi*, 192. The Young Marshall seems to have had a weak spot for Luo and his friends. In addition to bankrolling the NSP and lending Zhang Junmai money, he once paid off Luo's debts, amounting to $100,000 (yuan?). USDS, R.G. 84, China Diplomatic Post Records (Peiping), 1934, vol. 40, 800 decimal series, Willys R. Peck, counselor of legation, to Johnson, American minister, Peiping, 30 July 1934, on the general political situation in Nanjing.

73. Zhang, *Shehuizhuyi*, 3.

74. Carsun Chang to Richard Wilhelm, 14 July 1927, Wilhelm Papers.

75. Zhang, *Shehuizhuyi*, 3.

76. Zhang later implied that he had heard a pair of Wilhelm's lectures at the China-Institut in late 1929. Carsun Chang, "Richard Wilhelm, Weltburger," *Sinica* 5, no. 2 (1930): 73.

77. BDRC, 1: 32.

78. Chang, *Third Force*, 24-25.

79. Jeans, "Syncretism in Defense of Confucianism," chap. 7.

80. Cheng Cangpo, "Zhuiyi Zhang Junmai," 28; GS 4, no. 5, 71-72.

81. Zhang, *Shehuizhuyi*, 3. Carsun Chang to Richard Wilhelm, 14 July 1927, Wilhelm Papers.

82. Carsun Chang to Richard Wilhelm, 30 August 1928, Wilhelm Papers.

83. Carsun Chang, "Der Idealismus in der chinesischen Philosophie zur Zeit der Sung-Dynastie," *Forschungen und Fortschritte* 6, no. 17 (1930): 224-25; Carsun Chang, "Philosophisches Ringen im heutigen China," *Die Tatwelt* 6, no. 1 (1930): 25-33; Carsun Chang, "Die Hauptfragen in der Konfuzianischen Philosophie," *Sinica* 5, nos. 5/6 (1930); 213-26.

84. Carsun Chang, "Die Stellung der Kanonischen Literatur im modernen Geistesleben Chinas," *Sinica* 6, no. 1 (1931): 13-26; no. 3 (1931): 97-108.

85. Ibid., 103, 107-8.

86. Li Huang, "Jingdao Zhang Junmai," 18.

87. Carsun Chang, "Die staatsrechtliche Krisis der chinesischen Republik," *Jahrbuch des offentlichen Rechte der Gegenwart* 19 (1931): 316-55.

88. Zhang, *Bianzheng weiwuzhuyi*, 192; Zhang, *Shehuizhuyi*, 3-4.

89. Philip West, *Yenching University and Sino-Western Relations, 1916-1952* (Cambridge: Harvard University Press, 1976), 116-21.

90. In the fall of 1930, Dongsun, like Junmai earlier, left Shanghai. He moved to Peiping to take up an appointment in the Department of Philosophy at Yenching University. He was serving as department chairman (1931-33) when Zhang was offered the post. BDRC, 1:131.

91. Zhang, *Bianzheng weiwuzhuyi*, 192; YX, 22.

92. Chang, *Third Force*, 91

93. In Jiangxi, Sun executed hundreds of students, teachers, and GMD members suspected of cooperation with the NRA. Jordan, *The Northern Expedition*, 85.

94. Jeans, "Syncretism in Defense of Confucianism," 31, 84-86.

95. Ibid., 105-7.

6

Heaven or Hell:
Soviet Russia through the Eyes of a Third-Force Intellectual at the Beginning of the Nanjing Decade

During the years following the 1917 Russian Revolution, many Chinese intellectuals turned their gazes westward toward the newly arisen Soviet Russia. Disillusioned by their treatment at the hands of the Western powers at the Versailles Conference, they were impressed by the promise of the new Bolshevik regime to abrogate all unequal treaties imposed on China by czarist Russia. Those attracted by the new regime included, of course, leaders of the Chinese Communist Party (CCP), and during the 1920s three of the party's leaders—Chen Duxiu, Li Dazhao, and Qu Qiubai—visited the Soviet Union.[1] Prior to the bloody split with the CCP and its Comintern (hereafter, CI) advisers in mid-1927, some Guomindang (GMD) leaders—such as founding father Sun Yat-sen; theoretician Hu Hanmin; and dean of the future Nanjing Government's Central Political School, Luo Jialun—were also inspired by the Russian experiment.[2] Hence, CCP and GMD reactions to the new Soviet Union are well known to students of modern Chinese history and Sino-Soviet relations. In contrast, the views of those politicans and intellectuals opposed to the CCP and GMD—the so-called "third-force" figures—are not so well known. Yet, during the 1920s and 1930s, they often expressed their views of Soviet Russia in books, journals, newspapers, and speeches.

One of those "third-force" intellectuals was Zhang Junmai. He had become an anticommunist as early as 1920 (chapter 3). As this chapter will demonstrate, though, during the Nanjing Decade his views became more complicated; that is, while continuing to oppose the Soviets' political methods and express his disgust with the Chinese communist "bandits," he was quite impressed with the economic programs of the Soviet regime. His opinions were exhaustively set forth in two books, *SuE pinglun* (A Critique of Soviet Russia) (1927), and *Shitailin zhixia zhi SuE* (Soviet Russia under Stalin's Rule) (1933), and hence these works serve as the primary sources for this and the next chapter. Since by 1927 Zhang had been keenly aware of communism for several years, though, it might be helpful to briefly review his earlier assessments of that ism and its Russian homeland.

Pre-1927 Views on Russia and Communism

By the time of the GMD-CCP split in mid-1927, Zhang had a long-standing mistrust of both Russia and communism. While a student at Jiangnan Higher School in Nanjing in 1903, he joined a student volunteer corps organized to drive the Russians out of territories they had seized in Manchuria under cover of the Boxer Rebellion. For his temerity, he was immediately expelled from school and handed over to the local authorities for "stringent supervision," one of the Qing government's methods of dealing with students involved in revolutionary activity.[3] Four years later, he expressed skepticism concerning Russian willingness to adhere to the principle of nonintervention in Tibet, as Anglo-Russian talks had agreed in a convention signed in August 1907.[4] A year after the 1911 Revolution broke out, he broke with Yuan Shikai over the issue of Russian support for an independent Mongolia. Zhang termed the Russians' action "foreign aggression" and worried that if Mongolia was "lost," Inner Mongolia, Manchuria, and Tibet would also be swallowed up.[5] Three years later, he was still smarting from the Russian action, as became clear when he bitterly referred to the "so-called autonomy" of Mongolia in the Russo-Mongolian Protocol.[6]

Fleeing the wrath of Yuan, in 1913 Zhang traveled to Germany to study. On the way, he lingered in St. Petersburg for two or three months (his first and longest visit to Russia), enjoying the hospitality of his cousin, Liu Jingren, who was minister to Russia from 1912 to 1918.[7] In his sparse writings on the experience, Zhang eschewed criticism of Russia, preferring instead to mention his contact with Paul M. Miliukov (1859-1943), the head of the Constitutional Democratic Party (Kadets). As a moderate and a constitutionalist himself, Zhang must have welcomed the opportunity to meet the famous Russian liberal, whose Kadet party had dominated the first Russian parliament (Duma) in 1905. Moreover, the Russian party's political platform must have reminded Zhang of his own pre-1911 Revolution beliefs, for the Kadets favored a reformed monarchy rather than revolution.[8] Zhang also witnessed celebrations of the three hundredth anniversary of Romanov rule. Two decades later, he still recalled "the clamor of the festive occasion in the city." His political comments, however, were restricted to a brief discussion of the tensions between Russia and the Austro-Hungarian Empire on the brink of war.[9]

After an exciting three years in Germany and England, in 1916 he returned home the same way he had come. After two years of brutal warfare, Russia was a much different place from that he had visited in 1913. It had suffered two million casualties in 1915 alone, with three million refugees wandering the land. Hence, when Zhang arrived in March 1916, the Russian military situation was grim, while government had fallen into the hands of Rasputin and the empress.[10]

By this time, Zhang was beginning to fancy himself something of a Russian specialist (as well as a German expert). Whereas during his first visit he had noted signs of war on the horizon, when he passed through in March 1916, Minister Liu, after asking Zhang whether he thought the Germans would advance on Russia, told him the Russians were suffering from a shortage of military equipment, as well as from hunger and cold, and hence could not last much longer.[11] However, Liu's warnings were premature. In the spring of 1916, the Russian army was still capable of mounting an offensive on the Eastern front, while the Central Powers were by no means free from the pervasive war weariness. Moreover, in contrast to Minister Liu's assessment, the munitions and supply situation was greatly improved. Hence, the final crisis in Russia was not to begin until the fall of 1916,[12] several months after Zhang's visit.

Following his return to China in 1916, Zhang participated in the successful struggle against Yuan Shikai's attempt to revive the monarchy. Continuing his political activity after Yuan's death, Zhang opposed federalism in China, argued in favor of Chinese participation in World War I, and cooperated with the government of warlord Duan Qirui.[13] In the meantime, Russia was passing through the storm of the October Revolution. At the time, it was very difficult for Chinese to get accurate news of developments in Russia, but Zhang was fortunate. Following the European armistice in November 1918, he had the opportunity to travel again to Western Europe (thanks to his friendship with Liang Qichao), where reports of the new Russia were readily available.

During his three-year stay in war-ravaged Europe, he made clear his interest in—and even admiration for—the experiment in Russia by producing the first Chinese translation of the 1918 Soviet constitution, which he obtained in Switzerland. In doing so, he later claimed, he coined the Chinese term for soviet–*suweiai*.[14] In the fall of 1920, he also called for negotiation of a treaty establishing diplomatic relations with the Soviet Union.[15] Nor could he repress his admiration for Lenin, the leader of the Russian Revolution. Reflecting his belief in the Ming philosopher Wang Yangming's theory of the unity of knowledge and action, Zhang praised Lenin for possessing both knowledge and the ability to act.[16] Finally, he praised the Soviet emphasis on educating the poor and lamented China's lack of a leader like Anatole V. Lunacharsky (1875-1933), the people's commissar for education.[17]

Most curious, in light of his reformist political views, was his praise, during the years 1920-1922, for "revolution." In fact, he sounded much like his future enemy, Mao Zedong, when he argued that continuous revolution was a characteristic of history. "The reason human society progresses daily without ceasing," Zhang argued, "is due to revolution."[18] Hence, he was quite willing to use revolutionary means to rid China of the warlords.[19]

This endorsement of revolution seems to have been an "armchair-radical" position, though, for when faced with the real thing he was repelled, just as he had recoiled from Sun Yat-sen's advocacy of revolution prior to 1911. Instead, Zhang chose to emulate the peaceful path of German social democracy during these years in Europe and rejected the violent revolutions supported by the communist parties of Soviet Russia, Germany, and other European states. In this position, he had plenty of company. The statesmen of Western Europe, he wrote in late 1919, viewed Lenin and Leon Trotsky as "a snake and a scorpion," and "the capitalists particularly hated them."[20]

Although as a socialist Zhang was not fond of capitalists, he came to share the statesmens' view of Communists. In part, this was due to his growing fear of social revolution, which seemed to him to lurk everywhere in postwar Europe. In late 1920, he expressed his fear that it would eventually engulf China as well. As we have seen (chapter 2), he advocated the adoption of German-style socialism as a means of avoiding such class warfare.[21]

He first made his general opposition to Russian communism clear in 1920, during the course of a debate with his old friend and fellow member of the Research Clique, Zhang Dongsun (chapter 2). This opposition to Leninist-style revolution was intensified by his witnessing the abortive communist uprising in Jena (where he was studying) in March 1921. Moreover, following his return to China in 1922, he clashed in print with the CCP and its allies, the GMD and Russia (chapter 3).

Views of Soviet Russia at the Beginning of the Nanjing Decade

Until late 1927, Zhang's writings on communism were fragmentary and scattered. In December of that year, however, he published a book-length study of Russian communism, *SuE pinglun*. The GMD had crushed the CCP in Shanghai in April of that year, but, as this work showed, Zhang remained obsessed with communism.

In analyzing that ism for his countrymen, he focused on the experiences of the Soviet Union during the decade since the October Revolution, rather than the Communist movement in his own country. This was natural, for at that time Russia was the only communist state in the world. Moreover, materials on the CCP—at that time, an underground party hiding from the White Terror—were hard to come by, and even if they had been available, Zhang did not consider the CCP in the same class as the Communist Party of the Soviet Union (hereafter, CPSU). In addition, it was not safe to publish on the "Reds" then; hence, just as in the case of his translation of Harold Laski's *A Grammar of Politics*, he had to resort to a pseudonym to avoid the GMD censors. This time he hid behind the name "Master of the World Chamber" (*Shijie shi zhuren*), an anonym that probably referred to his strong interest in foreign affairs. Although *SuE pinglun* was published in December 1927, he later asserted that it was drafted during 1926. It is possible, then, that it was based on the anti-Marxist lectures at the Institute of Political Science that his students later remembered so well.

Is Soviet Russia China's Friend?

Zhang's book may have been a delayed response to a debate that erupted in Beijing academic circles in October 1925 and continued for two or three months. Focused on the question of whether Russia was China's "friend," it attracted the participation of such luminaries as Liang Qichao, Zhang's mentor since youth; Ding Wenjiang, his arch opponent in the "Science and Metaphysics Debate"; Hu Shiqing, who later joined Zhang in founding the NSP; and Li Huang, a leader of the CYP who became one of Zhang's closest friends in adversity during the critical period, 1927-1928. Considering his close relationships with these men and his interest in communism and Russian affairs, the debate could hardly have escaped his notice. Even though he was then residing in Shanghai, the articles generated by the debate were published in at least three major newspapers, including *Chenbao*, the organ of the Research Clique of which Zhang was a member.[22] Given the participants, the subjects, and Zhang's lifelong inability to avoid a good "pen war" (*bizhan*), it seems reasonable to conclude that this debate may have have played some role in stimulating the drafting of *SuE pinglun*.

The book also may have been a response to the rosy views of the Soviet "experiment" that seemed to prevail among some of his fellow intellectuals, views that could be glimpsed, for example, in the writings of Hu Shi and Ding Wenjiang, two of the leading liberal intellectuals of the period (Hu had also clashed with Zhang in the debate over science and metaphysics). Writing from Moscow to a friend in the summer of 1926, Hu glowed with admiration for the Russians, even though he was careful to add that "we who love freedom" could not "completely" approve of their ideals. They were "conducting a political experiment of unprecedented magnitude," he enthused. "They have ideals, plans, and an absolute faith, and these alone are enough to make us die of shame. . . . How are our drunk and dreaming people worthy to criticize the Soviet Union?" In lectures delivered in Chicago in 1933, he reiterated his praise of the "great Soviet experiment." His admiration lasted until after World War II, although this did not mean that he approved of authoritarianism for China. He recognized, to be sure, that such a system would leave no place for independent thinkers like himself.[23]

Ding traveled in the Soviet Union during September and October 1933 (just before the publication of Zhang's second book on Soviet Russia). Although he expressed reservations about the Soviet experiment, he was sufficiently attracted to ask himself why he was not a communist. As in Zhang's case, though, he drew a sharp line between communism in power in Russia, with its national strength and technical progress, and communism in the rural areas of China, led by leaders he viewed as uneducated. Ding also resembled Zhang—who supported the economic programs of the Soviets while opposing their political measures—when he declared that he sympathized with a portion of communism but opposed the Communist-style revolution.[24]

In Zhang's foreword to *SuE pinglun*, he made it clear he wanted to expose the truth about Russian communism. Anyone who had lived in Europe since 1918, he insisted, realized that "the Soviet Russian system was absolutely not worth imitating." Yet unexpectedly, he admitted, the communist movement had been able to gain influence in China. For Zhang, the source of that influence was China's northern neighbor. "What I dislike about Russia is its communism," he added, "[and] . . . its use of communist theory to delude the world."[25]

Moreover, Lenin was a hypocrite, he insisted (putting himself at odds with many Peking University students), for while the Russians were restoring capitalism in the form of the New Economic Policy (NEP), Lenin's "supreme headquarters for inciting world revolution, the Third International, day and night still called on [other] peoples to overthrow capitalism and stamp out the bourgeosie." Alas, he concluded, "Are these not words that deceive oneself as well as others?" (p. 75). Russia, he continued, relied on its capitalistic NEP to raise secret funds to purchase and ship arms to assist other countries' revolutions. Russia told people, he complained, "This is socialist revolution, this is overthrowing capitalism." Those who believed it, he asserted, had not thoroughly investigated Russian affairs (p. 88).

In addition, like the May Fourth activists a few years earlier, both Zhang and his mentor, Liang Qichao, were worried about China's youth and with good reason. In the mid-1920s, students at the best school in the land, Peking University, were enthusiastic about communism. They noisily welcomed Leo Karakhan, the Soviet diplomat who negotiated the 1924 treaty with the Peking warlord government in which the Soviet Union became the first power to relinquish extraterritoriality; when he visited campus to speak, they shouted "Ten thousand years of life for the Soviets!" and "Long live the people's revolution!" Moreover, a poll taken on campus during the winter of 1923-24 also indicated strong pro-Soviet and leftist sympathies, with Russia winning four times as many votes as the runner-up (the United States) in response to the question, "Which country is China's true friend?" In the same poll, Lenin was voted the "greatest man in the world."[26]

In some case, students were already leftists when they arrived at Peking University. As one young student put it, even though he had not yet joined the CCP, by the time he left for Peking he "had already purged myself of the last vestiges of Hu Shih's and Liang Ch'i-ch'ao's values, and . . . gone over completely to the left-wing positions of Ch'en Tu-hsiu." Pro-leftist sympathies, however, did not mean that many students joined the CCP. According to a member of the underground CCP at Peking University, only twenty to thirty of almost two thousand students belonged to the Party during the period 1925-1926.[27]

By way of contrast, Liang Qichao and Zhang's answer to the question of whether the Soviet Union was China's friend was a resounding no. Hence, they may have been the sort of people a young communist student at Peking University had in mind when he recalled that politicians in the pay of the northern warlords who controlled the government in Peking "regularly published articles attacking the 'Red menace.'" The pieces were "so absurdly argued," he claimed, "that people simply laughed at them."[28]

In the 1925 debate over Russia, Liang harshly attacked the Soviets. Labeling them imperialists, he called on China's youth to wake up to the truth of communism.[29] As a professor and former head of his own school, Zhang also worried about China's young people. "What I least understand," he lamented, "is why the young people in this country regard Soviet Russia as an immortal in heaven and will be unhappy until it descends." "What they [the Leninists] hang out to show others," he complained, "is paradise and gold. In reality, it is nothing more than hell, dung, and dirt" (p. 43). He had written *SuE pinglun*, he explained, to show that Russia's actual situation was the complete opposite of its overseas propaganda (foreword, p. 1). When the chips were down, he simply could not understand the popularity of Soviet Russia and communism among China's youth. The Reds, he complained, argued that bourgeois democracy was false democracy. Yet, "six or seven people have seized the sovereignty of millions of Russians, but . . . our country's young people sing their praises" (p. 52).

He deeply feared a repeat of the Russian experiment in his own country. Even in an experimenting China, he wondered, how could some people want to surpass Russia? He was determined to do battle with them, he wrote, and passionately declared that he was willing to "change myself into one billion tongues and mouths in order to one by one identify and correct errors for [the sake of] my four-hundred-million compatriots" (p. 52).

Admiration for Soviet Russia

And yet, as the preceding survey of his pre-1927 views as well as his later 1933 work on Soviet Russia reveal, the great anti-Communist's attitude toward Soviet Russia, like those of Hu and Ding, was an ambivalent one. While there was much he rejected, he could not help but admire some aspects of the new state (which may have contributed to the tense relationship in 1927 with his elder, Liang Qichao). Although he rejected the Bolsheviks' revolutionary means, for example, he admired their willingness to act, which was hardly surprising considering that one of the major effects of his 1919-21 European experience had been to turn him into an ardent voluntarist.[30] The Bolsheviks' policies, he declared, "tallied with the condition of the people, [their] means tallied with the times, [and they] stressed implementation and disparaged empty talk. While the whole world was helpless and lacked a policy, [they] alone did what others did not dare to do. [They were] really valiant fighters for the revolution and extraordinary men in the world" (p. 25).

He also admired what he viewed as the Soviets' efficiency. Although he preferred the democracy of Western Europe, when it came to getting things done he seemed to sympathize with those Chinese in the 1930s who favored "efficient dictatorship" over democracy (chapter 8). The CPSU's administrative effectiveness, centralization of power, and swiftness of implementation, he admitted, were superior to the "numerous discussions and few achievements" of the multiparty governments in Britain, the United States, France, and Germany (p. 127). Perhaps with the fragmentation of China— divided among Nationalists, Communists, and warlords—in mind, he also admired the CPSU's unity. The Red Army defeated the Whites, he concluded, because it had a united will and organization (p. 38).

In addition, he thought the Russians' "willingness to sacrifice for the world's people" admirable. He hastened to add, however, that "the price they have paid has been too great." Revealing the common tendency at that time to think of the Soviet regime as an "experiment" (Hu Shi referred to the "Soviet experiment"), he hoped that his fellow Chinese would not "view important national affairs as experimental objects for Russia's political laboratory." Ever the professor and Confucianist, he placed his faith in education, noting that more people studied foreign affairs every day, and thus each day there was less uncritical imitation of others (foreword, p. 2).

It also was clear, as it had been in Europe during 1919-21, that Zhang admired Lenin. When the latter was alive, Zhang wrote in 1927, his "intelligence, ability, and sagacity were sufficient to control the Communist Party. Hence, the flaws of dictatorship were not yet revealed to the outside [world]" (p. 128). He also admired Trotsky, whom he described as possessing a creative spirit and being good at formulating and implementing plans (p. 41). Trotsky, he exclaimed, was "Soviet Russia's Napoleon, who awed the entire world" (p. 107).[31]

Although he did not like Russia's "open talk about world revolution," he could not help but be impressed by its success in pacification, in view of the ongoing struggles in China among warlords, Communists, and Nationalists in 1927. Chinese should study this Soviet success, he insisted. On the other hand, Zhang, whose brother was then assistant general manager of the Bank of China,[32] did not recommend copying Russia's financial administration and currency system. It had a reputation for chaos, he pointed out, and thus in the financial realm—as in the NEP—the Russians had adopted the practices of capitalist nations. The budget, he added, was "purely a West European-type budget" (pp. 77-83). In discussing expenses of government, he thought the Russian leadership had awakened to the mistakes of the communist experiment, for it charged people for what it had provided free in the past (with the exception of medicine and education). Hence, its financial administration was becoming more stable. The regime had finally recognized, he asserted, that the principle of "from each according to his abilities and to each according to his needs" could not be applied. As a result, the Russian system had failed to escape the profit-seeking economy of the present world. Thus, he concluded, "one may know without asking whether Russia is communist or capitalist" (pp. 85-88).

Of all the things he admired about Soviet Russia, he was most intrigued by its NEP, although the Soviets had not embraced that policy out of conviction. Instead, it was a response to an increasing number of peasant uprisings. In the absence of an international socialist revolution, the regime was forced to compromise with the peasantry, or, as one Bolshevik put it, to conclude a "peasant Brest," a temporary armistice with the peasants similar to the truce with the Germans formalized by the Treaty of Brest-Litovsk in March 1918. At the Tenth Congress of the Party in March 1921, Lenin called for abandonment of the requisitioning of supplies under War Communism, to be replaced by a tax in kind on a percentage of the peasants' production. The obstinacy of the peasantry, in short, forced the Soviets into a "retreat from communism." However, the retreat was tactical and temporary, not a permanent surrender. As it happened, the policy was to outlive Lenin himself and be dismantled only following the rise to power of Stalin, who conquered the countryside by liquidating the kulaks and establishing collective farms.[33]

Zhang was not the first Chinese political figure to be impressed with the NEP. In 1921-1922, Sun Yat-sen, whom Zhang criticized for the alliance with the Communists, was quite taken with the plan. The Chinese people feared the communism of Soviet Russia, Sun told his followers in mid-1922, and did not realize that Russia's NEP had changed that communism to national capitalism. Russia, he added, had abolished its laws prohibiting private ownership more than a year before. In January 1924, Sun's GMD went so far as to assert that the NEP was the same as its Three Principles of the People.[34]

In 1927, Zhang viewed War Communism (1917-21) as a failure, both in industry and agriculture. The expropriation of private property and nationalization of industry, he wrote, had not promoted socialism but strengthened the people's faith in capitalism (pp. 53-55). As a socialist, he refused to admit that nationalization was wrong; the Russians had botched it, he wrote, by rashly, carelessly, and senselessly trying to nationalize all industry overnight, a failure that gave opponents of nationalization in the world an excuse to argue it could never be realized (pp. 53-54). As he had done since 1920, he contrasted Russian failure with German success. The Russians' plans for converting private property into public property failed, he noted, because they were "not careful and thorough beforehand like the Germans."[35] Moreover, the state's use of military force to collect foodstuffs in the countryside, he maintained, was careless and contrary to the human feelings of 85 percent of the population–the peasants. The popular revolts that resulted, wrote Zhang, forced Lenin to adopt the NEP that was the crux (*daguanjian*) of Russian politics (pp. 55-60, 62).

Zhang certainly recognized that the NEP represented a retreat from communism. The Russians, he wrote, had been trapped between a lack of food and warm clothes, on the one hand, and the world's ridicule if they restored industry to private individuals, on the other. Hence, echoing Sun Yat-sen's 1922 comments, Zhang wrote that the Russians strove for a "compromise between communism and private capitalism, and that was national capitalism (*guojia zibenzhuyi*)" (p. 65). Such a compromise could not help but appeal to Zhang, with his Confucian fondness for the "middle way" in economic matters (note his views on the mixed economy in chapter 2).

He went on to explain the nature of that "compromise." Under the NEP, major industries were nationalized in Russia, he explained, while the state and foreign capitalists shared control of other industries, such as textiles, coal, metals, and other mining. He praised the creation of national trusts, in place of the previous administration of industries by the centralized National Economic Council (*Guomin shengji huiyi*). He also admired Lenin's "open-door" policy toward foreign businessmen, which he viewed as a frank admission that foreign capital was necessary for the exploitation of Russia's natural riches (pp. 65-67). As a proponent of democracy, he thought he perceived another advantage to the NEP as well. A number of civil and commercial laws were adopted, leading him to enthuse (naively, to be sure) that "the spirit of the rule of law is being extended with each passing day, while the government's scope for acting at its own discretion is increasingly reduced" (p. 64). Unlike Sun Yat-sen, however, he was not fooled by the NEP, for he recognized that national capitalism was merely a temporary expedient on the road to communism for the Soviets (p. 68).

He realized, too, that the NEP was not without problems. The rich peasant class (kulaks), he reported, had seized power in the village soviets. Prices of industrial goods had risen and supply was insufficient for peasant demand, while the prices of agricultural goods had fallen; as a result, industry and agriculture were out of balance.[36] Finally, he noted, the new industrial enterprises lacked capable managers. Concerning the latter, he added, Trotsky had lamented "the difficulty of getting the right man for the job." That point, he added, was precisely the "mortal wound" in all problems of industrial society (pp. 72-74).

Clearly, for Zhang, as for Sun, the NEP had put Russia on the right track. Its goal was to ensure people sufficient food and clothing and the ability to live and work in peace, he explained, objectives consistent with the common reasons for founding a nation (*liguo*). Increases in production, the solicitation of foreign capital, and the reformulation of methods for paying wages were the acts of capitalists and not "secrets obtained by Lenin alone." Hence, Zhang argued, "this [the NEP] is really capitalism. How can it be called a New Economic Policy?" (p. 74). Lenin himself admitted this, wrote Zhang, when he conceded that capitalism was an essential element in the communist economy and Russians should utilize it (p. 75).

On the whole, however, Zhang was impressed with the NEP and enthused that it had "one hundred advantages and not one disadvantage." It satisfied the peasants, merchants, and workers, he wrote, and hence preserved the communist government. Otherwise, he added, he did not know "whose empire Russia would be today." Referring to the abandonment of War Communism, he conceded that one had to admit the CPSU's courage in correcting its mistakes (pp. 68-69).

And yet, a note of bitterness crept into Zhang's analysis when he pondered the costs. "The bloodshed in Russia lasted for years and the dead lay everywhere," he complained, "but the only lessons they [Communist Party members] obtained were that there is no absolute good and evil in [either] socialism or capitalism, and capitalism must be utilized" (p. 77).

Criticism of Soviet Russia

Soviet Dictatorship. Although Zhang found things to admire in Soviet Russia, he was still the unrepentant anti-Communist when it came to communist politics. In direct contrast to his favorable view of its economic policies in the mid-1920s, he was appalled at the Red Terror and factionalism practiced by the CPSU. The repression had been there all along, of course. Opposition parties of various stripes were suppressed following the revolution, and after 1922 no noncommunist organization was permitted in Russia. As for factionalism, at the Tenth Party Congress in 1921 Lenin had declared the time had come to put an end to all opposition. Hence, by order of the Congress, factionalism was prohibited and all extant factions eliminated. However, with the death of Lenin in late January 1924, factions reappeared with a vengeance. At first, it was Stalin, Zinoviev, and Kamenev against Trotsky, and within a year of Lenin's death they had succeeded in deposing Trotsky as head of the War Commissariat. Then it was NEP supporters Stalin, Bukharin, Rykov, and Tomsky against NEP opponents Zinoviev, Kamenev, and Trotsky. By the time Zhang's book was published in December 1927, Stalin and his "rightist" supporters were completely victorious with the expulsion of Trotsky, Zinoviev, and Kamenev from the party.[37]

Since his first exposure to communism during his 1919-1921 sojourn in Europe, Zhang had been opposed to the violent methods of the Soviets, for whom the end justified the means. The Communists wanted to abolish private property and implement communism to progress to the ideal society, Zhang noted, and declared that because they had such a "sacred goal, there is no harm in using cruel means." Zhang's angry response was that two million Russians had perished from being "cut and maimed," and several millions had starved to death. "How much have the people suffered spiritually and materially," he demanded, "and how much national strength have they lost?" He clearly thought it had been in vain, for under the NEP Russia had reverted to capitalism and a gap between rich and poor (p. 52).

He sounded like the reformer battling the revolutionaries in pre-1911 Japan again. "All modern revolutionists," he complained, "excuse suffering as something the revolutionary era cannot avoid" (p. 119). What about Cromwell in England and 1793 in France (the height of the French Revolution and the year of Louis XVI's execution)? they asked. For Zhang, there was no comparison. The cruelty of the CPSU's methods, he declared, was "one hundred thousand times greater than that of England and France in the past. Literature has been ruined and abandoned, families have been destroyed . . . and the experienced and accomplished people (*laocheng zhi lie*) have been driven to their deaths" (p. 119). In an eerie harbinger of the assault on the "Four Olds" in the Chinese Cultural Revolution to come, he complained that what had been cultivated for thousands of years in Russia had been destroyed in four or five. Yet, those fortunate enough to survive still could not rest easy. In the streets, they dared not speak, and in their minds, they dared not disagree. When a member of the British Labour Party returned from a visit to Russia, he noted, she reported that everyone dwelt in an atmosphere of Red Terror (p. 119).

He also was appalled at the class warfare. In carrying out their terror, he wrote, the Russian Communists particularly detested the bourgeosie; hence, they had wiped out the entire class. There was no need to gather evidence on someone who had been accused, he noted, for his fate was determined by his class (as in China after 1949). After the establishment of the Cheka in 1917,[38] he explained, those who were the least bit suspect were sentenced to death. According to Soviet Russia's own official statistics, he noted, 1.7 million persons were sentenced to death between 1918 and 1920. Citing a table giving the number of deaths in various categories—including 6,575 professors and teachers—he exclaimed that this made "everyone's hair stand on end" (pp. 119-21). It was true, he conceded, that one reason they killed so many was because anticommunists killed party members. However, for every party member killed, he noted, the Communists killed one thousand. In short, he complained, Lenin used murderous and bloody means to preserve his political power. That, he noted with Confucian-like self-righteousness, was "taking the country by unrighteous deeds and killing the innocent." Foreign newspapers, he reported, called this the "new" Red Terror (pp. 122-23).

He realized the Cheka was not the only instrument by which the CPSU enforced its reign of terror. There was always the Red Army to back up the authorities. The Leninists' ideal was a society of class equality, he grumbled, but their method of setting about it emphasized armed force. He recognized the Red Army was a major reason for the success of the October Revolution. Lenin, he wrote, realized he could not found a nation without soldiers (pp. 24, 30). Yet, Zhang opposed the composition and aim of the Red Army. Since an army's job is to protect the entire nation, he argued, the obligation of serving in it should be borne by everyone. The Red Army violated that principle, for it recruited only workers and peasants. Moreover, its goal was to protect Russia's dictatorship. Hence, he questioned whether such a class army for domestic use could last long (pp. 41-42).

But why the terror? he asked. Because the Stalinists feared the overturning of the government, he wrote, and hence wanted to arrest and wipe out all those suspected of opposition. They had placed under strict surveillance anti-government politicians and academic staff, while landlords and others were arrested and punished. And yet, Zhang was not surprised that so many were killed, for, as he complained, "Lenin's followers consider killing people as a method of ruling the nation" (pp. 122-24).

In 1927, he was well informed of the fates of Trotsky and Zinoviev. He was amazed that their "meritorious service" to Soviet Russia was considered harmful to the construction of socialism and that they (like Zhang himself in 1927) were labeled "counterrevolutionary criminals" due to political disputes (p. 124). On the other hand, he admitted Trotsky's group was no kinder to Stalin when it came to name-calling, for it had labeled him a "criminal counterrevolutionary dictator" (p. 131).

Searching for the source of all this mayhem, Zhang asserted that the CPSU had invented the theory of dictatorship. It was merciless, he noted, and eliminated the franchise of nonlaborers and the freedom of ordinary people to assemble and speak. However, he added, dictatorship's use of a single party to rule the nation had an important prerequisite—that the party did not split. Otherwise, there would be disputes over routine matters and no time to attend to "a great plan for the nation." Hence, party discipline was used to seek the party's unity and the dictatorship's longevity, and violations of discipline reaped harsh penalities (p. 127).

For Zhang, then, the party was the culprit. The Marxism that led to the birth of the CPSU was too extreme, he argued, since it had resulted in the rapid and complete overthrow of the former government and social order. Communist Russia's system of government and principles, he complained, "risked great disorder under heaven and showed contempt for the world's rules and regulations." As a result, he declared, the people of the world regarded the Bolsheviks as "great scourges" (pp. 12-13, 28, 32). Moreover, he was unhappy with the Leninists' view that, since the old regime had not been a constitutional nation and did not protect parliamentary politics, the key to communist success was absolute obedience of party members (p. 15). Nor, in fact, could this fervent Chinese patriot have liked the Leninists' opposition to the defense of the fatherland when WWI broke out (p. 18).

Once again he contrasted Russia with the nations of Western Europe. According to a proverb, he wrote, people's hearts were as different as their faces, which made it difficult to unify the people's will. The nations of Western Europe followed popular sentiments and protected the people's human rights. A political organization needed a parliamentary majority to organize a cabinet, and political parties took turns governing the nation. Politicians had the freedom to change their views and leave their orginal party. In Russia, that freedom was missing. Hence, denunciation and expulsion were used to discipline party members. His judgement was harsh: "This does not acknowledge the human dignity of mankind, the will of mankind, and—pushing it to the extreme—it does not consider humanity as humanity" (p. 128).

He also recognized the Soviet regime was an oligarchy. He was amazed that the retention or elimination of one or two persons could influence the entire Communist Party's prosperity or decline, life or death. He also realized that the system of dictatorship did not benefit from other people's criticism; in fact, it "definitely opposed the views of other parties." Although he admired Trotsky, he realized that the latter was aware of the need for democratization only within his own party and did not realize that democratization could not be limited to his party.

"Dictatorship and democracy," Zhang sighed, "are two incompatible names." "In a dictatorship, the entire nation is [governed by] a government monopoly; in a democracy, the entire nation [is governed by] the voice of the people. There is absolutely no such thing as dictatorship for the nation and democracy for the party" (p. 130). Dictatorship, he asserted, was like a "room without openings for ventilation." The denial of air to the individual was like the denial of freedom of word and deed to the citizenry (p. 131).

He was also disturbed at the rampant factionalism and lack of social harmony he perceived in Soviet politics. As a Confucianist, he (like the Japanese) believed in the importance of social harmony. Hence, what disturbed him most about Soviet Russia, perhaps, was the constant conflict. There was no peace in Russia, he wrote, for its government failed to achieve harmony among the various factions, with the results that some people were exiled overseas and the "mutual savagery of the civil war" occurred. There was no mutual trust, for the Russians extolled class struggle, and hence people of the same country "will not live under the same sky." There was no freedom and equality, for the bourgeosie could not participate in government and dissenting parties were denied the rights of assembly and speech. Finally, the world knew the Russians used bribery or coercion to impose on small and weak nations. His conclusion was harsh: "Which of these matters is not most savage and extremely cruel and without parallel in history? How can they shamelessly brag and bestow kindly and beautiful names [on these things]" (p. 46)?

The problem with autocratic government, he wrote, was that whether it was operated by an emperor or a class, it was dominated by one person. If this one person existed, there was internal unity and mutual assistance; if this person was not present, there was internal division and numerous fluctuations. "How strange it is," he concluded, "that the Russian government that takes the proletariat and the Communist Party as its props also cannot escape this general rule" (p. 99).

What he particularly had in mind was the power struggle that broke out while Lenin was on his deathbed. In December 1922, Lenin had suffered yet another stroke, and hence thought it time to prepare a will dealing with party and governmental affairs. He worried about the possibility of a clash between Stalin and Trotsky, both of whom he criticized. Although he thought Trotsky the more capable of the two, he emphasized that each had strengths and weaknesses. In early January 1923, however, he added a postscript to his will in which he called for the removal of Stalin from the office of general secretary. He went on to attack Stalin publicly and in the end broke personal relations with him. However, before he could carry through with this drive, he suffered a third stroke on 9 March, from which he never recovered. Although, following his death in January 1924, the will was read aloud in the Central Committee, Zinoviev spoke up for Stalin, and hence the will was not published and Stalin was saved.[39]

Since Zhang had not been to Russia since the revolution took place (his last visit was in 1916), for his analysis of the struggle over Lenin's will he relied on Max Eastman's book, *After Lenin's Death*, which he called a "unique work" and "an unprecedented book on Russian affairs."[40] It seems to have merely confirmed his beliefs. "My profound feeling after reading it," he asserted, "is that the system of dictatorship is a failure" (p. 100). Since the Communist Party did not recognize the word *people*, he continued, the outcome was simply decided by the likes and dislikes of Lenin's retinue. The suppression of Lenin's report criticizing Stalin, he argued, was very similar to the imperial edicts of powerful villains on the throne in China. Freedom of speech, which was normal under parliamentary government, was absent. The Soviet regime decided to print a copy of the report to show to Lenin on his deathbed but did not allow the public to see it. Where were those entrusted with responsibility under parliamentary politics? Zhang asked. Stalin and the others, he noted, also banned Lenin's letter naming Trotsky as his replacement. (Here Zhang was mistaken, for there was no such letter.)

Zhang was disgusted by this internal strife and contrasted what he called manipulative tricks and violence by two or three persons with the alternation of cabinets and election of presidents in democracies. Under Stalin and his cohorts, he explained, the lack of civil rights and banning of opposition parties were just like similar actions in Lenin's time. However, dictatorship had given way to a struggle between Stalinists and Trotskyites to "push each other aside." Was this personal maneuvering among political groups superior to open competition under democracy, he asked. Was it an orderly system that could be imitated? Those who engaged in long-range planning for China, he urged, should deeply consider this (pp. 100-3).

He believed that the alternation of political power was a major event in a nation. Monarchies selected heirs, while democracies resorted to presidential elections and alternation of cabinets. The CPSU, he complained, relied on a small number of people to direct all major affairs. The problem was that this same small number of people also were the interested parties in succession disputes. Hence, internal strife and "squeezing each other out" were the only means of settling the succession, an approach that Zhang considered tragic (pp. 103-4).

He traced this problem to the Soviet emphasis on discipline, the first duty listed in the CPSU constitution. The party sought obedience, he noted, and critical discussion was not allowed. One had to follow all rules and regulations; doing things on one's own initiative and accord was unheard of. The name was rule by the party, but where, he asked, was party rule in the competition between people such as Stalin and Trotsky (pp. 105-6)?

Here Zhang unleashed a diatribe against dictatorship, echoing his position in the debate over democracy and dictatorship that was to break out a few years later (see chapter 8). He first erroneously claimed that Lenin named his own successor[41] and then went on to criticize him for it, noting that such a procedure meant there was no genuine expression of the people's will. The Russians allowed two or three powerful people in the party to direct affairs, he continued, and that led to struggles between individuals. Obviously, he asserted, they could not use the good method of alternation of leaders. Those with extraordinary talents and abilities (he probably was thinking of Trotsky) were "the most valuable treasure of a nation." Hence, the nation's political system should tolerate them, Zhang insisted, and not use rules and regulations to restrict them (as Stalin did in the case of Trotsky).

He could have been speaking of the GMD regime then in power in China or the future People's Republic of China when he complained that dictatorships did not hesitate to sacrifice a nation's talent. He realized that the CPSU emphasized party discipline to unify party principles, duties, and responsibilities and seek administrative quickness and efficiency (the latter point had great appeal for Zhang). Yet, the policies of the past several years, such as the NEP, had set off disputes within the party. Hence, despite party discipline, dissent and administrative inefficiency proved unavoidable. In Zhang's view, the CPSU's actions were contrary to human feelings, and in the end the party would be unable to protect itself (pp. 108-9).

In Zhang's eyes, the problem lay with Lenin, who thought the democracy of Western Europe unsuitable for Russia. Therefore, Lenin relied upon "sacred and inviolable" party discipline, which produced centralization of party power and dictatorship in the Central Committee and Politburo. As a result, Zhang explained, the party "restricted ordinary people's civil rights . . . [arranged for] unequal numbers of peasant and urban delegates, and . . . eliminated the freedoms of assembly and speech for opposition parties" (p. 109). In addition, party dictatorship placed a taboo on factions within the party. Trotsky, he pointed out, violated that taboo and hence was charged with factionalism. Such issues as peasant policy and Lenin's real intentions concerning capitalism, Zhang pointed out, all resulted in the formation of factions (pp. 109-12).

Zhang was amazed when Zinoviev and Kamenev switched from enemies to friends of Trotsky and commented how "fickle" politicians were. Zhang thought the two had reasons to oppose Stalin, however, for while the rumors of "Napoleonic catastrophe" that Stalin previously aimed at Trotsky were dead, party discipline had resulted in people's loss of freedom of speech and action and was "something that people suffered from together" (p. 113).

The central problem, in Zhang's view, was the struggle between the Stalinists and the Trotskyites over the issue of capitalism versus communism, triggered by the NEP. Those who wanted to revert to a capitalism in which peasants and workers freely competed were described as traitors and heretics. Zhang was not surprised and wrote that a "lack of tolerance for minority factions is the reason the Communist Party is the Communist Party and what its party discipline depends on" (pp. 114-16). In the past, he noted, the party had been able to rely on Lenin to maintain discipline, thanks to his knowledge, experience, and proper management of affairs. Even though there were factions, Lenin himself did not form one. Sounding like a Confucianist, however, Zhang complained that the present Soviet leadership lacked the right people, while problems were more complex than in the past. "Could one," he wondered, "rely on empty words in the party constitution to restrain human feelings" (p. 116)? Hence, he expressed the hope that the Russian system was not long for this world: "The Russian government's foundation consists of party discipline. Once party discipline wavers, there will be no way to centralize party power, and the passing of dictatorship and fall of the Communist Party government will not be far off" (pp. 116-17).

The Soviet Constitution. Not only did Zhang oppose Soviet politics, he heavily criticized its constitution. By the time he published *SuE pinglun*, Soviet Russia was on its second constitution. The first was adopted in July 1918, and Zhang translated it while in Europe during the years 1919-1921. This document dubbed the new regime the "Russian Socialist Federated Soviet Republic." It stipulated an electoral system in which the urban population far outweighed the rural residents in representation. It provided for a Central Executive Committee (CEC), the CEC's appointment of the Council of People's Commissars, and a hierarchy of local and regional soviets. Ironically, it did not mention the real ruler of the country, the CPSU. Neither the popular will nor government machinery would possess any power; that was reserved to the central organs of the party, especially the Politburo. Democratic centralism, fortified by strict party discipline, would rule the day. Freedoms were granted, but only to the working class.

By 1921, there were six separate Soviet republics. Hence, a need arose for a "union" of these states. As a result, in December 1922 a "Union of Soviet Socialist Republics" was announced and a new draft constitution—"Stalin's constitution"—was approved. As finally ratified in January 1924, it contained no substantative changes from the 1918 constitution. Like the latter, it did not mention that real power lay with the party.[42]

It would have been extremely surprising if a "constitution-monger" like Zhang, who had already translated an earlier constitution, had failed to take up the new Russian constitution in his 1927 study. In fact, he saved his greatest vitriol for this document.

He began by criticizing the name bestowed on Soviet Russia by the 1924 constitution, the "Union of Soviet Socialist Republics." "Those youth who hear about Russia's system and want to imitate it," he complained, "are probably deluded by its beautiful name and have not carried out a thorough investigation." In fact, he argued, the name was empty. Russia did not have real "soviets," he argued, for its use of the word was merely a synonym for factory electoral districts and vastly different from the idea of industrial self-government. It was not "socialist," for Russia had revived capitalism with the launching of the NEP in 1921. After the implementation of the NEP, he insisted, Russia's policy for founding the nation was "different only in degree from that of capitalist nations; there was no difference in character." It was not a real "republic" but a dictatorship of the poor, while the will of the people could not influence politics. Finally, it was not a real "union" (*lianbangguo*), he continued, for the small states were forced by armed might and the dictatorship of the CPSU to join the union, an act of coercion that was incompatible with any real sovereignty of these states (pp. 44-45).

Moreover, he had other grounds for objecting to this document. It denied six classes—entrepreneurs, bondholders, merchants, priests, the old regime's royal family and police, and criminals and the mentally ill—the franchise and right to be elected to office. Second, representation in the various levels of soviets right up to the national soviet was slanted in favor of city dwellers, even though peasants constituted 85 percent of the population. This inequality, Zhang explained, could be seen in the elections to prefectural soviets, in which urban soviets elected one delegate for every two hundred people, while the rural soviets elected one delegate for every two thousand people. Third, the constitution provided no separation of the legislative and executive branches. The executive committees elected by the soviets, Zhang noted, were combinations of executive and legislative. Hence, when the Russian Congress of Soviets was not in session, the CEC took its place. Fourth, the primary characteristic of the constitution was its elimination of the political power of the capitalist class. The latter lost its civil rights, he explained, for the Communist Party "blames all evil in the world on the rich, while it attributes all virtues . . . to the poor." Although Zhang was a socialist, he argued (perhaps under the influence of his banker brother, Chang Kia-ngau?) that capital and capitalists were necessary for production. Yet, he pointed out, the Russian government denied any political power to capitalists, solely to revive hatred for the former rulers. Fifth, Soviet Russia's elections were by voice vote rather than secret ballot. If one voted against the Bolsheviks, he was labeled a member of the Whites or a counterrevolutionary or was threatened with arrest or had his bread coupons canceled. Hence, members of the CPSU passed everything unanimously, while other parties were silent. Finally, according to the constitution, the Congress of Soviets elected a CEC, and the latter selected the people's commissars of the ministries. Although that appeared to be just like a legislature's election of a cabinet, Zhang declared, everyone knew that the six or seven members of the Politburo controlled all power in the country. Without their agreement, "laws did not become laws and people's commissars did not become people's commissars." Hence, to speak of those "elected" to the Congress of Soviets or the CEC, he complained, was "deceptive talk."

In sum, this lifelong supporter of constitutionalism thought the Soviet constitution a farce. It eliminated the capitalist class, dissidents within the proletarian class, and even the right of 500,000 party members to speak and make decisions. "Millions upon millions of people obey the orders of 500,000 people. 500,000 people are totally controlled by a Politburo of six or seven people. Hence . . . the entire constitution is a mere formality and tool for obliterating the people's eyes and ears." Dictatorships, he declared, were incompatible with constitutions:

> A constitution is an expression of the people's will. Dictatorship is the product of a small number of people's arbitrary actions. If there is a constitution, it will not brook a dictatorship; if there is a dictatorship, then even if there is a constitution it will be as if there is none. *This is the basic disease Russia has contracted* [italics mine]. Even if it strives with all its might to use the people's will as an ornament, [the situation] will be impossible. (pp. 46-51)

Comintern (CI) Intervention in China. In late 1927, a Chinese scholar could hardly produce a serious book on Soviet Russia without some attention to the CI, whose four-year intervention in the Chinese revolution had collapsed in July 1927, just a few months before publication of *SuE pinglun*. Hence, Zhang was understandably keenly interested in that organization. "My countrymen," he declared, "want to be fully aware of Moscow's plans for the East" (p. 89). However, instead of focusing on CI political and military advisors in China, such as Borodin and General Blyukher and their spectacular failure by mid-1927, Zhang used an obscure and defunct Soviet organization as the vehicle for his discussion of Third International policy in the East. By June 1927, CI documents seized during Zhang Zuolin's 6 April 1927 raid on the Soviet Embassy in Peking had been published in the Chinese and Western press.[43] Moreover, during the months leading up to publication of Zhang Junmai's book, he resided in the International Settlement in Shanghai. In light of the "red scare" atmosphere prevailing in China and his own precarious political situation, however, he was obviously unable to procure up-to-date materials on the CI adventure in China.

Zhang's discussion of "Moscow's plans for the East" focused on the Union for the Liberation of the East (*Dongfang jiefang hui*), founded in Moscow in October 1918. Its goals, he noted, were to create a united anti-imperialist front in Asia and guide a struggle that would eventually lead, it was hoped, to a federal United States of Asia. It is not clear whether he realized that the Union had already been absorbed in 1919 by the Central Bureau of Communist Organizations of Eastern Peoples, established during preparations for the First CI Congress.[44] According to Zhang, in 1927 the Union's nineteen guiding principles, drafted by one K. Troianovskii, were "still adhered to by the Russian government." He went on to describe them so his country would "understand the plots of Soviet Russia's communist government."[45] These principles, he noted, were used to "scheme in the stead of Easterners" (p. 95). They called for expulsion of foreign economic presence in the East, especially that of foreign capitalism. However, the Soviets, he added, did not include themselves in those categories; instead, Troianovskii described Russia as the "daring vanguard" of socialist nations that did not "selfishly rob" (pp. 93-95).

Troianovskii also claimed the nations of the East were still in the era of early capitalism, and hence "implementation of the conditions of European-style socialism cannot be sought in the East" (p. 91), an argument that undoubtedly did not sit well with Zhang's belief in socialism. Yet, the Russian thought the future hopeful. Because domestic capitalism was weak in the East and the revolution had begun, argued Troianovskii, the East should be able to "avoid the suffering of capitalism" and move in one leap from the early stage of capitalism into socialism (p. 92). Zhang did not agree with this proposition. Referring to the capitalistic NEP, he objected that the Union did not realize that "Russia's communist experiment has already failed" (p. 95). In writing this, one might protest, Zhang was both unfair and ahistorical, for the Russian document was drafted in late 1918, before the replacement of War Communism by the "capitalistic" NEP in 1921.

As an intellectual himself, Zhang must have found equally dismaying the document's call to build nations on the laboring classes—laborers' republics—for, as the Soviet text put it, "it was impossible to expect too much from the classless intellectuals" (pp. 90-91). Moreover, he strenuously objected to the Soviets' proposal to divide Eastern countries into classes, while simultaneously calling for resistance to foreigners. He questioned how a country bogged down in internal strife (i.e., class warfare) could find the strength to cope with foreign aggression. He found this tactic "an enormous contradiction between national self-determination and communism, and something the Russians had failed to investigate" (p. 95).

As a federalist (see chapter 4), though, he found interesting the Union's appeal for an Asian federation, including Russia, and its rejection of the idea of "Asia for the Asians" (pp. 90, 92) (a slogan that would have its heyday later under the Japanese). Yet, he also viewed the proposal with more than a trace of cynicism, as well as a reiteration of his previous attack on the "Union" portion of Russia's new name in the 1924 constitution. The "Union of Soviet Socialist Republics" lacked true "federalism," he insisted, and so would this Asia-wide federation.

Russia's self-interest was obvious, he continued, for it wished to be the master in such a federation, while other nations would be vassals. Its behavior, he wrote, was clear from the treaties it had concluded with the Ukraine and other small nations (p. 96). The criteria always were Russia's interests and thus it exploited the small nations. When the principle of national self-determination was not advantageous to Russia, he complained, it had no scruples about completely eating its words. Armenia and Georgia both had been given independence in 1918, he pointed out, but in 1921 they were carved up or occupied by Russia. Hence, he wrote, "one may realize how sincerely the

Russian government unites with others, and those who sing the praises of communism may suddenly see the light" (pp. 96-97). In addition, he scoffed, the reason Russia wanted to abolish tariffs and make Asia a free-trade zone was that it assumed it was Asia's advanced nation and its industry, commerce, and technology were superior to others; hence, opening other nations would be a "great advantage" to Russia (p. 96).

Finally, Troianovskii's principles called for abolition of the militarism in China he claimed had resulted from the combination of foreign officers and native troops. Because they were dangerous, Troianovskii argued, foreign officers should be expelled from Asia. Sounding very much like Zhang in 1922,[46] Troianovskii called for the replacement of foreign mercenaries with a compulsory national militia (p. 94).

In 1918, the Russian could hardly have known that beginning in 1923-24 Russia would dispatch the first of a thousand military advisers to China to advise "native troops." Nor did Zhang miss this in 1927. The Russians' fifteenth principle, he wrote, spoke of doing away with foreign officers, yet the Russians "still allowed Borodin and others to flagrantly carry out intervention" in China (p. 96). Hence, Troianovskii's words, he concluded in disgust, were "all diplomatic tactics and not sincerely offered as principles (*zhuyi*)" (p. 96). Yet, here again he was being ahistorical, for five years elapsed between the promulgation of Troianovskii's principles and the dispatch of Borodin and other Russian advisors to China.

In conclusion, there was only one exception to his opposition to the CI's role in China, and that was his approval of its help in China's struggle against other foreign imperialists. No matter how grudgingly, in 1927 he conceded that "Soviet Russia helped our country's independence movement" (p. 28).

His Favorite Models

In the course of taking a close look at Soviet politics in 1927, he ended up affirming his previous political leanings. He was continually drawn to the contrasts between West European democracy and the means by which the CPSU ruled. In the course of lambasting the Soviet political system, Zhang often reminded readers of his own preference for democracy and socialism.

After criticizing lack of majority rule in Russia, for example, he conceded that critics might counter that neither England's political party governments nor America's presidential candidates represented majority rule and ask why his opposition to the Russian system was so profound. He rejected the criticism of Anglo-American government out of hand. Unlike the Russian rulers, he argued, the English and American governments did not deprive people of the franchise, use coercion in elections, and ban the existence of other parties. If the English or American governments made mistakes, the legislative assembly could invoke the responsibility article and overthrow the government. If one party was toppled, another party could replace it. Moreover, the English and Americans had two or three parties from which to choose. None of this was true in Russia.

In a powerful defense of Western democracy, Zhang declared, "England and America possess the will of the people, while Russia lacks the will of the people. Freedom is the main tenet (*zhigui*) of [Anglo-American] politics. Everything that can develop the people's will and promote the people's rights is good politics. Those things contrary to this are bad politics" (pp. 51-52). In short, democracy was strong in the modern world because it was based on the will of the people. Parliaments were representative, political parties alternated in power, and one faction followed another's path (p. 100).

Continuing, he contrasted Russia with his favorite European models. Germany's Social Democratic Party and England's Fabian Society, he asserted, relied on peaceful methods, such as elections, speeches, and public ownership of property (p. 12). What he really thought worthy of imitation, he wrote, were long-lived institutions that benefited the nation, made the people happy, and created a peaceful society. As always, for him that meant constitutions, parliaments, compulsory education, and universal military service (p. 43). In contrast to the emptiness of the "Union of Soviet Socialist Republics," he had faith that in England and the United States, cabinets, parliaments, presidents, and senates were real (p. 44). Complaining about the slaughters carried out by the CPSU, he reminded his readers that Karl Kautsky of the German Socialist Party opposed such violence.[47] If the ideas of the socialist revolution could be widely dessiminated, Kautsky had argued, there would be no need for "murderous and bloody cruelty." Why then, asked Zhang, was murder inevitable in the Soviet Union (p. 124)?

He invariably returned to the contrast between dictatorship and democracy (hence, making clear what his position would be in the future debate over democracy versus dictatorship in Chinese intellectual circles). In the former, he argued, there was no criticism by the people's will, political supervision was missing, and the usual practice of alternation of party leaders was unheard of. They simply fought to the bitter end. Driving home his point, he wrote, "Why do we not hear of . . . counterrevolutionary factions, large-scale arrests of political offenders, prisoners being executed without trial, and the establishment of a 'Cheka' in the nations of Western Europe?" Because, he declared, "Western Europe is democratic and Russia is a dictatorship." Western Europe based its government on the majority, while Russia based its on the minority. The establishment of Soviet Russia was the idea of several tens of thousands of CPSU members, and they did not "consult the will of the people and did not solicit the sympathy of other political parties. They presumptuously believed in the rightness of their proposals and were bent on having their own way. They expelled and put to death those who opposed them." Hence, they had always been in danger of being overthrown, Zhang wrote, making it necessary for the police and army to keep an eye on the people. In short, up to the present (1927), they had "relied solely on weapons to maintain themselves. . . . Alas, can this be a reasonable [and] lasting foundation" (pp. 125-26)?

Despite his approval of the NEP, in 1927 he still believed his models superior to Soviet Russia in the economic sphere—a faith that would be shaken in the late 1920s and early 1930s when the World Depression struck Germany and England, while the Soviets seemed to flourish under the First Five-Year Plan. The "soviets" in Russia lacked the concept of industrial self-government, he argued; it was Germany's Workers' Council Law that provided for laborers' participation in factory affairs (p. 44).

Moreover, he admired Germany's plans for nationalizing industry, even though they were never carried out. Germany had provided for nationalization in the Weimar Constitution, he explained, but also had made clear that after nationalization the enterprises should be profitable, maintain the spirit of individual initiative, avoid bureaucratism, and not allow self-seeking merchants to control the trade in nationalized goods. The German government established a Socialization Commission (*Shehui suoyou weiyuanhui*), he added, to investigate matters. If these points had been resolved, he lamented, the foundations of the nationalized enterprises would have been unshakeable, and Germany's economic organization could have transcended capitalism.

Sounding like a German nationalist, he blamed Germany's failure on those very powers whose democracy he so admired. Unfortunately, he noted, after 1919 the German government was spiritually exhausted by the Allied occupation and demands for reparations and had no energy to spare for the reform of domestic affairs. Hence, the nationalization bill was shelved (pp. 53-54), and Zhang was able to cling to his belief in nationalization.

Conclusion

It is clear from this discussion of Zhang's 1927 views that while he approved of the moderate economic policies of Soviet Russia, he continued to abhor its dictatorship. Hence, he admired the NEP, while despising the "new Red

Terror" and the factionalism manifested in the power struggles between Stalin and his opponents played out in the CPSU during the 1920s. In this viewpoint, he was to prove consistent, for in his 1933 work on Soviet Russia he once again praised its economic policies (the Five-Year Plan, including its collective farms) while excoriating its dictatorship.

Writing several years later, he claimed that his 1927 book had been influential, for those who had "done evil then regretted their errors and changed their course."[48] In 1927, though, he seemed uncertain. Would the Soviets follow in the footsteps of Western Europe, he wondered, and implement two-party government? Would Stalin step down and Trotsky take his place? One thing was clear to him, though, and that was the split in the CPSU. In the end, his entire book made clear which of the two alternatives—democracy or dictatorship—he preferred and which he was warning his countrymen against. "Can those who imitate foreign countries not be aware of what to guard against?" he asked plaintively (p. 132).

Six years later, he was to once again take up the question of the nature and inner workings of the Soviet Union. Ironically, that book was published in the same year the Weimar Republic, which had exerted such a tremendous influence on his political and economic thought, was replaced by Hitler's regime. If the shadow of the recent Bolshevik Revolution had hung over his earlier attempt to make sense of the Soviet experiment, in 1933 the specter of the World Depression that began in 1929 would lend urgency to his observations.

Notes

1. On Qu's and Chen's visits, see Jonathan D. Spence, *The Gate of Heavenly Peace: The Chinese and Their Revolution, 1895-1980* (New York: Viking, 1981), 137-46. In 1924, the GMD organ in Shanghai, *Guomin ribao*, published a laudatory account of Soviet life by Li Dazhao, then visiting the Soviet Union. Maurice Meisner, *Li Dazhao and the Origins of Chinese Marxism* (New York: Atheneum, 1970), 61-62, 235.

2. For a thorough treatment of Sun's views on the new Russia, see C. Martin Wilbur, *Sun Yat-sen: Frustrated Patriot* (New York: Columbia University Press, 1976). During Hu's 1925-26 visit to Moscow, he attended the Third CI Congress and had an interview with Stalin. BDRC, 2: 164. For Luo Jialun's favorable view of the Bolshevik Revolution, see Vera Schwarcz, *The Chinese Enlightenment: Intellectuals and the Legacy of the May Fourth Movement of 1919* (Berkeley: University of California Press, 1986), 119.

3. YX, 11; GS 4, no. 4, 33.

4. Zhang, "Waiguo bannian jishi," 11. In the 31 August convention, the two powers recognized Chinese sovereignty in Tibet and promised not to intervene in Tibet's affairs. MacKerras and Chan, *Modern China*, 222.

5. YX, 13-14.

6. Zhang Junmai, "Zhanshi Ouzhou waijiao zhi xin mishi" (A New Secret History of Europe's Wartime Diplomacy), *Da Zhonghua* 1, no. 7 (1915): 8.

7. Liu Jingren (Shixi), like Zhang, was a native of Baoshan and graduate of the Guang fangyan guan in Shanghai. He went on to a successful career in the diplomatic world. *Who's Who in China*, 5th ed., 165.

8. Miliukov went on to serve in the Provisional Government established following the February 1917 Revolution (March-May) as foreign minister and "most influential man in the cabinet." Donald W. Treadgold, *Twentieth Century Russia*, 8th ed. (Boulder, CO: Westview, 1995), 39, 50, 55, 95-98; Jesse Clarkson, *A History of Russia* (New York: Random House, 1962), 390.

9. This discussion of Zhang's visit to St. Petersburg is based on Zhang, "Wo cong shehui kexue," 9-10; STLZX, preface no. 1, p. 1. The tensions between the Russian and Austro-Hungarian empires, Zhang explained later, stemmed from the latter's annexation of Bosnia-Herzegovina, which Russia considered the Slavic race's territory. Hence, Zhang recalled, "at that time there were many reports that the possibility of war between the two nations was hanging by a thread." Ibid.

10. Treadgold, *Twentieth Century Russia*, 87-89.

11. STLZX, preface no. 1, 1. Zhang's reply to Liu's question was that the German Army was divided between the Western and Eastern fronts and used the railway to transfer troops back and forth between the two. If the main German force invaded Russia, it would be completely cut off and no longer available for the Western front. Ibid.

12. Treadgold, *Twentieth Century Russia*, 88.

13. Jeans, "Syncretism in Defense of Confucianism," chap. 5.

14. Zhang, *Zhonghua minguo minzhu xianfa*, introduction, p. 1; Chang, *Third Force*, 24; Zhang, "Yijiuyijiu," 20; YX, 16; Zhang, "Nianyu nianlai ," 4. However, in his book, *SuE pinglun* (Shanghai: Xinyue shudian, 1927), 19 (hereafter, SEPL), he used the term *suweiai* without claiming to have invented it.

15. Zhang, "Du *Liu xingqi zhi Eguo*," 62-63. He recognized this was something China's warlord government would oppose. Hence, in an appeal to direct democracy, he called on the people of China to demand the government negotiate peace and a treaty with Russia. Ibid.

16. XDG, 390. Stalin and Trotsky also were dedicated to the "unity of theory and practice." Treadgold, *Twentieth Century Russia*, 158.

17. Zhang, "Du *Liu xingqi zhi Eguo*," no. 2, 57. In late October 1917, Lunacharsky was selected as education commissar in the first Council of People's Commissars. The term *minister* was rejected by the Bolsheviks as echoing bourgeois government terminology. Treadgold, *Twentieth Century Russia*, 115-16

18. XDG, 377-80, 382, 388-89.

19. Zhang, "Zhongguo qiantu," 1-6, 8-9.

20. Zhang Junmai, "Ji Faguo zongxuanju ji zongtong xuanju" (Notes on the General and Presidential Elections in France), *Jiefang yu gaizao* 2, no. 9 (1920): 57.

21. Although Zhang did not approve of Sun Yat-sen's alliance with the CCP and the Comintern, Sun, like Zhang, was opposed to social revolution, class struggle, and violence. Wilbur, *Sun Yat-sen*, 8, 216.

22. For a summary of the debate, see Wu Xiangxiang, *Jindai shishi luncong* (Collected Essays on Events in Modern History), 3 vols. (Taipei: Wenxing shudian, 1964), 2: 303-12. On *Chenbao* as a Research Clique newspaper, see Zhang Pengyuan, *Liang Qichao yu minguo zhengzhi*, 233-34.

23. Grieder, *Hu Shih*, 194, 232, 280.

24. Furth, *Ting Wen-chiang*, 206, 208-14.

25. SEPL, foreword, 1; 77. Hereafter, page citations to this work will be noted in the text in parentheses.

26. Stephen N. Hay, *Asian Ideas of East and West: Tagore and His Critics in Japan, China, and India* (Cambridge: Harvard University Press, 1970), 237-38. Could the 1925 debate over whether Russia was China's "friend" have stemmed from the Peking University poll?

27. Wang Fan-hsi, *Memoirs of a Chinese Revolutionary* (New York: Columbia University Press, 1991), 11, 18. For his life as a secret CCP member at Peking University during the years 1925-26, see ibid., 13-21.

28. Ibid., 14.

29. Wu Xiangxiang, *Jindai shishi luncong*, 2: 307-09.

30. Jeans, "Syncretism in Defense of Confucianism," chap. 7 (esp. 224-47).

31. Although Zhang used "Napoleon" to praise Trotsky, Stalin applied it to his rival in a pejorative sense. Infra, p. 136.

32. BDRC, 1: 27.

33. Treadgold, *Twentieth Century Russia*, 141-44.

34. C. Martin Wilbur and Julie Lien-ying How, *Missionaries of Revolution: Soviet Advisors and Nationalist China, 1920-1927* (Cambridge: Harvard University Press, 1989), 43, 95. When Sun met with Comintern agent J. F. M. Sneevliet ("Maring") in December 1921, he questioned him about the NEP. Afterward, Sun told one of his followers of his great satisfaction in learning about the plan, which he considered similar to his Plan for the Industrial Development of China. Wilbur, *Sun Yat-sen*, 119-20, 124.

35. For a list of his reasons for the failure of nationalization in Russia, see STLZX, 59-60.

36. This disparity between rising urban and falling rural prices was labeled the "scissors crisis" by Trotsky. Treadgold, *Twentieth Century Russia*, 146.

37. Ibid., 155-65.

38. The Extraordinary Commission for Struggle with Counterrevolution and Sabotage—or "Cheka," after the initial letters of the first two words in the Russian title—was established in December 1917 under Felix Dzerzhinsky and immediately launched a Red Terror. Ibid., 120.

39. Ibid., 150-51, 157.

40. After publication, the Russian government banned Eastman from returning to Russia. SEPL, foreword, 1.

41. According to a Russian specialist, Lenin's will "did not point to any single individual as unqualifiedly worthy of his mantle." During his last months, however, he did express opposition to one potential successor, and that was Stalin. Treadgold, *Twentieth Century Russia*, 150-51.

42. Ibid., 151-55.

43. The first document was published on 19 April, with more released to the Chinese and Western press by the end of June. That same year, N. Mitarevsky published a collection of these materials under the title, *World-Wide Soviet Plots, as Disclosed by Hitherto Unpublished Documents Seized at the USSR Embassy in Peking* (Tientsin: Tientsin Press, n.d. [1927].

44. Branko Lazitch and Milorad M. Drachkovitch, *Lenin and the Comintern*, 2 vols. (Stanford: Hoover Institution Press, 1972), 1: 372, 375-76.

45. For a complete list of the nineteen points, see SEPL, 89-95.

46. For Zhang's opposition to a standing army and advocacy of a compulsory national militia, see his *Guo xian yi*, 67-72.

47. On Zhang's meeting with Kautsky, see supra, chap. 2.

48. STLZX, preface no. 1, 2.

7

Soviet Russia, the Comintern, and the Chinese Communists:
Views of a Third-Force Politician during the Early 1930s

After considerable adventure, including being kidnapped for ransom in Shanghai and forced into exile in Germany, in the early 1930s Zhang returned to his earlier fascination with Soviet Russia. Whereas *SuE pinglun* (SEPL) was an academic study, written in China with the help of English- and German-language research materials, his 1933 work, *Shitailin zhixia zhi SuE* (Soviet Russia under the Rule of Stalin; STLZX), included his observations while passing through Moscow on the way home from Europe in September 1931. Hence, it possesses an immediacy, demonstrated in tales of his experiences in Russia, not present in the 1927 book. Moreover, it is a broader study than SEPL; in addition to dealing with economics, politics, and the Comintern (CI), as he had in SEPL, he devoted considerable attention to Soviet education and ideology, in particular the state of philosophy under the Communists. Finally, while the attention of most Chinese was centered on the Japanese penetration of Northeast and North China, he sounded the tocsin to alert his country to the Soviet threat in Northwest China (Xinjiang).

While teaching in Germany in the summer of 1931, he accepted an appointment in the philosophy department at Yenching University in Peking, where his old friend, Zhang Dongsun, was chairman. As in 1913 and 1916, he returned home via Russia (in 1918 and 1921, he went to and from Europe by sea).[1] He had clearly been looking forward to this visit. When he arrived at the Soviet border, he recalled, he was admitted to the country he had been thinking about for a decade. Hence, he decided to stop in Moscow for a few days on his way back to China.[2]

His observations during his visit—his third in nineteen years—became the basis for several articles describing Russia since the launching of the First Five-Year Plan (FFYP) in 1928, which began appearing in the NSP organ,

Zaisheng, in March 1932, six months after his return. His visit also resulted in publication of STLZX, which took up where SEPL left off.[3] Published more than two years after his return to China, STLZX may have found an audience among Chinese university students, who in the early 1930s demonstrated strong interest in the FFYP (see below). The fact that it was published by *Zaisheng*, however, inevitably meant limited circulation in an era when opposition-party journals were not welcomed by the GMD regime.

Since he had been away from the academic world in China for two years, in his new book he did not emphasize the infatuation with communism of China's youth as his motive for publishing, as he had in SEPL several years earlier. Moreover, things had changed. While he had been away, the GMD's White Terror, combined with the Jiangxi Soviet's isolation, had threatened to cut off communist contact with the students, and as a result the CCP had lost many members. Thanks to its anti-Japanese propaganda and attacks on GMD misgovernment, though, communist *ideas* attracted the sympathy of the young, although membership in the CCP was too dangerous. That empathy usually took the form of praise of the USSR. "While the Chinese soviets were isolated from the world by government blockades, and news from the West revealed devastating economic depression," writes one China scholar, "reports from the Soviet Union indicated that Stalin's Five-Year Plans were transforming a backward nation into a modern industrial power."[4]

The Soviet ambassador described that progress in a June 1934 speech at Yenching University (while Zhang was in Canton), with student interest reflected in more than one hundred questions. Meanwhile, the West was impotent in the face of the Japanese advance in China, with the result that, as in the aftermath of World War I, Chinese looked to the Soviets for support. As a result, Chinese students were pleased when Sino-Soviet diplomatic relations were resumed on 12 December 1932.[5] In addition, Soviet success at repelling foreign encroachments provided a sharp contrast to Chinese inability to get rid of the imperialists. While Zhang was in Moscow in 1931, his countryman Mo Dehui told him that several days before he had encountered the English and Japanese ambassadors at a tea party. Since China sought complete sovereignty, they reminded Mo, if it did not revoke consular jurisdiction (extraterritoriality), then how could it "blame Chinese youth for admiring Russia"? (p. 84).

Admiration for Soviet Russia

It is a bit startling, for one used to thinking of Zhang as the consummate anti-Communist, to learn in SEPL and STLZX that he also admired certain aspects of the Soviet system. In the former book, as we have seen, he expressed his appreciation for the NEP. In the latter, he praised the FFYP, the educational system, and the forces he thought responsible for Soviet successes: Lenin and Stalin, the Russian people, and the powerful organization of the CPSU.

First Five-Year Plan

When he arrived in Moscow, Russia was on the move again after seven years (1921-28) of relative tranquility under the NEP. Spearheaded by the FFYP (1928-32) in industry and agriculture, it was in the midst of what has been called the "Second Revolution." This dramatic effort attracted intense interest from foreign observers and produced many admirers of the Soviet "experiment." By the time it was launched, Stalin and his followers had "neutralized" both the Right Opposition, led by Nicholas Bukharin, and the former Left Opposition of Leon Trotsky and Gregory Zinoviev, while the secret police ensured that the "masses" carried out the new orders. The slogan was Stalin's "socialism in one country," which he had used earlier in his struggle with Trotsky.

The NEP era of moderate treatment of the peasantry was now over. The party set out to rapidly industrialize and convert farmers into an agricultural proletariat. Far from being simply an economic scheme, the FFYP launched a new age in Russian history, in which, in the words of the late Donald Treadgold, "governmental fiat invaded every area of life in a manner unparalled in the history not only of Russia but of any other country up to that time. The . . . Plan marked the real beginning of Soviet totalitarianism."[6]

Even more than earlier (the NEP), Zhang was impressed with Soviet economic policies. During his European trip (1929-31), he later admitted, he had been "most interested" in the FFYP. With the speedy progress of industry and the collective farms, the administrative achievements of the CPSU had been established on an "unshakeable foundation," he enthused, and hence "we must completely alter our former attitude toward Soviet Russia" (p. 105; preface no. 2, p. 1). There was an important difference, though, in his appraisals of the NEP and FFYP; although he had approved of the former for its salutary effect on ordinary Russians, he had not proposed China emulate it, as he now did with the FFYP.

Evidence of the FFYP could not missed in Moscow. When he arrived, he recalled, the main poster he saw called on Russians to "Complete the Five-Year Plan in Four Years." He was struck by the form, as well as content, of the posters, and—in a passage censored from the 1971 Taiwan edition of STLZX—criticized the GMD from which he had fled two years earlier. "When

I wandered about the downtown streets of the Russian capital . . . what caught my eye was the neatness and uniformity of . . . the posters, which was vastly different from [GMD] headquarter's posters filling streets and walls throughout our country over the past several years." In Russia, he noted, there were no writings or papers on walls. Russian posters, he explained, contained government policies and were used to admonish people "to rush forward together" (*yizhi benfu*). It was all quite a contrast to Chinese practice. China's fondness for using "literary veterans" (*wenzhang laoshou*) to praise people, he wrote disdainfully, meant it had "fallen victim to a literary disease" (*zheng xianyu yizhong wenzibing*). His countrymen only knew how to "write set phrases" (*xiezuo chengwen*), he grumbled, and hence could not match the young Russian nation's following talk with action ([1933], p. 88).

Even before he set foot in Moscow, he had noted a new moderation and realism in Soviet policies (just as Sun Yat-sen years before had been attracted by the moderation and practicality of the Soviets' NEP). In Germany, he was impressed by newspaper headlines, such as "Change in Direction of Soviet Russia" and "The Collapse of Communism," which referred to Stalin's 23 June 1931 "Six Points" speech (an abridged version is included in STLZX) calling for moderation in the FFYP. The time for "wrecking" was gone, Stalin declared, and he called for a new approach toward the managers and technicians on whom the success of the Plan depended.[7]

In fact, Stalin's new policies may have reminded Zhang of the German Social Democrats he had admired in his sojourn in Germany in the early 1920s. The Soviet leader, he noted, wanted to adopt the capitalist countries' factory management laws (*jingying gongchang fa*) (which Zhang had studied in the early 1920s with the help of German Communist, Karl Korsch). That was one of the reasons Europeans used the phrase "change in direction" to praise Russia, he recalled. He also thought the Communists were becoming more realistic. In the beginning, he noted, the Communists relied on the loftiness of their ideals and thought they could establish a new system. However, they came to realize it was impossible, for they were restricted by production costs just like capitalist industry and commerce. Such a communist concession to reality did not lead him to conclude Stalin's speech represented a retreat, though; it was an advance, he insisted, for Stalin had discovered how difficult it was to escape material limitations (pp. 140-45).

In addition to reading about the FFYP in the German press, he studied and listened to reports. He rejected criticism by a German economist as the views of the irrelevant classical school of economics and opposition by Social Democratic Party bigwig Karl Kautsky as representing the Second International's jealousy of the Third International. On the other hand, he welcomed the conclusion of a French industrialist, after visiting Russia, that the success of the plan was no longer in doubt. Citing Russia's construction of factories, production of goods for the people, and sale of agricultural products to Europe, Zhang argued it was already a self-sufficient country—a goal he embraced for China at the 1934 NSP Congress—and had "launched a new phase in world history" (pp. 33-35).

His admiration for the FFYP was greatly strengthened by the contrast between the impact of the World Depression on England and Germany and on Soviet Russia. Having just traveled from Germany to Russia, he was in a good position to compare the two (as he had done in his debate in 1920 with Zhang Dongsun). Germany was in the midst of the World Depression, he explained, and he had seen numerous factories with no smoke rising from their chimneys. Hence, the "insolvable problem" of unemployment had arisen, with unemployed workers—some of whom had become beggars—everywhere. Government revenues had declined, with the result that the German government had retrenched two or three times since the summer of 1931, the salaries of government officials had been cut, and scientific research institutes had been closed (p. 27).

Russia, on the other hand, had avoided mass unemployment and concentrated capital in the hands of the state, which had enabled it to undertake large-scale construction, open numerous factories, graduate talented youths from schools, and strive to match supply with demand. "Everywhere in Russia," he marveled, "I heard people speak of recently built factories," and there was no talk of "having more hands than needed" (p. 27). Therefore, the returned student from Germany turned his attention eastward, although—as his writings during the 1930s on Germany showed—he by no means abandoned his admiration for German learning.

He went on to explain to his readers that Russia advanced while Germany floundered, because the latter was a capitalist country. That meant it was at the mercy of the world economy and thus suffered in the World Depression. Russia, on the other hand, had cut off contact with the outside world when it went communist. Because it had failed to obtain a major loan from the British in the mid-1920s,[8] beginning in 1928 it had to go it alone with the FFYP. Those two factors, he noted, meant it was not as exposed to the vagaries of world markets as Germany. Finally, it possessed advantages other countries lacked, such as vast natural resources and a large number of consumers. Hence, its success, he concluded, was really due to "natural elements" (pp. 27-28).

Emphasis on Russian resources did not mean he ignored the plan, the achievements of which he considered "on the whole . . . outstanding."[9] He recognized its problems were massive, such as where the Russians would get the necessary vast sums of money and large numbers of technicians, as well as engines, iron and steel, and machinery. Moreover, he acknowledged there had been failures to meet production goals and quality had been terrible. However, for him the real story did not lie in FFYP statistics, for, he stressed, "dull figures and percentages . . . cannot express one ten-thousandth of the Plan's difficulties and obstacles." Instead, he saw the FFYP as a grand historical event, and what is more, one much more difficult to carry out than Qin Shihuang's Great Wall, Sui Yangdi's Grand Canal, and Greece's glorious age of construction (pp. 30-34).

Although he claimed to be unbiased in his assessment of the plan, he accepted at face value Soviet claims, such as those by Molotov and the Russian Cultural Agency (pp. 35, 37-39). Although his anticommunism did not blind him to useful practices in the homeland of communism, accepting such Soviet claims uncritically was fraught with peril, for they neglected to mention the human cost of the FFYP in the countryside.[10]

Model for China

Zhang was not simply another scholar studying the FFYP but one who saw in it an answer to China's needs. Since he saw mainly the successes of the FFYP—thanks to his dependence on Soviet sources—it was easier for him to advocate it as a model for China. "The greatness of the Five-Year Plan," he gushed, "absolutely cannot be described on paper."

> Imagine ourselves setting up a factory, deciding on a plan, creating designs, erecting buildings, appointing engineers, recruiting workers, and even selecting the day to open the factory. In the course of doing this, there would be many days of great pain and worry. [However,] beginning with one factory, [we could] expand to one hundred and [then] one thousand factories. (pp. 39-40)

It was no doctrinaire anticommunist who now supported adoption of Russia's planned economy and national socialism or national capitalism. "We cannot reject them," he argued, "just because they stem from a communist government." "If the nation's private enterprises are placed under a state plan (*guojia jihua*)," he continued, "there will be no need to use . . . expropriation, and we will have the means to control the nation's businesses" (p. 49). It was no coincidence, then, that a planned economy and national socialism figured so prominently in the NSP program when it was drawn up a few months following his return to China.

It is clear that his willingness to imitate Russia was driven by intense nationalism. The majority of Chinese, he complained, wore foreign clothes, ate foreign food, used foreign newsprint, and hung foreign lanterns to light their boats. That, he exclaimed, was what the Russians meant when they called China a semicolony of Europe, America, and Japan. For him, the Russian model provided the solution, contradictory as it might seem as yet another example of reliance on foreigners. Hence, he advocated copying Russia's state-operated industries, appointing a large number of foreign engineers, purchasing lots of foreign machinery, and developing basic industries and becoming a self-sufficient nation. "This is an industrial policy we can adopt," he concluded proudly.

He also proposed emulation of Russia's foreign trade policy. Russia concentrated overseas trade powers in the hands of the government, he noted, to maintain a balance between exports and imports. This was designed to prevent the outflow of cash by limiting importation of foreign goods, while encouraging exports to build up foreign reserves for the purchase of foreign machinery. This, he wrote, "is something we can adopt from Russia's commercial policy" (preface no. 2, p. 3).

In addition, he advocated copying the Soviets' method of raising funds for the FFYP, namely, channeling what labor produced and earned into capital for industry. The government, he explained, had passed laws to repress those who ate but did not work; the workers labored one-half day each week for the nation; and the government offered prizes to compell people to labor and encourage efficiency. His Confucianist strain surfaced when he declared that the meaning of the following passage in *The Great Learning* (*Daxue*)[11] was "completely realized" in Soviet Russia: "Let producers be many and consumers few. Let there be activity in production, and economy in expenditure" (pp. 42-45). Undoubtedly thinking of his own country, he asserted that, "Except for everyone in the nation laboring, there is no other way to produce wealth, no other means to increase the national wealth. Those who forsake this and merely admire the wealth and power (*fu li*) of the West, are all trusting to luck, like people waiting for heaven to rain gold" (p. 47).

He also called for the imitation of a second Russian method of accumulating capital for industry, and that was for the people to economize on food and clothing (pp. 47-48). He was confident China could do this, too:

> Hereafter, new capital should be emphasized. If the increase in capital is swift . . . we will not suffer from enterprises being unable to expand, and industrialization will attain its goals. The first essential of what Russia has done is for new enterprises to absorb the people's earnings. This is what we should take as our model. (p. 49)

He supported his call to emulate Soviet capital-raising techniques by calling on yet another German scholar, who argued that because Russia had no capital and could not borrow from abroad, it had to pay for the plan by "mobilization of people's earnings," as well as their "enormous sacrifices" and "extreme austerity." Fortified by his German "authority," Zhang plugged the NSP's program:

> If our country's reformers are careful not to speak lightly of destruction and ground themselves on our national-socialism program, which will place everyone under a state plan characterized by the sacrifices of "many producers but few consumers," why worry that our country's industry and agriculture cannot progress. (pp. 54-55)

He had ample opportunity to observe the austerity imposed on Russians by the regime. While returning to China on the Trans-Siberian Railroad, for example, he met a Soviet doctor who had been unable to purchase books from Western Europe for over a decade, thanks to the regime's policy of restricting the outflow of funds. Difficult as it might be to imagine Zhang without his beloved Western books, he heartily approved of the Soviet policy, asserting that "for the sake of stabilizing the state's finances, our citizenry had the duty of not buying a new book from Western Europe for ten years" (p. 51).

He also approved of the Russian government's refusal to use its funds to purchase clothing and shoes abroad. He must have been reminded of Europe in the immediate post-World War I days when he observed that Moscow streets were filled with Russians wearing old clothes and worn-out shoes because the government preferred to import machinery. In addition, the government chose to export scarce foodstuffs in exchange for factory machinery. Russians chose not to eat well or wear good clothes, he wrote, and hence "suffered their entire lives to industrialize the nation." They had a saying, he reported: "We should exchange butter for bricks and tiles and meat for machines." Hence, in addition to striving for production, it was necessary to restrict consumption. If successful, he wrote with yet another allusion to *The Great Learning*, producers would be numerous but consumers few. Therefore, "the accumulation of wealth and power will be especially great and industrialization particularly swift" (pp. 52, 54, 99).

This was not to say Russia had no problems. However, although he described several (pp. 40-41), they did not alter his admiration for the plan. Despite difficulties, he wrote, Russia used its "ingenuity" and "steadfast and persevering strength" to control them. From the viewpoint of "our poor and chaotic country," he added, "how can we bear to censure [the Russians]. [We should] admire and praise [them]" (p. 41).

However, there was a limit beyond which he was unwilling to go in calling for emulation of the FFYP, revealed in his resistance to the argument that destruction by the CPSU had been the necessary prelude to its subsequent construction. In a possible slap at the CCP, he emphasized that "those able to imitate Soviet Russia's destruction cannot necessarily emulate . . . [its] construction, while those who imitate Soviet Russia's construction are not bound to begin with . . . [its] destruction." Undoubtedly with the CCP in mind, he urged those "adept at imitating Russia" to make every effort to "follow Russia's construction and avoid its destruction" (pp. 42-43).

He also was displeased that people were treated unequally in Russia. Party members and workers, he wrote, fared better than those who worked with their minds. Workers received a far greater food ration than intellectuals, and, as a result of government subsidies, workers' food and clothing costs were far lower than those of "intellectual laborers" (*zhishi laodongzhe*). Hence, the socialist ideal, "From each according to his abilities and to each according to his needs," had "absolutely not been realized in Russia." Thus, one might add, Russia had reversed Mencius's famous dictum that those who labored with their minds governed those who worked with their hands.[12] In addition, politics overrode economics in Russia, he pointed out, for the Soviet government charged the bourgeoisie more than workers for the same goods (pp. 79-81).

In proposing imitation of the FFYP, he was prepared for skeptics aware of his anticommunism. As we shall see later, though, it was clear that his admiration for Stalin's Russia was not a case of dropping that anticommunism for a new idolatry. In the past, he wrote in 1932, he had been opposed to Russia, because it opposed democracy and selfishly claimed political power for one party. At present, he praised Russia "due to its creative achievements, and because its policies are gradually becoming more humane (*heyu renxing*)." His standpoint, he declared—disingenuously in view of his involvement then in founding a political party—stemmed from "unbiased words about right and wrong, advantages and disadvantages, and are not the personal views of political parties and groups on the Left or Right" (preface no. 2, p. 4).

In addition to his fulsome praise of the FFYP, he saw lessons for China in the Second Five-Year Plan (SFYP), which went into effect two years following his trip to Russia (1933-37). This plan was, in his words, to eliminate the last "capitalistic elements" and "consolidate gains already won" (pp. 52, 54, 99). Moreover, there was a lesson in the fact that the Soviets had to wait until the SFYP to produce their own machinery. Those in China who "aspired to follow Russia," he wrote, should be aware that China, too, would have to wait for a second stage before "we can manufacture our own machinery" (p. 94). Finally, he was struck by a speech by Stalin, in which the latter noted that China, like the Soviet Union, lacked heavy industry and, as a result, its own war industry, and hence was open to partition by the "greedy and covetous." Concluding, Zhang wondered if his countrymen had heard and been moved by Stalin's warning concerning China's lack of heavy industry (pp. 146-48).

Collective and State Farms

It was not entirely true, as sometimes charged, that as an intellectual and university professor, Zhang ignored the countryside. As his lengthy analysis in STLZX of the agricultural side of the Soviets' "Second Revolution" demonstrates, upon his arrival in Russia he was immediately struck by the fact that it was a peasant country (like China) and hence was intensely interested in its collective and state farms (p. 56).

The seeds of the collectivization drives of the FFYP were planted at the Fifteenth CPSU Congress in December 1927 (the same month Zhang's *SuE pinglun* was published). The basic objective, according to Stalin, was to transform agriculture by amalgamating small peasant farms into large farms, "gradually but steadily, not by means of pressure, but by example and persuasion." Unfortunately for millions of peasants, that was far from the way collectivization was carried out.

Collectivization was launched in the summer of 1928. Although Stalin declared in May 1928 that "expropriation of the kulaks would be folly," in the summer of 1929 he ordered party workers to liquidate "as a class" the 5 percent of farmers classified as kulaks. At first, definition of a kulak was based on wealth, but the term soon came to mean any peasant opposed to "socialism." In what one historian calls a "war of urban Communists against the village," complete with chaos, pillaging, and murder, millions of peasants were driven onto collective and state farms. By the end of 1932, more than a year after Zhang's visit, 60 percent of peasant families had been collectivized.

There were two basic types of collective undertakings: state and collective farms. The former were the property of the Soviet government and utilized hired labor or "peasant proletarians." The latter, on the other hand, were supposed to be self-governing cooperatives of peasants who pooled their means of production and split the yield. In fact, there were three types of collective farms: the commune; the *toz*, a production cooperative; and the *artel*, under which the peasant retained his livestock and his own small garden plot. The latter was by far the most prevalent type, and by 1933 comprised over 96 percent of collective farms. Yet, as in the case of the NEP, the Soviets considered the *artel* a temporary concession.

Although collectivization proved a political victory for Stalin and his cohorts and a major contribution to construction of Soviet totalitarianism, it was an economic disaster. In 1932-33, millions of peasants died from human-made famine, and as late as 1937, the country was still struggling to regain pre-1928 production levels.[13]

As in the case of the FFYP's industrial side, Zhang's interest in Russia's collective farms was stoked while he was in Germany. West Europeans, he recalled, were fascinated. On the eve of his departure from Jena in September 1931, his German landlords naively termed the Russian farms "human paradises" (p. 60).

By the time he arrived in Soviet Russia in 1931, nearly 53 percent of peasants belonged to collective farms.[14] He made it clear that as a socialist he favored this policy. For the past several decades, he wrote, socialists had worried that peasant families' strong sense of private property would be a great obstacle to socialism. However, at present, Soviet Russia had invented a new pattern in agriculture. Oddly enough, though, he did not credit Stalin with that innovation but lumped it with the inventions of Newton and Watt as examples of serendipity (p. 58).

Once in Moscow, he did not waste any time. The day after his arrival, Mo Dehui (Liuchen), head of the Chinese delegation then in Moscow conducting negotiations concerning the Chinese Eastern Railway,[15] introduced him to the Russian Cultural Agency, where his first request was to visit a collective farm. He was immediately granted permission to visit one called "Keluomina" (Kolomna?), two to three hundred *li* (one *li* equals one-third of a mile) from Moscow.[16]

As the account of a Chinese—and a "third-force" one rather than that of a member of the GMD or CCP—Zhang's recollections of his visit to the collective farm and his conversations are interesting. When he arrived at "Keluomina" district, he was taken to the local office, where he met "proletarians" "full of heroic spirit." While there, he noticed a map that showed that "Keluomina" district had already achieved the FFYP goal of including one-half the land in collective farms, and hence collectivization had been halted. That map, he wrote admiringly, was "nearly a little Five-Year Plan in each district." Afterward, he visited a trolley factory. Told by his worker-guide that the plant produced 360 streetcars a year, he enviously wondered whether any of China's factories could manufacture streetcars and whether there was one that could produce 360 a year.

When he reached the collective farm, he noted that it was the commune type, adding that Russians believed this kind was closest to ideal agricultural socialism (pp. 61-62). It also, one might point out, was closest to the state farm. All tools and livestock were jointly owned by members, who lived in communal buildings. However, he was visiting a collective farm that was in the minority, for the majority were the *artel* type.[17]

Guided around by the farm director, it was clear to him—unlike to some Western visitors[18]—that the Russians' standard of living was "far below that of the German worker." These peasants, he declared, were "the equals of impoverished people in our country" (p. 62).[19] Poverty also was starkly evident in the canteen, where he received a cup of black tea and several pieces of black bread, but no butter or sugar. His curiosity aroused, he inquired in vain about the farm's finances, including workers' earnings. As he departed, a Western-style residence near the entrance was pointed out as the home of the former landowner, an exiled White Russian.

Reflecting later on what he had seen, he concluded that the collective farms were no different technically from areas under cultivation by the great landlords in Germany's East Prussia. The only difference, he explained (unnecessarily), were the property relationships. In addition, it was clear he did not find the farms examples of perfect socialism. The explanation was Stalin's "Dizziness from Success" speech the year before his arrival.[20] Calling for a retreat from crash collectivization, this address opened the way for some relaxation, and it was this type of collective farm he visited. As examples of the new atmosphere, he noted that executive committee members were free to withdraw from the farm, while their pay was distributed according to rank. Hence, although the farms were collectivized, he noted, their administration did not correspond to socialism's principle of pure equality, "from each according to his ability and to each according to his needs."

Despite the farm's asocialist character, he approved of other signs of thaw. In the past, he explained, no matter how much livestock or land an executive member brought to the *artel*, at the end of the year their reward had been equal. Was that not similar, he wondered, to Mencius's comment about large and small shoes bringing the same price?[21] To remedy that injustice, he reported, the Russian government allowed *artels* to pay 5 percent annual interest for families' capital. Moreover, he wrote, to prevent dissatisfaction, work had been divided into five grades worth different points. Finally, a distinction was made between hard workers and lazy ones, with the executive committee having the power to expel the latter from the farm. He approved of this "different treatment" in combination with the "equality of the *artel* system." That, he explained, kept the system from "going against human feelings" (pp. 63-65).

He also was interested in Soviet state farms. As "factories in the field" and "grain and meat factories," this type of farm was the communist goal.

However, since they were extremely inefficient, their main value was as agricultural experimental stations and ways to bring land under cultivation in new areas. The disastrous first quarter of 1930 proved a turning point for state farms, and by the time of Zhang's visit a large number had been dissolved and their holdings turned over to collective farms.[22]

What he learned about the state farms, he recalled, made him "wide-eyed and tongue-tied and at a loss as to what to say." He was stunned by the hugeness of the farms, which were examples of the "gigantomania" that Russians used to explain the fascination with the big that characterized the FFYP.[23] "Alas!" he declared, "this is absolutely unexpected by those of us brought up with villages of small farmers" (p. 75).

Writing about the Soviet state farms brought to mind two German estates he had visited, one in Kant's birthplace, Konigsberg, and the other near Weimar in Thuringia. They were huge, he recalled, with thousands of livestock, as well as their own ironworks and dairies. Moreover, they had scientific specialists in charge of livestock, bees, and fruit trees, and their continual experimentation was the reason Western livestock was fat and fruit trees, large (p. 74). In an amusing aside, he recalled chatting with a man in charge of raising pigs:

> Photographs of pigs hung everywhere in the room. He explained them to me, saying that such-and-such a pig won first prize this year, and another pig was second to an English Yorkshire pig's certain number of catties (*jin*). He loved the pigs in the room just as much as ordinary people loved their children. My brother, Kia-ngau, and I jokingly called him "Dr. Pig." (p. 74)[24]

In short, he wrote admiringly, the farms applied all the new inventions in science, industry, and sanitation. China could not compete with those German farms, he lamented, for the "grandness of their scale is beyond the wildest dreams of those who have seen only Jiangsu and Zhejiang's scattered rice paddies" (p. 74).

Models for China

There was no question but what he found the Soviet collective and state farms interesting, but could they be copied by China? When the director of the "Keluomina" farm asked him whether the collective farm system could be carried out in China, Zhang replied diplomatically that "it would not be impossible to implement the cooperative spirit in agriculture" (p. 63). However, in March 1932, a month after the NSP program was drafted, he went further and thought he saw a remedy for China's rural problems in the FFYP. Chinese agriculture could not satisfy demand within the country, he wrote, and hence China had to import rice from Annam and Siam. The way to increase Chinese production—and thus break dependence on foreigners—he argued, was to copy Russia's combination of collective farms with those under private ownership. That, he enthused, was "an agriculture policy we can adopt" (preface no. 2, pp. 2-3).

He saw even more concrete—and patriotic—uses for the Soviet state farm. Since they were used to reclaim wasteland, he argued, China could implement them in the undeveloped lands in the Northwest and beyond the Great Wall.

> [We can] designate large areas as experimental farms (*shiyansuo*) and use machine cultivation. At the same time, [we can] map out transportation routes between the interior and the Northwest or [the territory] beyond the Great Wall, so we can take what we have reaped from cultivating pastures and ship it to the interior, in order to resist importation of rice from abroad. This is what our country should immediately undertake. (p. 78)

Praise for Soviet Education

In addition to the FFYP, Zhang thought the Soviets were doing a good job in education. He had admired Lunacharsky, people's commissar for education, since the early 1920s (see chapter 6). Although in SEPL he had ignored education, choosing to concentrate on Russia's politics and economy, in his 1933 work he reverted to his original interest in the Soviet educational world.

He thought Soviet educational theory oversimplified. He took issue with its sharp delineation of bourgeois and proletarian education, which claimed the bourgeoisie glossed over class interests and believed in nationalism, idealism, religion, character development, and education for its own sake, while the Soviets stood for class interests, internationalism, materialism, opposition to religion, character as but one element in the society to which one should devote oneself, and education as but a means of attaining their goals. He thought the Soviets oversimplified the two approaches. Capitalist states, he wrote, had numerous types of schools, and their ways of educating talent were extremely diverse. As for the Soviets, they also stressed iron discipline and the homeland. Proletarian education was not limited to internationalism and materialism, he insisted, for none could be praised as educators who taught the "creation of disturbances but not the observance of law, materialist struggle but not moral training" (pp. 160-61).

As an educator himself, he had a broad concept of education, dividing it into direct (the school system) and indirect (libraries, museums, movie houses, theaters, and radio broadcasts). While in Russia, he seems to have seen more of the latter than the former. Mo Dehui, for example, took him to see an opera called *The Red Poppy*, about Chinese anti-imperialism and old customs of the Chinese family. In Germany, he had seen another Tretiakov production, *China Seething*, based on the Wanxian Incident.[25] It had already been performed in Shanghai, he remembered, under the title, *Roar! China!* He recognized the two plays contained "international political propaganda," but because they concerned Chinese patriotism, he did not condemn them. They stemmed from the same spirit, he concluded, as Schiller's play, *William Tell*,[26] adding that due to the later era, references to imperialism and the laboring class had been added to both plays (pp. 168-69).

He also praised Soviet films as rich in educational significance, though the one he saw seemed more like a political morality tale. In addition, he visited the Museum of the Revolution, where he was particularly struck by an oil painting depicting the "recklessness and depravity" of the Russian nobles. He did not miss its significance in the homeland of communism, noting that it was "an appropriate work in light of the class-struggle concept" (p. 169).

He was disappointed with the lack of opportunity to visit more schools, however, and noted that he had visited only a nursery in a workers' district, the Culture Park's kindergarten, and Moscow University. He very much wanted to spend one or two days at a middle school and elementary school to observe their new-style teaching, he wrote, but time did not permit. Hence, he had to settle for a day of lectures at the Museum of Education outlining the school system. Nevertheless, he was impressed and described the speaker's "warmth and sincerity" as "moving." "From the museum staff's 'tireless teaching,'"[27] he exclaimed, "one may infer the new atmosphere after the Russian Revolution" (pp. 169-70).

He was especially interested in Soviet experiments with new educational theories. Russia's educational system, he explained, adopted Germany's theory of uniform schools (*yiti xuexiao shuo*; *einheitsschule*), which was described in the Weimar Constitution he had translated a decade earlier.[28] The practical significance of this theory in Russia, he explained, was that those eager to learn had schools in which to enroll.

Of the three types of education in Soviet Russia—ordinary, vocational, and political—he thought the Soviets had done best in vocational education, which assisted Russia's industrialization. They had established industrial schools to produce skilled workers. The government also had established labor academies (*laodong yuan*) for workers and peasants, and graduates could take an examination to enter university. There also were night schools for workers, evening schools for peasants, a communist university, and a party affairs school (pp. 171-72).

He applauded Russia's experimentation and innovation in education since the revolution, although even the Russian authorities admitted they had failed to implement the "complex" and "project" (*sheji jiaofa*) methods. However, he added, it was not the methods that were at fault but that "what Russia used to apply them went beyond normal limits." The two approaches could certainly be utilized, he concluded, but China's educators should "take Russia's failures as object lessons and skillfully manage them" (pp. 174-77).

In 1933, he pointed out that there had been "changes in the direction of Soviet Russia's education" over the previous three years. In politics, Russia had retreated from world revolution to socialist construction in one country. In economics, it had retreated from the idea of "from each according to his ability and to each according to his needs" to adoption of a currency system and clear demarcation of wages according to rank. Finally, he concluded, there had been retreat in the educational realm. Stalin had warned his countrymen not to waste energy on unrealistic experiments, Zhang wrote, but to urgently seek regularization of work. Hence, during the past two to three years the complex and project methods had been attacked by party, government, and industries worried about the quality of workers and engineers (pp. 178-80). The result, he reported, had been restoration of traditional education, as well as the emphasis on individual, rather than collective, efforts.

In the end, he was a pragmatist. He did not think, he wrote, that "sticking to old ways is necessarily right and loving the new is definitely wrong. The appropriateness of all systems depends on their results. If the results reaped by a new system are inferior to those of the old system, then a swarm of blame arises, and it [the new system] cannot be sustained." He then addressed his compatriots:

> What I especially hope for from our country's intellectual and educational circles is that we ourselves should create, test, and carry out new theories and institutions, and should not consider following other countries our special skill. This would be an expression of the real creative power of our race's culture, and cannot be discussed in the same breath with those who today reject the familiar in favor of the exotic (lit., eschew chicken for wild duck; *she jiaji qiu yewu*). (pp. 183-84)

Models for China

Just as in other aspects of the Soviet experiment, he saw lessons for China in the educational realm. As a result of his philosophical studies in the early 1920s, he had adopted a voluntarist approach to life. Hence, he must have been impressed when the museum staff told him that Soviet elementary schools emphasized the voluntary spirit (*zidong jingshen*) and environment.

More important, however, was the Soviet schools' emphasis on nature and hygiene. "When I heard those words [nature and hygiene]," he wrote excitedly, "I felt this policy was extremely suitable for our country's urban and rural elementary schools. If urban and rural residents can learn the laws of nature and the importance of hygiene, then . . . a great reform must occur in life" (p. 171).

Since China and Soviet Russia both suffered from widespread illiteracy, he especially found inspiration in Soviet efforts in this realm, efforts of which the Museum of Education staff were proudest. For a change, Germany was no help, for it enjoyed nearly 100 percent literacy.[29] The museum staff told him that young people had been appointed as teachers to eliminate illiteracy and had been very successful. Illiterates were taught for six months and learned enough words to keep daily accounts. Later, they were tested, and if they had forgotten words, they were returned to the semi-illiterate list and forced to resume study.

He clearly saw the implications for China. "I believe if a nation has several tens of millions of illiterates," he declared, "then . . . there are a number of people who are unaware they have any relationship with the state." "If these kinds of people constitute the majority of a nation's residents," he continued, "there has never been one [nation] that has not perished." This then was another reason to admire the FFYP, for it had called for the elimination of illiteracy and the implementation of compulsory education. In addition, he reported, in July 1930 a CPSU Congress had passed a resolution stating that only if compulsory education was implemented would it be possible to achieve final political and economic victory, a sentiment with which Zhang obviously agreed (pp. 172-73).

Praise for Lenin, Stalin, and Trotsky

Since Zhang admired some things about Soviet Russia, the question arose as to who or what was responsible for those successes. In pondering this question, he concluded that the leaders, people, and CPSU organization were behind them.

Chinese students were drawn to the USSR in part because of their admiration for Lenin. Zhang shared that feeling, as seen in his writings in the early 1920s and his comments in SEPL. In the early 1930s, he broadened his perspective to include Trotsky and Stalin, as well as Lenin, as major figures. Lenin and Stalin were responsible for the dictatorship and the planned economy, he wrote, which were the key elements in the twentieth century's new political situation (p. 2).

During a long wait in the customhouse on the Soviet border in September 1931, he had an opportunity to scrutinize the portraits of Lenin and Stalin on the wall. Lenin's picture, he wrote, showed an "intelligent and wise" person, possessed of "firmness of will" (p. 1). As for Stalin, his forehead "lacked a noble and forthright air." This was a man, wrote Zhang, who was "expert at scheming and good at coping with his surroundings" (pp. 1-2).

He thought Trotsky superior to Stalin in thoroughness of views and consistency of theory, but concluded Stalin was better in controlling the strategems of political power and in tactics for coping with his surroundings (p. 15). In creative genius, Stalin was inferior to Lenin, but in steadiness he surpassed him. The excellence and apropos nature of Stalin's theories, he concluded, were inferior to Trostky's, but he surpassed him in ability to adapt to change while implementing matters (pp. 65-66).

The Support of the People

Since his student days in Japan before the 1911 Revolution, he had admired the "one or two men." Now, however, he admitted that Lenin and Stalin did not deserve all the credit for Soviet Russia's successes. After he had been in Moscow for a few days, he recalled, he realized the reason behind the two leaders' great deeds was the support of the populace. As six years earlier (SEPL), he admired the strivings and sacrifices of the Russian people. Sounding much like Hu Shi and Ding Wenjiang (chapter 6), he declared that even though he was not a Communist Party member, he had "great admiration" for the Russian people's "charging ahead and taking enemy positions" (p. 15).[30]

Admiration for the CPSU's Organization

In addition to the leaders and the "people," Zhang credited the strength of the CPSU organization for the successes of Soviet Russia. Part of his discussion of party organization proved sensitive enough for the GMD regime in Taiwan to censor from the 1971 reprint of STLZX (hence, pagination of the citations follows the 1933, rather than 1971, version). Perhaps with his own newly born NSP in mind, he asserted that great movements in history had to have strong organizations behind them. Like Sun Yat-sen and the GMD before him, he was impressed with the Soviet Party: "We [the NSP?] are not totally in agreement with Soviet Russia's politics," he wrote, "but the organization of its Communist Party must be praised as one of the great products of the twentieth century" ([1933], 116). That admiration was genuine, for the NSP's organization—like that of the GMD—was modeled after the CPSU's.

It may have been testimony to the missionary impact on China that the CPSU reminded him of the Jesuits. "Of those [organizations] that can be compared to Soviet Russia's Communist Party," he asserted, "none is better than the Society of the Cross [Jesus], founded in 1539 [1540]." The Jesuits were established by Ignatius de Loyola (1491-1556), who saw his times dominated by combat. Hence, he resorted to military discipline to control his priests and organize the Society, which dispatched Matteo Ricci and Ferdinand Verbiest to China.[31] The Society, Zhang declared, was a "combat organization for missionary undertakings," which adhered to the principles of fortitude (*jianku*), chastity (*zhencao*), and obedience (*fucong*). Except for chastity, he concluded, "what Lenin demanded from party members and Loyola, from fellow priests, were exactly the same."

In the early years of the century, he continued, Lenin had called for a "rigorous party" (*yanmi zhi dang*), which would place talent under iron discipline and give party cadres total power to manage them. Lenin's policy, Zhang pointed out, "exactly tallied with Loyola's proposal to replace the Church's life of idleness with the discipline of the military camp" ([1933], 116-17).

Zhang witnessed that "discipline of the military camp." While in Moscow, he viewed the Communist Youth Corps' anniversary celebration. Their VIPs wore plain clothing, he reported, and had a "worried, diligent, cautious, and disciplined" look (no doubt they were worried about being purged!). In more than ten years, he continued, they had never wavered from strict enforcement of the "fortitude" practiced by the Jesuits. He then reached a conclusion that could not have been popular with his communist countrymen. "The reason Communist Party members have held on to political power up to the present," he argued, "has absolutely nothing to do with their principles or the material conditions they greatly admire, but is entirely the result of their constantly bearing in mind these two great principles [fortitude and obedience]" ([1933], 117).

Quoting an American scholar, he declared the CPSU was like an army,[32] but he was not fooled by the apparent power of Soviet organizations. The Soviet system was a "one-man autocracy" (pp. 124-25), he wrote, with that man being Stalin, as clearly seen in the replacement of Lenin's policies with Stalin's. Under Lenin, the CI strove for "world revolution," while under Stalin the goal was "socialism in one country." The period after 1928, he stated bluntly, could be described as "Russia under Stalin's rule" (pp. 13-15).

Criticisms of the Soviet "Experiment"

Although he admired much in the "new" Soviet Russia under Stalin, he still abhored communist politics. "My impressions of Russia have changed a bit," he admitted in 1932, "but those . . . changes are limited to Russia's reconstructed economy and have nothing to do with the political aspect." Thus, he rejected the class state and ridiculed Soviet claims to a "classless society," expressed his disgust with CPSU intraparty power struggles, scoffed at the idea that the state would eventually "wither away," and made abundantly clear his distrust for the CI, as well as Soviet penetration of China's Inner Asian frontiers.

The Class State

While on tour in Russia, he made his disapproval of class warfare clear by clashing with his Russian guide, who had lived in China. When he insisted that China's class distinctions were not as extreme as Europe's, a position that echoed that of his mentor, Liang Qichao,[33] she asked if Shanghai's compradors were not bourgeoisie. Although she was right—compradors had become capitalists and "China's first modern entrepreneurs"[34]—he responded they were employees of foreign business firms and not bourgeoisie. He dismissed the fact that the guide frequently shook her head in disapproval with the explanation that "Marxist class theory was already deeply embedded in people" (pp. 60-61, 164).

He went on to note Lenin's argument that since democracy was a capitalist government, it was necessary to deprive rich people of the franchise and enable the oppressed to rule in order to progress to socialism. Hence, he concluded, Lenin's proletarian dictatorship was a dictatorship of the peasants and workers (p. 107).

He found plenty of evidence in the constitution and quotidian life that the Soviet Union was a "class state." The constitution denied the franchise to six classes, stipulated that only laborers were allowed to serve in the military, and even made sure house rents varied according to class, he noted. Moreover, administration of justice varied according to class. If the accused were workers, he explained, their punishment was light, but if they belonged to the nobility, priesthood, or a rich peasant family, the penalty was heavy. The Communists' goal, he declared, was not punishment befitting the crime but preventing "reaction" (*fandong*).

Class also determined the right of children to pursue education. He reported a conversation with the chancellor of Moscow University, who stated that 70 percent of the new students each year were children of workers and peasants, with only 30-35 percent of the places saved for bourgeoisie. His response was to fall back on his Confucianism by quoting the *Analects*. When he heard the chancellor's statement, he wrote, he felt it was "contrary to the aim of 'providing education for all people without distinction'" (*you jiao wu lei*) (p. 153).[35] He also heard that some elementary schools accepted only children of CPSU members, while some research institutes accepted only party members, for example, only those who had been party members for a decade were admitted to the "Party History Research Association" (*Dangshi yanjiuhui*) (pp. 107-9). Intellectuals also were discriminated against, he added, since it was difficult for them to join the CPSU (p. 121).

The result, he asserted, was that 2.6 million party members ruled 140 million Russians by shutting the bourgeoisie out of political power, while laborers who disagreed with the CPSU, such as the Socialist Revolutionaries, were either driven abroad or remained in the country "silent as winter cicadas." There also were political means of destroying dissidents (*yiji*), he noted, which assured concentration of political power in the party. In elections, for example, the party did not use the West European secret-ballot method but "raising your hand." Since people were aware that the slightest opposition would mean surveillance by the secret police, he explained, it was the rare person who lifted his hand in opposition.

The CPSU's rule over the Russian people, he continued, was also strengthened by the fact that members of soviets were indirectly, rather than directly, elected. Village soviets elected delegates to prefectural soviets, the latter elected delegates to provincial soviets, and these elected representatives to the All-Russian Congress.[36] The party monopolized those "elections" because executive committees, presidiums, and people's commissariats on every level were subordinate to it (pp. 110-11). Members of other parties were elected to soviets, he admitted, but they were not allowed to criticize government policies, as "commonly seen by people who travel to Russia" (he did not mention witnessing a meeting of a soviet). What is more, in the highest levels of soviets, the majority of executive committee members belonged to the party. Finally, the Central Executive Committee and the Council of People's Commissars were entirely made up of party members. These situations, he noted grimly, were due to CPSU "manipulation" and not the result of "popular will" (*minyi*).

The Leninists, he continued, claimed they had adopted dictatorship rather than democracy to abolish inequality in property and to attain a classless state.[37] He labeled a "dream" their argument that all inequalities would disappear after rich and poor were equal. As long as one person swept floors while another managed a factory, he argued, there would be a distinction in society between the ignorant and the intelligent. He also thought the CPSU's belief that political differences arose from the disparities between rich and poor to be nonsense. At present (1932), he noted, there were no capitalist interests behind either Stalin or Trotsky (exiled from the Soviet Union in January 1929), yet they still engaged in factionalism. The real reason behind such struggle was that rulers considered it glorious and pleasurable to wield power, he argued, with the result that even if they all belonged to the CPSU, they could not avoid scrambling for power and profit.

He saw little chance of eliminating inequalities, regardless of the Communists' arguments, and hence his view of Russia's future was grim. The classless society, he wrote, "was [like] a sacred mountain that is within sight but inaccessible. Russia's citizens will always suffer from dictatorship and be unable to extricate themselves." There would always be confrontation between political parties, he continued, giving the Russian government a pretext to maintain dictatorship. Even if opposition within Russia disappeared, he argued, as long as there were capitalist countries, the Russian government would strive to build internal defenses against invasion, which would yield another pretext for dictatorship. In his opinion, "Russia's dictatorship is a system of government that will probably never change. If the citizens do not rise to destroy it, the Communist Party members will never 'withdraw and take the path of the worthies'" (*tuibi xianlu*) (pp. 111-15).

CPSU Intraparty Struggles

Just as in 1927, he was dismayed by factionalism within the CPSU. This time he relied on political philosophy to explain it, and his views also may be seen as a salvo in the debate over democracy and dictatorship that was just beginning in China in 1933 (chapter 9).

West European political scientists used freedom (*ziyou*) and authority (*quanli*) to stand for democracy and centralization, he explained. In Western Europe, the balance between government authority and individual freedom was protected by constitutions. Members of a political party were free to debate the party's positions and, if they disagreed with them, could form a faction or switch to another party. All of this led to the development of their citizens' "voluntary spirit" (which he also mentioned could be found in Soviet elementary schools).

The CPSU was different, he continued, for it had authority but no freedom. Its "centralization" meant obedience, and its "democracy," that a member had to withdraw if his views differed from the party's. No parties were allowed outside the CPSU or factions within the party. Hence, he explained, political views did not arise out of party discussions but from the "cadre's approval," and those who objected were expelled. He traced this lack of freedom to the CPSU's emphasis on "careful and exact discipline." Within the party, "unity of action" was most important. Hence, CPSU members had to follow orders, and "freedom was sacrificed to authority" (pp. 126-27).

Even though he admired Soviet economic and educational policies, he still preferred the politics of Western Europe. Western Europe provided constitutional protection of citizens' rights, the equal right of people to participate in government and politics, the establishment of political parties based on freedom of assembly, the right of parties to join the government and organize cabinets, the right of those who left one party to join or organize another party, and a member's freedom to decide whether to observe party discipline (p. 128). In Western Europe, he continued, there were numerous parties and hence everyone could be satisfied; the adoption of theories advocated by a group's representatives depended on the popular will; each group had as a prerequisite a sense of responsibilty; and each had the opportunity to establish a government and satisfy its desire for power (p. 137).

The CPSU, on the other hand, stipulated that those who did not observe discipline would be expelled from the party and exiled (p. 128). Russians had "only the obligation to obey and absolutely lacked freedom of discussion." After the party came to power, he continued, there had been frequent internal disputes, with the losers labeled criminals and expelled from the party or exiled to Siberia (p. 129). The real reason for the expulsion of Trotsky from the Soviet Union, he added, was that there was no room for two heroes in the Russian system (p. 132). In his view, the CPSU's outlook closely resembled that of traditional Chinese politics, whereby the "victors are a nation's rulers, while the defeated are treated like prisoners."[38] Hence, in the Soviet system, he concluded, there was no balance between democracy and centralization (p. 129).

Not for the first or the last time, he suggested the Russian system was contrary to human nature. For people to advocate different ideas, he noted, was a "constant of the laws of human nature (*renqing wuli zhi chang*), and could not be forcibly made uniform" (p. 136). Hence, since Soviet Russia had only one party, it was natural for factions, such as the Trotskyites, to appear (pp. 136-37). Since Russia had only one kind of officially permitted political view, that determined by the party cadre, he explained, dessimination of other views was a violation of the law, and there was no opportunity for an opposition party to establish a government (pp. 137-38).

He was aware that some people believed that while the state was being transformed (as in the Soviet Union), it was necessary for the government to be all-powerful. However, he insisted that "freedom of the individual and concentration of political power are not mutually obstructive." The individual's freedom was manifested in speech and assembly, he explained, while the government's authority was displayed in the implementation of policies.

He took advantage of the opportunity to plug the NSP's program, which sounded suspiciously similar to Sun Yat-sen's division between "popular sovereignty" and "government power."[39] There was a compromise (*zhezhong*) between freedom and authority, Zhang explained. Citizens should be permitted freedom of speech and assembly and allowed to participate in the national assembly and discuss politics; in these ways, the will of the people would be expressed and the people's rights, protected. On the other hand, the national assembly would discuss and pass a three- or five-year administrative program (*xingzheng gangyao*), while the government would be jointly organized by leaders of the parties, he continued. The national assembly would grant the government full power to implement the administrative program as it saw fit. As a result, even though cabinet members came and went, there would be no change in policy, and authority would be concentrated in government.

He contrasted his plan with Russia's "centralization of authority and sacrifice of freedom." The Russian approach, he explained, created frequent unrest, with the result that the government ruled by way of Draconian laws and exiled the nation's leaders to distant and out-of-the-way places within Russia, as well as to foreign lands. Those out of power were compelled to form secret associations, he argued, and adopt revolutionary behavior to overthrow the government. Therefore, he concluded, his plan embodied order and safety, while Soviet Russia's offered only disorder and danger (pp. 138-39).

The "Withering Away of the State"

As a nationalist and statist, Zhang rejected the Marxist belief that the state was destined to "wither away." He did not believe the Soviets neglected the state in favor of the international arena, and based his arguments on Stalin's emphasis on "socialism in one country," the policies of the CPSU and the CI, and a study of Lenin's 1917 pamphlet, *State and Revolution*.

He confessed that not until he reached Moscow had he realized the importance of the latter, which he noted was revered as a "political bible" by the CPSU (pp. 16-17).[40] "If we say that Locke's [*Two Treatise of*] *Government* was the basic work of English parliamentary government," he asserted, "there is no doubt Lenin's *State and Revolution* is the basic work for Communist political proposals" (pp. 17-18). In this pamphlet, Lenin recognized the need for the state as an instrument of class domination in the immediate future. After destroying the bourgeois state, Lenin argued, the Communists would establish the proletarian state or "dictatorship of the proletariat." In the lower stage of communism, the state would still be needed, although it would "wither away" in the higher phase.[41]

Hence, the Communists awaited the day when the means of production would belong to the state and the ground would be cut from beneath the capitalists and their power to suppress others, eliminated. They called this, he explained, "the withering away of the state." He thought this was nonsense. The "withering away of the state" were "unheard of words for those who study political science." The state was inseparable from the nation, he explained, and each nation's language, history, and customs were different. Therefore, until confrontation between nations was eliminated, the state would not "wither away" (pp. 20-22).

Lenin was right, Zhang acknowledged, when he declared that a proletarian state would be needed in the first stage of communism. Although the proletariat had seized power in Russia, "I heard in the Russian capital that not only . . . has the state not perished, its position is increasingly secure." He found evidence of this in his observations of Russia's mililtary, economic, and foreign affairs.

Everyone who visits Moscow, he wrote, hears the Russians claim the capitalist nations will soon attack. That propaganda was widespread and had increased people's enthusiasm for national defense. "One afternoon," he recalled, "I joined our country's embassy staff and watched the Russians practice with motorcycles on an athletic field, while overhead airplanes soared up and down. A friend said I was simply watching Russia's preparations to attack others; how could one believe that other countries were coming to attack!" In addition, he recalled that when he visited the front during the 1929 Sino-Soviet War in Manchuria (chapter 5), the Red Army had scattered leaflets that clearly spoke of recovering Soviet Russia's national rights in the Chinese Eastern Railway.

He also found evidence of the persistence of the state in foreign relations, and cited as evidence a March 1931 speech by Molotov, chairman of the Council of People's Commissars. In discussing Soviet Russia's relations with other countries, Zhang pointed out, Molotov did not use class as his standpoint but spoke in terms of Russia opposing other nations, thus providing further evidence that the state had not withered away (pp. 22-23). Moreover, before the revolution, Russia had dealt with England, France, Germany, and Japan, and its policy was preservation of Russia's rights. After the revolution, it negotiated with the same countries, and its policy was still protection of

Russia's rights. "Changes in the internal distribution of wealth and power have had no impact on the state's foreign relations," he declared, and hence class theory was "a means of communist revolution, not a truth of the scientific world" (p. 24).

Finally, to promote industrialization, the Russians exported everything they could to earn funds to purchase foreign machinery. This approach, he explained, "considered Russia an economic unit and other nations separate economic units." Obviously, the state had not withered away in the economic realm either (pp. 23-24).

In Zhang's mind, then, there was no doubt that the Soviet Union was "based on the state," a position those who were pro-Russian loathed, he wrote, and considered an insult to the CPSU and the CI. In response to the communist argument that the state was the expression of irreconciable class conflict, he pointed out that when a nation was invaded, the people united in resistance. Under the system of compulsory education, all children—whether rich or poor, high or low—attended school. Where were the irreconciable classes in those two phenomena? he wondered (p. 18).

The Communists also believed, he continued, that the state was the tool of the capitalists and as a result approved of any action that could harm that entity. He may have had China in the 1930s in mind when he wrote that if people called for unity in the face of foreign aggression, the Communists objected it was the tune of warmongers. The Communists especially enjoyed creating internal disorder, he wrote, to overthrow the status quo. If someone tried to dissuade them in the name of resisting foreign aggression, they replied, "You are a running dog of the capitalists." He was critical of the communist view, scoffing that they "only know there are classes and do not know there is the state."

In sum, he argued the Soviet Union's policy was based on the state and criticized some of his countrymen. Those who "conduct propaganda for the Soviet Union," he argued, often asserted that they recognized only the existence of classes and did not acknowledge the existence of the state. That, he snorted, was just like the Russian federation basing its policy on the state, but if others used the words *state* or *patriotism*, they were "running dogs of imperialism or capitalism." Was that not what was called, he asked sarcastically, "permitting a *zhou* magistrate to commit arson, while not allowing the common people to light a lamp?"

In the final analysis, though, Soviet Russia was strong enough to get away with its absurd emphasis on class divisions. Its geographical superiority and the strength of its position were far above those of other nations. Even though it had used the theory of class to overturn its government, he admitted, that was no hindrance to its territorial integrity. He was almost certainly thinking of the Chinese Communists, however, when he went on to warn:

> If those whose geographical situation is inferior to Russia's and whose people's concept of the state is weaker each day insistently and clamorously place the theory of class before their countrymen, they are simply destroying their country and race. What social transformation can one speak of? (pp. 24-25)

Thus, for him, the state transcended classes and was definitely not "withering away," even in the homeland of class warfare, Soviet Russia. Hence, he was very much of a "statist."

The Marxist Dictatorship over Soviet Philosophy

In the early 1930s, Zhang was interested in more than just economics and politics. Since the early 1920s, he had been keenly interested in European philosophy—a fascination that was to persist until the end of his days. Moreover, in the fall of 1931, he had just completed two years studying and teaching philosophy in Germany. Finally, as a party leader himself by 1932, he took a special interest in the ideology propounded by the CPSU.

It was clear to him, following his arrival in Moscow, that materialism was a kind of a state religion in Soviet Russia (p. 159). As a result, Marx's authority was so overwhelming that "those who followed it prospered, while those who opposed it died." If a Russian philosopher presented an argument even slightly different from Marx's, he explained, he was denounced by the government as "blasphemous and lawless" (p. 153). Free to differ with the CPSU, Zhang promptly accused it of standing Marx on his head. Instead of political changes following those in the economic base, he pointed out, it had been the other way around in Russia, with War Communism, the NEP, and the FFYP changing the economic base. Production methods had been unable to affect politics, he argued, and hence it was clear the Russian Revolution was not due to the realization of Marxism but to the "Communists' skill in seizing political power" (pp. 156-57). He also criticized the Marxist idea that the economic base produced philosophy. The same base did not produce the same philosophy, he argued. Hobbes and Locke lived in the same environment, but their political thought was different, and the same was true of Fichte, Schelling, and Hegel, who, despite being from the same country and era, differed in thought (p. 162).

His views of the Russian philosophical world were reinforced by his meetings with leading figures in the Soviet capital. The chancellor of Moscow University informed him that whether students pursued the liberal arts, science, or engineering, they had to study *Dialectical Materialism*, *Sociology on the Basis of Historical Materialism*, and *The Economics of Marxism*. Zhang immediately saw parallels in Chinese history. What difference, he asked, was there between that Soviet requirement and Han Wudi's rejection of the Hundred Schools and praise for the Six Classics,[42] and the Ming Dynasty's compiling and fixing The Four Books and The Five Classics as standards for passing or failing for those who took the imperial examinations? The Soviets, too, went from one hundred schools contending to one school. How could that be called the "progress of human culture?" he complained (pp. 153-54).

He also found plenty of evidence of Russian philosophers who had been purged for straying from the party line. A White Russian philosopher and famous specialist on Hegel's logic, Ilyin, he reported, had been imprisoned, only to be released on Lenin's order and exiled to Siberia (p. 166). Zhang also was aware, from Anglo-American philosophy journals, that Abram M. Deborin (1881-1963) had been an authority in Soviet philosophical circles and an opponent of idealism. However, Zhang reported, Lunarchevsky, the former minister of education, had criticized him for the "stink of idealism,"[43] while Stalin had declared Deborin had made absolutely no contributions regarding the practical problems of proletarian revolution.[44] As a result, Deborin went mad and ended up in an insane asylum. Zhang concluded, not surprisingly, that it was "really difficult to be a philosopher in Soviet Russia" (pp. 158-59, 166).

Most exciting for Zhang, the possibility of meeting Nicholas Bukharin, whose *Historical Materialism* Zhang had read, was broached while he was touring the collective farm at "Keluomina." After a lunchtime discussion of historical materialism with members of an American delegation to a Pacific Conference who also were visiting the farm (p. 62),[45] one member asked him whence he came. When he replied Jena, the delegate then inquired whether he had known Rudolf Eucken, to which he replied he had studied philosophy under Eucken in 1920.

> The Russian Cultural Agency guide . . . was sitting beside me and heard I was fond of philosophy. Thus, he said: If you are interested in investigating Russia's philosophical circles, should the agency invite Bukharin, on your behalf, to chat with you? I replied: This is someone I wish to meet, and I am very willing to discuss philosophy with him.
>
> The American delegate heard I would meet Bukharin and, with an unhappy expression on his face, questioned me: You are a disciple of Eucken. Why are you studying materialism? I was aware of the childish directness (*zhiqi shuangzhi*) of Americans and did not . . . debate the matter with him but merely said: When we enter a country, we should inquire about its taboos and customs.

> This also is a point I should be aware of in my investigation of the Russian situation. . . . [The Russian guide's] suggestion that I should meet him [Bukharin] for a talk was just what I had hoped for. Who was to know that . . . [the guide] was not fully aware of the inside story of the relationship between Russian philosophers and politics. He knew only that Bukharin was a philosopher of the government faction (*zhengfu pai*), and still had not heard of his recent frustrating circumstances. In particular, . . . [the guide] did not anticipate that the government would not permit him to talk with a foreigner. . . . [the guide] at first invited me to go to the cultural agency on 7 [September]. When I arrived at the agency, he put off my questions, saying only that he would . . . invite a philosopher from the Communist Research Institute (*Gongchan yanjiuyuan*) to meet with me. Therefore, I . . . realized there was no chance of meeting with Bukharin. (pp. 163-64)[46]

Instead of Bukharin, on 8 September he had a rather depressing session with a scholar in the philosophy section of the Communist Research Institute, who was concurrently a professor at Moscow University.[47] He explained himself earnestly, wrote Zhang, and his appearance was that of a scholar. The conversation was held in German, with Zhang noting that even though Russian scholars were generally well versed in two or three languages, the professor's German was inadequate to express his ideas. When the latter explained that materialism was Russia's "sole central ideology" (*weiyi zhi zhongyang sixiang*), Zhang playfully asked whether it was modeled on Bukharin's theories. In reply, the professor vigorously denounced Bukharin's "errors," defensively adding that he had nothing to do with the "revisionists" (*xiuzhengpai*), but took revolution as his standpoint. In response to Zhang's inquiry about the other wayward philosopher, Deborin, the professor disdainfully explained that Deborin was a "Menshevik idealist." Unsatisfactory as it had been, Zhang tried to arrange another meeting, as well as a visit to Moscow University; however, the professor insisted it was impossible. Even though he was a scholar, Zhang concluded, the professor could not meet foreigners without the government's permission.

The deepest impression the professor made on him, though, was how swiftly philosophers in Soviet Russia could fall out of favor. Once top-notch materialists, Bukharin and Deborin had been replaced. Russia's society and economy had not changed, he pointed out, but the masters of the philosophical world had changed repeatedly. Hence, he declared, it was obvious that changes in philosophy stemmed from thought (or politics) and not the environment (pp. 164-66).

He was also interested in the Communists' opposition to religion. The materialists' opposition to religious principles, he noted, was "especially fierce." As a result, the CPSU opposed the Russian Orthodox Church. The Soviet constitution stripped priests of their civil rights, abolished religious subjects in the school curricula, and banned assemblies of more than three children under eighteen years of age for religious lessons. In recent years, he added, the CPSU had even established the "Union of the Godless," with sixty thousand members and twelve thousand branches. Restrictions on Soviet philosophers upset him, but he felt little empathy for the attacks on Christianity. "A person in Western Europe," he recalled, "angrily told me he regarded the Soviets as lawless and godless," adding that "all humanity should openly attack them." Zhang retorted that "I also came from a 'godless' (*wushangdi*) country. What's strange about that!" (pp. 159-60).

He even found evidence of philosophical struggle in the Museum of the Revolution in Moscow. Describing the displays in the "ideological section," he reached a rather optimistic—and bizarre—conclusion:

> Hegel's portrait hung on top and below it were [those of] [David Friedrich] Strauss and [Ludwig] Feuerbach. Even lower were the [portraits of] Marx and Engels. This [display] was used to show the order of transmission in Marxist philosophy. . . . Ilyin's release and the display of Hegel's portrait . . . show that . . . there are probably some who are dissatisfied with crude materialism and are moving toward Hegelianism. (p. 166)

Despite this rosy view, he ended his visit quite depressed about the state of philosophy in Soviet Russia. He cited a student's criticism of his professor to argue that Soviet "philosophers" were propagandists, incapable of training a new generation of scholars. Moreover, the Russian people were not allowed to think for themselves but had to mouth Marx's words. As a result, thought had been "completely abandoned," and there was no philosophy in Soviet Russia.

He saw hope for the future, though. Sooner or later, he declared, materialism and mechanistic realism (*jixieguan zhi shizailun*) would collapse. Even though the Russian government still would not grant people freedom of thought and speech, it would no longer be able to consider materialism its "sole central ideology." His own beliefs were crystal clear: under no circumstances, he declared, should a country's thought become like "an imperial edict [used to] instruct far and wide" (*shengyu guangxun*), but freedom of thought should be considered the proper way (pp. 166-67).

The Comintern and the Chinese Revolution

As he had throughout the 1920s, in the early 1930s Zhang vented his anxieties about the revolutionary activities of the CI. In SEPL, he had shown himself fairly ignorant of the CI's role in China, as revealed by his focus on an organization that had been defunct for years. By the time he published STLZX, however, six years had passed since the dramatic collapse of the CI effort in China; he had spent two years in Germany, where he had access to materials on the CI;[48] and he had visited "the capital of world revolution," Moscow. Hence, by the early 1930s, he was much more knowledgeable about the CI's activities, especially those concerning his own country.

Organization and Funding of the CI. When his compatriots heard the name "Third International,"[49] Zhang declared, they often associated it with the GMD's "admission of the Communists" (*rongGong*) era, and spoke of the munitions and the political and military advisers, such as Michael Borodin and Galin (General Vasily K. Blyukher), Russia sent to China. It was as if "Third International" came and went like a shadow, he added, and had unlimited assets and talent to assist revolutions in other countries. However, that was a misunderstanding, he asserted, for the "Third International" was "really the general-staff headquarters of world revolution."

He went on to describe how the Russians dominated the CI. They had five seats in the CI's Executive Committee (ECCI), he explained, while other nations had one seat each. In addition, funds for assisting other nations' revolutions came from Russia's Office of Foreign Trade (*Duiwai maoyi ju*), not the CI. Even though the Soviets repeatedly claimed the CI was separate from Russia, he noted, he was not fooled and observed that it was obvious "it is essentially not the 'Third International's' own power" (p. 185).

This time around, he had found the right documents. Even though the CI's operations were secret, he wrote, its goals had been openly recorded in the CI's Statutes.[50] Articles 8 and 9 made clear, he wrote, that more than half the work of the CI was shouldered by the CPSU.[51] Since the approval of the Twenty-one Conditions by the Second Congress of the CI in 1920, the Leninists had demanded that parties representing the laboring classes in other nations change their names to communist parties. Hence, in addition to socialist parties in the assemblies of other countries and the Second International, he explained, the Russians had made sure there were communist parties and the CI (pp. 185-87).

He reflected on his experiences with communism in Europe during the early 1920s. "When I was travelling in Europe in 1920," he recalled, "I often heard members of the German Communist Party mention the . . . Twenty-one Conditions." The objective, he wrote, was to sever relations with socialist parties and reject reformism (*gailiangzhuyi*). As a result, he complained, the conditions emphasized "revolution and insurrection." He went on to translate several of the conditions, the contents of which could not have pleased him.[52] Article 3, for example, opposed bourgeois legality and called on each communist party to create a parallel illegal organization, while article 6 opposed social patriotism and social pacifism (pp. 187-88). He also described the organization of the CI in 1928, as well as its 1927 budget (pp. 189-90). One item in the latter must have heightened his anxiety for China's future. Funds were set aside for a party doctrine school (*dangyi xuexiao*), he noted, that trained foreign students studying in Soviet Russia.[53]

Sun Yat-sen University. During his visit, he was keenly interested in visiting Sun Yat-sen University (SYSU), which had been established in Moscow in the fall of 1925 to commemorate the Chinese leader who had passed away earlier that year. Although it had a short life (1925-30), the school trained many of the future leaders of the CCP, including every one of the famous (infamous?) Twenty-eight Bolsheviks. It also turned out many of the leaders of the Trotskyite movement in China. Even some who were later to become prominent in the GMD also studied at the school, perhaps the most famous being Chiang Kai-shek's son, Ching-kuo. Zhang undoubtedly found it extremely worrisome that, after decades of studying in Europe and America, Chinese students by the hundreds were traveling to Russia to study at SYSU.[54]. As in the case of the CI, the university's funding was provided by the Soviet government.[55]

Despite his interest in SYSU, in 1932 he was confused about it. In recent years, he claimed, SYSU had been retitled the University of the East Named after Stalin (*Shitailin mingyixia zhi dongfang daxue*). This, however, confused it with the only other Russian school where Chinese youth received political training, the Communist University for Toilers of the East Named after Stalin. In addition, his chronology was wrong, for the Communist University had been founded in 1921, more than four years before SYSU, and thus could not have replaced it.[56] He also was unaware that SYSU had closed the year before his visit to Moscow, which makes it unsurprising that his September 1931 request to the Cultural Agency for an introduction was ignored. Even if it had still existed, he would have had a dificult time winning access, for even though, in the words of a former student, it was "not a completely secret institution, it was not open to the public either."[57]

He was right about one aspect, though, and that was the University's role in translating Marxist classics into Chinese. The school undertook a large-scale project to translate the works of Marx, Engels, Lenin, and others. Many such works were rendered into Chinese for the first time, and attempts also were made to standardize Chinese translations of Marxist terms.[58] In the early

1930s, Zhang showed he was aware of this project when he wrote he had heard the university "still had more than a thousand Chinese students who were solely engaged in translating books for importation into our country. Several boxcars (*chexiang*) filled with books, whose quantity may astonish people, have entered our country" (p. 191).[59]

Sometimes these printed materials ended up in the wrong hands when they reached China. Zhang was aware, for example, of the communist documents confiscated in a raid on the Russian Embassy in Peking carried out in early April 1927 by Zhang Zuolin (p. 191). A selection of those materials was published in English the same year in Tientsin.[60] They gave anti-Communists like Zhang clear evidence of Soviet and CI penetration of China. They recorded, wrote Zhang, that from October 1925 to April 1926 Russia spent U.S.$383,000 in China, while its expenditures in Guangdong were "incalculable." All those expenses, he added, were borne by Russia's national treasury (p. 191).

But why, he wondered, did the CI become involved in the Chinese revolution, when there were so many opportunities closer to home in Europe. After pointing out what he called the CI's "successful actions" in the 1918 German Revolution and in the establishment of the Hungarian and Bavarian soviets, he reminded his readers that the March 1921 insurrection in Germany had been put down. The Russians then realized there was no hope of revolution in the countries of Western Europe, he wrote, so they "cooperated with the members of Zhongshan's [Sun Yat-sen's] party." However, in 1927 the opposition to communism in Wuhan revealed the CI had failed again. Hence, as a natural consequence of this collapse of world revolution, the following year the Russians launched the FFYP at home.

The Noulens Affair. Someone asked Zhang why, if post-1928 Russia had abandoned world revolution, the Noulens case had occurred in China (pp. 193-94). In 1931, Hilair Noulens was in charge of the Organization Department of the CI's Far Eastern Bureau in Shanghai. The Department provided funds and agents, not only in Shanghai but throughout Asia. As a result of good detective work and lucky breaks, the Shanghai Municipal Police arrested Noulens and his wife in June 1931 and also seized a large number of communist documents. The Noulens were transferred to Nanjing to await trail by a military court. Sentenced to capital punishment, they ended up—partly as a result of an international campaign claiming their innocence—serving five years. When the Japanese took Nanjing, they were released from jail "somehow" and disappeared from sight.[61]

It was no wonder Zhang was asked about the case, in view of the notoriety of the Noulens. His reply was curious. In a politically corrupt nation (the GMD regime was notoriously corrupt), he argued, the Communist Party had more leeway for action. Even though Stalin had abandoned "world revolution," he explained, if there was an exploitable loophole, he would take advantage of it. The German historian Arthur Rosenberg's assertion that world revolution had been abandoned, Zhang concluded, referred to places where there were no such loopholes. How could Communist Party members be expected not to seize an opportunity? he asked (p. 194).

If he thought being in Moscow was going to offer an opportunity to snoop into the inner story of the CI's adventures in China, though, he was mistaken. "When I was in the Russian capital," he recalled in frustration, "I wanted to study the similarities and differences in the strategies of Russia's Stalinists and Trotskyites regarding the Chinese revolution. I sought [but] could not obtain records of Borodin's and Galin's China trip. I wanted to go to Sun Yat-sen University and question our country's students, but was not allowed to enter its gate."

However, the Cultural Agency did arrange for him to meet a China scholar at the Communist Research Institute, who told him Russia's China specialists were divided into three schools. In addition to the Leningrad and Vladivostock schools, which studied Chinese culture, literature, and languages, there was the Communist Research Institute, which focused on Chinese social history and social problems from a Marxist perspective. The academician told Zhang the Anglo-American-influenced view of China was wrong and reviled the book by Peking University sociologist and liberal, Tao Menghe, entitled *Zhongguo zhi jiating yu nongcun* (The Chinese Family and Village).[62] He told Zhang that Tao made the Chinese village sound like a "harmonious paradise." If it was really like that, the professor protested, how did one explain the White Lotus Society's rebellion, the Taiping Heavenly Kingdom's upheaval, and the 1911 Revolution? Tao's discussion of Chinese society, he told Zhang, plagiarized an Englishman's theory, which he insisted was a great error.

Zhang was not impressed. The professor's words, he wrote scornfully, used a Marxist perspective to investigate China. His conversation with the professor was not a novel and gratifying discussion, he snorted, and had absolutely nothing to do with what he wanted to hear about, namely, the similarities and differences in strategies for the Chinese revolution of Russia's various factions. Hence, he broke off the meeting after a half-hour. He did learn something, however, for the scholar told him there were seven or eight specialists in the China section of the institute. Hence, Zhang concluded ominously, "one may infer that Russia does not forget China for a single day" (pp. 195-96).

Theses on China of the Seventh Enlarged Plenum of the ECCI. Discouraged at his failure to break through the wall of silence in interviews, Zhang adopted another tact. "In Moscow," he recalled, "I sought Russia's strategy for the Chinese revolution but could not find [it]; therefore, I looked for it in the writings of the Russian Revolution's leaders." It was testimony to Trotsky's reputation among Chinese that Zhang placed his *Eguo zhenxiang* (The Real Situation in Russia) first on his list of such works.[63] When he read Trotsky's book, Zhang wrote, he realized that the resolutions of the 1926 Enlarged Plenum of the ECCI, obtained when Zhang Zuolin ransacked the Russian Embassy in Peking, really contained Russia's strategy for the Chinese revolution during the period of GMD-CCP cooperation (p. 196).

The ECCI's Seventh Plenum convened in Moscow from 22 November to 16 December 1926, with China the focus of the debates. It was at this meeting that Stalin reiterated his policy of supporting Chiang Kai-shek and the GMD, against increasing criticism from within the CPSU—leading Zhang to write later that the CPSU under Stalin had failed to "render the slightest bit of help" to the Chinese revolution of the 1920s (p. 135). In the theses, the ECCI ordered the CCP to remain within the GMD, penetrate and steer its government leftward, and implement a radical agrarian program.[64] These policies were laid out in the plenum's eight resolutions, published under the title "Theses on the Situation in China."[65] The version seized in Peking included additional articles (the "Extra Theses"), which Zhang included in the list of nine topics he cited in STLZX (p. 196).

In discussing the "captured" theses, he seemed a little incredulous. In November and December 1926, he recalled, the National Revolutionary Army had already captured Wuhan and Jiujiang, and the Nanjing anticommunist period was near. Yet, he wrote, the CI still firmly believed in GMD-CCP cooperation. Hence, throughout the resolutions the bourgeoisie were exonerated, and the resolutions even vigorously urged the CCP to join the National Government. Usually, he marveled, the CPSU used a class standpoint to decide whether to welcome or reject people, but in the China situation it allowed the CCP to unite with the middle and petty bourgeoisie and even said that some big bourgeoisie could act jointly with the revolutionaries.

His conclusion was harsh. Because the GMD-CCP alliance was unalterable, the Communists did not hesitate to "pervert their normal theory to seek a share of political power." Even though the Communists cooperated with the GMD, their intention of using the latter appeared in their writings. One might say, he wrote, that the Communists were good at pandering to the status quo, but this led to the sudden split and permanent destruction of their equality of power with the GMD (pp. 196-98).

Nearly forty years later, the GMD still smarted from Zhang's criticism. Hence, the following harsh words by Zhang were censored from the 1971 version of STLZX published in Taiwan. After Nanjing and Wuhan came out in opposition to the CCP, he wrote, Trotsky reviled Stalin and Bukharin, who were then in the CI directing the Chinese revolution. Trotsky censured the CCP's lack of an independent position before the Northern Expeditionary Army arrived in Shanghai and carried out its purge of Communists. "It was already crystal clear," Zhang added, "whether the National Government's revolution was a bourgeois or workers-and-peasants-dictatorship type." However, he wrote, the Russians continued to repeat their careless words and regarded the GMD as like-minded. Hence, Trotsky bitterly reproached them, pointing out that in an April 1927 speech, Stalin still praised Chiang Kai-shek as a faithful ally, while in a May speech he praised the Wuhan government as the revolutionary center, after it drove out the right wing. From a purely communist revolutionary standpoint, commented Zhang, all those critical words of Trotsky's took as self-evident that he was right and Stalin was wrong. However, Zhang obviously disagreed with both. Because there were "a thousand changes a day in the revolutionary cause, how can a nation ten thousand *li* away direct another country's revolution, with everything going as one wishes!"

He then excoriated the GMD, CCP, and Russian "politicians":

> I believe that at the beginning of the Sino-Russian alliance in 1922 . . . [Sun Yat-sen] took democratic unification as his goal. [However,] the ambition of the Russians and Chen Duxiu lay in communist revolution. The two [goals] were vastly different, but because of the Russians' strong and healthy organization and infiltration of the disorganized and undisciplined society of our country's gentry (*shidaifu*), Russia's power extended everywhere and was sufficient to send people to their deaths (*zhiren siming*). Moreover, those of my countrymen who love to be leaders simply submitted and obeyed in order to pander to the Russians and foster their own plans. Therefore, the workers and peasants and the military were everywhere controlled by the Communist Party. As for the government leaders, they were merely puppets at the front of the stage. When the Yangtze River [area] was pacified, what the two factions thought was no longer concealed. Each wanted to use the government's power to act, and Nanjing and Wuhan split. Yesterday, they regarded each other as close, while today they are enemies. One may term cooperation between Nationalists and Communists a great fraud among Chinese and Russian politicians, while national reform was just words. ([1933], pp. 200-202)

Writing in the early 1930s, he pointed out that Sino-Russian relations had been restored (supra, n. 5). Citing a 15 December 1932 editorial in *Dagong-*

bao, he noted that some people hoped Russia would repent of its previous errors. They argued:

> We should realize at that time innumerable lives were sacrificed as a result of each other's blind policies. If we really want to promote the old friendship again, we should deal together with the previous mistakes in the provinces. In the past, Russia was fond of using colored glasses in regard to China and believed false reports. Based upon impractical ideals, they forcibly carried out their plans [based on] wishful thinking. (p. 198)

Zhang's response to the editorial was to reiterate what he argued earlier in STLZX. The CPSU, he explained, profoundly believed in Marxism, the class struggle, overthrow of the bourgeoisie, and construction of a proletarian dictatorship. It had been consistent in theory and action and did not tolerate the adoption of one part of its program while rejecting another. It used those four points to execute its policies at home and in foreign countries. Hence, he scathingly criticized the *Dagongbao* editorial: "To say its [Soviet Russia] beliefs are blind and to expect it to abandon its revolutionary means in favor of another plan for China is just like discussing with Christian priests discarding and not reading the Bible or hoping that the Muslims will burn the 'Koran'" (pp. 198-99).

The CI's dessemination of revolution, he asserted, was a policy that brooked no changes. England, Germany, and France had communist parties, he pointed out, but they were all subordinate to the CI. Here again he stressed the differences between Europeans and Chinese, arguing that European communist parties did not harm their own nations. However—referring to the Chinese soviets and the GMD's attempts to "exterminate" them—because of the communist disaster in Jiangxi, Anhui, and Hubei, all China was "disturbed and without peace." Europe's situation was different from China's, he explained, because its governments were different. Its political parties had been founded under law and had the freedom to advocate their political views. They had no right, he added in a slap at the CCP, to raise troops and revolt. Even communist parties in the West, he added, were the same as other parties. In desseminating their views, they had the right to publish newspapers, assemble, and participate in politics. "These," he insisted, "were the only ways to obtain political power." Thinking of the CCP again, he argued that "in countries with complete educational and police administrations, naturally there was no leeway for exploiting the students in schools or colluding with the common people in the countryside." Concluding, he proved but another in a long line of anticommunist strategists in the twentieth century. "The only way to prevent the spread of the Communist Party," he argued, "is to reform the nation's internal administration, make it [the CCP] advance from a secret society to an open political organization, and limit its actions to the dessemination of political views and not allow it to affect the easily swayed peasants and ignorant young people (*nuoruo nongmin yu wuzhi zhi qingnian*)." To put it bluntly, he concluded, we should "first ensure our country has no exploitable political weaknesses, and then it will not be difficult to change the Chen Sheng and Wu Guang kind of Communist Party into an [Ernest] Thalmann and [Marcel] Cachin-style Communist Party"(pp. 199-200).[66]

The Soviet Threat to Northwest China

Although STLZX focused on Russian—and to a lesser extent, Chinese—Communists, following the Manchurian Incident of September 1931 it was the Japanese threat to China that loomed largest. Even though Zhang was busy railing against Japanese encroachments in the Northeast, he still found time to worry about the Soviet threat in the Northwest; that is, he was concerned that the loss of Manchuria would be matched by a similar disaster in Xinjiang. The common denominator in both regions, he argued, was the use of railway construction to carry out aggression against China.

Since the Russo-Japanese War, he explained in STLZX, Japan had created a railway network in Manchuria to carry out its plan to "annex the three provinces." While this "Northeast disaster" was still unresolved, he continued, outside the western frontier rail lines crisscrossed and connected with China's borders. "If there is a similar 18 September Incident in the future," he lamented, "I do not know how our authorities will resist it. My countrymen should urgently awaken to this" (p. 201).

Since it was too late to save the Northeast, he focused on the threat to the Northwest. In 1932, he recalled that when he resided abroad "one or two years ago," he had several encounters with people that made him "sense the danger of Xinjiang being coerced by Russia." He met a German employed by the commercial attache's office in the Chinese Embassy in Germany, he recalled, who was very well versed in Russian. He showed Zhang a Russian railway map, and only then did Zhang realize that the railways Russia had built and was about to build in Central Asia were approaching Xinjiang. Furthermore, in Germany he met two students from Xinjiang, who told him of the flood of Russian cotton imports in their area, which, Zhang added, was a result of the FFYP. Finally, while traveling home on the Trans-Siberian Railroad, he met two Chinese who boarded at a new Siberian station, on their way from

Errata in the Photograph Section

1. There should be a hyphen between the "Chi" and the "kai" in the caption for the top photograph on the first page.

2. The word "nee" in the caption for the bottom photograph on the first page should not be capitalized.

3. The caption for the bottom photograph on the second page should read "*Reproduced from*" (not "for").

4. There should be no hyphen between "Hsu" and "Chi" in the name, Hsu Chi-kai, in the caption for the top photograph on the third page.

5. There should be a comma after "Youyi (second from right)," in the caption for the bottom photograph on the third page.

6. There should be no hyphen in the word "Shanghai" in the caption for the bottom photograph on the fourth page, and the source, *Who's Who in China*, should be italicized.

7. The caption for the bottom photograph on the sixth page should read: "Zhang, his second son, Guochao ("Dragon") and his first son, Kuo-liu ("Tiger"), at Moganshan (Zhejiang), summer 1936." *Courtesy of Chang Kuo-liu.*

8. The caption for the top photograph on the last page should read: "Zhang's wife, Wang Shiying, surrounded by her children, Diana Chang and June Tung (front row from left to right), and Guochao, Kuo-liu, and Guokang (rear from right to left) at the Mid-Autumn Festival in Shanghai, 1940." *Courtesy of Chang Kuo-liu.*

9. The second name in the caption for the bottom photograph on the last page should read "Guokang," not "Guokong."

Zhang's father, Zuze (Runzhi). *Reproduced from the album of Hsu Chikai, with the permission of Pang-Mei Natasha Chang.*

Zhang's mother (Nee Liu). *Reproduced from the album of Hsu Chi-kai, with the permission of Pang-Mei Natasha Chang.*

The Political Information Society (Zhengwen she) in Japan, 1907; Zhang is in the front row, fourth from the left. *Reproduced from Zhenglun, courtesy of the Institute for Research in the Humanities, Kyoto University.*

Zhang in St. Petersburg, April 1913.
Reproduced for Xianfa Xinwen, courtesy of the East Asian Collection, Hoover Institution.

Zhang with the famous poet, Xu Zhimo, sometime before Xu divorced Zhang's sister, Youyi (Yu-i), in 1922. *Reproduced from the album of Hsu-Chi-kai, with the permission of Pang-Mei Natasha Chang.*

Zhang (left) with his sister, Youyi (second from right) and Liu Wendao and his wife, Liao Shishao, in France in fall 1921 or winter 1922. *Reproduced from the album of Hsu Chi-kai, with the permission of Pang-mei Natasha Chang.*

Zhang (right), Hans Driesch, and Qu Shiying, Beijing University, 1923. *Reproduced from H. and M. Driesch, Fern-Ost. Als Gaste Jungchinas, with permission from F. A. Brockhaus, Leipzig, 1925.*

Zhang as president of the National Institute of Self-Government in Shang-hai, 1925. *Reproduced from* Who's Who in China, 3rd. ed., 1925.

Zhang's wife, Wang Shiying, whom he married in 1925. *Courtesy of June Tung.*

Zhang (seated fourth from right) with his brothers and sisters in Shanghai in 1927 at the funeral of their parents. *Reproduced from the album of Hsu Chi-kai, with the permission of Pang-Mei Natasha Chang.*

Zhang and his wife during their 1929-31 stay in Germany. *Reproduced with permission from Zhuanji Wenxue.*

Zhang, his first son, Guochao "Dragon," and his second son, Kuo-liu "Tiger," in Lushan, summer 1936. *Courtesy of Chang Kuo-liu.*

Zhang (front left), brother Kia-ngau and his daughter, Rosemary (front right and center), and brother Jiahzu with his wife, Xiaomei, Chongqing, 1939. *Courtesy of Chang Kuo-liu.*

Zhang in Qingshuixi, Sichuan, March 1939. *Courtesy of Chang Kuo-liu.*

Zhang at the Institute of National Culture, Dali, Yunnan, 1939-41. *Courtesy of Chang Kuo-liu.*

Zhang's wife, Wang Shiying, surrounded by her children (front row from right to left) Diana Chang and June Tung, (rear from right to left) Guochao, Kuo-liu, and Guokang at the Mid-Autumn Festival in Shanghai 1940. *Courtesy of Chang Kuo-liu.*

Wang Shiying (front row, third from left) with her son Guokong "Leopard" (on her left), her daughter Diana (on her right), and the staff of the Institute of National Culture following their arrival in Dali in August, 1941. *Courtesy of June Tung.*

Xinjiang to the Harbin Engineering University. In response to his questioning, they told him it took only a few days to get from Xinjiang to the Trans-Siberian Railroad. These three meetings, he noted, made him keenly aware of Xinjiang's danger (p. 202).

He clearly associated Russian railway building with their encroachments in Asia. After the Trans-Siberian Railroad was completed (1903), he recalled, Outer Mongolia became an independent region, that is, was lost to the Chinese empire. At present, he added, some of Russia's Central Asian rail lines approached "our" Outer Mongolia, he added, and warned that because of those lines, "the doorway of Tianshan's northern route is already under control of the Russians" (pp. 202-5).[67] Moreover, in 1930, he continued, Russia completed the Turksib (Turkestan-Siberian) Railway, which "reached almost to the Chinese frontier."[68] According to an official in the Soviet Railway Commissariat, this railway, which paralleled the Xinjiang border for four hundred miles, was also built to "prevent the penetration of Western European capitalism into Sinkiang."[69] Clearly, Zhang thought that where Russian railways went, trouble could not be far behind. Hence, in 1932 he declared the "outbreak of a Central Asian war is not far off" (p. 202).

Sounding nostalgic for the lost Central Asian empires of the Han, Ming, and Qing, he called on his readers to remember how much territory China had lost in that part of the world during the last years of the Qing. "From Tannu Tuva in Outer Mongolia in the North to the Pamir Plateau in the South," he lamented, "how much territory have we given up without a fight?" Although the Russians' "plan to nibble away at our Western frontier had long been clear," in the past they did not have a rail line connecting Central Asia and Siberia. At present, though, they had the Turksib Railway, and thus the Red Army could "set out in the morning and enter Xinjiang in the evening," while China had only 20,000 to 30,000 extremely decadent soldiers in Xinjiang, divided between the routes north and south of Tianshan. There was absolutely no possibility, he complained, that troops would be sent from China proper. Hence, he morosely concluded, Xinjiang was at Russia's mercy, and he feared that only a lack of planning on Russia's part would keep Xinjiang from becoming another Outer Mongolia and Manchuria.

Russia's new line also would harm China economically, for Russia had built power stations, weaving mills, a chemical industry, and granaries, as well as planted cotton fields along the railroad. Thus, he concluded, "Xinjiang's economic power is completely in Russia's hands" (pp. 205-6).[70] Finally, although he did not mention it, completion of the Soviet line also contributed to an increase in the Russian political presence in Xinjiang.[71]

He then stressed the importance of good communications for warfare. He asked his readers to think of the fighting in Shanghai (1932) and Manchuria (1931-32), where there were roads between rear areas and headquarters. However, the situation in the rest of China was different. Because China lacked Japan's modern communications, it took far more time, he complained, for China to reinforce the provinces of Liaoning and Heilongjiang from Jehol (Rehe) and Chahar than for the Japanese to transport soldiers from Japan to the South Manchurian Railway.

When the Japanese Army fought the Nineteenth Route Army in Shanghai, he continued, it made sense that soldiers north of the Yangtze should cross the river. However, the Japanese prevented such a crossing by stationing one or two warships between Nanjing and Zhenjiang. A steady stream of Japanese troops arrived in Shanghai and even landed at Liuhe Harbor, while China was helpless, due to its lack of modern communications. Not surprisingly, he concluded that "if a nation has modern communications, its territory survives; otherwise, it perishes," which line of argument brought him back to the FFYP. Echoing Sun Yat-sen's obsession with creating a railway network,[72] Zhang argued that all projects mentioned in the FFYP section on communications "should be imitated by our country" (p. 202).

Having established that general principle, he urged his compatriots to consider whether Xinjiang would survive in the Republic. In fact, he added, the danger to the western frontier was not limited to Xinjiang. He insisted that "in the future, an international war will begin there" (pp. 206-7). At present, he added, there was no place west of Xinjiang that was not a "fuse for an Anglo-Russian war." In this instance at least, he believed Russia's claims that it was threatened by the outside world and granted that there was reason for Russia's "eagerness to make arrangements for national defense" (pp. 207-8).

Returning to the Russian threat to China, he noted that a German specialist on railways, A. Runkel, had divulged that Russia used its railroads in Central Asia to advance and spy on China, to press on toward China's door (pp. 208-9). Hence, Zhang could see nothing but disaster for China in the future in the Northwest. "Alas!" he wrote, "The Japanese Manchurian railways have already conquered three provinces. Even though the railway outside the gates of Xinjiang [Turksib Railroad] has not yet entered our territory . . . we have already been encircled. The Northeast trouble is not yet over, but disaster on the western frontier is already brewing." He worried that even though he repeatedly issued this warning, he would not be able to arouse his countrymen's "distressed feelings and perplexed anxiety" but would merely contribute to their "sitting anxiously and sighing," and "increase their feeling that national affairs cannot be managed" (p. 209).

Opposition to the CCP

While advocating emulation of much from Soviet Russia, Zhang lambasted the CCP. The Russian Revolution, he asserted, had taken the path of construction, which was "very different . . . from the Communist Party that burns and kills at various places in our country." In response, he advocated the age-old Chinese technique of using the weapons of barbarians to control barbarians, just as in 1920 he had proposed adopting socialism to ward off social revolution (chapter 2):

> If intelligent and broad-minded people in our country are unwilling to recognize Russia's value and understand the contents of Russia's plans, then the violence of our country's Communist calamity is just beginning. To save ourselves hereafter . . . [we must] adopt communism's constructive part in order to destroy its destructive side. (preface no. 2, pp. 3-4)

He was prepared for those who might argue that communism's achievements were inseparable from its beliefs and practices. Some maintained, he admitted, that what he proposed was precisely what Communists deeply loathed. It would be impossible, according to his critics, to adopt the FFYP while abandoning class struggle and one-party dictatorship, to reap the achievements of the communist revolution while refusing to sacrifice for it. His reply was to insist his words were "precautions against possible danger" and warnings that the Communist Party was in terrible shape. He did not neglect to point out that even though he had visited Russia for only a few days, he had studied Russian affairs for more than ten years. He had prepared before he went to Moscow, he insisted, and did not obtain everything from on-site observations (preface no. 2, p. 4). It was his usual practice, one might add, to combine travel and study, as he had done by sojourning in Japan and Europe, as well as traveling widely in China during the 1920s and 1930s.

In any event, in 1933 he was worried about the struggle between the GMD and the CCP, which then took the form of a series of encirclement campaigns carried out by the GMD against communist areas:

> How many youth have died, what have been the costs of the Jiangxi bandit areas, how great an influence has the Red calamity had on the loss of the four Northeastern provinces, what will be the final outcome of the struggle between the government armies and the communist bandits—I crane my neck and gaze southward. These are not groundless worries! ([1933], preface no. 1, p. 2)

When it came to communist politics, he expressed alarm and bitterness. Intellectual circles were unaware, he wrote, that it was he who had coined the

Chinese translation of *soviet* (*suweiai*). If a copyright could be granted, he insisted, then those three characters had appeared first in his 1919 translation of the Soviet Russian constitution, published in *Jiefang yu gaizao*. However, far from proudly claiming credit, as he had done so often before, in 1932 he hoped the three characters would be "stamped out of Chinese dictionaries of politics as soon as possible" (p. 105).

In addition to the problem of communism within China, there was the threat of its connection with the worldwide communist movement. There was no doubt in Zhang's mind that the Twenty-one Conditions imposed on all communist parties in 1920 meant the CCP was "part of the Third International and . . . under its direction." Now leader of the NSP, he complained that members of the CCP called opposition parties in China "bourgeoisie," "feudal forces," "the comprador class," and "running dogs of imperialism." They were "nearly at the end of their wits," he wrote, "to create new kinds of terms to describe them. Thus, [they] strive to meet the obligations of the word 'denounce' in Article 1 of the CI's conditions."[73]

He compared the CCP with communist parties in Europe and found it lacking:

> Its [the CCP's] work in the communist movement is completely unlike the workers' movements in England and France, which strove for factory laws and labor insurance when they began. It [CCP] comes straight to the point (*dandaozhiru*) to seize political power. Hence, it focuses on illegal organizations and propaganda in the armed forces. Their [the Communists] only fear is that civil war will not occur, in [their] pursuit of the worsening of the situation. If one talks of the awfulness of foreign aggression by enemy countries and says we should [put up] a united resistance to foreign aggression, it [CCP] simply makes light of this. Speaking from a class standpoint, they do not know that . . . "fatherland" was an unalterable dogma before the establishment of the proletarian dictatorship. (pp. 188-89)

He went on to clarify his own differences with the CCP (chapters 2 and 3). "In regard to foreign things," he explained, "the people of our group (*wobei*; he and his NSP colleagues?) have always calmly investigated their suitability to national conditions and then decided whether to accept or reject them. We have never ventured to eschew the familiar for the exotic, and we especially do not enjoy seeking to perfectly imitate the exotic (*qiu weimiao weixiao yu yewu*). This is where we are different from Chen Duxiu and his group" (p. 105).

As so often before and after, he retold his story of witnessing the communist uprising in Jena in March 1921, the origins of his profound opposition to communist parties and the CI, and his dismay after discovering, following his return from Europe in 1922, that communism had spread to China (pp. 105-6; see also chapter 3). As in 1927, he especially worried about communism's hold on Chinese youth. During the past several years, he wrote in 1932, "several hundred thousand young people have fallen into the Communist trap" (*wei gongchanzhuyi xianyu gangluozhe*). Moreover, he continued, "the Jiangxi-Hubei communist extermination districts have wasted ten and even one hundred million in national currency" (p. 106).

Thus, he considered the CCP much worse than European communist parties. In recent years, he wrote, the CCP had declared independence from both Russians and GMD. However, as early as the period in which they were admitted to the GMD, they had hidden among the peasants and in the army. During the Northern Expedition, he noted, they were thoroughly familiar with the strategically important terrain. Therefore, the Chinese Communists, he complained, were

> not like [the communist parties that act as] the masterminds (*zhunao*) of the workers' movement in European countries, but are bandits who assemble in the mountains and forests in response to a whistle (*xiaoju shanlin zhi tufei*). For assistance, they use the Red Army's organization and Marx's doctrines, and hope that in a short time they can seize political power. They cannot be compared to European socialist parties. One may say they are the twentieth-century's Chen Sheng and Wu Guang. (p. 198)[74]

In equating the CCP to these late-Qin peasant rebels, Zhang in effect excluded it from the ranks of the socialist movement. In addition to the socialist speaking, this might well have been his Confucian streak expressing the traditional distaste for peasant rebels.

Conclusion

Zhang went to Russia in 1931, just as he had in 1916, with questions weighing on his mind. Lenin and Stalin had been in charge for fourteen years, he mused. Was their longevity due to revolutionary sacrifices, he wondered. What had they achieved after the revolution? What were the similarities and differences between the governments of Lenin and Stalin (p. 2)? He made it clear, in addressing such questions, that he wrote from the standpoint of an outsider and a Chinese and was not prepared to "echo what others say and simply beat the drum for them" (preface no. 1, p. 2). Lest his readers suspect him of sympathizing with the CPSU, he also made it plain that he and the Communists were unequivocal opponents, that, as he put it, whatever he admired Communists considered wrong, while whatever they admired he thought wrong.

He pithily summed up his differences with communism. He considered one-party rule wrong, he declared, while Communists took it as the secret of revolutionary success. Having discovered that it was impossible to bring all land under the control of the state and collective farms, he continued, the Communists were forced to allow half of Russia's land to remain in private hands. Far from ruing that development, he praised it as a "sign that Russia's policies were gradually conforming to human nature." Finally, he saw nationalism winning out over communism in Soviet Russia. Despite the fact that class struggle was the communists' basic theory, he explained, since the CER incident of 1929, the Russian slogan had been "to protect Russia's rights." That, he crowed, was evidence that Russia "took state and nation (*guojia minzu*) as its standpoint" (preface no. 2, pp. 1-2).

The Soviet promise following World War I to return the territories czarist regimes had taken from China and cancel the unequal treaties, combined with the disappointments China had suffered at the Versailles Peace Conference, had reoriented some Chinese away from the West and toward the Soviet Union. Similarly, in the early 1930s, the World Depression turned Zhang's gaze—in economics, at least—away from his heretofore favorite models of England and Germany toward Soviet Russia. In STLZX, he no longer waxed eloquently on the superiority of Western Europe over Soviet Russia, as he had in SEPL in 1927.

It is clear there were four driving forces behind his reappraisal of Soviet Russia. One was certainly nationalism, which led him to search for ways to recover China's lost sovereignty. The second was his anti-imperialism (although he disliked facile slogans). The third was his animus against the home-grown variety of communism, the CCP, which he thought more like traditional Chinese peasant rebels than a modern political party. Finally, he worried that because China was poor and chaotic, it might have to endure party struggles like those between the Stalinists and Trotskyites in Russia before implementation of the Soviets' FFYP (p. 2).

His admiration for the Russian experience also could be viewed as part of the upsurge in popularity of the Soviet Union among West Europeans and Americans in the late 1920s and early 1930s. This was partly due to the estrangement of these people from their own societies, making them ripe for the appeals of a "model society" elsewhere.[75] Hence, the FFYP naturally attracted their admiration. Since Zhang had spent eight of his forty-four years in Western Europe by 1931, he was influenced by what he read and heard there when the time came to formulate his reactions to the Soviet Union. Hence, one can see a shift in his thinking, in his praise for Soviet economic policies coupled with his negative assessment of Western Europe's ability to cope with

World Depression.

However, he was not merely copying the attitudes of Europeans and Americans when he enthused about the Russian "experiment," for he had his own powerful motivation. Hailing from a backward China beset with imperialism, he was driven to find a model for his country's decades-old quest for "wealth and power." Whether the "pilgrims" were Western or Chinese like Zhang, both were disillusioned with the way things were going at home and hence both were open to the appeals of Stalin's FFYP.

Moreover, Zhang had an even more practical reason for his interest in the Soviet "experiment," for underlying his attempts to winnow Soviet policies for the best models for China was the fact that he was no longer simply a Chinese intellectual but leader of a political party of his own. Hence, much of what he admired in Stalin's Russia—such as the planned economy, state socialism, and the call for national economic self-sufficiency—showed up in the NSP platform he and his colleagues drafted two months before publication of his four-article series on Soviet Russia.[76]

Today's reader will be startled by Zhang's admiration for Stalinist industrial and agricultural policies and protest the price of those "victories." In his 1932-33 writings, he showed little sign of comprehending those enormous costs (although in SEPL he seemed fully aware of them). And why should he? He had, after all, stopped in Moscow for only a few days, hardly time enough to penetrate the secrets of the regime (as he often complained), and spoke mostly with those assigned by the CPSU to meet him. Moreover, the worst of the famine that killed millions of collectivized peasants occurred in 1932-33,[77] following his visit. Then too, in a China beset with the White Terror, perhaps it was difficult for him to secure up-to-date reports on the difficulties besetting his model collective farms. When all is said and done, however, the FFYP about which he enthused constituted the true beginning of Soviet totalitarianism.

Like many thinkers, he was not always consistent in his views. An anti-communist—although a selective one, we now know—he also was a socialist naturally opposed to capitalism. Was his standpoint that of capitalism? he asked in 1932. The answer was a swift and simple no. However, it was better than communism, he thought, for it corresponded to economic principles and avoided the corruption that came with government-operated enterprises, while communism engaged in forcible seizures and talked of obliterating everything (preface no. 2, p. 1).

The reader cannot help but be struck, after noting his descriptions of life under communism in Soviet Russia, with the obvious parallels to what was to come in China after 1949, for example, such cataclysmic events as the Anti-

Rightist Movement and the Cultural Revolution. He understood the cavalier approach to violence of the Communists and was deeply disturbed. In Bukharin's speech to the CI in 1921, he noted, the Russian had argued that it was impossible to make an omelet without breaking eggs–that is, revolution had its price. There was no need to fear temporary destruction, Bukharin insisted, for that was the way to an even higher level of economic life. Zhang, however, was outraged by this facile analogy between omelets and revolution. In the transformation of a nation, he wrote, some people toppled others, while some were eliminated:

> If we speak of eggs, they are . . . products consumed daily. In one day, one can break ten million without a thought. How can the worth of each individual who is being removed within the country be regarded as an egg? How can this [elimination] be viewed as insignificant as breaking an egg? Nevertheless, the Russian Bolsheviks regard revolution as simply the act of breaking eggs. (p. 3)

Books such as Zhang's on Soviet Russia clearly demonstrate that, unlike many of his countrymen, by the late 1940s he had long been acquainted with communist practices, such as treating party members and laborers better than those who worked with their minds. Thus, it was not surprising that he chose lonely exile in the spring of 1949 rather than stay in communist China and undergo the repression he clearly foresaw.

Notes

1. Since his wife and daughter were with him in Germany, they must have accompanied him on this return trip home via Russia. However, he did not mention them in the account of his journey in STLZX (hereafter, page references in the text in this chapter pertain to this source).

2. Ibid., preface no. 2, pp. 3, 105.

3. Ibid., 1; preface no. 1, 2; 105. Four chapters in this work were published earlier in the NSP journal. Zhang Junmai, "Wo zhi Eguo guan" (My Views of Russia), *Zaisheng* 1, nos. 1, 5-7 (1932). He then added seven chapters and published the result in November 1933 as STLZX. Preface no. 1 is dated 10 October 1933, while preface no. 2 is dated March 1932. The 1971 Taiwan edition of this work was censored; for expurgated passages, I have used the 1933 edition published by Zaisheng zazhi she in Peiping, which will be cited in the text as [1933]. This first edition was advertised repeatedly in *Zaisheng*, with Zhang praised as "utterly different from those ordinary [people] in the country who view Soviet Russia through colored glasses." *Zaisheng* 2, no. 4 (1934), back cover.

4. John Israel, *Student Nationalism in China, 1927-1937* (Stanford: Stanford University Press, 1966), 103.

5. The above description of communist influence on students during the early 1930s is drawn from ibid., 101-3. Resumption of Sino-Soviet relations, which had been disrupted in 1927, was announced in Geneva by China's representative to the League of Nations, Yan Huiqing (W. W. Yen), and the Soviet foreign minister, M. Litvinov. MacKerras and Chan, *Modern China*, 344; BDRC, 4: 51.

6. Treadgold, *Twentieth Century Russia*, 193-95.

7. Ibid., 196-97.

8. In a commercial treaty signed in August 1924, Prime Minister Ramsay MacDonald promised Russia a large loan. When his government was replaced by that of conservative Stanley Baldwin in November, however, the treaty was scrapped. When the Baldwin government remained in power for five years (1924-29), the Russians finally realized there was no hope of a British loan and in 1927 decided to go it alone. STLZX, 28; William L. Langer, comp., *An Encyclopedia of World History* (Boston: Houghton Mifflin, 1952), 968.

9. Unable to procure a copy of the plan, he relied on *The Economic Life of the Soviet Union* (New York: Macmillan, 1931), whose American author, Calvin B. Hoover, had spent three years working for the Soviet Social Sciences Research Council. He translated the sections on industry and agriculture in Hoover's chapter on the planned economy. For the English original, see Hoover, 307-9.

10. Treadgold, *Twentieth Century Russia*, 206.

11. James Legge, *The Four Books* (Taipei: Yishi chubanshe, 1971), 379 (with slight editing).

12. According to Mencius, "Those who labour with their minds govern others; those who labour with their strength are governed by others." Ibid., 249-50.

13. Treadgold, *Twentieth Century Russia*, 202-06.

14. Clarkson, *A History of Russia*, 595.

15. For details of Mo's negotiations, which involved twenty-two "fruitless" meetings in Moscow between April and November 1931, see BDRC, 3: 38.

16. He was not to be the last "liberal" Chinese intellectual to visit a collective farm. Ding Wenjiang visited one during his 1933 trip to the Soviet Union. Furth, *Ting Wen-chiang*, 209.

17. Treadgold, *Twentieth Century Russia*, 204-5.

18. On the astonishing blindness of Western visitors to the "new Russia," see Paul Hollander, *Political Pilgrims: Travels of Western Intellectuals to the Soviet Union, China, and Cuba* (New York: Oxford University Press, 1981; reprint, Harper Colophon, 1983), chap. 4.

19. The room in the log dwelling he was shown had nothing but a bed, bench, and photographs on the wall, as well as a "dirty quilt that was intolerable to look at" (p. 62). Arriving in Russia two years later, Ding Wenjiang was to form similar impressions of the collective farm's poverty and dirt. Eating lunch in a dining room with a dirt floor, wooden benches, and a view of the stable outside, he was reminded of the filthy teahouses in Yunnan. Furth, *Ting Wen-chiang*, 209.

20. Zhang demonstrated his belief that Stalin's speech was crucial by including a translation as an appendix to his chapter on the collective farms. The speech also revealed Stalin's character, added Zhang, as one reluctant either to rashly advance or to lag behind others. Zhang noted that between the lines Stalin always admonished party members neither to go too far nor to do too little. STLZX, 66-73.

21. According to Mencius, "If large shoes and small shoes were the same price, who would make them?" Legge, *The Four Books*, 256 (slightly edited).

22. Treadgold, *Twentieth Century Russia*, 204-5; Clarkson, *A History of Russia*, 593, 595.

23.Treadgold, *Twentieth Century Russia*, 211.

24. Chang Kia-ngau probably visited his brother in Germany in December 1929, while on a world tour lasting from May of that year until March 1930. He also visited Germany in early October but on that occasion spent three weeks in Berlin Hospital recovering from surgery for hemorrhoids. Like his brother, he stopped in Moscow (mid-June 1929), where he spent ten days studying the Soviet economic system. Yao Songlin, *Zhang Gongquan xiansheng nianpu chugao* (First Draft of a Chronological Biography of Chang Kia-ngau), 2 vols. (Taipei: Zhuanji wenxue she, 1981), 1: 94, 95-96; Phyliss A. Waldman, "Chang Kia-ngau and the Bank of China: The Politics of Money" (Ph.D. diss., University of Virginia, 1984), 268-69.

25. In early September 1926, the British shelled Wanxian in retaliation for the detention of two of their vessels and killed and wounded a thousand people, according to the Peking government. MacKerras and Chan, *Modern China*, 308.

26. In the early nineteenth century, Johann C. Friedrich von Schiller (1759-1805) taught history at Jena University. Will Durant, *The Story of Philosophy* (New York: Simon & Schuster, 1926; Washington Square Press, 1952), 293. Zhang taught philosophy at the same university during his 1929-31 stay in Germany.

27. Zhang took the term "tireless teaching," which Legge translated as "instructing others without being wearied," from the *Analects*. Legge, *The Four Books*, 195.

28. The Weimar Constitution had specified a uniform type of elementary school for all children (Articles 146, 147). It also stipulated admission to secondary schools on the basis of talent rather than parents' financial status. In the end, however, these fine principles were circumvented. Gordon Craig, *Germany, 1866-1945* (New York: Oxford University Press, 1978; Oxford University Press paperback, 1980), 423.

29. By the end of the nineteenth century, Germany's illiteracy rate was only 0.05 percent, the lowest in Europe. Ibid., 186-87.

30. In the 1933 edition, he used the German term, *Sturm tempo*.

31. On Ricci and Verbiest, see Jonathan Spence, *To Change China: Western Advisers in China, 1620-1960* (New York: Little, Brown,1969; Penguin, 1980), 5-6, 23-33.

32. Zhang probably was citing William Henry Chamberlain's *Soviet Russia: A Living Record and a History* (Boston: Little, Brown, 1930).

33. Levenson, *Liang Ch'i-ch'ao*, 210-11.

34. John K. Fairbank, *The United State and China*, 4th ed. (Cambridge: Harvard University Press, 1983), 229-30; John K. Fairbank, *The Great Chinese Revolution,*

1800-1985 (New York: Harper & Row, 1986), 96.

35. Legge, *The Four Books*, 305.

36. Zhang was behind the times, for in December 1922 this body had been renamed the "All-Union Congress [of Soviets]." Treadgold, *Twentieth Century Russia*, 153-54.

37. Elsewhere, Zhang asserted that communists always took class as their standpoint and considered owning property evil and unvirtuous, while being propertyless was thought to be good and virtuous. STLZX, 120.

38. Zhang's phrase echoed traditional Chinese sayings such as, "If you win, you become a high official; if not, you are boiled alive" (from the *Zuozhuan*), and "Winners become rulers, while losers are outlaws."

39. De Bary, Chan, and Tang, *Sources of Chinese Tradition*, 2:110-11.

40. It was common in Soviet Russia to refer to *State and Revolution* as a "new bible" for the Bolshevik Party. Clarkson, *A History of Revolution*, 462.

41. James P. Scanlan, "Lenin, V.I.," in Paul Edwards, ed., *The Encyclopedia of Philosophy*, 3 and 4: 434-435.

42. Literally, the Six Arts (*liu yi*). Traditionally, this term referred to the Six Classics: the Books of *History*, *Odes*, *Changes*, *Rites*, *Music*, and the *Spring and Autumn Annals*. The *Book of Music* was lost. Wing-tsit Chan, trans. and comp., *A Source Book in Chinese Philosophy* (Princeton: Princeton University Press, 1963), 17 (n. 10).

43. Zhang referred readers to Lunarchevsky's article, "Hegel in Russia," for details. STLZX, 158.

44. Deborin was an editor of the journal, *Under the Banner of Marxism*. In 1931, he and the other editors were attacked for "overevaluation of Plekhanov" and alleged "leanings towards idealism and Menshevism." Treadgold, *Twentieth Century Russia*, 265.

45. Although at first glance, this appears to be a reference to a conference of the Institute of Pacific Relations (IPR), this was not the case. The Soviets set up an affiliated council in 1931, but it did not join the IPR until 1934. Moreover, it did not participate in an IPR conference until 1936, when some Soviets attended the Yosemite meeting. John N. Thomas, *The Institute of Pacific Relations: Asian Scholars and American Politics* (Seattle: University of Washington Press, 1974), 16. The delegation Zhang encountered consisted of Carter and his son, a jurist named Carpenter, and another unnamed person. Zhang, *Shitailin zhixia*, 163. This sounds suspiciously like a delegation from the IPR, which was trying to persuade the Soviets to join then. "Carter" could have been Edward C. Carter, then serving as secretary of the American Council of the IPR. However, he did not travel to the Soviet Union until 1934. Thomas, *Institute of Pacific Relations*, 4, 11-12.

46. The romanization of the Chinese characters for the guide's name is "Bolaote." Elsewhere in STLZX, Zhang used *Gongchanzhuyi yanjiuyuan* for "Communist Research Institute."

47. The Russian's professor's name in Chinese was "Citefusike."

48. In his 1933 work, he drew on Arthur Rosenberg's *Geschichte des Bolschewismus von Marx bis zur Gegenwart* (Berlin: Europaische Verlagsanstalt, 1932). Rosenberg was formerly a member of the German Communist Party and the Executive Committee of the CI. STLZX, 191-93; Julius Braunthal, *History of the International*, trans. John Clark, 3 vols. (New York: Praeger, 1967), 2: 5 (n. 1).

49. Zhang often enclosed "Third International" in quotation marks. Was it because, as a socialist, he thought it an upstart and not a true successor to the Second International?

50. The statutes had been adopted at the Second CI Congress, held in Moscow in July and August 1920. For the complete English text, see Braunthal, *History of the International*, 2: 533-37.

51. According to Article 8, the "chief work of the Executive Committee falls on the party of that country where, by decision of the world congress, the Executive Committee has its seat [i.e., the Soviet Union]." Article 9 describes the responsiblities of this Moscow-based ECCI. Ibid., 2: 536.

52. Zhang translated Articles 1, 3, 4, 6, 12, 13, 16, and 18. For an English text of all Twenty-one Conditions, see ibid., 2: 537-42.

53. This may have been a reference to the Communist University for the Toilers of the East, a school set up to train revolutionary cadres from the East. Wang Fan-hsi, *Memoirs of a Chinese Revolutionary*, 47.

54. Sheng Yueh, *Sun Yat-sen University in Moscow and the Chinese Revolution* (Lawrence: Center for East Asian Studies, University of Kansas, 1971), preface; 1-4, 11. Sheng was one of the Twenty-eight Bolsheviks.

55. According to a former student, funds were provided by the Profintern, whose main source of income was the Central Council of Labor Unions of the Soviet Union. Ibid., 42.

56. Ibid., 154.

57. Ibid., 31. In his reminiscences, Mao Yiheng argued that SYSU was closed to nonrevolutionary Chinese scholars following Hu Shi's 1926 visit. Zhang, Mao recalled, "tried unsuccesfullly to gain admittance while he was in Moscow." Mao Yiheng, *Emeng huiyilu* (Taipei: Wenhai chupan she, 1974 [1954]), 166; cited in Sheng Yueh, *Sun Yat-sen University*, 144. Apparently, neither Mao nor Sheng realized the university had closed the year before Zhang's attempt to visit.

58. Ibid., 4.

59. In a work published two decades later, Zhang wrote that the Soviets had founded the Communist University for the Toilers of the Orient [East] and Sun Yat-sen University, adding that "to both of these institutions thousands of Chinese young men were smuggled to receive training. The collected works of Marx, Engels, Lenin, and Stalin were translated into Chinese by the Chinese students, and millions of copies printed and sent to China on the Siberian railway." Chang, *Third Force*, 72.

60. N. Mitarevsky's *World Wide Soviet Plots* was published in Tientsin in 1927.

61. Frederic Wakeman, Jr., *Policing Shanghai, 1927-1937* (Berkeley: University of California Press, 1995), 147-51.

62. Born in the same year as Zhang (1887), Tao (L. K. Tao, Tao Lu-kung) was a returned student from both Japan and England. After serving as professor of sociology at Peking University, 1914-28, he became director of the Institute of Social Sciences, Academia Sinica. Again like Zhang, Tao was an unofficial delegate to the Paris Peace Conference in 1919 and served as a member of the People's Political Council during World War II. In 1915, he published (with Leong Yew Koh) *Village and Town Life in China*. *Who's Who in China*, 5th ed., 296; 6th ed., 193. For identification of Tao as a liberal, see Chow Tse-tsung, *The May Fourth Movement*, 216.

63. Zhang probably read the English translation by Max Eastman published in New York in 1928. As we have seen, Zhang was an admirer of Eastman's *After Lenin's Death*.

64. Conrad Brandt, Benjamin Schwartz, and John K. Fairbank, *A Documentary History of Chinese Communism* (Cambridge: Harvard University Press, 1952), 32-33; Wilbur and How, *Missionaries of Revolution*, 356-58.

65. For an analysis and the English text, see Robert C. North and Xenia J. Eudin, *M. N. Roy's Mission to China: The Communist-Kuomintang Split of 1927* (Berkeley: University of California Press, 1963), 39-43, 131-45.

66. Although he was leader of the German Communist Party, Thalmann worked within a democratic framework, which was why Zhang praised him. In the presidential elections of 1925, the German Communist Party chief received 2 million votes, while in April 1932 he got 3.7 million votes. However, in view of Zhang's anti-CI views, one has to wonder about his admiration, for Thalmann had a reputation as a Soviet stooge. Craig, *Germany*, 558; Pinson, *Modern Germany*, 417. In the 1930s, Cachin was a member of the triumvirate that dominated the French Communist Party. Braunthal, *History of the International*, 2: 423.

67. The Tian Mountains are north of the Tarim Basin in Xinjiang.

68. Martin R. Norins, *Gateway to Asia: Sinkiang, Frontier of the Chinese Far West* (New York: Day, 1944), 54-55.

69. Andrew D. W. Forbes, *Warlords and Muslims in Chinese Central Asia: A Political History of Republican Sinkiang, 1911-1949* (Cambridge: Cambridge University Press, 1986), 41.

70. Zhang was not alone in this gloomy conclusion. According to a 1944 study, by 1930 Sinkiang was "already falling economically into the hands of her Soviet neighbor." This was thanks in good part to the Turksib Railway, which gave Russia an advantage over its rivals in the Xinjiang markets. By 1931, Russia had procured "new and considerable trade and communications privileges in the Chinese province." Norins, *Gateway to Asia*, 55, 69. A more recent study reached the same conclusion, noting that due to the Turksib Railway, "the Soviet economic stranglehold on Sinkiang became all but complete." Forbes, *Warlords and Muslims*, 41-42.

71. Ibid., 42.

72. Wilbur, *Sun Yat-sen*, 23-26.

73. It was necessary, according to Article 1, to "denounce, systematically and unrelentingly, not only the bourgeoisie, but also their assistants, the reformists of all shades." Braunthal, *History of the International*, 2: 539.

74. Chen and Wu were peasant draftees sent by the Qin authorities in 209 B.C. to guard a town. When rains delayed them, making the death penalty a certainty when they reported for duty, they decided to revolt and attacked the Qin forces in the first major uprising against that dynasty. In the end, both men were killed by their own followers for absuing their power. Sima Qian, *Historical Records*, trans. Raymond Dawson (Oxford: Oxford University Press, 1994), 140-45.

75. For an interesting but depressing treatment of the fervor with which Western intellectuals responded to the Soviet "experiment" in the late 1920s and early 1930s, see Hollander, *Political Pilgrims*, chap. 6.

76. The NSP's program, "Women suo yao shuo de hua," was dated 28 February 1932, while Zhang's articles on Soviet Russia were published in the May, September, October, and November 1932, issues of *Zaisheng*.

77. Treadgold, *Twentieth Century Russia*, 206. Estimates of the numbers of people who perished in the famines range from ten million (Stalin) to 14.5 million (Robert Conquest). Ibid.

8

Third Force:
The National Socialist Party of China, 1932-1937

In September 1931, the Japanese engineered the Mukden Incident, and by March 1932 all of Manchuria was in their hands. This was not the first example of Japanese aggression in China in those years (in 1928, the Japanese clashed with troops of the Northern Expedition in the Ji'nan Incident). Moreover, opposition to the Guomindang (GMD) following its assumption of state power in 1927 was not unknown (the Chinese Youth Party [CYP] had been in existence since 1923). Nevertheless, as a result of this intensified threat to the survival of the Chinese nation, a number of minor political parties and groups appeared during the 1930s.[1] Dissatisfied with the GMD's equivocation in the face of aggression, as well as its one-party dictatorship, they preached opposition to the government and resistance to the Japanese. Among these parties was the National Socialist Party of China (NSP), founded by Zhang Junmai and his colleagues in 1932.

Previous studies of the 1930s have neglected the role of minor parties such as the NSP, in favor of an exclusive focus on factional struggles within the GMD, the rise of the Chinese Communist Party (CCP), the continued warlord threat, and Japanese aggression. Undoubtedly, these were the main stories of the decade, along with the impact of the Great Depression on China. However, they were not the whole story. To fail to grant them their "day in history" is to overlook an opportunity to weave a few more threads into the intricate tapestry of the Chinese past.[2] Parties like the NSP and men like Zhang, in both thought and action, contributed to the rich political ferment of this era.

This chapter focuses on Zhang, one of the leading figures in the ranks of third-party figures opposed to both the GMD and the CCP in the 1930s. He was the leader—though by no means the only one—in the NSP from the

This chapter is reprinted, with permission and minor changes, from *Republican China* 19 (November 1993).

Mukden Incident to the outbreak of the War of Resistance in July 1937—and beyond. He was repeatedly elected head of the party, was the primary drafter of its program, was a mainstay of its journal, and, in his travels throughout prewar China, relentlessly pushed its cause with a diverse collection of regional power holders. In short, it is hard to imagine the history of the NSP during the 1930s without him.

This chapter attempts to trace Zhang's contributions to NSP activities and thought, as well as his impact on Chinese politics in general, during the period 1932-1937. The outbreak of the War of Resistance in the latter year ended this early phase of the party's history. During the war, the NSP (like other minority parties) participated in the United Front against Japanese invasion, and hence was largely dormant (there were no party congresses) until the end of the war and the outbreak of civil war brought a renewed burst of activity.

The Founding of the National Socialist Party of China

As we have seen, Zhang was teaching in Germany when Yenching University invited him to join its philosophy department in 1931. On the way home, he narrowly escaped being trapped by the outbreak of war in Manchuria; he arrived in Peiping just one day before the Mukden Incident of 18 September. After several months of uneventful teaching at Yenching, his luck evaporated when the Japanese attacked Shanghai while he was spending the Chinese New Year's holiday there with his brother, Kia-ngau. In a lecture at Yenching following his return, he made the mistake of criticizing the GMD's National Government for its failure to resist the Japanese at the beginning of the conflict, while praising the Nineteenth Route Army for its unyielding stand. Pressured by the GMD authorities, Yenching Chancellor Wu Leichuan dismissed Zhang from his teaching post.[3]

Again, as in 1927, his teaching career had been suspended due to politics. Perhaps this was the last straw, for he now began to devote all his energies to establishment of the NSP. The roots of this organization lay in the pre-1911 Revolution Society to Protect the Emperor and Political Information Society, as well as the post-Revolution Progressive Party and Research Clique.[4] Hence, it represented another link in the chain of organizations influenced by Kang Youwei and especially Liang Qichao, for a number of NSP members had been followers of one or both of these gentlemen. Zhang himself had belonged to the Political Information Society, the Progressive Party, and the Research Clique, while another major leader of the NSP, Zhang Dongsun, had been a member of the Progressive Party and the Research Clique.[5]

The two Zhangs had been thinking of founding a party for some time. With the death of Liang Qichao in 1929, the way was clear for his disciples to take the initiative. In 1930, Zhang Dongsun reportedly published an article in *Shishi xinbao* in which he advocated national socialism and called for the organization of a NSP.[6] During discussions following Dongsun's move to Peiping in the fall of that year, however, it was proposed the party be named the Constitutional Party . In testimony to their regard for Zhang Junmai, it was decided to wait until his return from Europe before proceeding further with the organization of a political organization. When Zhang returned, he argued that the name "Constitutional Party" was too old-fashioned and proposed that the organization be dubbed the NSP instead. Hence, in October 1931, the group began laying the groundwork for the organization. First came the founding of a National Renaissance Society (*Zaisheng she*) and the publication of a journal, *Zaisheng* (The National Renaissance). Although GMD accounts claimed the NSP was not officially established until 1934, according to NSP histories it was founded on 16 April 1932.[7]

The motives behind the formation of the party were clear. During much of the time it was being organized, the Japanese were transforming the Mukden Incident into the Manchurian Incident by occupying all of that huge province. Hence, Zhang wrote later, he and his friends and colleagues "sought to organize a new party to rescue the nation from the desperate situation."[8] Although there is no doubt the Japanese threat was the stimulus, there were other reasons, such as opposition to the GMD's one-party dictatorship, the Communist threat in South China, China's long-standing internal disorder, and personal ambition.[9]

The NSP's program contained three elements (echoing Sun Yat-sen's Three People's Principles): nationalism, democracy, and socialism. Although it was no different from the GMD in championing nationalism, its explanation linking that ism with Soviet practice could not have appealed to Chiang Kai-shek. The NSP, wrote Zhang, was influenced by Stalin's saying "socialism in one country." Hence, "we also took the nation as the starting point." The NSP also favored Anglo-American democracy—hardly surprising given the two Zhangs' decades-long admiration for it—and opposed GMD dictatorship and its suppression of human rights. Zhang Junmai placed the matter on philosophical grounds when he argued that for a people to lack freedom did not correspond to human nature. Finally, the party believed the implementation of capitalism was impossible in China. Hence, it proposed "socialist reform under national planning," with recognition of both public and private property. Heavy industry would be nationalized, while light industry would remain under private management.[10]

In this support for a planned economy, Zhang may have been influenced by his classes with Adolph Wagner and Gustav von Schmoller at the University of Berlin on the eve of World War I, as well as by his favorable view of the Soviet economic model. In the 1870s, Schmoller and Wagner had spearheaded a revolt in German universities against laissez-faire economics and free trade. Like Zhang and the NSP, the two German scholars argued for economic planning by the state, insisting that it alone could rise above selfish class interests.[11]

Zhang and the NSP during the 1930s

Opposition parties were illegal in GMD China during the 1930s. Hence, throughout the period from its founding in 1932 until the GMD recognized its existence in 1938, the NSP was an illicit organization.[12] As a result, Zhang and his party were under a good deal of pressure from the government. On the surface, there seemed little reason for the GMD, which had its hands full with the communist, warlord, and Japanese threats, to worry about this minuscule group. Beginning with one hundred or so members in 1932, it probably enrolled no more than a few hundred (mostly professors and their students) by the outbreak of war in 1937.[13] However, the NSP—like its brother party, the CYP—aroused the anger of Chiang Kai-shek and the GMD by its repeated attempts to link up with one or another of China's warlords or militarist factions. The NSP's motives were physical security, that is, protection from constant persecution by the GMD; its hope that these warlords and their provincial reconstruction efforts in the 1930s might prove viable governmental alternatives to the GMD dictatorship; and the need for funds to carry out the party's activities (as mentioned in chapter 5, one of the early supporters of the NSP was Zhang Xueliang).

The idea of launching the regeneration of China from a provincial base had a long lineage and could be traced to the 1898 reformers, Sun Yat-sen, and others before Zhang. For their part, the generals could tap the prominent intellectuals in the NSP for provincial reconstruction ideas, while at the same time winning some degree of legitimacy by their association with the intellectual class of China. As a result, Zhang was a peripatetic character in the 1930s, going from warlord to warlord offering his services and seeking protection, just as during an earlier era of disunity in China, the Spring and Autumn period, his hero Confucius had gone from state to state seeking a ruler to employ him and his political ideas. This may have made it hard for the GMD secret police to catch up with him, but it also has made it difficult for the biographer to trace his movements across China during those tumultuous years.

The Fujian Rebellion

In the spring of 1933, Peiping became an even more dangerous place. As a result of the infamous Tanggu Truce, concluded in May between the National Government and the Japanese, anti-Japanese resistance was outlawed in Peiping, and the Chinese government was obliged to help crush it.[14] This pressure forced Zhang to go south. He made the most of it and in his travels recruited members and established party branches in several provinces. By the fall, he was back in Peiping as editor of the party organ, *Zaisheng*,[15] which managed to outrage all sides with its opposition to the GMD, the Communists, and the Japanese. Hence, it was not long before it felt the heavy hand of the regime. Following a visit by the Peiping military police, the journal was branded "reactionary," and the chairman of the Peiping Branch Political Council, Huang Fu, was ordered to dissolve the NSP and arrest its members. Owing perhaps to Huang's personal relationships with Zhang's mentor, Liang Qichao, and Zhang's brother, Kia-ngau, he did not carry out the government's order.[16]

About the same time, Zhang's attention was caught by the Fujian Rebellion, one of many similar incidents in the 1930s. A short-lived affair, it lasted from its formal beginning on 20 November 1933 until GMD troops captured Changzhou on 21 January 1934. Led by the Nineteenth Route Army so admired by Zhang, the movement established a People's Revolutionary Government.[17]

The launching of this regime brought a swarm of sympathizers to Fujian. In addition to those involved in its founding, such as the Nineteenth Route Army and the leftist Third Party, there were Trotskyites, nonpartisan intellectuals, and members of the CYP.[18] Not the least among its attractions was that it offered an escape from the unremitting pressure in Peiping.

It did not take Zhang long to join this migration. When he received a telegram from a party member in Fujian, with the party's concurrence he traveled to that maritime province.[19] His memoirs are silent concerning his specific reasons for undertaking this dangerous trip. In light of his and the NSP's beliefs, he was probably drawn to Fujian by four features of the regime. It opposed Chiang Kai-shek, the GMD, and even Sun Yat-sen; it possessed a socialist character; it claimed to be in favor of democracy; and its platform called for resistance to the Japanese.[20] In addition, Zhang and his colleagues may have been influenced by their friends in the CYP, who were strongly attracted to the Fujian regime. CYP leaders Zeng Qi and Zuo Shunsheng, whom Zhang had known since the 1920s, traveled to Fujian.[21] On the other hand, in light of Zhang's anticommunism, he could not have been happy about the Fujian government's negotiations with the CCP, which were known throughout the country.[22]

In any event, he was too late, for within a couple of days of his arrival the GMD vise began to tighten on Fujian. Hence, with the help of the local Bank of China branch—thanks to Kia-ngau—Zhang fled by steamer to Guangzhou.[23] There he found a teaching post in philosophy at Zhongshan University (The National Sun Yat-sen University). At that time, dissident GMD leader Zou Lu was president of the school. The university was in serious financial difficulty when Zhang arrived, due to "political unrest." Hence, it appealed to the GMD central government for financial assistance. This strategy succeeded, and in December 1933, the central government began to remit a monthly subsidy to the school.[24]

This background probably explains Zhang's dismissal by Chancellor Zou before his one-year contract with the university expired.[25] The school got rid of Zhang, the anti-GMD party politician, in order not to jeopardize its petition for GMD government funds. Although disappointed, he was probably not surprised at this most recent intrusion of politics into the educational world. He had seen it all before, with the GMD's closing of his Institute of Political Science in 1927 and his dismissal from his teaching post at Yenching University in 1932. In any event, he may well have felt uncomfortable at Zhongshan University. Since he had refused to allow Sun Yat-sen's will, the "Zongli's Testament," to be recited at the Institute of Political Science,[26] he could not have been pleased with the inclusion in the curriculum of Zhongshan University's Department of Political Science of a course entitled "Principles of the Kuomintang."[27]

The First NSP Congress, 1934

Following his dismissal, he returned to Peiping. In the fall, the NSP convened its First National Congress in Tianjin, at which time it officially announced its establishment. Zhang was elected general secretary (*zongmishu*) and one of three chairmen of the presidium.[28] The party's manifesto continued the attack on the GMD, castigating its failure to resist Japan, its denial of the people's freedom, its erratic relationship with the CCP, its unstable foreign policy, and its imitation of first Russia and then fascist Italy. The NSP clearly thought it could do better. It called for national unity against foreign aggression, which challenged the GMD's monopoly on foreign affairs. In domestic politics, it advocated adoption of "the Anglo-American system," which meant democracy. It was a sign of the depression-ridden times that the manifesto devoted the most attention to economics. Yet, its advocacy of economic self-sufficiency for China hardly seemed the way to help end the worldwide economic collapse (although it did approve of trade to obtain the goods China could not produce). The great powers, the manifesto asserted, were abandoning laissez-faire economic policies and "gradually advancing toward socialism." The NSP clearly intended for China to be part of that wave, while eschewing communism. Hence, it advocated that China adopt "social justice" as its principle and reject those class concepts that destroyed society's "harmony" (a Confucian note). The state would manage large industries, while private individuals would continue to own them. Peaceful methods would be used to transform agriculture into a system in which peasants owned their land (echoing Sun Yat-sen's slogan "land to the tiller"), as well as to improve technology and promote cooperation. Finally, the manifesto emphasized nationalism (lit., "the nation as the central idea"; *minzu zhongxin sixiang*) and assured its readers there was no contradiction between it and freedom of thought and academic independence. In fact, it asserted, they complemented each other. Hence, it concluded, "the promotion of culture required the gradual development of nationalism in an atmosphere of freedom of thought."[29]

Discussions with Yan Xishan

In his political report to the congress, Zhang expressed his fear that Japan would launch an all-out invasion of China. Manchuria and Rehe (Jehol) had already fallen, he lamented, and Hebei and Shandong would be difficult to defend. Hence, he considered Shanxi important as a buffer in the Northwest.[30] Following the congress, he demonstrated his and the NSP's concern by traveling to that province, where he had discussions with its longtime ruler, Yan Xishan, concerning ways of preparing for Japanese attack.[31] Although the details of his talks with Yan are not known, while in Shanxi Zhang delivered a speech in which he stated he had come because he believed the provinces of the Yellow River valley were in "extremely great danger," in light of Japanese encroachments on Chinese territory in the North. If war should break out, he warned, there was no way Shanxi could remain aloof. If Japan and the Soviet Union went to war, he feared, Shanxi would suffer the fate of Belgium in WWI. The ultimate target of his criticism was the Nanjing government, which he accused of inaction in regard to the defense of Shanxi. As a result, it was up to the province's people to prepare to defend their territory against invasion. They stood in the "first line of defense of the nation," he insisted, and hence their responsibility was especially heavy. He hoped that they would not behave like Zhang Xueliang and fail to resist.[32]

There may have been other reasons for his visit to Shanxi. Like him, Yan was a strong anti-Communist. Moreover, Zhang may have been seeking protection from the GMD. Although Yan had proclaimed his loyalty to the central government and his relations with Chiang Kai-shek were cordial, he never allowed the GMD to develop its party strength in Shanxi.[33] Looking for signs of hope in the grim 1930s, Zhang also may have been interested in Yan's provincial reconstruction movement. In 1932, Yan had launched a ten-year program of economic development, in hopes of strengthening Shanxi sufficiently to hold off the Japanese and the CCP, both of whom were close by. He built roads and a railway, fostered light industry, increased the output from Shanxi's fields and mines, and even redistributed landholdings. He attempted to establish a state monopoly over commerce, industry, and agriculture to fund and control his development projects. He pared the power of the village gentry, developed a village school system, enhanced women's rights, and checked drug addiction. It was not for nothing that under Yan's rule Shanxi was referred to as the "model province."[34]

Despite Yan's achievements, there is no evidence that Zhang and his party made any effort to become involved in the Shanxi reconstruction movement. It may well have been too close to the onrushing Japanese invaders. Moreover, they may have shared the reactions of their friends in the CYP, who returned from visits to Shanxi with bad impressions of Yan's efforts. "How could this barren land with its impoverished people," wondered Li Huang, "manage to build up a model province in the North?"[35]

Chen Jitang and the Xuehai Institute

Once back in Peiping, Zhang was offered the opportunity to participate in a more promising provincial reconstruction effort. As he later recalled, "I unexpectedly received a letter from Guangdong. Chen Jitang invited me to lecture at the Mingde she, which was later transformed into the Xuehai Institute."[36] Zhang had met Chen the previous winter, while teaching at Zhongshan University,[37] and his invitation was welcome for the safe haven Guangzhou would offer from the "White Terror" in Peiping. American diplomatic dispatches around this time are replete with reports of arrests by the GMD, Blue Shirt activity, and pressure from the Japanese police and military in Peiping and Tianjin.[38] The arrest of Feng Youlan by a special agent of Chiang Kai-shek's provisional headquarters and ten policemen demonstrated that even philosophers—like Zhang—were not safe from the long arm of the GMD dictatorship. Moreover, the press speculated that the reason for Feng's arrest might have been his lectures on Soviet Russia, which were decribed as favorable to that country.[39] In that case, Zhang also had cause for worry, for in *Shitailin zhixia zhi SuE*, published in November of the previous year (1933), he had taken a favorable view of Russia's First Five-Year Plan (chapter 6).

He probably was already in Guangzhou when the ax fell on his party in Peiping. In December 1934, personnel from the Public Security Bureau burned more than three thousand issues of *Zaisheng*, and it was forced to suspend publication for several months. Nor was there any anonymity for Zhang, for the bureau also burned 161 offprints of one of his articles.[40]

Under these circumstances, it was understandable that he would take precautions. When he took ship from Shanghai to Guangzhou (via Hong Kong), he booked passage in third-class steerage, rather than in first or second class, where he would have drawn attention. After 1932, he later recalled, "I travelled between Hong Kong and Peking incognito, undetected by Kuomintang agents."[41] In addition, during December 1934 and January 1935, he reverted to the use of a pseudonym in his writings.[42]

In Guangzhou, he did more than lecture. He also joined with his friend and party colleague, Zhang Dongsun, to found the Xuehai Institute. It took some time to prepare for its establishment. Although Zhang Junmai arrived in Guangzhou in late 1934, the institute was not founded until the following August. Moreover, in contrast to his presidency of the Institute of Political Science in the 1920s, he did not head the Xuehai Institute.[43]

At that time, the philosopher Chan Wing-tsit met Zhang in Guangzhou and guessed that the main purpose of the latter's visit was "definitely political."[44] The evidence indeed suggests a link-up between the NSP and Chen's regime at this time. There was, for example, an NSP presence at the Xuehai Institute, and one observer went so far as to claim that the institute had been established by the NSP.[45] In addition to Zhang, who served as a tutor (*daoshi*) and dean of studies (*xuezhang*), several other members of the NSP served as administrators, faculty members, or were students at the institution, while the library contained NSP materials.[46]

This cooperation with Chen was part of the NSP's expansion, since Zhang's 1933 trip, into the Yangtze and Pearl River regions. In addition to party members at the institute, other important figures in the NSP, such as Luo Wengan, journeyed to Guangzhou to join the Chen regime.[47] According to one NSP member, while Zhang was in Guangdong and Guangxi many scholars in these provinces joined the party. Moreover, there is evidence that the expansion bore fruit in Southeast Asia as well.[48]

At the same time, the NSP founded a party organ for South China, *Yuzhou xunkan* (The Universe), to parallel *Zaisheng* in North China.[49] As one party member put it, *Yuzhou* "echoed" *Zaisheng* in the North.[50] The party was probably motivated by the persecution of the latter (it was no coincidence that *Yuzhou* was launched in the same month *Zaisheng* was being burned in Peiping), as well as the party's concurrent expansion in the South. Cautiously, the NSP established the magazine in Hong Kong, under the editorship of a pair of party members, one of whom was a former student of Zhang's. Its purpose has been described as the promotion of the democratic and anti-Japanese resistance movements.[51] Its contents also made clear the close connections between the NSP and the Guangdong and Guangxi authorities, for it carried articles by Chen Jitang, Li Zongren, and Bai Chongxi, as well as heavy doses of news concerning the two provinces.[52]

The Guangxi Clique

Although Zhang seems to have spent most of his time, during his year and a half in the South, in Guangzhou working on his educational, journalistic, and political party projects, he was also extremely interested in the reconstruction movement underway in Guangxi province. This was not surprising, for it was being praised throughout China, and its leaders—Li Zongren, Bai Chongxi, and Huang Shaohong—were viewed as "progressive and able administrators."[53] Moreover, Zhang thought the region important, in light of Japanese aggression. In his report to the First NSP Congress in 1934, he argued that the need for a base for revival, as well as dispersal of national defense industries, required emphasis on the Southwest.[54]

It is not clear how he became acquainted with the Guangxi leaders. He may have met them during his visit to Guangxi in the spring of 1933. It is also possible that he was introduced by Li Zongren's aide, Gan Jiehou, who taught at Zhang's Institute of Political Science in the 1920s and, like Zhang, was a Baoshan (Jiangsu) man.[55] In any event, the Guangxi authorities were interested in Zhang, for in 1935 they appointed him an adviser to their provincial government.[56] In addition, in the fall of 1935, Lei Binnan (Beihong), commissioner of education (1933-1936) and one of the most important civilian members of the Guangxi Clique, invited Zhang to lecture.[57]

There were probably several reasons Zhang was attracted to Guangxi. Its efforts seemed very promising to a man who spent the 1930s looking for viable provincial reconstruction movements. Whereas Yan Xishan was developing Shanxi for his and Shanxi's benefit, the Guangxi Clique was reforming its province as a way of strengthening China,[58] which may explain why Zhang was more enthusiastic about the latter. He seems to have been drawn to Chen Jitang's Guangdong for its educational opportunities, as well as protection and employment for his party members, while he was impressed by Guangxi's efforts to create a true "model province." Moreover, like Yan and Chen, the Guangxi Clique opposed both the central government and the Communists. Finally, Zhang was very much of a rationalist,[59] and hence he probably preferred the sober realism of the Guangxi leaders over the crass superstition practiced by Chen Jitang, who fervently attempted to incorporate phrenology and *fengshui* into his political and military strategy.[60]

Although it was reported that many scholars in Guangxi joined the NSP, the party's lack of influence in that province was in stark contrast to its penetration of Chen's Guangdong. One does not have to look far for the reason. The Guangxi leaders had belonged to the GMD since 1924, even though they had steadfastly refused to relinquish authority over the province to the party. Although they were hostile to the Nanjing government and attempted to maintain their independence from it, their quarrel was with Chiang Kai-shek, not his party. Hence, they were still influenced by GMD ideology in their policies.[61] As a result, when Zeng Qi, the leader of the CYP, tried to recruit Li Zongren in 1929 after Li had broken with the GMD authorities, Li responded that he opposed Chiang Kai-shek, not the GMD, and if he abandoned his high posts in his own party, "people would look at me scornfully, saying that I switched allegiances easily."[62]

During the 1930s, the Guangxi leaders launched the "three-self policy," which was described as self-government, self-defense, and self-sufficiency.[63] Judging from his past writings, Zhang agreed with all three objectives. He had been interested in the first two since the early 1920s, when he had repeatedly stressed the importance of self-government and self-defense. The key institution in the Guangxi program was the militia, which Zhang also had advocated since the early 1920s.[64] Moreover, as we have seen, in 1934 the NSP had called for self-sufficiency for China. There was also some German influence on Guangxi's reconstruction program,[65] which Zhang, as a returned student from Germany and German specialist, must have noted. In fact, his speeches and writings on Guangxi revealed a real psychological crisis in the minds of China's elite, for in case after case he condemned Chinese practice and compared it unfavorably to the way Europeans—especially the Germans—did things.

In addition to their governmental and military reforms, the Guangxi Clique recognized that more fundamental changes were necessary. Hence, in 1933 they launched the basic education movement, which called for compulsory education of children between the ages of six and twelve, as well as part-time instruction for illiterate adults. Large numbers of basic schools were established to give the impoverished a rudimentary education, prepare them for participation in local government, and imbue them with a national consciousness. Although the level of instruction was low, the movement was very successful.[66]

In addition, they pushed a social reform movement, which was similar in some respects to Chiang Kai-shek's New Life Movement. It strove to control dress; regulated prostitution, gambling, and opium smoking; railed against "extravagant" social behavior; and, in stark contrast to Chen Jitang, attacked superstition. In 1933, the Clique published a list of regulations for the "improvement of social customs."[67]

In his speeches and writings, Zhang lent his support to the basic education movement, as well as the campaign for social reform. In addition, he praised Guangxi's efforts to become a model province for all China. In doing so, he expressed gloom at China's predicament in the mid-1930s. Where was China's "way out" (*chulu*)? he asked. Japan's aggression was steadily increasing, and yet the "foundation for our country's revival work still had not been established." It was clear from his criticism of the central government and the Communists that he did not believe they had the answers. Instead, he placed his hopes in the two reconstruction efforts in the Southwest. With the exception of Guangdong's Three-Year Plan, he declared, only Guangxi had a "vigorous, youthful spirit." Therefore, each year during the period 1933-1935, he wrote, he had visited Guangxi to check on its progress.

As a result of those observations, he was hopeful that the Southwest province could prove the model for national reforms. "Guangxi's reconstruction," he wrote, "is not Guangxi's problem [alone], but involves the question of whether the Chinese nation can survive." He was blunt: "I hope that Guangxi's reconstruction will . . . turn into China's great reform. [Then] perhaps there will be a ray of hope for the nation's future." "What I have seen in Guangxi," he added, "for example, the hard work and thrift, the simplicity and frugality, and the achievements of the militia, have amply demonstrated that no other province can keep up." He called on the Guangxi people to strengthen their intellectual and moral powers and "serve as models for the people of the entire nation."[68]

His reference to moral powers, as well as the argument in another of his Guangxi speeches that good education produced good character and bad education led to bad character,[69] were reminders that Zhang was a Confucianist. Yet, it was perhaps the nature of his audience that led him to play down the Confucianism, while emphasizing European practices and successes. Although the Guangxi leaders were conservative, they were not as stubbornly traditionalist as Chen Jitang—which may have explained Chen's attraction for Zhang. Zhang's rival Hu Shi confirmed this upon his visit to Guangxi in 1935, when he wrote that "superstitious hankering after the past" was absent in that province.[70]

In a 1935 article published in Guangxi on the anniversary of the 1911 Revolution, Zhang reiterated his hopes for its reforms. If one looked around the country, he wrote, only the Guangxi reconstruction movement of recent years had perceived the real ailments of the Chinese nation and possessed the power to reform them. What ailments? The severed ties between people and nation; the separation of civilian and military; the isolation of the scholar-officials (*shidaifu*) from the peasants, workers, and merchants; and society's disorganization. Since the establishment of the Republic, few had been able to think of ways to cure those problems. In fact, "only Guangxi had been able to . . . put things right in one region." It had provided a thorough cure for three of the four ailments from which China had suffered for thousands of years, he declared.

He went on to explain how the clique had accomplished this. First, through conscription, the militia, and the militia cadre school, Guangxi had made the common people realize their connection with and responsibility for the nation. By implementing the militia system, it had also bridged the gap between civilian and military that Zhang had been complaining about since the early 1920s. Everyone, whether provincial chairman, department head, government functionary, or commoner, he marveled, rose at 6:00 A.M. for military training —even fifty-year-olds. Moreover, he credited Guangxi with initiating military training for middle-school students even before Europe. Finally, Guangxi had also begun to pay attention to rural reconstruction. In this way, he argued, "good commoners" could be trained to cooperate with good government and public officials. Without such commoners, he warned, government was "water without a source and a tree without roots." Even Guangxi, however, offered Zhang no solution to the isolation of the scholar-official. That was a national problem, he sighed, and could not be solved by one province. The solution to this problem, some would add, awaited Mao Zedong and the CCP's rise to power.

It was clear, then, that Zhang saw Guangxi as the model province for national reform. Referring to the above three areas of endeavor, he declared that Guangxi had "already begun the revival of the Chinese nation. So long as the people of the entire nation are able to follow this road, there is boundless hope for this country of ours."[71]

By the spring of 1936, though, his days in Guangzhou were drawing to an end. In mid-May, the Nanjing delegation to the funeral of the GMD elder, Hu Hanmin, demanded that the Southwest bow to the central government. In June, war came to the Southwest, and by mid-July Chen Jitang was in exile in Hong Kong.[72] Zhang seems to have seen the handwriting on the wall, for he decamped to the British colony in mid-May.[73] The Mingde she and the Xuehai Institute disappeared with the collapse of Chen's regime. Once again the GMD had closed a school with which Zhang was associated, and the professor was without a classroom. In an understatement, he later lamented that it was "impossible to found schools under a one-party dictatorship."[74] With the NSP's southern base in Guangdong gone, Zhang closed *Yuzhou* and left for Shanghai.[75]

The Second NSP Congress, 1936

Once in Shanghai, he took refuge in translation work, just as he had following the closing of the Institute of Political Science in 1927.[76] In addition, he continued his party activities. In the fall, the Second National Congress of the NSP convened in Shanghai for one week. Zhang was reelected general secretary of the party and a member of the presidium. The congress decided to move the party's headquarters from Peiping to Shanghai, a decision that was probably motivated by increased Japanese pressure in the North, continued political repression in Peiping, and the party's efforts to expand to the South (although prospects for this appeared gloomy in the fall of 1936).[77]

Although there were signs Chiang Kai-shek was beginning to shift to the anti-Japanese camp,[78] Shanghai was still seething with unrest aimed at the National Government's failure to resist Japanese encroachments on China's territory. This discontent had produced a spate of groups calling for national salvation, followed by the arrest of seven key leaders of the movement in late November 1936.[79] Hence, it was not surprising that the main topic of discussion at the NSP Congress revolved around the Japanese danger and the question of the NSP's attitude toward the GMD government if the Japanese launched a full-scale invasion of China. Some delegates argued, on the basis of the party's platform calling for the formation of a government of national unity and defense, that the NSP should cooperate with the GMD against Japanese aggression. The majority, however, thought that since the ruling party had not yet abolished its one-party dictatorship and did not tolerate the existence of other parties, it would be impossible to cooperate with it. Hence, the discussions were inconclusive, according to a party source.[80] There was no doubt about the party's opposition to Japanese aggression, though, and the congress issued a declaration advocating immediate resistance.[81]

Following the congress, Zhang traveled to Peiping to "promote resistance to Japan."[82] Having lost its base in the provincial reconstruction movements in the Southwest, the NSP now agreed to a merger with another minority party as a way of strengthening itself. In early November, he and several party colleagues concluded a draft agreement with the Constitutional Party, which had been headed by Kang Youwei until his death in March 1927.[83] War broke out before the merger could take place, however, and hence it was postponed until following the conflict.

In the meantime, Zhang began to edge toward eventual reconciliation with the GMD, as revealed by his participation in the Lushan Conference in mid-July 1937 and exchange of letters with Chiang Kai-shek in the spring of the following year.[84] In late November 1936, he visited Jiangxi province, drawn there more by his abiding anticommunism and interest in reconstruction movements than by any newfound love for the GMD. Since winning the province back from the CCP in 1934, the GMD had been busy pacifying it with the intent of making it a model province. No doubt the governor of Jiangxi, Xiong Shihui, helped make the visit possible, for he and Zhang's brother, Kia-ngau, were fellow members of the National Government's Political Science Clique. In fact, shortly after Zhang's visit, Xiong showed his approval by contributing an introduction to Zhang's translation of General Erich Ludendorff's *Der Totale Krieg*.[85]

In a speech to GMD administrators and educators in Ruijin, the former capital of the Jiangxi Soviet, Zhang made it clear that his view of communist politics and ideology had not changed since his first contact with it in Europe in the early 1920s. He praised the CCP's ends, while excoriating its means. He also blasted it for what he termed its blind imitation of Soviet Russia, its materialism, and its reliance on class struggle. Addressing the CCP's dramatic switch, following the Mukden Incident, from advocating class struggle to promoting national struggle, he argued that the latter "completely nullified the doctrine of class struggle," for under nationalism everyone was equal.

During the 1930s, as we have seen, he was fascinated with the reconstruction efforts in Fujian, Shanxi, Guangdong, and Guangxi and hoped they would show China the "way out." There was a difference in his approach to the GMD's reconstruction effort in Jiangxi, however, for he hoped that this effort would provide a model of anticommunism for the nation and serve as the "spiritual front line of defense against communism." The uselessness of China's old politics and culture had led to the appearance of the CCP, he admitted, and he hoped that the GMD's Four Great Policies (*si da zhengce*) in administration, education, welfare, and defense would create a Jiangxi that would not be misguided by the CCP again. If these programs were successful in the CCP's former soviet area, he argued, then Ruijin and Jiangxi anticommunism would bode well for national anticommunism.

In the final analysis, his anticommunism prodded him closer to the GMD. "During the past ten-odd years," he declared to his GMD audience, "I have not believed for one moment that the Communist Party that kills and burns can save China. Hence, hereafter I am willing to continue to serve as your supporter."[86] In short, when it came to a choice between the two evils of the GMD or the CCP, his fervent anticommunism won out over his distaste for the GMD one-party dictatorship.

Concluding his visit to Jiangxi, he returned to Shanghai, where he devoted himself to writings on education, culture, academic thought, philosophy, economics, and the CCP. With conflict with Japan looming, he also pursued his translation of Ludendorff's work and tried to prepare his country for a war of resistance. Unfortunately, when that war began with the Marco Polo Bridge Incident on 7 July 1937, he was in Peiping on party business.[87] When he finally was able to flee back to Shanghai on 10 July, the war that was just beginning would follow him for eight bitter years.

Conclusion

In the 1930s, there was a four-way struggle under way in China among the GMD, CCP, warlords, and the Japanese. Thus, the minor parties—such as the NSP and the CYP—are often overlooked by historians. Yet, one could argue that consideration of them is necessary for a full picture of the period. They were "third forces," for they opposed both the major parties on the scene in the Nanjing Decade, the GMD and the CCP (although there were signs of "leaning to one side"—the GMD—on the eve of the war). They enrolled some of China's "best and brightest" and hence offer the student of the 1930s insights into some of the most interesting ideas in circulation at the time. Moreover, they spread these arguments through their journals and newspapers.

As far as "might have beens" are concerned, who can deny that a China governed by social democracy would have been preferable to one under communism? Zhang Junmai and the NSP offered such an alternative and had the courage to do so in an extremely dangerous political environment, as made clear by kidnappings, arrests, assassinations, and executions. This does not make them saints. Zhang was not a pacifist, nor was he a proponent of non-resistance. He approved of war, if it was for the right cause. However, he rejected the idea of establishing his own party-army.

In thinking about the significance of Zhang and his party in the 1930s, one reviewer's rude comment concerning a book's thesis comes to mind: "So what?" Did the man and party have any *power*? In fact, they did, by virtue of their links with provincial reconstruction movements, especially those in Guangdong and Guangxi. These sorts of links angered Chiang Kai-shek and rightly, for the juncture of guns, model provinces, and the political and cultural ideas offered by such minor-party figures as Zhang was a very real threat. Whether the warlords themselves took these figures seriously or merely treated them as "window-dressing" and instruments of political legitimacy is another question.

In sum, the NSP had important men, operated its own journals and newspapers, and had links with those who possessed territory, soldiers, and money, and hence deserves further study.

Notes

1. For mention of some of these parties and groups, see Ch'ien Tuan-sheng, *The Government and Politics of China*, 351.

2. For a collection of essays, as well as a lengthy introduction, on minority parties and their leaders, see Roger B. Jeans, ed., *Roads Not Taken: The Struggle of Opposition Parties in Twentieth-Century China* (Boulder, CO: Westview, 1992).

3. Zhang Junmai, *Bianzheng weiwuzhuyi*, 192. On Wu, who was appointed chancellor of Yenching University in 1929, see West, *Yenching University*, 62-66.

4. Xiao Wenzhe, comp. and ed., *Xiandai Zhongguo zhengdang yu zhengzhi* (Modern Chinese Political Parties and Politics) (Nanjing: Zhongwai wenhua she, 1946), 43.

5. Xiang Goufu, "Minchu xianzheng jianwen lu" (A Record of My Experiences with Constitutional Government during the Early Republic), *Koushu lishi* (Oral History), no. 1 (October 1989): 94; Yang Hanhui, *Xiandai Zhongguo zhengzhi jiaoyu* (Modern Chinese Political Education) (Peiping: Renwu shudian, 1932), 45.

6. BDRC, 1: 132.

7. YX, 22; Xiao Wenzhe, *Xiandai Zhongguo zhengdang*, 43; Wang Peihuai, *Geming de baojian* (The Sword of Revolution) (n.p.: Weihuang she, 1936), 350; *Zhongguo ge xiao dangpai xiankuang* (The Present State of Affairs of Minority Parties in China) (n.p., 1946), 65-66; GS 4, no. 5, 72.

8. Zhang, *Bianzheng weiwuzhuyi*, 192.

9. Chou Hsiang-kuang, *Political Thought of China* (Delhi: Chand, 1954), 183.

10. Zhang Junmai, "Wu guo zhengdang fazhan," 3.

11. Agatha Ramm, *Germany, 1789-1919: A Political History* (London: Methuen, 1967), 341, 363.

12. The GMD had implicitly acknowledged the existence of the NSP before 1938, when it invited General-Secretary Zhang Junmai to participate in the Lushan Conference in July 1937.

13. BDRC, 1: 31; Wang Peihuai, *Geming de baojian*, 353-54; *Zhongguo ge xiao dangpai xiankuang*, 73.

14. Li Huang, "Reminiscences," 447-49.

15. Zhang, *Bianzheng weiwuzhuyi*, 192.

16. YX, 23; "Shelun" (Editorial), *Yuzhou* 14, no. 8 (1984): 2 ; Huang Shen Yi-yun (Madame Huang Fu), "My Husband and I: Personal Reminiscences of an Eminent Chinese Woman," condensed, ed., and trans. by Te-kong Tong, 1960, Special Collections Library, Butler Library, Columbia University, 115-21, 125, 338, 355-56, 384, 443.

17. MacKerras and Chan, *Modern China*, 346, 348. For an excellent analysis of the rebellion, see Lloyd E. Eastman, *The Abortive Revolution: China under Nationalist Rule, 1927-1937* (Cambridge: Harvard University Press, 1974), chap. 3.

18. Ibid, 104.

19. Zhang, *Bianzheng weiwuzhuyi*, 192.

20. Eastman, *The Abortive Revolution*, 99-100, 109, 106-8; BDRC, 1: 216.

21. Zuo Shunsheng, "Reminiscences," 105-6.

22. Eastman, *The Abortive Revolution*, 120-21.

23. Zhang, *Bianzheng weiwuzhuyi*, 192; Wu Xiangxiang, "Zhang Gongquan xiansheng de qinglian dianfan" (Mr. Chang Kia-ngau's Honest and Upright Example), *Zhuanji wenxue* 36, no. 4 (1980): 87.

24. Zhang, *Bianzheng weiwuzhuyi*, 192-93; Zhang, "Nianyu nian lai," 5; BDRC, 3: 317-18; J. D. Bush, ed., *The National Sun Yat-sen University: A Short History* ([Guangzhou: The National Sun Yat-sen University], 1937), 5-6, 10-12.

25. Zhang, *Bianzheng weiwuzhuyi*, 192-93.

26. Zhang, *Shehuizhuyi*, 3. On Sun's last will and testament, see Wilbur, *Sun Yat-sen*, 278.

27. Bush, *The National Sun Yat-sen University*, 49-50. In view of his animus toward facile slogans, he could not have liked the inclusion in the same department's curriculum of a course entitled "Imperialism." On the other hand, the leader of the National Socialist Party of China probably approved of the department's course entitled "History of Socialism." Ibid.

28. Zhang, *Bianzheng weiwuzhuyi*, 193; "Zhongguo minzhu shehui dang jianyao shigao," 19; YX, 22-23; Xiao Wenzhe, *Xiandai Zhongguo zhengdang*, 43.

29. *Zhongguo ge xiao dangpai*, 66-68.

30. "Zhongguo minzhu shehui dang jianyao shigao," *19*.

31. Ibid. For an analysis of Yan's career as ruler of Shanxi, see Donald G. Gillin, *Warlord: Yen Hsi-shan in Shansi province, 1911-1949* (Princeton: Princeton University Press, 1967).

32. Zhang Junmai, "Shanxi duiyu weilai shijie dazhan de zeren" (The Responsibility of Shanxi in Regard to the Future World War), in *Minzu fuxing zhi xueshu jichu* (The Academic Basis for National Revival), 2 vols. (Peiping: Zaisheng she, 1935), 2: 109-13. In the fall of 1941, a member of the NSP reported that Zhang Xueliang's financial support of the party had ceased "some years ago." "Transmitting a Memorandum of a Conversation with the Representative in Hong Kong of the 'Chinese National Socialist Party,'" p. 4 of the memorandum. Although this was probably a reference to the December 1936 Xi'an Incident, which left the Young Marshall a prisoner of the Generalissimo, Zhang Junmai's 1934 speech, with its criticism of Zhang Xueliang, was published in 1935 and hence may have come to the

attention of and angered the Young Marshall.

33. James E. Sheridan, *China in Disintegration: The Republican Era in Chinese History, 1912-1949* (New York: Free Press, 1975), 188; Chalmers A. Johnson, *Peasant Nationalism and Communist Power: The Emergence of Revolutionary China, 1937-1945* (Stanford: Stanford University Press, 1961), 95.

34. Sheridan, *China in Disintegration*, 188; BDRC, 4: 49; Furth, *Ting Wen-chiang*, 170.

35. Li Huang, "Reminiscences," 350-53.

36. Zhang, *Bianzheng weiwuzhuyi*, 193.

37. Xie Youwei, "Wo yu Zhang Junmai," 10.

38. USDS, R.G. 84, Peiping Post Files, vol. 41, 800 decimal series, November 1934 monthly political report.

39. "Sensation Caused by Arrest of Professor at Tsing Hua," *The Peiping Chronicle*, 30 November 1934, in USDS, R.G. 84, Tientsin Post Files, 1934, vol. 24, decimal series 800, political situation—news clippings.

40. YX, 25; "Benzhi disannian zhi yunming yu shiming" (The Fate and Mission of This Journal in Its Third Year), *Zaisheng* 3, no. 1 (1935): 2-3.

41. Chang, *Third Force*, 25.

42. Sun Chengzhai, "Du Wang [Housheng] zhu 'Zhang Junmai sixiang' hou de ganxiang" (Reflections after Reading "Zhang Junmai's Thought" by Wang Housheng), *Zaisheng* 4, no. 20 (1953): 54.

43. Zhang, "Nianyu nian lai," 5; Xie Youwei, "Wo yu Zhang Junmai," 10.

44. Chan Wing-tsit to author, 28 July 1977.

45. Xiao Wen-che, *Xiandai Zhongguo zhengdang*, 43.

46. Xie Youwei, "Wo yu Zhang Junmai," 10; YX, 25; Xie Fuya, "Zhang Junmai xiansheng er san shi," 23. The library subscribed to both of the NSP's party organs, *Zaisheng* and *Yuzhou xunkan*. In addition, it had four copies of Zhang's *Minzu fuxing zhi xueshu jichu*, as well as his translation of Harold Laski's *A Grammar of Politics*. The catalogue also included a section entitled "Party Principles" (*dangyi*), which listed works by Sun Yat-sen and the GMD but no works by or about the NSP. *Xuehai shuyuan tushuguan shumu* (Catalogue of the Xuehai Institute) (Guangzhou: Xuehai Institute, 1936), 253-55 and p. 2 of a separately paginated section on periodicals and newspapers.

47. USDS, R.G. 84, Canton Post Files, 1936, 800 decimal series, American Consulate General, Canton, dispatch to USDS, 11 June 1936, p. 2; "Political Report for June 1936," 36.

48. Zheng Xiaoyuan, "Tianmo liangfeng huai Zhang Junmai xiansheng" (At the End of the Day When a Cold Wind Arises, I Think of Mr. Zhang Junmai), *Minzhu Zhongguo* 4, no. 23 (1961): 8.

49. Sun Baoyi, "Junmai xiansheng yu minzhu shehuizhuyi," 24.

50. YX, 25.

51. Sun Baoyi, "Junmai xiansheng yu minzhu shehuizhuyi," 24; GS 4, no. 5, 73.

52. See *Yuzhou xunkan* 4, no. 1 (1936).

53. Sheridan, *China in Disintegration*, 197.

54. "Zhongguo minzhu shehui dang jianyao shigao," 19.

55. YX, 21; *Who's Who in China*, 5th ed., 118-19; Li Zongren, "The Reminiscences of General Li Tsung-jen," as told to Te-kong Tong, 1964, Chinese Oral History Project, Special Collections Library, Butler Library, Columbia University.

56. *Who's Who in China*, 5th ed., 3.

57. Zhang Junmai, "Jiaoyujia yu guomin qizhi de bianhua" (Educators and Changes in the National Character), *Yuzhou xuankan* 3, no. 10 (1935): 1; *China Handbook, 1937-1943*, "Chinese Who's Who," xxxvii; Diana Lary, *Region and Nation: The Kwangsi Clique in Chinese Politics, 1925-1937* (Cambridge: Cambridge University Press, 1974), 152, 216, 237(n69).

58. Ibid., 202.

59. Tan, *Chinese Political Thought in the Twentieth Century*, 276; Zhang Junmai, *Guonei zhanzheng Liujiang* (Six Lectures on Civil Wars) (Wusong: Guoli zhengzhi daxue, 1924) and Zhang Dongsun's introduction.

60. USDS, R.G. 84, Canton Post Files, 1936, 800 decimal series, Clarence E. Gauss, American Consulate General, Shanghai, to Nelson T. Johnson, Peiping, dispatch no. 294, 14 July 1936, Hu Shi's views of the political situation in China.

61. Lary, *Region and Nation*, 200-201; Sheridan, *China in Disintegration*, 195.

62. Li Zongren, ""Reminiscences," chap. 24, 1-3.

63. Sheridan, *China in Disintegration*, 195.

64. See, e.g., his *Guonei zhanzheng liujiang*.

65. Sheridan, *China in Disintegration*, 196.

66. Lary, *Region and Nation*, 181-82.

67. Ibid, 185-86.

68. Zhang Junmai, "Zhonghua minzu zhi zili anzai?" (Wherein Lies the Chinese Nation's Own Strength?), *Yuzhou xunkan* 3, no. 3 (1935): 1-4.

69. Zhang, "Jiaoyujia yu guomin qizhi," 1.

70. Sheridan, *China in Disintegration*, 196-97.

71. Zhang Junmai, "Guangxi jianshe yu Zhonghua minzu zhi gaizao" (Guangxi Reconstruction and the Reform of the Chinese Nation), *Yuzhou xunkan* 3, no. 4 (1935): 5-8.

72. Eastman, *The Abortive Revolution*, 251-60.

73. On 18 May, he lectured at Hong Kong University. Zhang Junmai, "Hanxue Songxue duiyu wu guo wenhua shishang zhi gongxian" (The Contributions of Han Learning and Song Learning to Our Country's Cultural History), *Yuzhou xunkan* 5, no. 3 (1936): 2.

74. Zhang, *Bianzheng weiwuzhuyi*, 193; Zhang, "Nianyu nian lai," 5.

75. Zhang, *Bianzheng weiwuzhuyi*, 193; BDRC, 1: 32-33.

76. Zhang, *Bianzheng weiwuzhuyi*, 193.

77. "Zhongguo minzhu shehui dang jianyao shigao," 19; YX, 26.

78. Lloyd E. Eastman et al., *The Nationalist Era in China, 1927-1949* (Cambridge: Cambridge University Press, 1991), 46.

79. Parks M. Coble, "The National Salvation Association as a Political Party," in Jeans, *Roads Not Taken*, 140.

80. "Zhongguo minzhu shehui dang jianyao shigao," 19.

81. YX, 26.

82. GS 4, no. 5, 73.

83. BDRC, 2: 333-35; 3: 433-36; Hu Yinghan, *Wu Xianzi xiansheng zhuanji* (A Biography of Mr. Wu Xianzi) (Hong Kong: Published by Author, 1953), 18; Wu Xianzi, *Zhongguo minzhu xianzheng dang dangshi*, 138; YX, 26. A leading member of the Constitutional Party, Li Daming, arrived in Peiping on 4 November. Li Daming, *Bei you yinxiang* (Impressions from a Northern Journey) (Shanghai: Dongfang wenhua chubanshe, 1937), 33. Zhang Junmai was in Jiangxi by 22 November. Hence, the meeting between leaders of the NSP and the Constitutional Party probably occurred sometime during the first half of November.

84. Zhang, *Bianzheng weiwuzhuyi*, 193; Council of International Affairs, *Chinese Yearbook, 1938-1939* (Chungking: Commercial Press, 1939), 4: 341-45. Convened on 16 July 1937, the Lushan Conference was called to exchange opinions on national problems. In addition to GMD invitees, the four hundred guests included leaders of minor parties, such as the NSP, the CYP, and the Third Party, and outstanding nonpartisans, such as Hu Shi. Eastman et al., *The Nationalist Era in China,* 126.

85. MacKerras and Chan, *Modern China*, 350; William Wei, *Counterrevolution in China: The Nationalists in Jiangxi During the Soviet Period* (Ann Arbor: University of Michigan Press, 1985), 55; BDRC, 1: 28; 2: 114; Xiong Shihui, "Xiong xu" (Introduction by Xiong [Shihui]), pp. 5-6, in Ludendorff, *Quan minzu zhanzheng lun*. Xiong's introduction was dated January 1937.

86. Zhang Junmai, "Ruijin shi jingshenshang fangGong de diyixian" (Ruijin is the Front Line in the Spiritual Defense against Communism), *Zaisheng* 4, no. 4 (1937): 6-10.

87. Zhang, *Bianzheng weiwuzhuyi*, 193.

9

In Search of the Middle Way:
The Debate over Democracy and Dictatorship during the 1930s

Our present problem is the existence of our state, not what type of state we should have.

—Jiang Tingfu[1]

The only hope is for the intelligentsia to unite in the task of transforming our present old-style dictatorship into a new-style dictatorship.

—Ding Wenjiang[2]

I do not believe in dictatorship.

—Hu Shi[3]

We neither completely approve of nineteenth-century-style parliamentary government nor abandon democracy. We oppose dictatorship but definitely are not completely unaware of the strong points of dictatorship.

—Zhang Junmai[4]

The Debate

During the 1970s and 1980s, the world was startled by a series of protests that demonstrated that interest in democracy was not dead in China, despite totalitarianism. One of the most famous of the dissidents, Wei Jingsheng, wrote a manifesto entitled "The Fifth Modernization: Democracy,"[5] while yet another

This chapter is reprinted, with permission and extensive revisions, from *Republican China* 10 (June 1985).

asserted that democracy was "highly valued and eagerly sought by the people" and hence "irresistible."[6]

Those expressions of lingering faith in democracy amid the realities of dictatorship were reminiscent of an earlier period in Chinese history. During the 1930s, there was a fervent debate among Chinese intellectuals between proponents of dictatorship and those who favored democracy.[7] Zhang Junmai seldom missed a good intellectual fracas in the Republican period, and he did not overlook this one. However, his contributions to the polemic have been virtually ignored in English-language writings; only one scholar (Chester Tan) has written of Zhang's views in the debate, and then only briefly.[8] Since Zhang may have been acting as a spokesman for members of the National Socialist Party of China (NSP), a look at his views might offer insights into their thinking as well.

The controversy was officially launched in December 1933 by publication of an article by an American-educated historian, Jiang Tingfu.[9] The debate it unleashed lasted until the outbreak of war in 1937, with the high point occurring in 1934-35. A number of intellectuals (mostly college professors who had studied in the West) participated,[10] and their articles were published in several prominent newspapers and journals. Influential men such as Jiang Tingfu, Ding Wenjiang, and Luo Jialun argued for dictatorship, while Hu Shi, Luo Longji, and others defended democracy.

The debate was stimulated by a pervasive sense in Nationalist China of domestic and world crisis. At home, the 1930s were characterized by a severe but inefficient and corrupt Guomindang (GMD) dictatorship; by constant warfare against warlords, Chinese Communists, and Japanese invaders; and by an economy in disarray. Abroad, democracy, under the crushing impact of the Great Depression, was suffering setbacks in Germany, Italy, Spain, Japan, and Poland. It was but a small step, in the minds of some Chinese intellectuals, from a "crisis of democracy" to a "failure of democracy" in the world, a view that seemed to be validated by the pessimism of some European thinkers and the weak roots and dismal record of democracy in China itself. At the same time, these Chinese were impressed with the achievements of the dictatorships of Mussolini, Hitler, Stalin, and Ataturk. Some even interpreted Roosevelt's and Ramsey McDonald's governments as moves in the direction of dictatorship.[11] Thus, these crises at home and abroad led some Chinese intellectuals to yearn for strong government, for an efficient dictatorship that might create order out of chaos, while others maintained their faith in democracy.

The issues of the debate have been characterized as "difficult and nebulous ones."[12] One problem was the legitimacy of China's claim to be a modern nation. Another was the question of unification and centralization of a country as large and diverse as China. A third was that of "national salvation," and a fourth, the question of the price to be paid for political order (some argued, e.g., that freedom could be omitted if a dictatorship advanced the majority's welfare).[13]

Certain common themes emerged from the participants' arguments about these issues. One of the most important was a yearning for capable government, one that was "efficient as a great sword, fast as lightning" and could "sweep away yesterday's planless, unorganized, anarchic conditions, and implant social, economic and political controls that are organized and planned."[14] Another was widespread agreement on the need for a planned economy. A third was a desire for government by experts, while a fourth addressed the question of which political model, democracy or dictatorship, could best achieve the above three goals.

Zhang Junmai Enters the Lists

Zhang published a number of articles in the early and mid-1930s that could be construed as contributions to the debate. In only one, however, did he tackle the controversy—and several of the participants—head-on. Published in February 1935 and entitled "The Third Type of Government Besides Democracy and Dictatorship," this article is the best single source for his views in the debate. Hence, this chapter will analyze this essay.

His position in the controversy was more complex than that of some of the other participants. Part of that stance was a refusal to abandon belief in democracy, although he very carefully defined what he meant by that term. This position was not surprising in view of his political career and thought prior to the 1930s. As we saw in chapter 2, since his student days in Japan before the 1911 Revolution he had consistently supported constitutional government as the best form of government. While at Waseda University, he read some of the classics of Anglo-American political thought (Locke, Mill, etc.) and later wrote he had been "particularly profoundly influenced by . . . democratic and constitutional thought." A disciple of Liang Qichao, in Japan he joined Liang's Political Information Society, which aimed at a speedy but peaceful and orderly transition to a constitutional government.

After the establishment of the Republic, he maintained his interest in constitutionalism. While in England during World War I, he visited the British Parliament to watch democracy in action in its homeland.[15] In the early 1920s, he commented on warlord constitutions and participated in attempts to draft an alternative.[16] After the founding of the GMD regime in 1927-28, he opposed its one-party dictatorship.[17] Following two years of self-imposed exile in Germany (1929-31), he joined with a number of other intellectuals to found an opposition party with the misleading and unfortunate name, the National Socialist Party of China.[18]

In fact, the 1930s debate over democracy versus dictatorship had been in progress for some time before Zhang got around to chiming in. One could have predicted he would leap into the fray, however, for he rarely missed an opportunity to take part in the many intellectual controversies of the 1920s and 1930s. He first made a name for himself—although not a very progressive one in the eyes of some Republican intellectuals—through his role in the 1923 polemic over "Science and a Philosophy of Life."[19] Battle lines were realigned in the 1930s debate, however; whereas in 1923, Hu Shi and Ding Wenjiang ganged up on Zhang, in the 1930s controversy, it was Zhang and Hu against Ding. Zhang's article "The Third Type of Government" was first published in February 1935 in *Dagongbao* and then reprinted the following month in the NSP's *Yuzhou xunkan*.

He was explicit about the reasons for his interest in the controversy. During the past year, he explained, there had been a lot of articles in *Duli pinglun* (The Independent Critic), *Dagongbao*, and other periodicals debating national reconstruction and autocracy, democracy and dictatorship. At the same time, Italy, Russia, and Germany were overthrowing "old-style democracy" (*jiushi minzhu*) and putting into effect dictatorship. Even in the "supreme headquarters" of democracy, England and America, political forms had greatly changed, compared with the nineteenth century. Hence, he concluded, the debate in China had to arise, partly as a reaction to trends in world thought and partly because everyone hoped to find a solution to China's failure, in an era of national crisis, to establish a national polity (*guoti*).

In his view, there were two major problems in the controversy. Seeing the nation's disunity, he wrote, some thought the debate would yield the solution to unifying the country. Others focused on the problem of democracy or dictatorship, which Zhang referred to as the "question of the disposition of political power." In his view, the former was more crucial, for "only after unification is it possible to discuss what to do about the form of political power." He recognized, though, that the two were not easily separated, that many of his countrymen, in their urgent desire for unity, were searching for a political form, albeit one suitable to national conditions, that could accomplish unity.

His own position seemed ambiguous. If a new form of political power could be found, he wrote, "*perhaps* [italics mine] the entire nation could be fairly rapidly unified." When he faced the question of whether democracy or dictatorship would provide this "new pattern," though, he reverted to his earlier argument, that unification would have to precede discussion of the disposition of political power. He made it clear where his sympathies lay, however, when he declared that not only would dictatorship fail to obtain unification, it would have the opposite effect. Democracy, on the other hand, involved questions of state organization (*guojia zuzhi*), such as the people versus the government and freedom versus authority.[20]

Critique of Views of Jiang, Ding, and Hu

Zhang devoted the first half of his article to an evaluation of the arguments of several major participants in the debate, evenly divided between those who sided with dictatorship—Jiang Tingfu and Ding Wenjiang—and those who were pro-democracy—Hu Shi and the journalist Zhang Jiluan.[21] Jiang, explained Zhang, focused on the problem of founding the state and unifying the nation, while Ding and Hu concentrated on the form of political power—democracy or dictatorship—following unification.[22] Zhang barely noted Zhang Jiluan's views, but it was clear he agreed with the latter's stance in the debate. The views of these participants (with the exception of Zhang Jiluan) have been repeatedly described in English-language works,[23] but Zhang's role in the debate has been neglected.

Jiang Tingfu

Jiang likened China's situation in the 1930s to that of England, France, and Russia before the Tudor, Bourbon, and Romanov absolutisms.[24] Unlike those despotisms, he argued, China's emperors did not "fulfill their historic duty," with the result that when the Qing was overthrown the state became a "heap of loose sand," and China was still a "dynastic state" (*chaodai de guojia*), not a nation-state (*minzu guojia*). Hence, Jiang declared the "unifying forces are the vital forces of our polity, and we should foster them; the forces that destroy unity are the enemies of our polity, and we should reduce and eliminate them." China's problem, in the 1930s, was "the existence of the state, not the question of what kind of state."

Jiang emphasized unity, explained Zhang, and did not care whether the government was a democracy or dictatorship. Since he implied that China should have an absolutism like those of the Tudors and Bourbons, Zhang noted, some suspected he wanted China to have a "capable autocratic monarchy." Zhang defended him, labeling that suspicion an "exaggeration" that arose from Jiang's hopes for unity and concentration on European absolute monarchies.

However, he also took issue with Jiang. China, in fact, had passed through an age of autocracy like those of the Tudors and Bourbons, he argued, for the actions of Qin Shihuang, Han Wudi, Tang Taizong, and Ming Taizu were similar to those of England's and France's autocratic monarchies. More importantly, he rejected Jiang's argument that China in the 1930s was similar to Europe in the fifteenth and sixteenth centuries. China's disunity, he protested, was not due to "remnants of the feudal system"—that is, to the fact that China had missed out on the accomplishments of the absolute monarchies of England and Germany—but to the vastness of China's territory, the ignorance of its people, and the failure of those in the central government to observe the law.

Because of the hugeness of China's territory, he explained, it was easy for a dissident province to revolt against the central government and impossible for a hero to rule according to a fixed pattern, as in Europe.

As for his analysis of the "ignorant people," it had two sides to it. On the one hand, he acknowledged that if the people were illiterate and ignorant, national unity would be impossible. Yet, he remained attracted to the notion that the voting populace was the equivalent of judges who decided right and wrong during elections. Since the establishment of the Republic, he wrote, the scholar-official, not the masses, had wielded political power, with the moderates outside and the radicals inside the GMD. This small group engaged in disputes, he explained, while the majority of the populace was viewed as unimportant. The result had been that universal education still had not been realized. He was discouraged and complained that in the past two decades and more, "one saw only the destruction of the law today and its protection tomorrow; allying with the Communists today and opposing them tomorrow." For the most part, he concluded, it had been a story of struggle between GMD and non-GMD forces. As for the majority of the four hundred million Chinese, "they had never occupied the position of masters in deciding right and wrong and deciding who should assume power and who should step down." That failure, he concluded, had resulted in government instability and national disunity.

Despite the burdens of geography and the failure of the people to assume their rightful role as "masters," he argued, if the leaders had knowledge and experience, good faith, and observed the nation's constitution (*genben dafa*), China definitely would not be as disturbed as it was at present. He criticized Yuan Shikai and Duan Qirui, with both of whom he had cooperated in the early years of the Republic. He was on infinitely more dangerous ground, during the Nanjing era, in criticizing GMD cult-figure Sun Yat-sen for first protecting the constitution and then abolishing it in favor of copying Soviet Russia's one-party dictatorship. The GMD could not have been amused when Zhang lumped Sun together with the militarists Yuan and Duan by writing that all three possessed "identical shortcomings." Regardless of whether political leaders were in or out of office, he complained, their "vacillations" caused disputes within the country, which resulted in local revolution.

Although his mentor and friend, Liang Qichao, had died several years before, Zhang was still haunted by his influence. Liang had argued that Europe's revolutions took place in their capitals, and hence once they were over, there was no further trouble. In China, however, revolutions often began in areas beyond the reach of government authority, and thus there were multiple revolutionary centers. As evidence, Zhang cited the Wuchang Uprising in 1911, the revolt against Yuan Shikai, the struggle between Nanjing and Hankou, the clash between Chiang Kai-shek and the Guangxi Clique, and the war between Chiang, Yan Xishan, and Feng Yuxiang. From these, he argued, the "greatness of local power may be inferred." If revolutionary politicians were in power, they wanted the central government to unify localities; if they were ousted, they hoped that local power would be sufficient to resist the central government. The "habitual nature of local revolutions," he concluded, had been a regular occurrence since the establishment of the Republic and was the third reason for China's disunity.

He was not a historian like Jiang but rather a political party leader and, he hoped, a "statesman." Hence, he thought attempting to "find a way out" by merely comparing China with European history, as Jiang had done, would never work. Instead, he offered a "prescription" based on his analysis of China's problems.

First addressing the problem of China's huge size—it was really a continent rather than a country, he pointed out—he spoke up for constructing railroads as a way to reduce its vastness. Better communications would bring China closer together, he explained, and hence the national language, economy, and "feeling" (*qinggan*) could be unified.

As for the problem of the populace, he acknowledged the argument that if the people were ignorant, there was no way they could come up with a good government. On the other hand, he was tempted by the view that if a good government was created first, the people then could be educated. His approach was a practical one: "If . . . we wait until we have a good people to establish a good government, that would be tantemount to people growing old waiting for a river to run clear." Instead, he advocated planning a democratic government, even though the majority of the people were illiterate and ignorant.

He admitted that the problem of government was the toughest and could not be solved without the "daring of the Qin Emperor or Han Wu[di]." The central government's destruction of law and the localities' revolts were really two sides to the same problem, he pointed out. If there was instability in the central government, then the result would be local revolution; if local revolution became habitual, then central government would be unable to maintain its prestige. Both those phenomena dated from the beginning of the Republic, he wrote, and everyone was aware of the suspicion between the central authorities and the localities. In addition, he wrote, there were the separatist warlord regimes and financial disunity. Jiang Tingfu's argument, he continued, was to point out there were several dozen autocrats in China and to propose using a "major dictatorship to abolish the minor dictatorships," that is, the second-rate warlords. To do this, Zhang commented, armed might would be necessary, but he made it clear that this was a simplistic solution. "China's unity," he insisted, "absolutely cannot rely merely on armed might but is a political problem." An army required administration, talent, arms, and pay and provisions. All those depended on finances, which in turn relied on taxes drawn from the national economy. The latter, in turn, was dependent on industry and commerce, which required talented technicians, a good currency system, and ways to protect that industry and commerce. If at present there was a first-rate soldier able to unify China, and he wanted to develop his armed might, Zhang explained, he should be aware that the military involved administration, finances, the economy, and even education. If successful, that kind of man could expand his power and would be praised by people in the provinces. Concerning China's future political direction, he could take into account China's national conditions, as well as the strengths of Europe and America, with the caveat that it would be impossible solely to copy Europe. In short, Zhang's ideal leader sounded like a *junzi* for modern China: "He must be able to accomodate numerous currents [of thought], know men and wisely employ them, and be completely unselfish." Then the roots of the disease of instability that had thrived since the founding of the Republic could be severed at one blow, and the provinces would cease local revolution and causing trouble for the central authorities. China, he concluded, could come up with a "Bismarck."

In the final analysis, though, he recognized he was verging on wishing for a hero. China, he hastily added, was a republic, not a warlord nation. Hence, in addition to a leader, it also needed participation of the popular will. Showing off his Western learning, he wrote that there were only two ways to accomplish that. One was to convene a "Philadelphia" convention, as in America, and draft a constitution, which would be used to elect a president after its ratification by the nation. The second was to copy Prussia and use a national assembly to express the Chinese people's wishes and establish a united China. In short, while he granted the importance of armed might, administrative achievements and expressions of the popular will were also crucial. Someday unification would be accomplished, he wrote hopefully, when "armed might, administration, and the popular will simultaneously advance together." The problem of national unity would not be as difficult as Jiang Tingfu thought, he concluded, if those who rose to meet the challenge in the future in the legal aspect "observed the law of the land" and in the moral realm "spoke frankly and sincerely."

Hu Shi and Ding Wenjiang

Whereas Jiang discussed the problem of national unity, Zhang continued, Hu and Ding discussed democracy and dictatorship in terms of which was easiest to implement.[25] According to Ding, "dictatorship and democracy are both impossible, but democracy is even more impossible than dictatorship." Hu, Zhang noted, sided with democracy, writing that it was "a kindergarten political system, most suitable for training a nation that lacks democratic experience." According to Hu, "democracy is the government of common sense, and enlightened dictatorship is the government of especially outstanding men. We cannot be certain of getting especially outstanding men, but common sense is relatively easy to instill."

Difficulty in implementation, Zhang commented, was inseparable from experience. During its twenty-odd years, the Republic had not really attempted democracy, while over the past ten-odd years, a Russian-style one-party dictatorship had failed. The foundations of neither kind of government had been established. Since the debate over which was easiest was inconclusive, he concluded, he would analyze their contents and then decide whether they were possible in China.

He began by citing Ding's views on democracy in Western Europe. Ding argued that even though Europeans had universal suffrage, "actual political power had fallen into the hands of those who pay party expenses, run newspapers, and operate radio stations." In short, he maintained, professional politicians had "discovered a tool to swindle others—propaganda." Zhang's response was to wonder whether Ding was talking about the suitability of democracy for China or simply discussing the advantages and disadvantages of democracy itself. It was clear that Zhang was more interested in the former. He revealed himself to be a practical politician when he listed five characteristics of democracy: there was investigation of voters; there was no manipulation or destruction of ballots following the elections; the majority party was allowed to assume power after elections; if there was no majority party, the parties could form a coalition party; and the ordinary and proper political morality of other nations was observed. If one argued that democracy was not applicable to China, he insisted, one should reply by denying China possessed his five conditions. If one found China had some of those conditions, then one should say China's level was not yet adequate and could not say that "democracy is even more impossible in China than dictatorship."

The strangest aspect of Ding's argument, wrote Zhang, was his assertion that universal suffrage was the major prerequisite of democracy. Yet, Zhang objected, although England's constitutional government was established in the seventeenth and eighteenth centuries, general elections were not held until after World War I. Hence, in his view, Ding used "this absolute standard [universal suffrage] as the crux of democracy . . . to overpower democracy and highlight his proposals on dictatorship!"

For his part, Zhang believed "democracy is not impossible in China." He defended that position by comparing his five conditions for democracy with Chinese reality. It was true, he admitted, that since the launching of the Republic, China had never had accurate voter rolls. Nevertheless, in investigations of inaccuracies, the voters came to vote and count ballots. Moreover, as long as there were impartial supervisors, the government and opposition parties would not hire people to forge and swap ballots, and hence "fair elections are still possible in China." Once the practice of elections was established in China, then majorities and minorities would be clear. If presidents of chambers of commerce and student class presidents could be chosen by elections, then "the habit of the minority obeying the majority will not be entirely lacking in China." In fact, the most important condition for the existence of a democratic country, he argued, was that the minority party should obey or cooperate with the majority party. He cited as an example of the violation of that principle Yuan Shikai's refusal in 1912 to allow Song Jiaoren to organize a cabinet, as well as Yuan's disbandment of the GMD. Those acts had created conditions in which China's political situation had been instable for twenty years. In the views of optimists, Zhang noted, if the hostility between political parties could be reduced, then organizing a cabinet would not be "as difficult as ascending to heaven." Even if China could not organize a cabinet that lasted three or five years as in England, he pleaded, at least it could establish one like France's that frequently alternated in power. He admitted the French example was not a good one but argued "at least it is better than using armed might to fight for political power."

He recognized that the GMD local and central party headquarters were elected. However, the central government permitted neither a parliament nor a multiparty cabinet. Thus, even though the upper level was a dictatorship, the lower level was democratic. He was clearly puzzled. "The most incomprehensible thing for those of us who advocate democracy," he declaimed, "is that [the GMD] obtains an upper level of dictatorship from a lower level of democracy."

Having made clear his objections to Ding's belief that democracy was impossible in China, Zhang tackled the latter's four conditions for a "new-style dictatorship." Perhaps getting revenge for the riducule he had endured from Ding during the "Debate over Science and a Philosophy of Life" over a dozen years earlier, he pointed out that, in his version of dictatorship, Ding had overlooked problems that "make one split a gut laughing." Ding maintained, Zhang explained, that the leadership of a dictatorship must consider the nation's interests its own. Yet, did not the leadership of a democracy believe that? Zhang objected. In a democracy, the popular will is the criterion of national interest. Under a dictatorship, the words of dictators were the highest authority (*kouhan tianxian*), leading Zhang to wonder what they relied on to distinguish national from nonnational interests.

In response to Ding's assertion that the leadership of the dictatorship must thoroughly understand how to modernize a nation, Zhang queried whether the leadership of a democratic nation did not understand the nature of a modernized country. Like a good philosopher, Zhang insisted on definition of terms. How should the term *modernization* be interpreted? he wondered. Was it the modernization of England, America, or the Soviet Russian dictatorship? Did the soviet represent modernization? Was it the modernization of the Italian corporate state, capitalism, or communism? He asked for a clear reply from Ding as to whom he could rely on for resolution of that kind of dispute.

According to Ding, the leadership of a dictatorship must make adequate use of the country's trained manpower. Was it possible, Zhang huffed, that the leadership of a democracy did not utilize the talented specialists of the nation? What was the talent British and American factories used?

Finally, Ding asserted that the leadership of a dictatorship must use the present national crisis to gather under its own banner all people capable of participating in government. Zhang's rejoinder was familiar by now. Was it possible, he inquired, that the leadership under a democracy did not need to utilize the present national crisis to appeal to the people? To what was Ramsey McDonald appealing when he took advantage of England's abolition of the gold standard to organize a national unity cabinet? To what was Roosevelt appealing when he advocated American economic revival?

In fact, Zhang scoffed, Ding's four conditions were not characteristics of a "new-style dictatorship" but simply minimum requirements for a modern state. The real characteristics of dictatorship he found in countries like Italy and Russia and summarized as replacement of the legislature by a central executive committee, replacement of English- and French-style party cabinets responsible to the assembly by a long-lasting one-party dictatorship, abolition of oppositionists' freedom of speech and of all opposition parties and groups, and replacement of the separation of the legislative and executive branches with the freedom of the government to act arbitrarily without restraint by the parliament.

These characteristics certainly would strike proponents of modern democracy as good reasons to avoid dictatorship. However, just as he had found positive lessons in Soviet Russia, Zhang found "special features" in dictatorship. If one party held power, and there were no opposition parties in parliament or criticism by public opinion, he argued, it would be easy to attain consensus, actions would be consistent, and it would be easy to continue policies and concentrate strength. These were the "advantages" of dictatorship, wrote Zhang, but Ding misunderstood and thought the achievements of Soviet Russia's planning represented the merits of dictatorship.

Although Zhang himself had profusely praised certain aspects of the Soviet experiment less than a year and a half earlier, now he lambasted Ding. Had he considered Soviet Russia's suffering? In the early stage of the revolution, they murdered dissidents; how many dead were there? Because the White Russians' views were different, civil war broke out; what about the cruelty? Because White Russia and Red Russia were incompatible, foreign intervention was launched; what about the damage to Russia? "Even though the civil war has ended now," he wrote, "the . . . result of dictatorship has not been 'to monopolize but not decide' but 'to monopolize and decide.'" In other words, he declared, the result of dictatorship has definitely been one-man autocracy." Hence, at present there was still competition between Stalinists and Trotsky-ites, and Kamenev and others were still opposed to Bukharin. The result of dictatorship, he asserted, was internal conflict.

He approvingly quoted Hu's comment that the "difficulty in imitating dictatorship is not only that leaders and talented experts are hard to find, but it also is extremely difficult to find the two to four million toadies of des-potism (*zhuanzheng adou*)." "Only if you give them sweets to eat and blood to drink," wrote Hu, "can you make them wholeheartedly shout long live for you, and eradicate reaction and support dictatorship for you. The danger of advocating dictatorship today is not only to 'encourage wicked people to do wicked things,' it is simply to teach three-year-old children to engage in arson." In contrast to his stance during the "Science and Philosophy" polemic of yesteryear, Zhang now approved of Hu as on the side of the angels. He admired Hu's conclusions, although he confessed to some trepidation concerning Hu's statement in *Dongfang zazhi* (Eastern Miscellany) that if China truly had autocratic leaders, then dictatorship would not be bad. Although that made people suspect Hu lacked firm beliefs concerning democracy, Zhang reflected, the views he expressed in his reply to Ding Wenjiang were "about the same as ours."

Zhang's "Third Type of Government"

Having made clear his views in debate with Jiang, Ding, and Hu, Zhang went on to lay out his plan for a new system of government, one that would combine the advantages of democracy and dictatorship. In doing this, it was clear that he, like many of his fellow Chinese intellectuals, was deeply worried by the crises he saw in the West and China in the mid-1930s. As in the cases of others, his anxiety led him to question the efficacy of democracy as a means of dealing with these emergencies. However, he did not reject democracy in favor of dictatorship, for if he knew the weaknesses of the former, he was even more acutely aware of the dangers of the latter. Instead, he proposed a system that strove for a compromise between the two.

Obviously, 1929 was the critical year for his analysis (as for so many others). The "great panic," as he put it, in the world economy threw into sharp relief what he saw as inadequacies of parliamentary and political party government. First, in an age of plenty, such as nineteenth-century England, political parties could indulge in the freedom of disagreement. However, in the current economic crisis, he declared, that liberty had to give way to a powerful government able to make decisions and act at will. Second, in an age of plenty, there was time for leisurely discussion and freedom of speech and assembly for the people and for political organizations. But the situation in England or Germany during 1930-1931 left no time for such discussions but rather demanded prompt decisions and actions, emergency orders, and dictatorial authority. Finally, in a parliamentary government, everything was decided by passage in the assembly and could not by changed by the executive. After the World Depression struck in 1929, he argued, the industrial nations began to suffer from decreasing revenues and increasing expenditures. There was no way to meet that crisis except to grant government the power to issue emergency orders and do whatever needed to be done.

It was clear from this desperate situation in the West, he continued, that a new type of government had grown up alongside nineteenth-century parliamentary government. He and his colleagues in the NSP, he noted, had proposed such a new type of government two years before in *Zaisheng*.[26] The goal, he asserted, was to transcend both dictatorship and parliamentary government and seek a "third type of government" that would strike a balance between government authority and individual freedom.

Like their countrymen, he and his colleagues were painfully conscious that China was in the midst of a national crisis. Like many of their fellow intellectuals, they turned to the West in search of principles their new type of government might follow to cope with this emergency. As a result of studying a democracy (England) and three dictatorships (Italy, Russia, and Germany), they identified three essential elements for their new-style government. First, it should embody the spirit of national unity. At a time when the Japanese were invading the interior, Zhang argued, political parties and groups should drop differences of opinion to solve the national crisis, for "only if there is a united will, is it possible to cope with a critical situation." Second, the new government should be capable of acting forcefully. Representative government was "government by discussion" (Zhang's English), but in a crisis, "empty words and fine talk are entirely useless," for it was essential that government be able to "act strongly." Third, there should be concentration of authority. The way to deal with difficulties on all sides, he explained, was to place all power in the hands of the government and give it a free hand to act. "There is no need to be able to check the government in every way," he insisted, "like the nineteenth-century parliaments."

To realize these three principles, he continued, government organization should be based on eleven points, the sum of which he described as "national democracy that concentrates mental and physical efforts (*xinli*)." By this, he meant that all parties and groups should "pool their strength and advance toward the same goal." The relative strengths of the parties should be ignored, for the interests of the nation must take precedence over those of parties and groups.

His program included a unified government, clearly necessary in an era of warlord separatism; a national assembly in which a certain percentage of the membership would be technocrats; political parties; and a civil service free from party interference. The national assembly would supervise the budget and discuss and draft laws but would not make use of the vote-of-confidence system.

Clearly, the most important provisions for Zhang were those involving the relationship between the national assembly and the central executive yüan (*zhongyang xingzheng yuan*). In his scheme, the national assembly would elect administrators to serve in the executive yuan. Leaders of the various political parties would be included, so the result would be a "government of national unity." The national assembly would pass a five-year "administrative outline" (*xingzheng dagang*), which would have equal effect with the constitution and could not be altered by the executive yüan. The national assembly would decide on the outline, but "experts" would take part in its formulation.

As for implementation of the administrative outline, the national assembly would grant the government power to act as it saw fit. There would be only two ways, in his plan, to remove ministers of the executive yuan. They could be stripped of office for financial malpractice or obvious violations of the law. Second, at the conclusion of each year or stage in the administrative outline, the national assembly, or personnel jointly elected by other citizens' organizations, would investigate the accomplishments of the outline. If they were poor, the national assembly could approve removal from office of ministers.

There were important principles infusing this program, and he devoted quite a bit of effort to their elaboration. In his view, there were five essential points in the eleven articles. The first was unanimity of policy. National unity was essential in tackling four urgent tasks: (1) the dismissal of useless soldiers and training of useful ones; (2) the elimination of local bandits to preserve peace and order; (3) the establishment of industry to vigorously develop the national economy; and (4) the implementation of universal education to enable all Chinese to possess political knowledge and understand their duties as citizens. Discussion of foreign affairs, he insisted, should be postponed until internal order was consolidated. Empty talk about foreign affairs before dealing with the critical issues of national defense, local bandits, industry, and education would be impossible and like "a destitute person wanting to associate with the family of the highest graduate (*jinshi*) in the imperial civil service examination system." Instead, once the national crisis had unified the nation's will and goals, in the period of government reform the first national assembly should pass a five-year administrative outline.

The second essential was concentration of the popular will. "Since we are a republic," he wrote, "the government cannot deviate from the will of the people." He agreed with Zhang Jiluan's view that China should consolidate the political center, while carrying out preparatory training in the development of freedom. Italy and Germany had reacted against individualism and parliamentary splits, he continued, and totally abolished parliament and political parties. In his view, the Nanjing government wanted to imitate Russia and Italy and use the methods others applied to trim excessive parliamentary authority in European democracy. "This is the wrong medicine for the disease," he objected. China's "disease" was that it still had not undergone the great political emancipation of nineteenth-century Europe; hence, Chinese were still unwilling to participate in politics and voice their views. The question, then, was how China could overcome this "illness" and make democracy a reality? His answer was to "temporarily utilize the literate people as voters"; "this kind of limited election has been very common in nations since the nineteenth century, and [it] absolutely cannot be said it is not democracy." Political parties, as long as their programs and actions were public, could participate in the government, but in the period of national crisis, "everyone should strictly implement Europe's so-called truce among political parties."

Third, China needed a powerful government. The nineteenth-century parliamentary system was too strong for him, for "the government's right to survive was controlled by the parliament." The post-1929 situation, he argued, was the exact opposite. At present, he wrote, "It is possible that the most important [element] within a state is the executive," for it was impossible to do without it. Moreover, in a time of emergency, the parliament was "not indispensable." In short, experiences since 1929 had taught the importance of the executive branch and the unimportance of the legislative branch, in his view.

In his system, the first national assembly would draw up the administrative outline. Although the parliament would continue to convene every year, the question of policy would have been decided. Even though it would have legislative power, its legislation would have to follow the administrative outline and hence could not "shake the government." Parliament's budgetary power would also have to conform to the administrative outline and could not be used to influence the rise or fall of a government. As a result, "the executive branch can remain in its post for a long time, and not change at any moment as a result of the approval or disapproval of the parliament."

Fourth, the government should possess the power of discretionary action. In his system, various specific items in the administrative outline and government bills would still be given to the parliament for discussion and decision. Simultaneously, though, the government could explain to the parliament the emergency nature of financial problems and request the power of discretionary action, as Germany and the United States had done. But this power would have a time limit, and parliament could revoke it when it wished.

Fifth, cabinet members would be appointed and dismissed on the basis of administrative efficiency. Zhang recognized that in a cabinet made up of members of different political parties (what he termed a "government of national unity"), there would inevitably be differences of opinion and conflict. However, if a member resigned, he argued that he should be replaced by someone from his own party, to maintain the spirit of national unity. If a member proved incompetent, then he could be removed. Dismissal would thus not be due to differences in policies or views but would be based on the criterion of administrative efficiency.

In his view, this program would combine the strengths of dictatorship with those of democracy. Because of the administrative outline, there would be continuity in policy and cabinet members would not be removed lightly, and thus experienced people would be retained. Since parliamentary authority would be limited, fragmentation of government could be avoided. If China wanted a Russian-style five-year plan, it would be easy, since political power would be concentrated, and government would have great freedom in administration and employment of personnel. At the same time, he continued, literate people would have the franchise and all political parties could participate in the parliament or in organization of a cabinet. The people's freedom of speech and assembly would still be protected by the parliament's legislative power. Once again, as with his earlier advocacy of German-style social democracy, he adopted the "middle way":

> To put it simply, the advantages of democracy are preserved in our system as of old. We neither completely approve of nineteenth-century-style parliamentary government nor abandon democracy. We oppose dictatorship, but definitely are not unaware of its strong points.

In a world characterized by democracies and dictatorships, the Chinese, according to Zhang Jiluan, had to "create our own [system]" and could not simply imitate Italy, Germany, and Russia or England and America. This, wrote Zhang Junmai, was what he and his colleagues had striven to do since establishing the NSP. As for Ding Wenjiang and Hu Shi, he advised his old adversaries to abandon the debate over democracy versus dictatorship and seek a compromise method. Their own third type of government, Zhang and his friends hoped, would provide a "way out" for China during that crucial period.

In closing, he admitted there were those who misunderstood his program, viewing the third type of government as opposed to democracy. He attempted to answer their criticism:

> In this essay, we have advocated a popularly elected parliament with legislative power. Moreover, according to our proposals, the people's freedom must still be protected in the constitution. Therefore, the third type of government . . . still takes democracy as its spirit. [However,] the nineteenth-century type of laissez-faire policy and unplanned government is difficult to apply in today's period of national crisis. Therefore, this article proposes adoption of an administrative outline and a powerful government. We have imposed strict limitations on the parliament's ability to shake the government. Hence, [it is] called a third type

> of government, meaning we have adopted the strong points and rejected the shortcomings of [both] democracy and dictatorship.

Conclusion

It is clear that Zhang's program was a reflection of his times—in particular, what was transpiring in the West. Hence, it reveals concerns similar to those of many other participants in the debate. His ideas were deeply influenced by the worldwide "crisis of democracy," as well as the concurrent rise of dictatorships in the 1920s and 1930s. Like others, he felt that parliamentary government—what he repeatedly called "nineteenth-century-style parliamentary government"—had weaknesses that the onset of the Great Depression in 1929 had highlighted. In short, he was fully aware of the impact of economics on the chances for democracy. Again, like many Chinese intellectuals, he thought the solution a strong and administratively efficient government staffed by technocrats or "experts."

He parted ways with those participants in the debate who favored dictatorship, though. Instead, he supported a democracy strengthened by what he saw as the strong points of dictatorship. Thus, while Ding Wenjiang argued for a "new-style dictatorship," Zhang tried to replace what he viewed as old-fashioned democracy with his "third type of government," or "national democracy." This view of democracy as "old-fashioned" was certainly not unique in the 1930s.[27] Moreover, Zhang and other Chinese intellectuals may have been influenced by British Fabians, who thought that nineteenth-century democracy was unable to cope with new problems and who leaned toward what one scholar has termed "state-generated administratively oriented social engineering."[28]

There is also evidence that his "national democracy" was not particularly original. A recent study has pointed out that even many of the advocates of dictatorship merely saw it as a means to the ultimate end of democracy. That democracy, they hoped, would be based on economic equality and the whole people, rather than a single class or party. It would be run by men of ability, selected by an examination system, and hence would be "real," "improved," or "new-style" democracy.[29] In the years following the debate, Zhang continued to propose a form of government that would combine the advantages of democracy and dictatorship. By 1938, however, he was calling the mixture "revised democracy" (*xiuzheng de minzhu zhengzhi*) rather than "the third type of government."[30]

Clearly, China was in trouble in the 1930s, and Zhang, as throughout his career, was preoccupied with the question "What's wrong with China, and what can be done to make it right?" Part of the answer was to be found in the piece we have been summarizing. The first part represented his participation in the debate, while the section on his new government represented both Zhang's view and the NSP platform.

Just as clearly, there were problems (or potential problems, since Zhang and his party never got the chance to implement their program) with his proposals. One is struck repeatedly by his reliance on the West for his inspiration, and even for his sense of crisis. The vast majority of Chinese and their problems, especially in rural China, seemed entirely outside his purview. He truly seemed to be part of the "While China Faced West" phenomenon.[31] His borrowings from the West were certainly deliberate, for he felt that the best from Western culture was necessary to make up for deficiencies in Chinese culture.[32] The problem, of course, was would such borrowings work in GMD China?

Another problem was his stress on unity. In a China fragmented by warlordism, Chinese Communist opposition, and Japanese invasion, it is not difficult to empathize with his motives. But was such "unity" possible in a China torn asunder by different visions?[33] Could different political parties cooperate, for example, in drawing up the five-year administrative outline and holding to it? What were the implications for Zhang's "democracy" of this unity?[34]

These musings also raise the question of motives behind his democracy. Since he was writing while elements of the GMD were trying to come up with a constitution, he may have been attempting to influence that process by publication of his party's program.[35] In view of his lifetime interest in constitutionalism, this would not have been surprising. Moreover, according to one scholar, those who defended democracy against dictatorship did so out of "discontent with the Kuomintang rather than from deep conviction in democratic values."[36] Zhang certainly opposed the GMD; on the other hand, he had been interested in democracy for a long while. It is difficult to say with certainty whether his "discontent with the GMD" outweighed his democratic convictions. It does make one uneasy, though, when Zhang implied in the midst of the World Depression that full democracy was only possible during "an age of plenty."

His assertion that democracy could be implemented at once with a limited electorate also was not unique. Such figures as Hu Shi and Chen Zhimai also took this position.[37] This may have been practical politics, but it also opened the way for abuses, in light of the sordid history of elections in Republican China.

Perhaps the most serious question concerning Zhang's blending of the best of democracy and dictatorship is "Was it feasible?" In arguing for a strong executive branch, he came uncomfortably close to the position of the dictator-in-waiting, Chiang Kai-shek. In 1935, the latter also argued for a powerful executive. The Central Executive Committee of the GMD, in a message to the Legislative Yuan in October 1935, asked for an "efficient system that can concentrate national strength" and an executive not "limited by inflexible regulations."[38]

In addition, in arguing that the legislature could create the administrative outline but then could not interfere with its implementation by the executive yuan (except in the case of illegal actions or incompetence, which he clearly hoped would be rare), Zhang's thinking began to resemble Sun Yat-sen's less-than-democratic distinction between sovereignty of the people and the government's ability, the people's right of sovereignty and the government's right to govern. Sun did not want the people to interfere with the government they had sanctioned; Zhang did not want the legislature to "shake the government" (by employing the vote of confidence). Were these, then, real similarities between Zhang's plan and the Sunism he professed to detest?[39] In fact, in attempting to come up with a democracy modified to fit China's circumstances, Zhang resembled both Sun Yat-sen and Mao Zedong. Sun's democracy was to be made different from the old by incorporation of the idea of the Five-Power Constitution. Mao's form was to be "New Democracy," as he called it in 1940. However, while Zhang argued for a "third type of government," Mao ultimately denied any validity to a "third way."[40]

Perhaps the most fundamental and widespread question posed by the debate and Zhang's arguments was whether democracy was a feasible model for China. Many participants in the debate thought not. Although distant in time and space from China in the 1930s, in the early 1970s some Western scholars agreed. In an exchange in the *Bulletin of Concerned Asian Scholars* some years ago, an American historian referred to "Western bourgeois democracy" as a fatally flawed model.[41] Another historian, after a thorough study of the debate, concluded that the nature of Chinese society and political traditions made it "perhaps one of China's tragedies during the twentieth century that, in the quest for a viable political system, attempts have been made to erect democratic institutions." "In a profound sense," he continued, "Anglo-American democracy was not suited to China." Instead, he argued, "In China, an authoritarian system of rule is perhaps better able to produce the 'greatest happiness of the greatest number.'" Most Chinese in the Nanjing period, he concluded, would have agreed with the statement: "We oppose a dictatorship that is for private benefit, but approve of a dictatorship that is for the public welfare."[42] In contrast to these positions, other historians have demonstrated a strong belief in the efficacy of democracy and an equally strong admiration for those such as Hu Shi who have defended it in China.[43]

My own position is closer to the latter. Anglo-American democracy may not have been suited to China, but its appeal to some Chinese has never ceased. It would have been far easier for Zhang to have abandoned democracy for dictatorship rather than struggle in the 1930s to find a "middle way" to shore up democracy (the end) with the strong points of dictatorship (the means). It would have been far easier—and safer—for the "Democracy Wall" and subsequent dissidents of the 1970s, 1980s, and 1990s to have remained silent and stayed out of jail.

Ultimately, the conclusion one reaches on the question of the suitability of democracy for twentieth-century China depends on one's views on the applicability of democracy outside the Western world. One thing seems clear, though—Zhang Junmai and Chinese before and after his time have felt the attractions of democracy strongly enough to risk their freedom and even their lives in its defense.

Notes

1. De Bary, Chan, Tan, *Sources of Chinese Tradition*, 2: 132.

2. Jerome B. Grieder, *Intellectuals and the State in Modern China: A Narrative History* (New York: Free Press, 1981), 346.

3. Grieder, *Hu Shih*, 232.

4. Zhang Junmai, "Minzhu ducai yiwai zhi disanzhong zhengzhi" (The Third Type of Government Besides Democracy and Dictatorship), *Yuzhou xunkan* 1, no. 6 (1935): 11.

5. Grieder, *Intellectuals*, 355-56.

6. John Fraser, *The Chinese* (New York: Summit Books, 1980), 303.

7. The best summary of the debate is Eastman, *The Abortive Revolution*, chap. 4.

8. Tan, *Chinese Political Thought*, 253-66 (esp. 259-60).

9. While most writers on the debate agree that Jiang's article ignited the controversy, Charlotte Furth argues that the debate was provoked by a "veiled" GMD attempt to defend itself from charges of despotism by asserting that "Chinese conditions" did not permit the establishment of a fascist government in China. Furth, *Ting Wen-chiang*, 215. Furth neither explains the circumstances surrounding the GMD statements nor gives sources for them. It is possible that she is referring to Chiang Kai-shek's March 1934 denial that he was planning to establish a dictatorship. USDS, China Diplomatic Post Records, Peiping, R.G. 84, vol. 46, 800 decimal series, American Consulate General, Shanghai, to Nelson T. Johnson, American Minister, Peiping, No. 7840, 5 March 1934, "Political Report for February 1934."

10. Tan, *Chinese Political Thought*, 235.

11. Eastman, *The Abortive Revolution*, 146. Tan refers to this trend in England and the United States as the "augmentation of executive power" and "centralized democracy," not dictatorship. Tan, *Chinese Political Thought*, 241.

12. Grieder, *Hu Shih*, 260.

13. This summary of the issues is based on ibid.; Furth, *Ting Wen-chiang*, 214-15; Eastman, *The Abortive Revolution*, 148-51.

14. Ibid., 145, 147, 152.

15. Jeans, "Syncretism in Defense of Confucianism," 129-31.

16. Ibid., 353-63.

17. See, e.g., his "Pi xunzheng shuo" (A Refutation of the Theory of Tutelage), *Xinlu* 1, no. 7 (1928): 1-14.

18. On the NSP, see supra, chap. 8.

19. Jeans, "Syncretism in Defense of Confucianism," 465-97.

20. Zhang, "Minzhu ducai," 1.

21. For brief biographies of these four men, see BDRC, 1: 20-22, 354-58; 2: 167-74; 3: 278-82. One scholar has described Jiang and Ding as "the most forthright advocates of dictatorship who were not merely acting as apologists for the Kuomintang." Furth, *Ting Wen-chiang*, 216.

22. Zhang, "Minzhu ducai," 1.

23. In addition to the works already cited, see Charles R. Lilley, "Tsiang T'ing-fu [Jiang Tingfu]: Between Two Worlds, 1895-1935" (Ph.D. diss., University of Maryland, College Park, 1979), 440-46; Jerome Chen, *China and the West: Society and Culture, 1815-1937* (Bloomington: Indiana University Press, 1980), 193-94 (on Ding Wenjiang and the debate in general); Y. C. Wang, *Chinese Intellectuals and the West*, 384-86 (on Ding).

24. The following discussion of Jiang's views is based on Zhang, "Minzhu ducai," 2-4. For Jiang's original article, see his "Geming yu zhuanzhi" (Revolution and Autocracy), *Duli pinglun*, no. 80 (December 1933): 2-5; translated in De Bary, Chan, and Tan, *Sources of Chinese Tradition*, 2: 129-32.

25. The following discussion of the views of Hu and Ding are based on Zhang, "Minzhu ducai," 4-6. For discussions of their respective roles in the debate, see Grieder, *Hu Shih*, 259-77; Furth, *Ting Wen-chiang*, 214-21.

26. "Guojia minzhu zhengzhi yu guojia shehuizhuyi" (National Democracy and National Socialism), *Zaisheng* 1, no. 2 (1932): 1-38. This article dealt with "national democracy." The piece on national socialism was published in *Zaisheng* 1, no. 3 (1932): 1-40.

27. Grieder, *Intellectuals*, 346.

28. Furth, *Ting Wen-chiang*, 217, 235.

29. Eastman, *The Abortive Revolution*, 151.

30. Zhang, *Liguo zhi dao*, part 2, chap. 4.

31. James C. Thomson, Jr., *While China Faced West: American Reformers in Nationalist China, 1928-1937* (Cambridge: Harvard University Press, 1969); Y. C. Wang, *Chinese Intellectuals and the West*.

32. Tan, *Chinese Political Thought*, 264.

33. Like Zhang, Ding Wenjiang worried that the Chinese did not share the most basic beliefs. Furth, *Ting Wen-chiang*, 221.

34. Tan assessed Zhang's hopes as "more ideal than practical." Tan, *Chinese Political Thought*, 260.

35. Eastman, *The Abortive Revolution*, 166-68.

36. Ibid., 153.

37. Grieder, *Hu Shih*, 271; Tan, *Chinese Political Thought*, 244-45.

38. Eastman, *The Abortive Revolution*, 175-76.

39. For discussions of Sun's theories, see Franz H. Michael and George E. Taylor, *The Far East in the Modern World*, 3d ed. (Hinsdale, IL: Dryden, 1975), 380-81; Grieder, *Hu Shih*, 270; Eastman, *The Abortive Revolution*, 171-72. Another NSP leader, Luo Longji, also drew a distinction between ability and authority. Grieder, *Intellectuals*, 345.

40. Mao Tse-tung, *Selected Works of Mao Tse-tung*, 5 vols. (Peking: Foreign Languages Press, 1961-77), 2: 339-84; 4: 170.

41. The author, Marilyn Young, agreed with Joseph Esherick in writing that "Chinese efforts to preserve her [their] sovereignty against imperialism" were a failure as long as they followed a fatally flawed model—Western bourgeois democracy." See "Imperialism in China: An Exchange," *Bulletin of Concerned Asian Scholars* 5, no. 2 (1973): 34.

42. While arguing against the suitability of democracy in China, Eastman also conceded that the National Emergency Conference in Luoyang in 1932 demonstrated "democratic rule was still an effective rallying cry in national politics." Eastman, *The Abortive Revolution*, 179-80, 163.

43. Grieder, *Intellectuals*, 350.

PART FOUR

Unity and Disunity during the War of Resistance against Japan

10

The "Other United Front":
The National Socialist Party of China, the Guomindang, and the Chinese Communists, 1937-1938

Most studies of the United Front (UF) formed as a result of the outbreak of the Sino-Japanese War in 1937 have focused on the roles played by the two major forces, the Guomindang (GMD) and the Chinese Communist Party (CCP). Little attention has been paid to the small parties and groups—such as the National Socialist Party of China (NSP)—and their leaders. It is quite true, of course, that the NSP was a small party during the war. Despite estimates ranging from approximately ten thousand to as many as two hundred thousand members, its wartime ranks probably numbered in the hundreds rather than the thousands.[1] And yet, its influence was greater than its size, for a number of famous Chinese intellectuals and statesmen belonged at one time or another. Its membership included, for example, Luo Wengan, Zhang Dongsun, Luo Longji, Pan Guangdan, and a number of other important intellectuals, as well as Zhang Junmai himself.

The minor parties and their leaders were very active during the formation of the UF and in its heyday, 1937-38. By tracing the role of one of these figures, Zhang Junmai, leader of the NSP, one may see the rise and beginning of the fall of the UF from a perspective other than that of the GMD-CCP struggle. This viewpoint should add another dimension to the history of China during the early years of the war and help us to attain a fuller sense of what the possibilities were a half-century ago in that war-torn land.

In Zhang's case, his involvement in the UF (like that of a number of others) began with the Lushan Conference, continued through the short lifetime of the National Defense Advisory Council (NDAC), and reached its culmination with the establishment of the People's Political Council (PPC), which he later termed "the beginning of the great cooperation of the political parties of the entire nation."[2] On the other hand, the decline of unity was reflected in his clash in late 1938 with the CCP, as well as the defection to the Japanese—beginning during the second half of 1938 following the adjournment of the First PPC—of some of the key leaders of the NSP. Perhaps surprisingly, in light of the GMD's persecution of him during the Nanjing decade (1927-37) and his consequent hostility toward that party and all it represented, the relationship between the two survived—despite the strains occasioned by Zhang's participation in the Association of Comrades for National Unity and Construction and the League of Chinese Democratic Political Groups—until late 1941, when Chiang Kai-shek finally cracked down on him. Let us first turn to a description of Zhang's role during 1937-38.

The Lushan Conference

When the first shots of WWII in Asia were fired in the Marco Polo Bridge Incident during the early morning hours of 7 July 1937, Zhang was just leaving a dinner with the GMD mayor of Peiping, General Qin Dechun.[3] Such company was certainly not standard fare for Zhang during the Nanjing Decade, which witnessed the closing of his Institute of Political Science in Shanghai by the GMD, his kidnapping for ransom, his exile in Germany from 1929-31 when things became too hot for him in China, and the hounding of him and *Zaisheng* during the years following the founding of the NSP in the spring of 1932. Yet, toward the end of the decade, there had been signs that, in the face of the Japanese and communist threats, the enmity between Zhang and the GMD was weakening.[4] Hence, when the GMD moved to garner support for what looked increasingly like war on the horizon by inviting over four hundred members of China's "unofficial parties and cliques," as well as representatives of the academic world, to attend a conference at Guling in the Lushan mountains, Zhang was included.

The Lushan Conference was the first public indication of a political truce in the making between the GMD and other parties and groups in China. It was the first substantive step toward the UF that would carry China through the horrible first year of the Japanese invasion. It launched the process of creating national unity and rallying China's population behind the National Government.[5]

Preparations for the meeting began in June 1937, the month before the conference convened. The final list of invitees was drawn up, the conference agenda prepared, and the summer capital of the government, Guling in Jiangxi province, was chosen as the site of the deliberations.[6] GMD notables, minority party leaders, and nonpartisans were among the participants, with Chiang Kai-shek and Wang Jingwei acting as cohosts and personally greeting the conferees.[7] The only notables absent were representatives of the CCP and the Guangxi Clique. By the time the conference opened on 16 July, fighting had begun in the North. Hence, what had been billed as a meeting for an exchange of views became a platform for calls for resistance to Japan and the creation of a united front. The meeting lasted a mere four days, adjourning on 19 July.[8]

Zhang's acceptance of an invitation from a man and party he had fought against for a decade revealed the influences on him at that time. Having just come from a Peiping under attack by the Japanese, he certainly was more than aware of the Japanese threat. In accepting the invitation, he also was acting in accord with the general sentiment expressed at the Second Congress of the NSP, held in the fall of 1936.[9] Finally, his brother, Kia-ngau, later recalled that after the war broke out, the government asked him to persuade Zhang to cooperate with it. His brother, wrote Kia-ngau, "accepted my advice to participate in the National Affairs Conference [Lushan Conference]."[10]

The time Zhang spent in Guling was critical for China. It was then that the negotiations that were to lead to war, rather than peace, were carried on. Zhang was in the audience when Chiang Kai-shek delivered his famous speech the day after the conference opened. Drawing the line against further Japanese inroads on Chinese territory, Chiang declared that, "If we allow one inch more of our territory to be lost, we shall be guilty of an unpardonable crime against our race."[11] Zhang supported Chiang Kai-shek's stance. In fact, Zhang had been the first speaker at the meeting. According to his memoirs, he was "the first to express support for the government's strategy of a war of resistance against Japan."[12] The foreign press reported Zhang's statement that "in the face of the present national crisis, the existence of the nation must be placed above everything else. Under the slogan of national unity . . . all those who have retired from the political limelight should place absolute confidence in the National Government and should offer, if any, constructive criticism."[13] When his speech was finished, Zhang later wrote, "Feng Yuxiang and others came [over] to shake [my] hand."[14]

The government thus got what it wanted at the Lushan Conference. It had convened the meeting, wrote Zhang, "with the object of forming a united front." When Chiang Kai-shek was quite sure of unity, as a result of negotiations with the CCP and the Guling talks with representatives of the "democratic parties" and nonpartisan leaders, he was ready to resist Japan. According to Zhang, he himself was "the first to agree to such a united front."[15] Hence, he recalled, he signed the declaration that called for unity of the entire nation against the foreign invader.[16] As so often in history, then, the threat of foreign aggression overrode—at least for the time being—domestic political struggles.

Following the conclusion of the conference, Zhang lingered on at Guling, taking what he described as "a month's summer holiday in the mountains." When he saw that the "situation in the outside world was abnormal (*budui*)," he decided it was time to leave.[17] Later, he vividly described what it was like to be nearly trapped by the eruption of warfare all around:

> On the day of the outbreak of war at Shanghai [13 August 1937], I went to the travel bureau of the Shanghai Commercial Bank [in Guling] to book passage on the Yangtse River, and received my steamer ticket. A few minutes later, when passing the office again, I was asked to give back the ticket. The reason was that Kiang-ying [Jiangyin], a strategic point on the Yangtse, had been blocked, and no boat could go down to Shanghai. The agent did not wish to tell me the news openly, and took me to his room. I booked another passage as far as Nanking. My arrival at Nanking on 17 August coincided with the Japanese bombing of that city. The steamer was anchored on the other side of the river, and when the bombing was over I landed.[18]

To conclude the story, after landing Zhang went to see his brother, Kia-ngau, then minister of railways, and asked for a ticket to Shanghai. Traveling by either rail or car was unsafe, though, and he had to abandon the idea of joining his family in Shanghai.[19]

The National Defense Advisory Council

When the government heard that Zhang was in Nanjing, it informed him that he had already been appointed a member of the newly formed National Defense Advisory Council (*Guofang canyi hui).* "But at that moment," he later wrote, "I was frankly more interested in seeing my family than in political discussions." When it proved impossible to travel to Shanghai, though, he had to resign himself to a life of politics sans family until—as it turned out—1940.[20]

The NDAC was established by the Organic Articles of 10 August 1937, passed by a new Nationalist organization, the Supreme National Defense Council (SNDC). The latter had replaced the GMD's Central Political Council as the nominally supreme political organ in wartime China. The NDAC was to "advise the government and hear reports from the government."[21] Its first meeting was held on 17 August, the day of Zhang's arrival in Nanjing, and its sixty-fourth and last session on 17 June 1938.[22] Along with the conclusion of a formal agreement between the GMD and CCP in August and September, it was the first manifestation of the new UF, and its membership eventually reached a total of twenty-four or twenty-five delegates.[23]

After his arrival in Nanjing, Zhang wired seven key members of the NSP to join him in the capital to discuss ways in which the party might render service in the War of Resistance.[24] As he later wrote, "my friends in the party all came to Nanjing for consultations and declared that [since] the Government was already fighting Japan, we should stay in Nanjing and participate in the national plans."[25] Hence, he and the seven NSP members "unanimously held that the only thing to do was to cease party disputes at home and stand together against the enemy."[26] As a result, in addition to Zhang, the NSP was represented in the NDAC by Zhang Dongsun, Jiang Yong, and Hu Shiqing.[27]

Li Huang, a representative of the Chinese Youth Party (CYP) in the NDAC, described the sessions in this way: "When the . . . Council convened, we first listened to reports from the war front. Next everyone listened to reports and ideas concerning war strategy, wartime resources and manpower, and there was a lot of empty talk and discussion."[28] Zuo Shunsheng, Li's party colleague and fellow delegate in the council, however, remembered the NDAC as a "good organization": "We were really able to talk because of the small membership. The attitude of the chairman, Wang Jingwei, was good. He gave us complete freedom to express our views in detail." The government could not completely disregard the resolutions of the council, Zuo argued, because "its members were responsible men capable of discussing concrete issues." Moreover, he added, the council operated at the beginning of the war "when there was spiritual unity against the enemy" and the "atmosphere was excellent."[29]

Nevertheless, the council was merely an advisory organ and possessed no legal or constitutional powers. The government had the power to dissolve it at will.[30] Moreover, it was too small. Those in the GMD and other parties who had been left out wanted in.[31] As Zhang Junmai recalled, "After the first days of panic were over, many party leaders who believed in democracy came to me to express their opinion that the fifteen-member [*sic*] . . . Council could not meet the needs of a united front, and they pressed for a reorganization of the Council."[32] Hence, negotiations with the SNDC ensued. During the course of these talks, Zhang later wrote, "the military defense of Shanghai was abandoned, and the government was so busy with the withdrawal from Nanking to Hankou that the question had to be postponed."[33] In late October, the members of the NDAC joined government personnel in leaving Nanjing by ship, amid continuous Japanese bombing.[34]

Hankou, part of the tri-city complex known as Wuhan, served as a temporary capital from the abandonment of Nanjing in December 1937 until the move to Chongqing in October 1938. The First UF had reached its zenith in Wuhan in 1926-1927,[35] and the Second UF was also to experience its heyday there, with the flourishing of the so-called "Hankou spirit." In late 1926, Zhang had traveled up the Yangtze to Wuhan to investigate the GMD in the full flush of its revolutionary enthusiasm during the Northern Expedition.[36] Now he again ascended the river, this time, though, as an ally of a conservative GMD.[37] During the depressing retreat, which took him further and further from his family and native province, he found comfort in reflecting on heroes of the Chinese past:

> When in those days I was going with the government from Nanking to Hankow and finally to Chungking [via Guilin], the example of Wen Tien-hsiang was continuously in my mind. He was Prime Minister during the Sung Dynasty when China was invaded by the Mongols, and he died a martyr. So also, when the Ming Dynasty came to an end, there were patriots everywhere who were loyal to the Chinese throne, fought against the Manchus to the bitter end, and, refusing to collaborate with the enemy, went underground when their cause was all but lost.
>
> This spirit among the Chinese, this willingness to fight for their country, was fully manifested during the war against Japan.[38]

Therefore, Chinese patriotic heroes were very much on his mind during the early, dark days of the war (as we have already seen in the prospectus he drafted for the Institute of National Culture in the winter of 1939). Perhaps inspired by this sort of martyrology, during the early months of the war he is said to have regretted he could not give his life on the battlefield.[39]

Threat to the United Front

Such patriotic spirit was not universal among Chinese at that time, however. There also was the possibility of a negotiated peace with Japan, if decent terms could be had. Since the Japanese were adamantly anticommunist, such a peace probably would have split the GMD-CCP UF. The 5 November Japanese demands, for example, called for a "common fight against Bolshevism," while those communicated to the Chinese Government on 26 December insisted that the latter "abandon her pro-Communist . . . policy and cooperate with Japan and Manchukuo in carrying out their anti-Communist policy."[40]

The major peace effort spanned the period between late October 1937 and mid-January 1938 and was carried on through the good offices of the German ambassador to China, Dr. Oscar Trautmann. When Trautmann approached Chiang Kai-shek in early November with the Japanese terms, the latter rejected them, declaring that he "could not accept any Japanese demands so long as the Japanese were not prepared to restore the *status quo ante*."[41]

By the end of November, however, things had changed, and the Chinese government was in an extremely perilous situation. The Japanese landing at Hangzhou had transformed the stalwart Chinese defense of Shanghai into a rout by the third week of November. The best Chinese armies appeared shattered, and the GMD capital, Nanjing, was menaced.[42] Nor would there be any help from the Western allies, for the 15 November declaration of the Brussels Conference amounted to empty words.[43]

In view of the drastically altered situation, Chiang Kai-shek and his generals concluded that the time had come to make peace. On 2 December, Chiang met with Trautmann in the soon-to-be-abandoned capital of Nanjing and, having been assured that the Japanese terms were the same as in early November, stated that China would accept them as a basis for negotiations, so long as the talks and peace terms were kept secret.[44]

It was too late for talk, however. On 13 December, the Japanese occupied Nanjing and launched the infamous "Rape of Nanking." The result was a new and harsher set of terms, which Trautmann communicated to the Chinese on 26 December.[45] The Chinese government wavered between acceptance and rejection. When it stalled by requesting further details, on 16 January 1938 the Japanese government dropped its efforts to make peace with the Chiang regime.[46] Hence, the GMD-CCP UF against the Japanese, which probably would have been split by the GMD's acceptance, survived.

Following the war, Zhang praised Chinese determination to resist the Japanese invasion. But what was his view in the early, dark days of the struggle? He certainly was aware of the peace negotiations, as well as the German mediation. His brother, Kia-ngau, with whom he was very close, was in touch with Trautmann.[47] However, there is evidence that Zhang was not in favor of peace at any cost. He was present at a secret meeting of minority-party leaders called by Zhang Qun, who served as the Chinese government's representative in the Trautmann mediation. Zhang Qun told those in attendance that a telegram had arrived from Chiang Kai-shek in Nanjing, reporting that Trautmann had proposed a ceasefire and peace and requesting that Zhang Qun solicit the views of those at the secret meeting. Former Minister of Foreign Affairs Luo Wengan, a member of the NSP, testily pointed out that Zhang Qun had not mentioned terms and declared "there is nothing for us to discuss here." Zhang Qun then volunteered that the Japanese generals had promised to retreat to Shanghai if the Chinese armies fell back west of Nanjing; only then would it be possible to speak of peace. Silent until that point, Zhang Junmai then protested that he was "afraid it is a ruse of the enemy. If our troops do withdraw, then . . . [there will] be great confusion, and we might not be able to restore order."[48]

He also heard about the peace negotiations as a result of his participation in the NDAC. Again, the evidence suggests he was not a "peacemonger." The meeting probably was held to discuss the 26 December Japanese terms communicated by Trautmann to the government. One of Zhang's colleagues in the council described the session:

> In the Council, Wang Ching-wei expressed that there was great hope for peace and requested the Council members to study the terms for peace. Since this was an important matter, everyone did not give speeches, but there was a violent reaction to express that Generalissimo Chiang had promised that we would "sacrifice to the end and would never speak of peace midway." However, no one continued to talk and gradually everyone returned home.[49]

Although Zhang had ample opportunity to learn of the peace feelers, one wonders whether he knew the extent to which Chiang Kai-shek was willing to negotiate. Usually very critical of Chiang, following the war he praised him: "The fact that he had no hesitation in turning down the Japanese conditions showed that he had little in common with the mentality of the Axis powers. . . . Chiang simply kept on fighting the Japanese, without worrying much about the consequences to himself."[50] Yet, as the evidence shows, on 2 December Chiang agreed to the Japanese terms as a basis for negotiation, and, when the Japanese torpedoed peace negotiations in mid-January, his government had not yet formally rejected the harsher 26 December terms. Moreover, there is evidence that Chiang *did* worry about the "consequences to himself." When presented with the 5 November peace terms, he told Trautmann that there would be a revolution in China, and the Chinese government "would be swept out by the tide of public opinion," if he accepted them.[51]

Guomindang Recognition of the NSP

Although it was clear that Chiang Kai-shek would have preferred merging all other political parties into a single party, and the NSP was said to have "expressed its readiness to consider the idea,"[52] the plan collapsed when the CCP, perhaps recalling the disasters of the "bloc within" days of 1927, refused.[53] Chiang then had to settle for convincing other parties to cooperate with the GMD under his leadership.[54] The first step was to obtain the parties' recognition of the paramountcy of Sun Yat-sen's Three People's Principles (TPP) and the supreme leadership of the government and the GMD in the anti-Japanese struggle. In return, Chiang and the GMD offered recognition of the existence of those parties, which had been living in a twilight zone of illegality throughout their brief lives. The method chosen was a public exchange of letters between the leaders of the NSP and CYP and Chiang Kai-shek and Wang Jingwei of the GMD.

Zhang was the first of the small-party leaders to write, and in his 13 April 1938 letter, he measured up to the GMD's expectations.[55] The NSP's program, he wrote, "is really much the same as Sun Yat-sen's racial, political, and economic democracy," though he was careful to add "the two may differ somewhat in phraseology." Moreover, he and his colleagues were ready, he declared, to discuss political problems and "questions that arise on the spur of the moment but defy an off-hand solution" with government and GMD leaders in "a spirit of cordial cooperation." Finally, he assured Chiang and Wang that "at the present critical moment, nothing is more important than whole-hearted and unreserved support for the National Government."

Having told the GMD leaders exactly what they wanted to hear and bearing in mind the public nature of the exchange, he then put in a plug for human rights, as well as GMD tolerance for his party. In doing so, he communicated to a wider public what the NSP stood for. According to the "Program of Armed Resistance and National Reconstruction," he wrote, "in the course of the war, the freedom of speech . . . press, and . . . assembly shall be fully guaranteed to the people, provided they do not contravene Dr. Sun Yat-sen's revolutionary principles or the provisions of the law." That, he emphasized, was "entirely in accord with the opinion of the National Socialist Party."

While he argued for GMD tolerance toward his party, he again revealed the influence of Confucianism on his politics. The Confucian Classics, he wrote, taught a *Weltanschauung* that "allows all things to grow great in common and all systems of philosophy to propagate at the same time and in the same place. Since the interests of the Chinese are catholic, their views do not tend to be biased or exclusive." Citing Sun Yat-sen's beliefs, as well as what he viewed as the CCP's dropping of class struggle in favor of nationalism and the "totalitarian theorists" abandonment of fascism as inapplicable to Chinese conditions, he argued that all of these showed the Chinese love for "compromise and the golden mean."[56] This feature of the Chinese character, he claimed, was "peculiar to us." Then he brought the philosophical lesson closer to home: "The recent declaration of the Emergency Session of the Kuomintang National Congress is an important document showing how the rule of the golden mean should be applied in practical politics. . . . If now the Kuomintang shows toleration to other political parties, a toleration that comes from the depths of the Chinese heart, can there be any doubt that this is a sure sign of the regeneration of the Chinese nation?"

Finally, he devoted a good bit of his public letter to his party's program. It stood for nationalism, a "reformed form of democratic government," and socialism, he wrote, going on to add brief explanations of each of its "three principles" (echoing Sun Yat-sen's famous TPP).

Having paid the price, he and his colleagues in the NSP had the satisfaction of seeing their party's name mentioned in the perfunctory GMD reply,[57] thus granting it instant public recognition. Moreover, the texts of the letters were printed in the Chinese press.[58] An editorial in *Dagongbao*, for example, referred to the exchange of letters as an event "rich in political history significance," with great importance for "the promotion of political unity." Through the exchange of letters, the NSP and the CYP had obtained "a position of open existence." The paper concluded by calling for absolute unanimity in support of the government, the Leader (*lingxiu*), the War of Resistance, and the TPP.[59]

Foreign correspondents also reported the exchange of letters. As in the case of some Chinese reports, though, the similarity of the NSP's name to that of Hitler's party in Germany created misunderstanding. Perhaps the most influential foreign report was that of John Gunther, author of the popular "inside" books. His 1939 work, *Inside Asia*, which sold over 250,000 copies, described the NSP as a "semi-fascist" party. Despite its protests, the 1942 edition continued to describe the party in that fashion.[60] As leader of the party, Zhang Junmai did his utmost to rebut these reports. In a letter to an American scholar, he complained that when reporting his exchange of letters with Chiang Kai-shek, foreign correspondents "referred without a second thought to our party as 'Nazi', thus creating all [those] distortions which might have occurred [even] without such mischief."[61]

The People's Political Council

The final cornerstone in the UF during 1937-38 was the establishment of the PPC. A foreign observer termed it "the first step toward decentralization of power since 1927."[62] Taking it even further, one participant later argued that the names of the members of the First PPC "were sufficient to show that during the war, there was a trend towards the development of democracy."[63] As a result of that sort of viewpoint, a common name for the PPC has been "China's Wartime Parliament."[64]

Negotiations concerning establishment of such an organization had begun while the government was still in Nanjing. At first, the discussions centered on possible expansion of the NDAC.[65] Interrupted by the move upriver, the question was revived when the government settled in Hankou.[66] According to Zhang, the GMD representatives displayed a frank and sincere attitude throughout the talks that led to the establishment of the PPC. Reflecting the government's desire to broaden its base of support during the national crisis, they proved willing to compromise.[67] The discussions concluded that the PPC should be much larger than the NDAC, that it would be advisory like the NDAC, and that the membership would be partly appointed and partly elected.

Having reached agreement, Article 12 of the "Program of Armed Resistance and National Reconstruction," adopted by the Extraordinary National Congress of the GMD held in Wuchang from 29 March to 1 April 1938, declared, "An organ shall be set up for the people to participate in affairs of state, thereby unifying the national strength and collecting the best minds and views for facilitating the formulation and execution of national policies."[68] Immediately following the congress, the GMD's Central Executive Committee met and passed the Organic Law of the PPC, which was promulgated on 12 April and published in the press.[69]

The First PPC was held from 6 to 15 July 1938. It had a total of two hundred members, of whom one hundred constituted category 4, which was where the parties were seated. Representation in that group was the subject of hard bargaining between the GMD and other parties prior to the PPC's convocation. In practice, each party was given a quota to fill as it saw fit, with the list then submitted to the GMD for approval. The NSP was allocated eight seats.[70] In fact, eleven members of the NSP found their way into the first council, due perhaps to what a CYP leader called "the Kuomintang's lack of clarity about the membership of [other] parties."[71] In addition, Zhang and Jiang Yong were elected to the council's Resident Committee, which functioned as a PPC "in miniature" when the council was not in session, hearing government reports and promoting the implementation of resolutions passed by the PPC.[72]

The First PPC seems to have represented the height of the UF. According to a minority-party councilor, "Members were in high spirits. Morale was excellent. Mr. Chiang [Kai-shek] was not prejudiced. Nor did he take a guarded attitude toward the other parties."[73] Even foreigners, the "old China hands," seemed swept up in the enthusiasm, with one calling the First PPC "an epoch-making event in Chinese history . . . and . . . the most representative . . . [body] ever assembled in this country."[74]

The GMD-CCP UF did not keep the NSP and CYP from attempting to cooperate with each other in the PPC, as they had done elsewhere ever since their first substantial contacts in Shanghai in 1927. A CYP leader recalled that on important issues his party held joint meetings with NSP members of the

PPC. Those meetings were infrequent, he added, noting that the two groups met "whenever it seemed necessary to discuss questions involving both parties. For instance, we exchanged views concerning the Communist Party." According to his testimony, the UF with the GMD, at least, was healthy: "At that time [the First PPC], we [the CYP and NSP] did not think of the Kuomintang as a problem requiring joint discussion."[75]

The Decline and Breakdown of the United Front

The beginning of the decline of the UF is usually dated from the summer or fall of 1938, with the renewed GMD crackdown on the CCP.[76] In May 1938, even before the PPC's convocation, the government eliminated all non-GMD youth organizations.[77] Even earlier—in January—the office of the CCP organ, *Xinhua ribao* (New China Daily), had been wrecked by a group of men.[78] During the summer, the government began to suspend newspapers and prohibit public meetings. By the winter of 1938, according to one foreign observer, "political prisoners began once more to fill the jails and concentration camps."[79]

Moreover, no sooner had the First PPC adjourned than the government adopted new censorship laws. Toward the end of July 1938, it adopted the "Regulations for Censorship of the Manuscripts of Wartime Books and Periodicals." Described as one of the most restrictive of the new regulations being imposed by the government to tighten its grip, it required all manuscripts to be checked and approved by authorized government agencies before publication. Despite passage of a resolution in the PPC calling for its repeal, it was written into law in 1940 and remained in effect throughout the war.[80] In addition, in 1938 the "Revised Standards of Censorship of Wartime Books and Periodicals" was promulgated. Its effect was sweeping, as it forbade criticism of the GMD, the National Government, and the Supreme Leader.[81]

Zhang largely escaped the effects of that gathering cloud of reaction. During the period from May to July 1938, he had been drafting a detailed explanation of the NSP's program. Originally entitled *Liguo zhi dao* (The Way to Found the State), it was subtitled, *Guojia shehuizhuyi* (National Socialism). He had no difficulty obtaining approval of the manuscript from GMD Central Party Headquarters, and in September 1938 it was published in Guilin, where he was lecturing while enroute fron Wuhan to Chongqing.[82] Moreover, the GMD allowed it to be advertised in *Zaisheng*.[83] As a result, by 1939 a third edition had been published, and, according to an admittedly biased source, it was said to have sold over 100,000 copies.[84]

By allowing the NSP to publish a program that could easily be considered a challenge to Sun Yat-sen's TPP, the GMD clearly showed that at that point in the war it had a more benign view of the NSP than of the CCP. Some hint of an explanation may be found in the earlier comment of a CYP leader, when asked about Chiang Kai-shek's idea of creating one party from those then in existence. The GMD, CYP, and NSP, he argued, were "like milk in water—it is easy for them to mix together. But as for the CCP and us, they are like stones in water which cannot mix together."[85]

Part of a flood of refugees of all kinds,[86] Zhang arrived in Chongqing prior to the opening of the Second Session of the First PPC. That city was to remain the capital of China from the fall of 1938 until the National Government's return to Nanjing in May 1946.[87] An inferno in summer and fogbound in winter, it was a "medieval" city, riddled with disease, profiteering, and inflation. Perhaps its only good point was the air-raid protection offered by its rocky topography.[88]

It was duty that brought Zhang to Chongqing. He had to be there in time for the PPC session, which met from 28 October to 6 November 1938.[89] The influence of his party suffered a decline at that meeting; instead of the eleven seats it occupied at the first session in Hankou, it held only eight places in the second session.[90] *Zaisheng* was tolerated, though, and resumed publication in Chongqing. It was registered with the government there, as it had been in Hankou.[91]

While waiting for the session to begin, Zhang showed his continued committment to the UF. As a result of rumors that the government might make peace with Japan, on 26 October he joined a group of councilors, including Wang Jingwei, who urged continued resistance. As a result of that motion, and perhaps helped along by a flattering message from the Generalissimo, on 2 November the council adopted a resolution reaffirming its faith in Chiang Kai-shek and calling on the country to maintain resistance.[92] At the meeting, Zhang's NSP colleague, Luo Longji, argued that the first session had expressed the unity of parties and factions, while the second should emphasize plans and methods of armed resistance.[93]

Underneath the surface of that unity, though, the strain of war was beginning to take its toll. During the second session, Zhang later recalled, there were reports of a rift between Wang Jingwei and H. H. Kong (Kong Xiangxi), who was president of the executive yuan, minister of finance, and one of Chiang Kai-shek's closest associates during the war.[94] As the fog settled over the city in December, Zhang made his own contribution to the erosion of the UF. In an open letter to Mao Zedong, he criticized the vaunted leader and his party. That attack understandably elicited a counterattack from a CCP spokesman. Zhang's letter and the CCP response set off a round of polemics between members of the two parties, adding tension between the CCP and a minority party to that already existing between the GMD and CCP (for a fuller discussion of this clash between the CCP and the NSP, see chapter 10).

The UF was further undermined when some leaders of the NSP defected to the Wang Jingwei regime, which was formally inaugurated on 30 March 1940. These figures included two men, Zhu Qinglai and Lu Dingkui, whose close associations with Zhang predated the establishment of the NSP.[95] Moreover, the defectors adopted the party's name, an action that the NSP in Chongqing wasted little time in denouncing: "We hear that in Shanghai there is . . . [an organization] using the name 'National Socialist Party, Special Committee for Governmental Affairs' (*Zhengwu te weihui*) that has issued a declaration in support of Mr. Wang [Jingwei]. This is obviously theft of [our] name."[96] In addition, the "National Socialist Party" (quotations in the original) was listed as one of the organizing elements of the Wang regime's Central Political Council, organized on 20 March in Nanjing.[97]

Even though Zhang officially denied his party's participation in the Wang regime,[98] the defection of his longtime colleagues must have constituted a severe blow to the prestige of the NSP. The final collapse of Zhang's participation in the UF came in late 1941. Having incurred Chiang Kai-shek's ire, the school he had founded in western Yunnan, the Institute of National Culture, was shut down, and he was placed under "city arrest," that is, forbidden to leave Chongqing.[99] With that blow, the UF was dead for him, for he was at odds with both its dominant parties, the CCP and the GMD.

Conclusion

The UF was important to China while it lasted. It enabled the country to make it through the early years of the war without completely disintegrating and concluding a disastrous peace settlement with the Japanese. However, it was probably fated not to last. Although the GMD granted the NSP public recognition, it did not give it legal rights. In short, the ruling party did not abandon political tutelage. It was interested in broad support for the war and the government, not in implementing democracy in China. The NDAC and the PPC, those gestures in the direction of representative assemblies, were both advisory in nature. They existed at the sufferance of the GMD, and the latter was completely free to ignore the resolutions that came pouring out of the assemblies (as it repeatedly did).

It was perhaps to be expected that a man who was a supporter of a

Western-style parliamentary system and had strenuously opposed the GMD's one-party dictatorship ever since the Northern Expedition of 1926-1927 would not be able to avoid clashing with Chiang Kai-shek for very long. What is perhaps remarkable is that the clash was so long in coming (the fourth year of the war). Nor was it possible for Zhang to subsume his anticommunist feelings. Hence, it was perfectly in character for him to chastize Mao Zedong and the CCP in late 1938, and not—as some might suspect—a put-up job backed by the GMD. If anything, his criticism of the CCP won him even more tolerance from the GMD. Finally, the defection of some of the key leaders of the NSP weakened the party by the spring of 1940. Those who would slight or persecute it thus had less to lose by doing so.

Notes

1. For the high tallies, see Zhang Zhiyi, comp., *Kangzhan zhong di zhengdang he paibie* (Political Parties and Groups in the War of Resistance) (Chongqing: Dushu shenghuo chubanshe, 1939), 79; John Gunther, *Inside Asia* (New York: Harper, 1939), 271; Xu Fulin, "Guojia shehui dang zhi chengli shi" (History of the Founding of the National Socialist Party), *Guojia shehui bao*, 7 July 1940, 4. For estimates placing the membership at less than 1,000, see *Zhongguo ge xiao dangpai*, 73; Ch'ien Tuan-sheng, *The Government and Politics of China*, 354.

2. Zhang, "Wu guo zhengdang fazhan," 3.

3. Zhang Zhiben, "Some Personal Reminiscences of Zhang Zhiben," condensed, edited, and transcribed by Zai Gaifu (Taipei: Institute of Modern History, Academia Sinica, 1960), 48. Zhang Zhiben later recalled, "As soon as I returned to my hotel, I heard the sound of gunfire. This was the Marco Polo Bridge Incident." Ibid., 49.

4. As we have seen in chapter 8, Zhang lectured in GMD-controlled Jiangxi in late 1936 and supported that party's attempts to wean the province from Communist influence.

5. Lawrence N. L. Shyu, "The People's Political Council and China's Wartime Problems, 1937-1945" (Ph.D. diss., Columbia University, 1972), 28-29.

6. Ho, "Reminiscences," 180.

7. Lloyd E. Eastman, "Nationalist China during the Sino-Japanese War, 1937-1945," in *The Cambridge History of China*, vol. 13, part 2: *Republican China, 1912-1949*, ed. John K. Fairbank and Albert Feuerwerker (Cambridge: Cambridge University Press, 1986), 558; "General Chiang Kai-shek Returns to Nanking; Leaders Discuss Nation's Problems at Kuling," *China Weekly Review* 81 (July 1937): 270.

8. Ho, "Reminiscences," 183.

9. That congress had issued a declaration advocating immediate resistance to Japan. YX, 26.

10. Zhang Gongquan [Kia-ngau], "Wo yu jiaxiong Junmai" (My Elder Brother, Junmai, and I), in *Zhang Junmai qishi shouqing jinian lunwen ji*, 102.

11. James B. Crowley, "A Reconsideration of the Marco Polo Bridge Incident," *The Journal of Asian Studies* 22 (May 1963): 286.

12. Zhang, *Bianzheng weiwuzhuyi*, 193.

13. "General Chiang Kai-shek," 270.

14. Zhang, *Bianzheng weiwuzhuyi*, 193.

15. Chang, *Third Force*, 25, 96-97.

16. Zhang, "Zhuiyi [Zeng] Muhan," 3.

17. Zhang Junmai, "Wuren chu kangzhan shidai zhong zhi taidu" (The Attitude of Those of Us Living in the Era of the War of Resistance), *Dongfang zazhi* 37, no. 13 (1940): 60.

18. Chang, *Third Force*, 110-11.

19. Ibid., 111. On 27 August, Japanese planes machine-gunned the car of the British ambassador, Sir Hugh Knatchbull-Hugessen, and severely wounded him. Leonard Moseley, *Hirohito: Emperor of Japan* (Englewood Cliffs, NJ: Prentice-Hall, 1966), 171.

20. Chang, *Third Force*, 11, 25. Sometime after 30 May 1940, Zhang's wife and four children flew from Shanghai to Yunnan to rejoin him. YX, 31; Zhang, "Wuren chu kangzhan shidai," 60.

21. Ch'ien Tuan-sheng, *The Government and Politics of China*, 280; Shyu, "The People's Political Council," 30.

22. Huang Yanpei, *Huang Yanpei riji zhailu* (Extracts from Huang Yanpei's Diary), comp. Center for Research on Republican China, Chinese Academy of Social Sciences (Beijing: Zhonghua shuju, 1979), 4.

23. For a summary of the GMD-CCP agreement, see Shyu, "The People's Political Council," 29 (n. 2). According to some reports, there were only twenty-four members of the NDAC. Ibid., 30 (n. 1); Ch'ien Tuan-sheng, *The Government and Politics of China*, 280. Others assert there were twenty-five members of the council. "Democracy versus One-Party Rule in Kuomintang China: The 'Little Parties' Organize," *Amerasia* 7, no. 3 (1943): 99; Li Huang, "Reminiscences," 542. The whole problem hinges on whether NSP member Luo Wengan was a member of the council. According to the *Amerasia* article and BDRC, 2: 441, he was.

24. "Zhongguo minzhu shehui dang jianyao shigao," 19. Those summoned by Zhang included Zhang Dongsun, Hu Shiqing, Luo Longji, Zhu Qinglai, Lu Dingkui, Jiang Yuntian, and Feng Jinbai. Ibid.

25. Zhang, *Bianzheng weiwuzhuyi*, 193.

26. "Zhongguo minzhu shehui dang jianyao shigao," 19.

27. Shyu, "The People's Political Council," 228. Shyu identifies Jiang Yong and Hu Shiqing as "independents" in the NDAC. In fact, both were NSP members, and the memoirs of another member of the council identifies them as such. Zuo Shunsheng, "Reminiscences," 139.

28. Li Huang, "Reminiscences," 543.

29. Zuo Shunsheng, "Reminiscences," 140.

30. Ibid.; "Democracy versus One-Party Rule," 98-99.

31. Ch'ien Tuan-sheng, *The Government and Politics of China*, 280.

32. Chang, *Third Force*, 111.

33. Ibid.

34. Li Huang, "Reminiscences," 546.

35. John Israel and Donald W. Klein, *Rebels and Bureaucrats: China's December 9ers* (Berkeley: University of California Press, 1976), 157.

36. For his report on that visit, see *Wuhan jianwen*.

37. For historical perspective on this political "backsliding" on the part of the GMD, see Wright, *The Last Stand of Chinese Conservatism*, chap. 12.

38. Chang, *Third Force*, 19.

39. LHWLX, 23.

40. F. C. Jones, *Japan's New Order in East Asia: Its Rise and Fall, 1937-1945* (London: Oxford University Press, 1954), 60 (n. 4), 65.

41. Ibid., 60-61; Shyu, "The People's Political Council," 66-71. For an early postwar study of the "Trautmann Mediation," see James T.C. Liu, "German Mediation in the Sino-Japanese War, 1937-1938," *The Far Eastern Quarterly* 8 (February 1949): 157-71. For a complete list of Japanese terms, see Jones, *Japan's New Order*, 60 (n. 4).

42. Ibid.

43. The declaration of the Brussels Conference called for a ceasefire in China and condemned Japan for violating the Nine-Power Treaty of 6 February 1922. In the circumstances, those were empty words, and Zhang was probably right when he asserted that the conference had convened without the slightest result. Zhang, "Wu guo zhengdang fazhan," 4.

44. Jones, *Japan's New Order*, 62. For the conditions, see ibid., 62-63, 63 (n. 4).

45. See ibid., 63-64, for a detailed discussion of those new demands.

46. Mackerras and Chan, *Modern China*, 368, 370.

47. Wu Xiangxiang, "Zhang Gongquan xiansheng de qinglian dianfan," 88.

48. Li Huang, "Reminiscences," 548-49.

49. Ibid., 547.

50. Chang, *Third Force*, 97.

51. Jones, *Japan's New Order*, 60-61.

52. William Tung, *Revolutionary China: A Personal Account, 1926-1949* (New York: St. Martin's, 1973), 241.

53. During the First UF of 1923-1927, CCP members were coerced by Comintern discipline into joining the GMD as individuals, thus forming the famous "bloc within." The Chinese Communists would rather have concluded a party-to-party alliance with the GMD, or a "bloc without."

54. Lloyd E. Eastman, *Seeds of Destruction: Nationalist China in War and Revolution, 1937-1949* (Stanford: Stanford University Press, 1984), 89.

55. The following discussion of Zhang's letter is drawn from the English version published in *The Chinese Yearbook, 1938-39*, 341-45. For the Chinese text of Zhang's letter and the reply by Chiang Kai-shek and Wang Jingwei, see *Zhongguo guojia shehui dang xuanyan* (Manifesto of the National Socialist Party of China) (n.p., n.p.), appendix. The foreword of this document is dated April 1938.

56. This was not, of course, the first time he had praised the "golden mean" concept of Confucianism. Earlier, he had applied it to the programs of the German Social Democratic Party (chap. 2).

57. For the full English text, see *The Chinese Yearbook, 1938-39*, 4: 343.

58. See, e.g., the Hankou dispatch of 21 April 1938 in the Yokota Minoru Newspaper Collection (Toyo Bunkyo), Scrapbook No. 41 (large size).

59. Zuo Hongyu, *Kangzhan jianguo zhong zhi Zhongguo qingnian dang* (The Chinese Youth Party during the War of Resistance and National Reconstruction) (n. p.: Guohun shudian, 1939), 16-19.

60. Gunther, *Inside Asia*, 271, 291. According to Harper & Row, *Inside Asia* sold over 150,000 copies in the hardcover edition and over 100,000 in the Book-of-the-Month edition. Corona Machemer, Harper & Row, to author, 10 March 1980. For an earlier NSP reply to its critics, see "Deguo de Guoshedang" (The National Socialist Party of Germany), *Zaisheng*, no. 9 (1938): 2.

61. Zhang to Paul M.A. Linebarger, 24 October 1940, in Linebarger, *The China of Chiang Kai-shek: A Political Study* (Boston: World Peace Foundation, 1941), 179-80.

62. Graham Peck, *Two Kinds of Time*, 2d ed., rev. and abr.(Boston: Houghton Mifflin, 1967), 77.

63. Li Huang, "Reminiscences," 723.

64. Lawrence N.L. Shyu, "China's 'Wartime Parliament': The People's Political Council, 1938-1945," in *Nationalist China During the Sino-Japanese War, 1937-1945*, ed. Paul K.T. Sih (Hicksville, NY: Exposition, 1977), 273-313.

65. Ch'ien Tuan-sheng, *The Government and Politics of China*, 280-81, 422 (n. 4).

66. Chang, *Third Force*, 111.

67. Lawrence N.L. Shyu interview with Carsun Chang, 7 June 1966, Berkeley, California; cited in Shyu, "The People's Political Council," 31-32.

68. *The China Handbook, 1937-1943*, 61.

69. Shyu, "The People's Political Council," 33. For the text of the Organic Law, see *China Handbook, 1937-1943*, 110-12.

70. Shyu, "The People's Political Council," 38, 40; Shyu interview with Carsun Chang, cited in ibid., 43-44.

71. Zuo Shunsheng, "Reminiscences," 162-63.

72. Ibid., 166; Shyu, "The People's Political Council," 51, 54.

73. Zuo Shunsheng, "Reminiscences," 161.

74. H. G. W. Woodhead, ed., *The China Year Book* (Shanghai: North China Daily News & Herald, 1939), 230.

75. Zuo Shunsheng, "Reminiscences," 165.

76. Hsu Lee-hsia Ting, *Government Control of the Press in Modern China, 1900-1949* (Cambridge: Harvard University Press, 1974), 126; Shyu, "The People's Political Council," 161.

77. Randall Gould, *China in the Sun* (New York: Doubleday, 1946), 96; Israel and Klein, *Rebels and Bureaucrats*, 169.

78. Ibid., 159.

79. Gould, *China in the Sun*, 96.

80. Shyu, "The People's Political Council," 161; Ting, *Government Control of the Press*, 22.

81. Shyu, "The People's Political Council," 162.

82. Zhang Junmai, "*Liguo zhi dao* xinban xu" (Preface to the New Edition of *The Way to Found the State*), in *Liguo zhi dao*, 1; Zhang Shiming, "Zhang Junmai xiansheng yu Guangxi" (Mr. Zhang Junmai and Guangxi), *Ziyou Zhong* 1, no. 2 (1970): 29. On Guilin as a liberal publishing center during the war, see Graham Hutchings, "A Province at War: Guangxi during the Sino-Japanese Conflict, 1937-1945," *The China Quarterly*, no. 108 (1986): 658-59.

83. *Zaisheng*, no. 4 (1938): 16.

84. *Guojia shehui bao*, no. 118 (1941): 4.

85. Li Huang, "Reminiscences," 551-52.

86. White and Jacoby, *Thunder Out of China*, 7-8.

87. On 5 May 1946, a ceremony was held to mark the formal return of China's capital from Chongqing to Nanjing. Mackerras and Chan, *Modern China*, 420.

88. Y. P. Mei, "Thus We Live in Chungking," *Asia*, July 1941, 349-51. For a fuller description of Chongqing during wartime, see White and Jacoby, *Thunder Out of China*, chap. 1.

89. Shyu, "The People's Political Council," 40.

90. Xu Fulin, Lu Dingkui, and Wang Youqiao are not included in the list of those who attended the second session. "Guomin canzheng hui lijie canzhengyuan xingming suoyin" (Name Index of Councilors in the Various People's Political Councils), *Zhuanji wenxue* 35, no. 2 (1979): 21-24.

91. Ting, *Government Control of the Press*, 262(n47).

92. *Dagongbao*, Hong Kong, 27 October 1938, 3; cited in P'an Wei-tung, *The Chinese Constitution: A Study of Forty Years of Constitution-Making in China* (Washington, D.C.: Catholic University Press, 1945), 95.

93. GBFO 371 [F810/189/10], A. Clark Kerr, Shanghai, to F.O., 16 December 1938.

94. Shyu interview with Carsun Chang, cited in Shyu, "The People's Political Council," 77-78 (n. 1).

95. Zhu had been elected to the Central General Affairs Committee (*Zhongyang zongwu weiyuanhui*) at the NSP's First Congress in 1934 in Tianjin and to the five-member presidium at the NSP's Second Congress in the fall of 1936. YX, 23, "Zhongguo minzhu shehui dang jianyao shigao," 19. He and Zhang had been acquainted since at least 1911. GS 4, no. 4, 34. Lu also was elected to the Central General Affairs Committee at the First Congress. At the Second Congress, he was chosen secretary-general of the meeting. YX, 23; "Zhongguo minzhu shehui dang jianyao shigao," 19. His association with Zhang appears to have begun when he taught at Zhang's Institute of Political Science in the 1920s. YX, 21.

96. "Guojia shehui dang xuanyan" (Declaration of the National Socialist Party), *Zaisheng*, no. 43 (1940), n.p. [inside front cover].

97. Wenhua gongying she, comp., *Minguo sanian shiyong guomin nianjian* (1941 Citizens' Yearbook for Practical Use) (Guilin: Wenhua gongying she, 1941), 211.

98. "Outstanding Events in the Sino-Japanese War: A Day-to-Day Summary," *China Weekly Review* 92, no. 8 (1940): 278.

99. Chang, *Third Force*, 103-4. For a fuller treatment of Chiang's suppression of Zhang and his school, see infra, chap. 12.

11

A Letter to Mao:
The Polemic over Zhang's Attack on the CCP, 1938-1939

Formation of the Wartime United Front

With the arrival of war between China and Japan in the summer of 1937, the long-brewing Second United Front (UF) between the Guomindang (GMD) and the Chinese Communist Party (CCP) finally came to fruition.[1] On 8 July, the day following the Marco Polo Bridge Incident, the Communists cabled the GMD and pledged their cooperation in resisting Japanese aggression. On the following day, the CCP requested reorganization and assignment of the Red Army. In a document delivered to the Nationalists on 15 July but not released until 22 September, the Communists promised the GMD that they would (according to a summary) "strive for the realization of Sun Yat-sen's Three People's Principles . . . abandon its policies of armed revolt, sovietization, and forcible confiscation of land . . . abolish the present soviet government . . . and abolish the term 'Red Army' and place Communist troops under government command." The following day Chiang Kai-shek praised the manifesto: he declared it

> shows clearly that national interests supersede all other considerations. . . . Since the Communists have discarded their former opinions and have come to realize the importance of national independence and national interests, I hope they will sincerely carry out what is contained in the declaration, and further expect that they will work in unison with the rest of the nation to accomplish the task of national salvation.[2]

It was with such fine words from both parties that the Second UF was launched in the summer and fall of 1937. At first, there were deeds to back up the words. In August, the CCP was included in the membership of the National Defense Advisory Council, established to "advise the government and hear reports from the government."[3] In the spring of 1938, that group was expanded to two hundred members and reorganized as the People's Political Council (PPC), with seven Communist members.[4]

It was not long, however, before the spirit of unity began to sour, and the two parties, whose rivalry could be traced back nearly two decades, resumed their long-standing conflict. In January 1938, a group of men wrecked the offices of the *Xinhua xinbao* in Wuhan, while in May all non-GMD youth organizations in Nationalist territory were eliminated.[5] In August, other mass organizations were disbanded. In what has been described as the "first serious breach in the united front" and the beginning of a steady deterioration in the GMD-CCP relations, the two parties bitterly quarreled over the issue of how to respond to the Japanese assault on Wuhan in the fall of 1938.[6] Finally, at the end of 1938, the disagreement became an armed one, with a clash between the Eighth Route Army and Central Government troops in northern Henan.[7]

Zhang Junmai's Letter to Mao Zedong

It was at this point that Zhang entered the fray. As we have seen, he was clearly an anti-Communist by the time he left Europe in 1921, an animus he maintained throughout the 1920s and 1930s. In light of this ideological opposition and the fact that he was bound to the GMD by the earlier exchange of letters, it was perhaps natural that he would side with the GMD in the growing dispute and attack the CCP.

Alarmed at the increased tension between the two major forces in the UF, he entered the lists. In doing so, he added friction between the CCP and the National Socialist Party of China (NSP) to that already present between the CCP and the GMD, and thus further strained the anti-Japanese UF formed following the outbreak of the war.

As the fog settled over Chongqing in the early winter of 1938, he published an open letter to Mao Zedong.[8] The timing could not have been worse, for his missive criticizing the CCP was published in *Zaisheng* on 16 December, just two days before Wang Jingwei, deputy director-general (*fuzongcai*) of the GMD and speaker of the PPC, fled China[9] and two weeks before the publicizing of Wang's telegram in which he accepted the Japanese anti-communist position. In fact, it was in the midst of CCP alarm at the call by Wang and the Japanese prime minister, Konoe Fumimaro, for "joint defense against Communism" that Zhang's letter was reprinted in the GMD organ, *Zhongyang ribao* (Central Daily News) and reported in the Shanghai periodical, *The China Weekly Review*.[10] Hence, it would have been difficult for the Communists to ignore Zhang's criticism.

It was the resolution adopted by the Enlarged Sixth Plenum of the CCP's Sixth Central Committee, which met in Yan'an from 28 September to 6 November 1938, that aroused the NSP leader's ire. Entitled, "On the New Stage of Development in the National Self-Defense War and the Anti-Japanese National United Front," it was based on the report Mao delivered on the final day of the meeting. The latter advocated a united front based not on formal agreements but on "consultation in settling whatever problems occur between the two parties." That policy of independence within the UF, Mao vehemently argued, would avoid the disastrous results of the First GMD-CCP UF during the 1920s, for the revolutionary bases and the Red Army would be retained, thus enabling the CCP to maintain its autonomy.[11]

It was the CCP's determination to retain its territories and army, along with his usual criticism of its ideology, on which Zhang focused in his letter.[12] "If all of us are sincere in resisting the enemy, saving the fatherland, and mindful of the supreme national interests," he argued, "why can't we all forget the interests of individual political parties and groups?" The policies of the CCP, he continued, had created a "three-way stumbling block" in the way of the "long-term cooperation in the form of a national alliance" that Mao himself had suggested. Those blocks, Zhang declared, were the CCP's "separate party with its own armed forces, its own special region, and its Marxist goal."

In Mao's report to the Sixth Plenum, Zhang complained, he had endorsed two military systems, the GMD's and the CCP's. Zhang made it clear that he objected; the armed forces should belong to the state, he asserted, not to a particular political party or ideology. He made his expectations of Mao quite clear: "It is our [the NSP's?] hope that you will take the initiative to completely entrust to Mr. Chiang Kai-shek the training, appointment, and command of the Eighth Route Army. This would be a first step towards promoting national unity and the success of protracted war."

Second, Zhang argued, "no political party in any country should occupy a special geographical area to enforce its particular policies." A unified system of law and administration, in his view, was a prerequisite for building a modern state. Yet, Mao and the CCP, he complained, maintained a "special region as an enclave," with its own government, taxation, and schools. It is apparent that, for Zhang, the CCP's separatism raised the specter of the warlordism that had torn China apart during the 1910s and the 1920s, when he was a young man. "Should all the organized political parties in China follow your example," he lectured Mao, "China would be divided into many administrative regions under different parties, and the country would revert to a state of feudalistic division." He made clear that it was "our hope that you will abolish the system of special regions."

Finally, there was the question of ideology. As we have seen, Zhang had been a consistent critic of Marxism since returning from Europe in 1921. He had attacked it in his contributions to the "Debate over Science and a Philosophy of Life" in 1923, maintained his offensive in lectures at his National Institute of Political Science, and continued to condemn the Communists' ideology right up until the eve of the war.[13] In view of that long-standing ideological opposition, the hostility he expressed in his letter was quite understandable.

He first applauded the CCP's decision, following the 18 September 1931 Mukden Incident, that class struggle was not suitable for China and the party's adoption of the strategy of national war in its place. He was clearly suspicious, though: "This switch of yours is indeed fortunate for our country, but you have yet to prove yourself."[14]

He also was troubled by what he saw as Mao's attempt to equate Marxism and the Three People's Principles (TPP). Even before the outbreak of war, that is, in the spring of 1937, the CCP had declared that the TPP were compatible with its minimum or short-term program.[15] In their September 1937 manifesto, the Communists declared themselves "prepared to fight for the realization of Dr. Sun Yat-sen's revolutionary principles because they answer the present-day needs of China."[16] Mao himself forcefully argued for the "realization of the Three People's Principles" a week later (29 September 1937), in an article entitled "Urgent Tasks of the Chinese Revolution Since the Formation of the KMT-CCP United Front." In doing so, he took issue with one of the leaders of Zhang's NSP. Zhu Qinglai of Shanghai, wrote Mao, "has maintained (in a certain periodical in Shanghai) that communism and the Three People's Principles are incompatible." That, Mao countered, was "the point of view of formalism," since communism was to be implemented in "a future stage of the revolutionary development." The task at present, according to Mao, was to "carry out immediately a revolutionary policy compatible with the Three People's Principles."[17] Finally, the above-mentioned resolution of the Enlarged Sixth Plenum, based on Mao's 6 November 1938 report, repeatedly called for the creation of a Republic of China based on the TPP, a goal Zhang vehemently opposed as tantamount to a one-party state.[18] During the first two years or so of the war, then, the CCP paid close attention to the TPP, which, in one scholar's view, "seemed to suggest that the CCP was moving away from Marxism-Leninism."[19]

Like his party colleague Zhu, Zhang had his doubts about the compatibility of the TPP and communism. The former, he pointed out in his 1938 letter, were based on nationalism and entirely different from the Marxist concept of class as the controlling force in history. Hence, he complained, an argument equating the two "not only confuses our people about the content of the Three People's Principles but [also] misrepresents Marxism." The same, he added, went for Mao's argument that "patriotism is the practice of internationalism in the national revolutionary war." Zhang was blunt: "Personally, I think you had better put aside Marxism when you engage in a national war against a foreign enemy. . . . Thus, the different schools of thought in our country will find a basis for mutual cooperation, to save the nation and to become unified."

His letter has been described as a "bitter attack" on Mao and the CCP.[20] In fact, it sounded more like an earnest plea for cooperation in the life-and-death struggle against Japan:

> We have read your report and have faith in the bright future of all political parties in this country. Therefore, we cannot choose to remain silent but offer instead our sincere views as a friendly admonition. Your acceptance will certainly lead to a much stronger unity from which all people will draw encouragement. Otherwise, if the present state of affairs is not changed, how much more of our strength will be dissipated by suspicion and friction! Future generations will definitely blame the failure of our resistance on the conflict of parties now in our country. You have demonstrated your love for our nation and our country in recent years; this nobody can deny. But you can yet take a further step! If so, the success of our armed resistance will be assured and the foundation of our Chinese national existence will be laid. With best wishes for your devotion to the nation.[21]

The CCP Reaction

The CCP reaction was not long in coming. Its first response, drafted by one of the CCP's lesser lights, appeared in the 14 January 1939 issue of *Xinhua ribao*, the newspaper that presented the Communist line in Nationalist-held areas.[22] Subsequently, three writers—including one of Zhang's former students who had also taught at Zhang's Institute of Self-Government in the 1920s—leapt to his defense in the pages of *Zaisheng*.[23] The three most important contributions to the polemic, however, were the attack on Zhang by a leading figure in the CCP and one of the "Twenty-eight Bolsheviks," Chen Shaoyu (a. k. a. Wang Ming);[24] Zhang's reply; and the entry into the debate —more than a year after publication of Zhang's open letter—of the target of that broadside, Mao Zedong.

On 15 January 1939, Chen, the leader of the CCP delegation in the PPC and director of the United Front Department of the CCP Central Committee,[25] addressed the Mass Conference for Anti-Japanese Resistance and Condemnation of Wang Jingwei, held in Yan'an.[26] Much of his talk, delivered to an audience of six thousand, was an attack on Wang, who had defected the previous month. Mindful of Zhang's letter to Mao, however, Chen also attempted to discredit Zhang by linking him with Wang. "I wish to ask about Chang Chun-mai [Zhang Junmai]," Chen declared, "because he is closely and intimately related to Wang Ching-wei." During the first session of the PPC, he charged, "Chang never spoke upon any question, except to support the resolution thanking 'virtuous and reputed' Chairman Wang." Just before the latter's flight,[27] he declared, Zhang published an open letter to Mao, which was "nothing but opposition to the Communist Party, the 8th Route Army, the Border Region of Shensi-Kansu-Ningsha [Ningxia], and advances the same arguments as Wang Ching-wei's circular telegram of December 29th last year." Following publication of Zhang's missive, he continued, "the Japanese immediately broadcast news that Chang Chun-mai, of the Wang Ching-wei clique, had opposed the Communists by publishing his open letter to Mao Tse-tung, and chanted him a beautiful paen of praise." Chen then led his audience to the expected conclusion:

> On the strength of all this, we cannot but suspect Mr. Chang's political position. Some say that he belongs to the same gang as Wang Ching-wei; some say that he, being a university professor and lacking political experience, has been utilized and exploited by Wang. . . . As to why Chang Chun-wai's [mai's] activities are closely related to Wang Ching-wei's, we expect that he himself can best explain to our fellow countrymen.[28]

One's first inclination is to dismiss Chen's charge as merely an attempt to tar Zhang with the same brush used on Wang Jingwei. However, during the first session of the PPC, there were bitter clashes between the Communists and Wang Jingwei's group, with the latter advocating abolition of the Eighth Route Army and the Border Governments.[29] Moreover, Wang's 29 December statement contained a passage that closely resembled the argument in Zhang's letter to Mao. In his statement, Wang argued that "since the Communist Party of China has already pledged itself to the cause of the 'Three People's Principles,' it should completely abandon its party organization and propaganda work, abolish its 'frontier' government, as well as its special military system, and be absolutely subject to the legal institutions of the Republic of China."[30]

This similarity between Zhang's and Wang's public statements, when viewed in the context of Zhang's consistent anticommunism, may well have aroused the suspicions of the CCP. It also was true that Zhang shared the fervent anticommunism expressed by Tokyo.[31] The Japanese invasion, however, excited Zhang's even more ardent nationalism and thus ruled out any cooperation with Japan on the grounds of a mutual anticommunism. Finally, the defection of some NSP leaders to the Wang Jingwei puppet regime lent credence to Chen Shaoyu's charges, and perhaps account for the zeal with which NSP members threw themselves into the quarrel with the CCP.

Chen also accused Zhang of opposition to Chiang Kai-shek. In the second session of the PPC, Chen charged, Wang Jingwei "insisted that Chang Chun-mei [mai] should report on his anti-Chiang . . . bill in the People's Political Council in order to blast the prestige of the leader of the resistance, to weaken the morale of the nation, and to influence national policy." Zhang then brought up a proposal, Chen continued, "virtually opposing the Generalissimo, while, despite our objection and with the support of Wang Ching-wei, he reported against the Generalissimo in the conference [Council]."[32]

In fact, that accusation was sheer nonsense, for at that time Zhang *supported* the Generalissimo. On 26 October, during the second session of the PPC, Zhang was among a group of councilors—including the speaker of the PPC, Wang Jingwei—who urged continued resistance in order to dispel rumors that the government might negotiate peace with Japan. As a result of that motion—and perhaps helped along by a flattering message from Chiang Kai-shek—on 2 November the council adopted a resolution reaffirming its faith in Chiang and calling on the country to continue resistance.[33]

In conclusion, it seemed Chen had forgotten about Wang Jingwei and the peace movement in defining "traitors." Instead, he broadened his attack to include Zhang's NSP as well. "Traitors," he declared, were those who "oppose the Generalissimo and the Communists simultaneously." It was clear that opposition to the Communists was the real charge against Zhang and his party. "If they [those who cause friction between the GMD and the CCP] oppose the Communists now, objectively they help the Japanese aggressors and Wang Ching-wei; if they oppose the Communists now, actually they oppose the war of resistance, the Kuomintang, the leader of the Chinese resistance, and the emancipation of the Chinese nation." During the second session of the PPC, Chen charged:

> Certain individual representatives put forth arguments for peace and refused to vote support of Generalissimo Chiang . . . and his declarations on the 30th of October; and as it so happened, these people were members of the National Socialist Party. We hope that the National Socialist Party will take a firm stand on the question of the basic National Policy; we hope the other leaders and members will rise up and put right Chang Chun-mai's thoughts and deeds, which are counter to the National Policy of Resistance.[34]

Zhang's Response to Chen's Attack

Chen's speech was published in *Xinhua ribao* on 7 February 1939. Since that newspaper was published in Chongqing, it was in its pages that Zhang read the attack on him. He responded almost immediately. In a rejoinder dated 10 February, he took issue with each of the accusations made by his fellow councilor in the PPC.[35] The first matter Chen inquired about, wrote Zhang, was the proposal to pass a resolution thanking Speaker Wang Jingwei. The first person to sign that resolution was Hang [Han] Liwu (a GMD member), asserted Zhang.[36] "I was asked by others," he continued, "so I was the one who rose to make the motion." Madame Wu Yifang, he recalled, then delivered the formal speech of gratitude.[37] He had not used the phrase "of good moral standing and reputation (*degao wangzhong*)" to describe Wang, he insisted, and urged Chen to check the original text of Wu's speech to see whether the words appeared there. Even if that phrase could be used as proof that he was close to Wang, argued Zhang, Chen had been among the councilors present; "why," Zhang asked, "did I not hear one word of protest?" Moreover, after Madame Wu's expression of gratitude, Chen and the other CCP councilors "rose together in approval." "At the very least," Zhang complained, "you . . . agreed with the motion. Why do you conceal the complete records of the matter today, blame others, and instead use this to make yourself look good?"

Chen also charged him with not making a single speech in the first session of the PPC, Zhang continued. Defending himself from this charge of indolence, he declared that he was "one of the conveners of the Military Affairs Group (*Junshi zu*)."[38] From the speakers' platform, he had spoken to the council on the investigative report, "[Carry] the War of Resistance to the End (*Kangzhan daodi*)." There were minutes concerning these matters, he insisted, so " how can you distort them?"

Chen also accused him, he continued, of having brought up a motion in the second session of the PPC opposing Chairman Chiang Kai-shek. The aims of the PPC, Zhang explained, were to "draw on [our] collective wisdom and absorb all useful ideas, [and] unify [our] strength (*jisi guangyi, tuanjie liliang*)."[39] If an individual disagreed with Chiang, he argued, he could not ignore his conscience and remain silent just because he might offend the authorities. That was the reason, he added, for the inclusion of the clause, "clearly distinguish the limits of authority and clarify responsibility (*qing quanxian ming zeren*)," in the motion. Only in that way, he insisted, could they help Chiang and the GMD to complete, at an early date, the great tasks of the War of Resistance and national reconstruction. The more help Chiang and the GMD received, he argued, the earlier the nation would be reconstructed. That was our responsibility, he concluded, and we should not be afraid to express our views just because they were true. That was the reason for the devotion of all our loyalty and knowledge, he wrote, adding in a swipe at the CCP that this was "naturally different from those who publicly support [Chiang and the GMD but in private] have other plans!"

Chen's attack did not end with the above charges, though; he also criticized Zhang's letter to Mao as "anti-Communist, anti-Eighth Route Army, and anti-Shen-Kan-Ning Border Region." In his rebuttal, Zhang was prophetic:

> [When] I wrote that letter, I really thought that, at a time when the entire nation's four-hundred-million compatriots were each sacrificing their most valuable things in order to fight for national survival, you and your comrades surely would not stingily hold on to the Eighth Route Army and the border regions, in order to delay internal unification and national reconstruction. Otherwise, two armies and governments will coexist in the same nation, and, even though the War of Resistance against Japan is over some day, internal problems will arise again, or, what will be worse, they will produce upheavals. Then when will it be possible to realize national unity? [40]

Zhang challenged other assertions in Chen's speech as well. The latter asserted, he wrote, that "Japanese bandits and Chinese traitors oppose Chairman Chiang, the Guomindang, and the National Government. We Chinese must support Chairman Chiang, the Guomindang, and the National Government." He had investigated the substance of what Chen termed support, he declared, and it did not include the abolition of the Eighth Route Army, the Border Regions, or the independence of the Communist Party. That, he complained, was "support in name, not in substance." Was that not something that knowledgeable people all realized? he asked.

Chen also stated, according to Zhang, "The Japanese bandits and the Chinese traitors oppose the Communist Party, the Eighth Route Army, the New Fourth Army, and the Shaan-Gan-Ning Border Region. We Chinese certainly support the Communist Party, the Eighth Route Army, the New Fourth Army, and the Shaan-Gan-Ning Border Region." If that logic was followed, complained Chang, "everyone in the country who opposes the Communists could be called a traitor and . . . relegated to the same category as the Japanese bandits." If everyone knew that certain gentlemen in the PPC were patriots but expressed views contrary to Chen's, would the latter then look down upon them as traitors? How could an argument like Chen's, Zhang wondered, support internal unity and carrying out the War of Resistance to the end?

In closing, he turned sarcastic. Chen had demanded that he explain the charges against him to his countrymen. "This served to show," wrote Zhang, "that in the Yan'an conference you still did not deliver the final guilty verdict on me. How can I be ungrateful!" What he really believed in, Zhang explained, was "the virtuous man's reason that shines brightly in the darkness (*junzi anran er rizhang zhi li*)." It was impossible, he confessed, to try to defend himself from Chen's "words of reproach." His countrymen were all familiar with his words and deeds over twenty to thirty years; there was no need to further explain himself. His final exhortation to Chen was natural, coming from the head of the *National* Socialist Party: "Take good care of the nation!"

Mao Zedong Enters the Fray

At first, Mao did not directly respond to Zhang's letter, preferring to let other Communist figures lead the counterattack. Zhang Wentian (a. k. a. Luo Fu), like Chen Shaoyu, was one of the infamous "Twenty-eight Bolsheviks." He lashed out at Zhang Junmai, writing about "people like Carson [Carsun] Chang" that "we must ask them to give an open expression of their attitudes toward the national policy for a resolute war of resistance. . . . And they should demonstrate their loyalty to the Nation in practical action in order to cleanse the crime in their political [lives]."[41]

Zhang Junmai's criticism of Mao clearly hit home, though, and finally the CCP leader struck back. In his famous article, "On the New Democracy," which appeared in January 1940, he wrote that Wang Jingwei had already defected and "Another section lurking in the anti-Japanese camp would also like to cross over":

> But, with the cowardice of thieves, they fear that the Communists will block their exit and . . . the common people will brand them as traitors. So they have put their heads together and decided to prepare the ground in cultural circles and through the press. Having determined on their policy, they have lost no time in hiring some "metaphysics-mongers" . . . who, brandishing their pens like lances, are tilting in all directions and creating bedlam. Hence, the whole bag of tricks for deceiving those who do not know what is going on in the world around them . . . the tales that communism does not suit the national conditions of China, that there is no need for a Communist Party in China, that the Eighth Route Army and the New Fourth Army are sabotaging the anti-Japanese war and merely moving about without fighting, that the Shensi-Kansu-Ningsia Border Region is a feudal separatist regime, that the Communist Party is disobedient, dissident, intriguing, and disruptive.[42]

There was no doubt the disparaging term "metaphysics-monger" was a reference to Zhang. As a note later attached to Mao's article explained, the "metaphysics-mongers" were "Chang Chun-mai and his group." The CCP had never forgotten Zhang's role in the 1923 "Debate over Science and a Philosophy of Life": "After the May Fourth Movement, Chang openly opposed science and advocated metaphysics, or what he called 'spiritual culture,' and thus came to be known as a 'metaphysics-monger.'"[43]

The real point of Mao's attack, though, was Zhang's letter to him over a year earlier, as a note attached to Mao's article made clear: "In order to support Chiang Kai-shek and the Japanese aggressors, he [Zhang] published 'An Open Letter to Mao Tse-tung' . . . at Chiang Kai-shek's bidding, wildly demanding the abolition of the Eighth Route Army, the New Fourth Army, and the Shensi-Kansu-Ningsia Border Region."[44]

In fact, as we have seen, one of Chen's charges against Zhang at the time had been that he *opposed* Chiang Kai-shek. Hence, the CCP editors were conveniently forgetting that the policy of Mao and his party during the war also had been to support Chiang. Moreover, Zhang never mentioned the New Fourth Army in his original letter.

However, Mao was not finished with Zhang. In the same article, he argued that the second stage of the united front of the four classes had begun with the fall of Wuhan. During that stage, he continued, one section of the big bourgeoisie had capitulated to the enemy, while another desired an early end to the War of Resistance. "In the cultural sphere," he concluded, "this situation has been reflected in the reactionary activities of . . . Chang Chun-mai."[45]

The following month (February 1940), Mao continued his offensive against Zhang. In a speech to a mass rally in Yan'an held to denounce Wang Jingwei, Mao declared, "Anti-Communism is the main objective both of Japan and Wang Ching-wei." Therefore, he continued, they were trying to break up the cooperation between the GMD and the CCP and "set them to fighting each other." To accomplish that, they had "used the die-hards within the Kuomintang to create trouble everywhere." In addition, they had "hired that metaphysics-monger Chang Chun-mai to make reactionary proposals for the liquidation of the Communist Party, the abolition of the Shensi-Kansu-Ningsia Border Region, and the disbandment of the Eighth Route and New Fourth Armies."[46]

At the end of the war, Mao had still not forgotten—or forgiven—Zhang's letter. While visiting Chongqing from late August to early October of 1945 (Zhang was in the United States at that time) to discuss peace with Chiang Kai-shek and the GMD,[47] he met with Jiang Yuntian, a charter member of the NSP and graduate of Zhang's Institute of Political Science.[48] According to Jiang, Mao "voiced his dissatisfaction" with Zhang's 1938 letter. The latter, he declared, "advised me to hand over [my] army. Frankly speaking, if we did not have those 10,000-odd worn-out rifles, we undoubtedly could not have existed. No one pays any attention to your fears." According to Jiang, Mao politely added, "It really is a matter for regret that I cannot meet Mr. Junmai this time to convey my sincere admiration of many years standing."[49]

Over two decades after the meeting between Mao and Jiang, Zhang wrote that Mao "constantly bore in mind my letter in Hankou [Chongqing], which advised him to disband [his] army and work for national unity." For that reason, he continued, Mao told Jiang that the negotiations in Chongqing with Chiang Kai-shek were possible "only [because I] relied upon my 20,000 worn-out rifles to fight." That, Zhang commented, was proof of Mao's consistent view that political power grew out of the barrel of a gun (*qianggan chu zhengqiang*).[50]

Other Reactions to Zhang's Letter

The Communists were by no means the only ones to respond to Zhang's letter. Various newspapers in the country competed to reprint it, and it was said to have had a lot of influence on public opinion.[51] It was even adopted by overseas Chinese schools in Southeast Asia as teaching material for Chinese literature classes.[52] The government-controlled press strongly supported Zhang, no doubt because his letter agreed with their own basic beliefs concerning the "Communist problem."[53] Later, Zhang was even defended by a GMD writer, a position he seldom enjoyed following the GMD victory in 1927. Zhang's letter, the GMD author wrote, was "meant as a sincere admonition to the Communists, but it merely enraged them to respond with unwarranted invective. So . . . Chang was accused of being a follower of Wang Ching-wei, the traitor."[54]

In all fairness, the CCP was not alone in its hostility toward the political position expressed in Zhang's letter. According to a member of the NSP, "the newspapers and journals of fellow-travellers," as well as the "entire country's left-wing newspapers and magazines," condemned Zhang.[55] For example, Israel Epstein, a left-wing writer resident in China, followed the CCP line in attacking Zhang in 1939. At the moment of Wang Jingwei's defection, he wrote, Zhang, "one of his [Wang's] associates" and the leader of the NSP, assaulted the CCP in a letter to the *Zhongyang ribao*, which was "still in the hands of Wang's followers." "Characteristically," he continued, "he argued that the existence of the Communist Party made not capitulation, but resistance more difficult. This was only another aspect of the disruptive activity of Wang Ching-wei's clique."[56]

Later, one of Zhang's own associates in the budding "third-force" movement, the League of Chinese Democratic Political Groups (*Zhongguo minzhu zhengtuan datongmeng*), denounced Zhang's letter. While lecturing in Guilin in the spring of 1942, Shen Junru, a leader of the National Salvation Association criticized for being too close to the CCP,[57] publicly castigated Zhang's message, which had urged Mao to hand over his military power. Many in the audience, according to an NSP member who was present, agreed with Shen. The NSP members did not, and attempted to refute him: "[If] military power is unified, then [that] will constitute a great foundation for securing national unification . . . . does Mr. Shen not desire national unification?" Shen's reply revealed his lack of faith in the GMD: "Mr. Zhang longs for democracy with all his heart and does not realize that [if one] seeks unification in Guomindang hands, will there be any democracy to speak of?"[58]

Criticism of Zhang's missive also appeared outside China. In his popular work, *Inside Asia*, John Gunther asserted that Zhang had "fiercely attacked the United Front . . . and early in 1939 [*sic*] demanded that the Red Government in Shensi give up its semi-autonomy."[59] Since his book sold well, that view of Zhang's letter was no doubt widely held wherever Gunther's volume was read. The NSP promptly took issue with him. In a letter to the American author published in a Hong Kong newspaper in October 1939, a member of the party wrote that Gunther had asserted that Zhang had disrupted the UF, because he had demanded that the Red Army and government abolish their semi-independent positions. "If Mr. Zhang . . . wanted to disrupt the UF," argued the letter-writer, "then he [would] not [have] advised the Red Army and government to abolish their independent government." Zhang's "advice to the Red Army to abolish its independent organization," he continued, "proves he is demanding unity and a concentration of strength in order to guard against foreign aggression." Therefore, the author triumphantly concluded, Gunther's belief that Zhang's demand for the abolition of the Red Army disrupted unity "is self-contradictory."[60] Although it may have had nothing to do with the NSP's protest, the offensive sentence was deleted from the 1942 edition of *Inside Asia*.[61]

Conclusion

Although the reverberations continued until the end of the war, the months between the appearance of Zhang's letter in December 1938 and the publication in September 1939 of a collection of views expressed by the various combatants marked the height of the polemic.[62] According to a GMD confidential publication, it ended—at least for the NSP participants—because Zhang Dongsun and other members of the party felt there was no benefit for them in continuing the dispute with the CCP.[63] As for Zhang Junmai, he turned his attention to the possibility of constitutionalism in wartime China, as well as the establishment of his Institute of National Culture.

It has been argued that Zhang's criticism of the CCP changed Chiang Kai-shek's opinion of him. Hence, Chiang ceased to regard him as a "reactionary figure" (*fandongpai renwu*), and even ordered the National Military Council to provide funds for Zhang's Institute of National Culture.[64] Chiang also subsidized the NSP. In October 1941, a leader of the NSP in Hong Kong, Xu Fulin, told a U.S. diplomat that the NSP was receiving a subsidy "paid in Chinese national currency to Dr. [*sic*] Carson [Carsun] Chang, the party's chairman, by the Generalissimo, Chiang Kai-shek." Part of the funds, according to Xu, was distributed through the Institute of National Culture, "an organization which . . . is run to provide a more or less respectable means of supporting a number of destitute intellectuals of this type."[65] In November 1941, the U.S. Consulate in Kunming confirmed that, following the incorporation of the NSP into the UF, "there has apparently existed a National Government subsidy to the Party [NSP]." The report added that the information was based on "several reliable sources" and that "the present annual grant is said to be NC 150,000."[66]

It has been suggested that in criticizing Mao and the CCP, Zhang was siding with the right-wing GMD.[67] When viewed in light of the subsidy to the NSP and Zhang's school, it would be easy to suspect him of attacking the Communists in return for financial support. The evidence argues against that conclusion, however. First, the GMD subsidy seems to have followed rather than preceded the December 1938 letter, although it is possible that it was promised if Zhang would carry out his public attack on Mao. Second, the letter was first published in *Zaisheng* and only later reprinted in a GMD newspaper; that is, it seems to have been aimed at NSP members and those who read their journal rather than the GMD. Third, those were the days of the UF, when parties were supposed to be cooperating; with the hostility between the NSP and the GMD sublimated, at least for the moment, Zhang's acceptance of a subsidy was understandable. Finally, and most conclusive, Zhang came by his anticommunism honestly, having maintained that position since at least 1921, as we have seen. Hence, although his acceptance of a GMD subsidy, after years of opposition to that party, was certainly evidence that he could be a politician and not above it all,[68] as has sometimes been claimed, it is doubtful that he was bribed to write the letter to Mao.

As for the CCP, it may well have wanted to see an end to the dispute (despite Mao's later remarks), so it could pursue its highly successful UF policy. The polemic may have been an aberration in that strategy, which stressed cooperation with other parties and, according to some sources, infiltrating and attempting to control them. According to a leader of the CYP, the CCP attempted to control the NSP and CYP, which the CYP leader labeled a "fearsome scheme."[69] A ranking GMD member agreed, arguing that during the war the CCP's tactic was to win over the NSP and the CYP to form a united front against the GMD.[70] Finally, a plainly anticommunist organization has claimed the United Front Department of the CCP targeted the NSP, with CCP members to be placed in "friendly parties" with instructions not to reveal their status. By uniting with other parties and factions, it was argued, the CCP could isolate and overthrow the National Government.[71]

For a moment, at least, the UF had cracked, allowing all of the old animosities to escape. That, in turn, threatened the alliance between the various parties at a time when China was fighting for survival against the Japanese invasion. Hence, after a few vitriolic exchanges, the various participants in the dispute seemed to have reached a tacit agreement to table the argument over complete unification in China to preserve the UF. That unity was finally attained in 1949, but scarcely in a form Zhang and his party found palatable. Moreover, even though Zhang indirectly carried the torch for the GMD in the 1938-39 polemic, it proved ungrateful. Hence, Zhang was destined to live out his old age in an alien land far from China, dreaming about the democracy that might have been if it had not been crushed in the combat between the two dictatorships.

Notes

1. For an analysis of the roots of that UF, see James P. Harrison, *The Long March to Power: A History of the Chinese Communist Party, 1921-1972* (New York: Praeger, 1972), chap. 12.

2. Lyman P. Van Slyke, *Enemies and Friends: The United Front in Chinese Communist History* (Stanford: Stanford University Press, 1967), 92-93. For a fuller description of this manifesto, see *China Handbook, 1937-1943*, 51.

3. Ch'ien Tuan-sheng, *The Government and Politics of China*, 280.

4. Van Slyke, *Enemies and Friends*, 94; Harrison, *Long March,* 279.

5. Israel and Klein, *Rebels and Bureaucrats*, 159; Gould, *China in the Sun*, 96. The GMD's method was to order organizations to register with the government but then refuse registration to those considered undesirable. Ibid.

6. Kenneth E. Shewmaker, *Americans and Chinese Communists, 1927-1945: A Persuading Encounter* (Ithaca: Cornell University Press, 1971), 88.

7. Lawrence K. Rossinger, *China's Wartime Politics, 1937-1944* (Princeton: Princeton University Press, 1945), 38.

8. Zhang Junmai, "Zhi Mao Zedong yifeng gongkaixin" (An Open Letter to Mao Tse-tung), *Zaisheng*, no. 10 (1938), 1-2. The letter was dated 10 December. There is an English translation in Warren Kuo, *Analytical History of the Chinese Communist Party*, 4 vols. (Taibei: Institute of International Relations, 1970), 3: 547-51.

9. BDRC, 3: 374. On 16 December, Wang, who served as speaker of the PPC during its first two sessions, met with Chiang Kai-shek for the last time. Ibid.; Shyu, "The People's Political Council," 49.

10. Kuo, *Analytical History*, 3: 514; *The Chinese Communist Movement: A Report of the United States War Department, July 1945*, ed. Lyman P. Van Slyke (Stanford: Stanford University Press, 1968), 68; *The China Weekly Review* 87 (31 December 1938), 145.

11. Harrison, *The Long March*, 288-89. For the text of part of Mao's 6 November report, see "Problems of War and Strategy," in *Selected Works of Mao Tse-tung*, 2: 219-35.

12. The following summary of Zhang's letter is based on Kuo, *Analytical History*, 547-51.

13. See, e.g., Zhang, "Ruijin shi jingshenshang fangGong de diyixian," 6-10; Li Chai [Zhang Junmai], "Gongchandang biangeng fangxiang yu renlei dexing zhi juewu" (The Communist Party's Change of Course and the Realization of Humanity's Moral Character), *Zaisheng* 4, no. 9 (1937): 1-11.

14. In the official version of Mao's speech to the Sixth Plenum, he reiterated that policy: "To subordinate the class struggle to the present national struggle to resist Japan—that is the fundamental principle of the united front." Harrison, *The Long March*, 288.

15. Ibid., 311.

16. *China Handbook, 1937-1943*, 51.

17. Brandt, Schwartz, and Fairbank, *A Documentary History of Chinese Communism*, 247-57.

18. Kuo, *Analytical History*, 488, 491-93. See also the report of Zhang's discussions with GMD veteran Zhang Zhiben concerning Article 1 of the May Fifth Draft Constitution, which stated that the Republic of China was based on the TPP. Zhang Zhiben, "Some Personal Reminiscenses," 48; Zhang Zhiben, "Zhang Zhiben tanhua bilu" (A Record of Conversations with Zhang Zhiben) (Taipei: Academia Sinica, Institute of Modern History, 1960), 63a, 63b.

19. Van Slyke, *Enemies and Friends*, 155-56.

20. *The Chinese Communist Movement*, 68.

21. Kuo, *Analytical History*, 551.

22. Lin Beili, "Qingjiao Zhang Junmai xiansheng" (A Request for Advice from Mr. Zhang Junmai), *Xinhua ribao*, 14 January 1939, 4. According to a middle-school classmate of Lin's, she was not a leading cadre (*fuzeren*) of the CCP. Yang Mingwei, "Guanyu Zhang Junmai xiansheng de gongkaixin" (Concerning Mr. Zhang Junmai's Open Letter), *Zaisheng*, no. 14 (1939): 11. *Xinhua ribao* was published irregularly,

first in Hankou and thereafter in Chongqing. In 1940, it had a circulation of around 25,000. Harrison, *The Long March*, 319.

23. Liu Jingyuan, "Yifeng gongkaixin de fanying: da Lin Beili nushi" (A Response to an Open Letter: A Reply to Madame Lin Beili), *Zaisheng*, no. 13 (1939): 1-2; Yang Mingwei, "Guanyu Zhang Junmai," 11-12; Zeng Youhao, "Minzhu zhengzhi de jingshen shi rongxu yidang shanyi piping de quanli—taolun Chen Shaoyu xiansheng dui Zhang Junmai xiansheng de zhiwen" (The Spirit of Democracy is the Right of Toleration for Other Parties' Well-Intentioned Criticism: A Discussion of Mr. Chen Shaoyu's Questioning of Mr. Zhang Junmai), *Zaisheng*, no. 17 (1939): 8. Liu and Yang concentrated their fire on Lin's letter, while Zeng focused on Chen Shaoyu's speech (to be taken up later). Liu quoted nearly all of Lin's published letter, in an attempt to rebut the latter's criticism of Zhang's appeal to Mao and the CCP to place the Eighth Route Army under Chiang Kai-shek's control, to abolish the border regions, and to "put aside Marxism." Yang also concentrated on defending Zhang's three major points. Zeng Youhao had studied under Zhang, served as a member of the faculty at Zhang's National Institute of Self-Government in 1925, and written several books on Chinese government, diplomatic history, and legal and political philosophy. John K. Fairbank and Liu Kwang-ching, eds., *Modern China: A Bibliographical Guide to Chinese Works, 1898-1937* (Cambridge: Harvard University Press, 1961), 46; Tseng Yu-hao [Zeng Youhao], *Modern Chinese Legal and Political Philosophy* (Shanghai: Commercial Press, 1930), 251.

24. Ironically, while Chen was attacking Zhang, he himself was being attacked by Mao and his associates, with the UF policy and leadership of the party the issues. The dispute came to a head at the Sixth Plenum. Harrison, *The Long March*, 284-89; Van Slyke, *Enemies and Friends*, 105-06, 106 (n. h). It is the latter's conclusion that Mao's criticism of Chen was "more a matter of factionalism than of doctrinal disagreement." For a GMD view of the dispute between Chen and Mao, see Kuo, *Analytical History*, chap. 29.

25. "Guomin canzheng hui lijie canzhengyuan," 23; BDRC, 1: 233. A CYP member of the PPC later asserted that Chen Shaoyu was the "most active communist during the Wuhan period. His position was higher than Chou En-lai's. He was the leader of the Communist Party fraction in the People's Political Council. . . . As Party spokesman, Ch'en . . . was eloquent and effective. . . . Sometime he spoke so firmly that he made people uncomfortable." He added that Chen had a "tendency to show off." Zuo Shunsheng, "Reminiscences," 169.

26. Chen's speech was first published in *Jiefang*, no. 62 (1939) and *Xinhua ribao*, 7 February 1939. The following summary is drawn from an English translation, *Old Intrigues in New Clothing*, Bulletin No. 7 (Chungking: New China Information Committee, 1939), 1-19 (especially 11, 17-18).

27. Wang left Chongqing on 18 December, while Zhang's letter to Mao was published on 16 December.

28. Ch'en Shao-yu, "Old Intrigues," 17.

29. Helen E. Busche, "Minor Parties and Political Groups and Their Efforts to Expand Democracy in China, 1927-1947" (M.A. thesis, University of Chicago, 1948), 120-21.

30. "Wang Ching-wei's First Statement," *Oriental Affairs* 11, no. 2 (1939): 100. For further discussions of the contents of this telegram, see John H. Boyle, *China and Japan at War, 1937-1945: The Politics of Collaboration* (Stanford: Stanford University Press, 1972), 223-24; Gerald E. Bunker, *The Peace Conspiracy: Wang Ching-wei and the China War, 1937-1941* (Cambridge: Harvard University Press, 1972), 119-20. Zhang undoubtedly disagreed with Wang, however, when the latter went on to assert that "the 'Three People's Principles' are the fundamental principles of the Chinese nation, and consequently, in fulfillment of our duty to protect our country, we must automatically and positively suppress all organizations and propaganda which run counter to them." "Wang Ching-wei's First Statement," 100. In light of these sentiments, it is clear that Zhang would have been no happier with Wang, rather than Chiang Kai-shek, leading China.

31. On Japan's anticommunism, see Saburo Ienaga, *The Pacific War: World War II and the Japanese, 1931-1945* (New York: Pantheon, 1978), 75-84. According to another analysis, the *Bokyo* ("Resist Communism") slogan that accompanied Japan's invasion of China was "sincerely and deeply felt." Robert M. Spaulding, "Detour through a Dark Valley," in *Japan Examined: Perspectives on Modern Japanese History*, eds. Harry Wray and Hilary Conroy (Honolulu: University of Hawaii Press, 1983), 255.

32. Ch'en Shao-yu, "Old Intrigues," 11, 17.

33. *Dagongbao*, Hong Kong, 27 October 1938, 3, cited in P'an Wei-tung, *The Chinese Constitution*, 95; *The China Weekly Review* 86 (19 November 1938): 386. According to the latter, the motion was passed on 1 November, not 2 November. When the council convened in Chongqing, it was praised by Chiang Kai-shek. "Although the Council has had only a short history," he wrote, "its existence has been fully justified." Chiang Kai-shek, *Resistance and Reconstruction* (New York: Harper Row, 1943; repr., Freeport, NY: Books for Libraries Press, 1970), 55-56.

34. Ch'en Shao-yu, "Old Intrigues," 17-18. I have seen no evidence that any of the eight NSP members of the PPC voted against the resolution, supported by Zhang, calling for support for Chiang Kai-shek.

35. Except where noted, the following discussion of Zhang's rebuttal of Chen's charges is drawn from Zhang Junmai, "Da Chen Shaoyu Yan'an yanci zhong fudai zhiwen" (A Reply to the Questions Appended to Chen Shaoyu's Speech in Yan'an), *Zaisheng*, no. 16 (1939): 1-2.

36. Although his surname should be romanized as *Hang*, he preferred *Han*. See the thumbnail sketch in "Chinese Who's Who," in *China Handbook, 1937-1943*, chap. 25, lxvi. Han later became Minister of Education in the GMD government. BDRC, 2: 269.

37. For a short biography of Wu, see BDRC, 3: 460-62. She was appointed to the PPC in 1938 and became a member of the five-person presidium in 1941 when Zhou Enlai withdrew. Ibid., 461.

38. Zhang later confirmed that he was a member of the PPC's committee on military affairs. Chang, *Third Force*, 111. For a description of the standing committees of the PPC, see Shyu, "The People's Political Council," 51-53. During the first session of the council, the standing committee that dealt with military matters had twenty-five members. PPC members were free to select their own committee assignments, with each member usually limited to one committee. Councilors tended to shun the military committee, because Chiang Kai-shek was in charge of military and defense matters and tolerated little criticism. Ibid., 51-52, 51 (n. 1).

39. According to Article 12 of the "Program of Armed Resistance and National Reconstruction," adopted by the GMD Extraordinary National Congress on 1 April 1938, the PPC's purpose was "unifying the national strength and collecting the best minds and views for facilitating the formulation and execution of national policies." *China Handbook, 1937-1943*, 61.

40. Zhang, "Da Chen Shaoyu," 2.

41. Luo Fu [Zhang Wentian], "Common Defense against Communism Means China's Downfall," *Jiefang*, nos. 63 and 64, 16 February 1939, quoted in Kuo, *Analytical History*, 513.

42. Mao Tse-tung, *Selected Works*, 2: 359.

43. Ibid., 383 (n. 10). For a discussion of Zhang's role in this debate, see Jeans, "Syncretism in Defense of Confucianism," chap. 13.

44. Mao Tse-tung, *Selected Works*, 2: 383 (n. 10).

45. Mao Tse-tung, *Selected Works*, 2: 377. Mao also mentioned Ye Qing (Ren Zhuoxuan). Ye broke with the CCP in 1928 and went over to the GMD side. Following the outbreak of the Sino-Japanese War, he became a fervent supporter of the TPP as the key to the solution of China's problems. BDRC, 2: 216-19.

46. Mao Tse-tung, *Selected Works*, 2: 389-90. Mao's entire speech was a rebuttal of those who, like Zhang, called for an end to the CCP, its armies, and the border region.

47. Accompanied by Zhou Enlai and the U.S. Ambassador, Patrick Hurley, Mao arrived in Chongqing on 28 August, met Chiang Kai-shek the following day, signed and issued a "Summary of Conversations" on 10 October, and returned to Yan'an on 11 October. Mackerras and Chan, *Modern China*, 414.

48. Max Perleberg, *Who's Who in Modern China* (Hong Kong: Ye Olde Printerie, Ltd., 1954), 44; YX, 22.

49. Jiang Yuntian, "Zhang Junmai xiansheng yisheng dashi ji," 26. In a dispatch four years later, the U.S. ambassador to China, John Leighton Stuart, made what appears to have a reference to that meeting between Mao and Jiang: "Mao . . . remarked to a prominent member of the Democratic Socialist Party [NSP] in September 1945 that in view of the KMT reliance on the United States he had to turn to the Soviet Union. He was also quoted as having said that because of that factor he had almost been defeated in 1927, whereas the success of the present revolution is due entirely to himself and his Chinese colleagues." Stuart to State, USDS 893.00/1-2049 confidential, 20 January 1949, 2.

50. Zhang Junmai, "Mao chao yu Qin zheng, Xin Mang, Sui Yang" ([A Comparison of] Mao [Zedong's] Dynasty with the Qin Government, [Wang] Mang [of the] Xin [Dynasty], and [the Emperor] Yang [of the] Sui [Dynasty]), *Ziyou zhong* 3, no. 9 (1967): 2.

51. *Zhongguo ge xiao dangpai*, 68-69.

52. LHWLX, 23. Wu Xiangxiang went on to assert that the entire nation admired Zhang's spirit, as revealed in the letter to Mao.

53. Jiang Yuntian, "Jiang xu" (Jiang [Yuntian's] Introduction), in YX, 3.

54. Kuo, *Analytical History*, 514.

55. Jiang Yuntian, "Zhang Junmai," 26; Jiang Yuntian, "Jiang xu," 3. According to the latter, those publications publicly denounced Zhang for his "crimes."

56. Israel Epstein, *The People's War* (London: Gollancz, 1939), 351-52 (n. 1). Epstein became a Chinese citizen following World War II. Born in Poland, he also had visited the United States. During the war, he served as correspondent for several U.S. newspapers and magazines, including the *New York Times* and *Time* magazine. During the Hankou period (December 1937-October 1938), when he was a correspondent for United Press, he spent some of his time in the buildings that housed the *Xinhua ribao*. After the establishment of the PRC, he was employed as an editor by the Foreign Languages Press in Beijing, until his arrest during the Cultural Revolution. Shewmaker, *Americans and Chinese Communists*, 90, 161, 163 (n. 17). One of his later works, *The Unfinished Revolution in China* (Boston: Little, Brown, 1947), has been described as "essentially a paean to the Chinese Communists," with a "'pretty clear bias.'" John N. Thomas, *The Institute of Pacific Relations*, 61.

57. Zhang later described Shen as a "fellow-traveller of the Communists," who "kept silent or expressed sympathy with them, but worked well with the League nevertheless." Chang, *Third Force*, 115. According to a leader of the CYP, others in the league also felt that the members of the National Salvation Association were too close to the CCP. Zuo Shunsheng, "Reminiscenses," 186. In October 1941, e.g., Shen and Zhang Bojun (a leader of the Third Party) visited Zhou Enlai in Chongqing to inquire whether the CCP would be willing to participate in the League of Chinese Democratic Political Groups. Moreover, most of the later contacts between the Democratic League and the CCP were handled by Shen and Zhang Bojun. Van Slyke, *Enemies and Friends*, 176-77, 183. After the establishment of the PRC, Shen served the regime in various capacities, including taking over as chairman of the Democratic League in 1956, until his death in 1963. For a short biography, see BDRC, 3: 99-101.

58. Jiang Yuntian, "Jiang xu," 3.

59. Gunther, *Inside Asia*, 271-72. This book was based on a trip Gunther took to Asia in 1937-38. He also included a few facts about Zhang's life, which he apparently harvested from *The China Weekly Review*'s *Who's Who in China* (his bibliography included the 1936 edition). After asserting that an earlier work, *Inside Europe*, contained very few errors, he wondered whether he could "dare to hope that the same general level of accuracy is maintained in this book [*Inside Asia*]. Facts are evasive and elusive in oriental lands. But I have arduously checked and double-checked every name, every date, every event, and parts of the manuscript have been checked by

experts." Gunther, *Inside Asia*, 576. Despite such care, he was clearly mistaken in his description of the NSP as "semi-fascist." Moreover, his work has been described elsewhere as a contribution to the "romantic image of the CCP." See Shewmaker, *Americans and Chinese Communists*, 263-65.

60. "Dabian liangze" (Two Responses), *Zaisheng*, no. 32 (1939): 1-2. The author, one Borcheng Huang, was probably the same man as Huang Bocheng, who served the NSP's successor, the Chinese Democratic Socialist Party, as a delegate to the Constituent National Assembly in November 1946, as well as being elected a reserve member of the DSP's Central Executive Committee in July and August of 1947. YX, 38, 42. In light of this letter, it seems clear that Huang was a member of the NSP during the war as well.

61. Gunther, *Inside Asia*, rev. ed., 291. This edition, however, continued to refer to the NSP as "semi-fascist." Ibid.

62. *Tongyi wenti lunzhan* (The Polemic over the Problem of Unification) (Chongqing: Duli chubanshe, 1939). This fifty-two page work reprinted Zhang's letter to Mao along with several contributions to the ensuing debate.

63. *Zhongguo ge xiao dangpai*, 69. One wonders, in view of Zhang Dongsun's interest in Soviet communism during the 1920s and his contact with CCP guerrillas during the war, what his motives were in favoring an end to his party's polemic with the CCP. Supra, chap 2; Tan, *Chinese Political Thought*, 268-69.

64. GS 4, no. 5, 73.

65. "Transmitting a Memorandum of a Conversation with the Representative in Hong Kong of the Chinese 'National Socialist Party,'" 4-5. According to Xu, each month Chiang appropriated CNC 30,000,000 to a secret fund, used to make payments to "ex-leaders and dissident intellectuals who might otherwise make trouble [diplomat's summary of the conversation]." According to Xu, none of what he termed the fairly generous subsidy given Zhang reached Hong Kong. Ibid., 4-5.

66. NA, Diplomatic Branch, R.G. 84, Kunming Post Files, 800 series, confidential correspondence, 1941, American Consulate, Kunming, to State, "Chinese National Socialist Party's Cultural Institute at Tali, Yunnan," 21 November 1941, 1.

67. "Democracy versus One-Party Rule in Kuomintang China," 112. According to yet another scholar, "The National Socialists under the leadership of Carson [Carsun] Chang supported the right-wing Kuomintang" by calling for an end to the Eighth-Route Army and the Border Governments. Busche, "Minor Parties and Political Groups," 120-21.

68. According to Zhang's brother-in-law, a professor at the Institute of National Culture, Zhang's acceptance of funds from Chiang Kai-shek was further evidence that Zhang was a politician as well as a statesman. Vincent Y. C. Shih, interview by author, 29 June 1976, Taipei, Taiwan.

69. Zuo Shunsheng, "Reminiscences," 202.

70. Huang Jilu, "Huiyi yu Junmai xiansheng yiduan tanhua" (Recollections of a Conversation with Mr. [Zhang] Junmai), *Zhuanji wenxue* 28, no. 3 (1976): 22.

71. Chu Wen-lin, *China's Struggle with the Red Peril* (Taipei: China Chapter, Asian People's Anti-Communist League, World Anti-Communist League, 1978), 163, 185, 191.

12

The Philosopher and the Generalissimo:
The Life and Death of the Institute of National Culture, 1939-1941

With the coming of the Pacific War in December 1941, the pace of political repression in Nationalist China was stepped up. Relieved by the news of the United States entry into the conflict that China had been fighting almost alone for four years, Chiang Kai-shek and the Guomindang (GMD) felt less pressure to make concessions to internal political opposition. Earlier tendencies toward some modification in the one-party structure of the GMD came to a grinding halt. "What was the need," asked an American observer, "for 'representative popular government' now? Was not America going to send to Chungking all the airplanes, tanks and guns necessary to build a great army? What internal opposition could then challenge Kuomintang rule?"[1] Hence, Generalissimo Chiang moved to increase the power of reactionary elements in the party.[2]

This chapter focuses on just one of the casualties of this political crackdown, the closing of a small and obscure school in western Yunnan, far from the Nationalist Government's wartime capital of Chongqing. This institution was founded by Zhang Junmai, and its fate was a direct result of his political beliefs and activities.

The Institute of National Culture, 1939-1941

With Chiang Kai-shek's approval (a real turnabout, in view of the closing of the two schools with which Zhang had been associated in the 1920s and 1930s),[3] Zhang established the Institute of National Culture in July 1939 near Chongqing. Because of Japanese bombing, though, by the fall of that year he had decided to move the school to Dali in western Yunnan.[4]

Two other factors contributed to that decision. First, Zhang had been deeply impressed with the climate, scenery, history, and ethnic diversity of Dali, when he visited during a May 1939 trip through western Yunnan and Southeast Asia.[5] Second, Long Yun, the governor of Yunnan, who had a reputation for shielding liberals from the GMD, donated one hundred *mu* (one *mu* is about one-sixth of an acre) of land for the school.[6] With assistance from both Chiang and Long (an unusual act of cooperation between the two rivals), in October 1940 the institute formally opened its doors in Dali.[7]

According to one account, Zhang founded the school to produce talent for the War of Resistance.[8] Its intellectual objectives, in a nutshell, were to develop the traditions of the Chinese nation, adopt the spirit of Western learning, and establish new directions in the spirit of China's scholarship. At the time, Zhang explained that he had adopted the *shuyuan* system because, unlike ordinary universities that merely emphasized intellectual attainments, China's native system placed equal emphasis on morality and knowledge. The institute would devote attention to self-cultivation and self-examination and use these as keys for the transformation of current customs.[9]

Along more political lines, the establishment of the institute may have been encouraged by Chiang Kai-shek and the government in an effort to compete with the Chinese Communist Party's (CCP) schools, which were attracting young people to Yan'an during the war.[10] It also may have been a way for students to escape GMD pressure, especially as exerted through the Three People's Principles Youth Corps, branches of which were established in every educational institution.[11] Moreover, founding it in western Yunnan, with its numerous minorities, fit in with the government's emphasis on border education during the war. A former student at the institute wrote that the school was moved from the environs of Chongqing to Dali at the request of trustee Zhou Zhongyue to "help the cultures of the border areas progress."[12] Finally, the institute may be seen as another blow in Zhang's running battle with New Culture activists during the Republican period. Probably because of his prominence as a supporter of "total Westernization," it was Hu Shi who drew Zhang's fire. While presiding over the institute, Zhang published a lengthy article attacking the "Hu Shi line."[13] This essay was described as the embodiment of Zhang's reasons for founding the institute, namely, "to correct the unhealthy trends since 'May Fourth.'"[14]

The institute was not large enough to pose a threat to either Communists or New Culture intellectuals, however, or sufficiently long-lived to accomplish much in the way of education of minority peoples. Zhang himself later recalled that it enrolled only ten to twenty students, with the same number of professors.[15] Moreover, it survived a mere two years.

The Closing of the Institute

In October 1941, Zhang journeyed from Dali to Chongqing to attend the second session of the Second People's Political Council (PPC), held from 17-30 November.[16] At first, there were no signs of trouble, and he continued to serve as a member of the council's presidium.[17] Following the Pearl Harbor attack and the beginning of the Pacific War, however, Chiang Kai-shek lowered the boom on Zhang. His institute was ordered closed, and he was confined to Chongqing and dropped from the PPC's presidium.[18]

Back in Dali, the students were anxious, suspecting the worst when their beloved teacher did not return on time from the PPC session:

> We all knew he was unwilling to remain very long in Chongqing. Each time after the People's Political Council adjourned, he hurried back to Dali to teach. When he went to Chongqing this time, however, by the end of November he still had not returned. Everyone was in suspense. Could he have been detained by the Guomindang in Chongqing?[19]

Those at the institute did not have long to wait. In early December, Zhang sent a telegram from the capital informing them the institute had been closed. "This telegram," recalled a former student, "really hit us like a bolt from the blue. The matter was settled, however, and there was nothing that could be done about it."[20] By March 1942, the Kunming press had announced the institute's closure.[21]

Yet, just a short time before, the school had been deemed worthy of receiving a government subsidy and had seemed to be serving Chiang's and the GMD's interests in opposing the Communists, fostering border education, and criticizing the May Fourth spirit. Hence, the question naturally arises: Why did Chiang Kai-shek suddenly change his mind?

After the war, Zhang published his own explanation. Chiang cracked down, Zhang recalled, because he was convinced that Zhang and his political party were involved in the student demonstrations in Kunming at that time. The cause of those protests was Madame H. H. Kong, wife of the minister of finance. According to press reports, the last plane to leave Hong Kong before its fall to the Japanese—at a time when people were desperately seeking transportation out of the city—carried Madame Kong's dog, as well as the madame herself. The cutting editorials published in the press led to angry student demonstrations.[22]

When in Chongqing, Zhang stayed with his brother, Kia-ngau, who was minister of communications. According to Zhang, Chiang Kai-shek chose his brother to convey his suspicions:

> During a cabinet meeting one day, Chiang showed him [Kia-ngau] a telegram saying that a student demonstration, then going on in Kunming, was taking place at my instigation. I told my brother I knew nothing about it, but that I would write to my political friends in Kunming to make an inquiry. Next day, my brother went to Chiang to transmit to him what I had said, whereupon Chiang jumped to the conclusion that "it must have been started by his political friends." Since at that time, Lo Lung-chi . . . was supposed to be my agent in Kunming, a letter of inquiry was sent to him. Lo answered that ten days prior to the student demonstration he had had an attack of typhoid and had been confined in Room 214 of the Municipal Hospital, so that he knew nothing of the demonstration. Since my Institute of National Culture was established in Talifu [Dali], and since it is a two-day trip by bus from there to Kunming, I do not see how my thirteen students doing post-graduate work could have had anything to do with the student demonstration in Kunming.[23]

Although Zhang saw Chiang's action in closing his institute as just another instance of the Generalissimo's emotional and impulsive behavior, by late 1941 there were several other reasons for Chiang's action.

First, because of Long Yun's protection, the opposition to Chiang in Kunming was effectively out of the latter's reach. Since Zhang's school was in Yunnan and he often passed through Kunming on his way to and from PPC meetings, Chiang may have repressed Zhang as a way of striking at Long. As long as Zhang was confined to the capital, he was in Chiang's power, unlike those liberals who remained in Kunming.[24]

Second, the crackdown may have been yet another instance of the GMD—freed from the necessity of being nice to its opposition by the entry of the United States into the war—deciding to knock dissidents down a peg or two.

Third, after 9 December, when the government declared war on Germany, the institute may have become an embarassment. Not surprisingly, in view of Zhang's earlier periods of study and teaching in Germany and intense interest in German culture, as well as the strong German influence on China during the 1930s,[25] the institute's main foreign connections were with that country. In the fall of 1940, following the collapse of France, the German National Academy invited Zhang to lecture. At the same time, authorities at the universities of Berlin, Jena, and Frankfurt established thirty scholarships for study in Germany for institute students. As a result, the institute appointed a German teacher to prepare its students to study in that country. In addition, there was a German historian, as well as a German anthropologist, on the faculty.[26] A former teacher at the institute recalled that there were two young (in their thirties) Germans at the institute, whom he described as "handsome and bright." They stayed several weeks, he noted, but had to leave following the

Pearl Harbor attack.[27] According to a former student at the school, those professors had been employed by government organizations, but because they were angry at the breaking of Sino-German relations (on 2 July 1941), they had gone to the institute to teach.[28]

German cultural organizations also joined those from Britain, France, and the United States in donating large numbers of books.[29] In addition, a German counselor stationed in the Far East contributed books to the institute's library.[30] All this, recalled a former student, made "certain people in the Guomindang still more suspicious and jealous."[31]

The institute also had contact with representatives of the German government. The U.S. Consulate in Kunming reported that the German Embassy representative in charge of the German consular office in Kunming was "known to have visited Tali in the summer of this year [1941] prior to the closing of this office, and he is believed to have inspected the Institute at that time." It was not known, the report added rather darkly, whether the institute had "any direct affiliation with or support from the German Nazi movement."[32]

The influence of things German did not go unnoticed by the outside world. In January 1939, a writer in a CCP newspaper complained that Zhang "worshipped" the Germany that had extended recognition to Manchukuo.[33] In November 1941, a report from the U.S. Consulate in Kunming, after noting that Zhang's German studies "appear to have aroused his particular interest. . . ," went on to assert that a comparison of the institute with the Haushofer Geopolitical Institute in Munich "instantly suggests itself."[34]

Fourth, there were the provocations of the NSP organ in Hong Kong, the *Guojia shehui bao* (National Socialism). Its anti-GMD line had led to several heated exchanges with the GMD newspaper in that colonial city, the *Guomin ribao*, prior to the fall of Hong Kong.[35] Moreover, it had the audacity to call for the release of the former Manchurian warlord, Zhang Xueliang,[36] which may well have angered the Generalissimo. Finally, the NSP leader in Hong Kong was strongly critical of Chiang and the GMD and, as a result, had been the target of threatening visits and letters.[37]

Fifth, Chiang Kai-shek, who was a regular reader of the newspaper that published the inflamatory editorial concerning Madame Kong, was said to be a protector of the Kong family.[38] Hence, his reaction to the student demonstrations in Kunming could have been motivated by a desire to punish those he imagined were behind the criticism of his sister-in-law.

Sixth, there was the question of NSP influence at Zhang's institute. If the school was a hotbed of opposition-party activity, then to the ordinary onlooker, Chiang and the GMD's subsidizing of it would look pretty foolish.

In fact, Chiang and his party subsidized *both* Zhang's party and school.[39] Hence, it would be inconsistent of the Generalissimo and the GMD to object if the NSP was active at the school. On the other hand, one-party dictatorships do not pretend to be consistent, when it comes to maintaining their power.

We are left, finally, with the question of whether the institute was used as a NSP cadre training school. No sooner had the subsidy begun than the ruling party insisted the institute was an NSP school. According to a postwar confidential GMD publication, the NSP established the institute to "expand its organization and intensify the training of [its] cadre. . . . It openly recruited young students from universities and middle schools who were dissatisfied with our party. It also made use of the party's Liang Shiqiu, Luo Wengan, and others to pull in young people."[40] Moreover, according to a former student, Zhang's plan to eventually establish five national-culture universities in China, and the authorities' support for the idea, aroused the GMD's "suspicion and jealousy." Hence, some Chongqing newspapers charged that he was using government funds to support NSP cadre at the institute.[41]

Leaving aside the obvious point—that Chiang Kai-shek's intention was to subsidize both Chang's school and party—was the institute a center for training NSP cadre? An NSP history later admitted the school was a party endeavor. The NSP advocated schools for education in national thought during the early years of the war, it noted, and one result was the Institute of National Culture directed by Zhang, the party head.[42] In addition, Zhang tried to recruit other leaders of the party for the institute. According to a former student, Luo Wengan served as chairman of the Department of Social Sciences; Mou Zongsan was a professor in the Department of Philosophy; and Hu Shiqing was appointed to the Department of History.[43] It is not clear, though, how much time Luo and Hu, who both passed away in 1941, spent in Dali. Moreover, although listed as members of the faculty, other well-known members of the party—such as Zhang Dongsun, Luo Longji, and Pan Guangdan—chose to teach elsewhere.[44]

Despite its acknowledgement of NSP influence, the party's involvement in the institute was not overt. In fact, Zhang seems to have taken pains to play down the party's connection with the school. According to a report by the U.S. Consulate in Kunming in November 1941, although prospective students had to take an entrance examination, "there is no evidence that the political views of the Party [NSP] must be subscribed to or that any pledge or oath is required prior to entrance."[45]

In addition, a former student recalled that Zhang—no doubt in deference to Chiang Kai-shek and the government who were supporting the school and its students—did not allow students to read *Zaisheng* and *Guojia shehui bao*.

Still suspicious, the Ministry of Education sent an inspector to investigate. He searched in the library for a long time, recalled the student, but failed to find a copy of Zhang's 1938 book explaining the NSP's program, *Liguo zhi dao* (The Way to Found the State).[46] By thus sticking to academic matters and avoiding politics, Zhang may have hoped that this time (unlike 1927 and 1936) his school would be able to survive.

Finally, more decisive than any of the above for the repression of Zhang in late 1941 was his participation in the League of Chinese Democratic Political Groups. The league was founded by leaders of the small political parties and groups, who concluded that a strong "middle organization" with a "distinct third-party stand and viewpoint" was needed to improve China's domestic political situation.[47] Chiang Kai-shek, however, was adamantly opposed to the league from its very inception.

Zhang played a prominent role in the organization. In addition to service on its executive committee, he was chairman of its Committee on International Relations.[48] Those responsible for the league resided in Chongqing, with Zuo Shunsheng, a leader of the Chinese Youth Party (CYP), serving as secretary-general. According to Zuo, he worked very closely with Zhang.[49] Shortly after the establishment of the league, the repressive political environment forced it to establish its official journal, *Guangming bao* (Light), in Hong Kong, with league leader Liang Shuming as its editor.[50] This group and its organ attracted contributions from various provincial militarists,[51] a fact that could only have increased Chiang Kai-shek's anger.

On 10 October 1941, *Guangming bao* published the league's program. It called for, among other things, an end to one-party rule, the separation of political parties and the military, rule of law, and academic and other basic freedoms.[52] Termed by one scholar "as much a condemnation as a program,"[53] it promptly elicited a hostile GMD response. As Zhang Junmai recalled, the GMD reaction was "openly unsympathetic and unfriendly." "After having had its own way," he complained, "it regarded with displeasure any challenge of its unrivalled authority, and it decided to dispatch Sun Fo and Wu Tieh cheng [Tiecheng] to Hong Kong to curtail the League's activities."[54] In a speech in Hong Kong, Sun argued that the anonymous program was, in the words of one scholar, "a sign of bad faith, if not of actual subversion."[55] A pro-GMD newspaper in Hong Kong launched a series of attacks on the league, and the British were formally asked to evict its leaders on the grounds that it was a purely Hong Kong phenomenon.[56] In China, futile attempts were made to suppress the program, which had been smuggled into the interior.[57]

As usual, it was Chiang Kai-shek's views that mattered most, and he had had his eye on the league since its establishment in the spring of 1941. During the summer of that year, he spoke at length with Zuo Shunsheng, and probed for information about his opponents, including Zhang Junmai. According to Zuo, Chiang "seemed somewhat disturbed." "He wanted me," recalled Zuo, "to discuss the strong point of each man." The interview ended on a rather ominous note, with Chiang exclaiming, "So they want to organize a party!" The Generalissimo's attitude, according to Zuo, was that the leaders of the league were not qualified to do so.[58]

Hence, Chiang tried to derail the league when it went public in October 1941. A leader of the CYP later recalled how Chiang went about it:

> In the beginning, Chiang requested Chang Ch'un and Wang Shih-chieh to remonstrate with Chang Chun-mai and Tso Shun-sheng . . . but both Tso and Chang indicated that the KMT had promised that in November [1940] . . . [it] would convene a National Assembly, but because this had been stopped, circumstances had led the opposition parties to take this step. This idea had been settled by the majority, and since the organization had been publicly established [October 1941], it would be difficult for the two of them at this mid-course to change their attitude and prohibit it. [59]

The CC Clique, a right-wing faction in the GMD led by Chen Guofu and his brother, Chen Lifu, also opposed the league. According to a leader of the league, the Chen brothers "assumed an obstinate attitude on problems relating to the participation of other parties in political affairs . . . [and] . . . failed to understand the function of the . . . League."[60]

The GMD also opposed the league on other grounds. Since the latter's program had been issued without signatures, the GMD "called the League's existence into question." It was to be considered an "anonymous organization," insisted the GMD. When the question was brought before the standing committee of the PPC, Zhang leaped (literally) to the league's defense —thereby, sealing the fate of his institute: "I stood up and said that I myself, together with Mr. Huang Yen-p'ei, Mr. Tso Shun-sen [sheng], and Dr. Lo Lung-chi, would be responsible for anything concerning the League. The question was then dropped."[61]

On 19 November, two days following the opening of the second session of the Second PPC and hence a time when leaders from all over China were in Chongqing, the league and its program were formally introduced. According to a foreign observer, Zhang Junmai and other leaders of the group "entertained Chinese liberals and National Salvationists and foreign pressmen and diplomats at a discreet tea party in Chungking itself. Here, secret police or no secret police, the declaration of principles was read aloud and circulated."[62]

The league next tried to introduce its ten-point program in the PPC, but that move was rebuffed.[63] According to Zuo Shunsheng, Chiang Kai-shek considered the resolution intolerable. When Zuo discussed it with him, Chiang's "face reddened," and he asserted that "we [the League leaders] were disturbing the situation." He was determined to kill it, reported Zuo, and thus planned to attend the council, a move that raised the specter of face-to-face conflict.[64]

As a result of Chiang's intransigent opposition, Zhang Junmai and his colleagues drafted a compromise resolution, which proved acceptable to the council. It called for convention of a National Assembly to adopt a constitution following the war, the strengthening of organs for the expression of public opinion, establishment of a wartime political organ in which all political parties could express their views, and employment of government staff on the basis of ability rather than party affiliation. By sponsoring a more moderate resolution, argued Zuo Shunsheng, "we demonstrated our loyalty to Mr. Chiang. We did not wish to hurt his position of leadership." Moreover, the leaders of the League wanted to "avoid a split . . . [and] we realized that our original resolution did not stand a chance of passage."[65]

In contrast to the GMD, the CCP response to the league was, in the words of one scholar, "very favorable."[66] Unlike the GMD, wrote one league leader, "the Communist Party understood our function, that of standing between the two parties."[67] There also may have been some assistance; the *Xinhua ribao*, for example, was said to have provided press facilities for league propaganda.[68] Nevertheless, a league leader asserted that the organization did not accept funds from the CCP.[69]

Conclusion

The reasons for the closing of the Institute of National Culture and the crackdown on Zhang were clear. It should be obvious from the previous discussion that Zhang, his party, and his institute had given the Generalissimo—by all accounts, a suspicious, emotional, and impulsive man—plenty of reasons to conclude that his subsidizing of the NSP and the institute was a mistake. Made more dictatorial by the onset of the Pacific War; perhaps troubled by the pro-German slant of the school, now that China was at war with that Axis power; stung by the anti-Chiang and anti-GMD viewpoint of the NSP mouthpiece in Hong Kong, *Guojia shehui bao*; angered by the connection between a liberal like Zhang and the most irksome of the provincial militarists, Long Yun; bothered by the attacks on the Kong family, to which he was inextricably tied by marriage; and angered by rumors that Zhang's institute was a cadre training center for the NSP, Chiang and the GMD probably were itching to put Zhang in his place.

Zhang's participation in the League of Chinese Democratic Political Groups was the final straw. The league was established despite Chiang Kai-shek's opposition; it gave every appearance, with its talk of serving as a "third force," of mounting another challenge (like the CCP's) to the one-party tutelage of the GMD; it received funds from provincial militarists who were Chiang's archrivals; and it seemed to get along far too well with the GMD's longtime enemy, the CCP. Moreover, with the fall of Hong Kong to the Japanese on 25 December 1941, the league lost its sanctuary from GMD repression. Leaders such as Liang Shuming were forced to return to Southwest China, where they were at the mercy of an intolerant GMD that had been the target of much of their previous criticism.[70]

It was clear that Zhang was one of the key leaders of the league, a fact that did not escape Chiang Kai-shek's notice. It also was obvious that, like the emperors of imperial China and Mao Zedong, Chiang took such dissidence personally. Not for him the Western concept of a loyal opposition. When Zhang Junmai stood up in the PPC's standing committee meeting to announce his willingness to be responsible for an organization the Leader opposed, and when he helped distribute the program of that group in a meeting in the capital of the GMD regime, he became a lightning rod for Chiang Kai-shek's anger, which the latter had been nursing for several months, over the activities of a political organization he opposed. Is it any wonder that, when he found Zhang within reach (while in Chongqing for the meeting of the PPC) and a good reason at hand (the student demonstrations in Kunming), he lashed out, closing the institute and confining Zhang to the capital?

Sadly for China's attempts to find a stable and fair political system, this was but one of a host of similar examples of political abuses to be found in the decades since the Republic was founded in 1912. In this sense, Zhang, described by a friend as "such a good man" and one whose "strong point was [his] refusal to sacrifice principles,"[71] was another of the many victims of his times.

Notes

1. Edgar Snow, *People on Our Side* (New York: Random House, 1944), 278. With outside aid, Chiang's government became less dependent on other, "more purely political and domestic, sources of support than might otherwise have been the case." Fairbank, Reischauer, and Craig, *East Asia: The Modern Transformation*, 717.

2. Michael Schaller, *The U.S. Crusade in China, 1938-1945* (New York: Columbia University Press, 1979), 89.

3. Although Zhang and his party were already part of the United Front, Chiang may have been further won over by Zhang's public letter, published a few months before the establishment of thc institute, criticizing Mao Zedong and the Chinese Communists (supra, chap. 11). On the earlier schools, see supra, chap. 4.

4. Zhou Xiangguang, "Ji Minzu wenhua shuyuan," 13; BDRC, 1: 33; Zhang Junmai, "Zhongguo zhanshi xianzheng shishi ji qi buzhou" (The Implementation of Constitutional Government in Wartime China and Its Steps), *Zaisheng*, no. 32 (November 1939): 3; Zhou Xiangguang, "Zhanshi chansheng de Minzu wenhua shuyuan" (The Institute of National Culture that Emerged during Wartime), *Guojia shehui bao* (Hong Kong), 6 April 1941, 3.

5. For accounts of Zhang's travels through Yunnan and Southeast Asia, see Zhang, "Dian you zagan," 26 July 1940, 3; 27 July 1940, 4; Zhang Junmai, "Nan you suo jian" (Observations During [My] Travcls in the South), *Zaisheng*, no. 28 (August 1939), 1-3; Zhang Junmai, "Yizhe xu" (Translator's Introduction), in Henry R. Davics, *Yunnan ge yizu ji qi yuyan yanjiu* (Studies of the Tribes of Yunnan and Their Languages) (Changsha: Shangwu yinshuguan, 1941), 1-9.

6. Eastman, *Seeds of Destruction*, 25-27; Zhou Xiangguang, "Ji Minzu wenhua shuyuan," 12; Zhou Xiangguang, "Zhanshi chansheng," 3; BDRC, 1: 33.

7. LHWLX, 24.

8. Shi Yi, "Wo suo zhidao Zhang Junmai," 2. For a fuller discussion of the school's curriculum and structure, see supra, chap. 4.

9. YX, 30.

10. Zhou Xiangguang, "Ji Minzu wenhua shuyuan," 12. For a discussion of the flight of educated youth to Yan'an, see Israel and Klein, *Rebels and Bureaucrats*, chap. 5.

11. Chou Hsiang-kuang, *A Modern History of China*, 161.

12. Zhou Xiangguang, "Ji Minzu wenhua shuyuan," 12. For the government's emphasis on border education, see *China Handbook, 1937-1943*, 403-4.

13. Zhang Junmai, " Hu Shi sixiangjie luxian pinglun (A Critique of the Hu Shih Ideological Line), *Zaisheng*, no. 51 (1940).

14. GS 4, no. 5, 74.

15. Zhang, *Bianzheng weiwuzhuyi*, 193.

16. Zhou Xiangguang, "Ji Minzu wenhua shuyuan," 13; Shyu, "The People's Political Council," 40.

17. GBFO 371/31644 [F1021/113/10], dispatch, A. Clark Kerr, Chungking, to Anthony Eden, Foreign Office, 11 December 1941, encl. 1.

18. Chang, *Third Force*, 103; Zhang, *Bianzheng weiwuzhuyi*, 194; Lawrcnce K. Rosinger, *China's Crisis* (New York: Knopf, 1945), 69.

19. Zhou Xiangguang, "Ji Minzu wenhua shuyuan," 13.

20. Ibid.

21. USDS, R.G. 84, Kunming Post Files, 1942, 800 decimal series, Troy L. Perkins, Kunming, to Clarence E. Gauss, Chungking, dispatch no. 104, 15 April 1942, "Political Report for the Month of March 1942," 6.

22. Ward to State, USDS 893.00/7-2244, 5, cited in Fredric J. Spar, "Liberal Political Opposition in Kuomintang and Communist China: Lo Lung-chi in Chinese Politics, 1928-1958" (Ph.D. diss., Brown University, 1980), 196.

23. Chang, *Third Force*, 103.

24. According to one observer, the GMD liked to keep its opposition in Chongqing, where it could keep an eye on it. Graham Peck, *Two Kinds of Time*.

25. See Kirby, *Germany and Republican China*. For the government of Chiang Kai-shek, argues the author, the Nanjing Decade was "a period of German influence on China." Ibid., 3.

26. Zhou Xiangguang, "Ji Minzu wenhua shuyuan," 13; Zhou Xiangguang, "Zhanshi chansheng," 3.

27. Vincent Y. C. Shih, interview by author, 29 June 1976, Taipei, Taiwan. The anthropologist's name was Inez de Beauclair. Ibid. A former student at the institute gave the German-language teacher's name as "Baokelan." Zhou Xiangguang, "Ji Minzu wenhua shuyuan," 13. It is possible that Beauclair and "Baokelan" were the same person.

28. Ibid.; Mackerras and Chan, *Modern China*, 388.

29. Zhou Xiangguang, "Zhanshi chansheng," 3.

30. Zhou Xiangguang, "Ji Minzu wenhua shuyuan," 13.

31. Ibid.

32. "Chinese National Socialist Party's Cultural Institute," 3.

33. Lin Beili, "Qingjiao Zhang Junmai," 4.

34. "Chinese National Socialist Party's Cultural Institute," 4.

35. Xu Fulin, "Xu Fulin xiansheng huiyilu," 14.

36. The editorial, "Zhengfu ying ji jiefang Zhang Xueliang" (The Government Should Immediately Release Zhang Xueliang), was included in the volume, *Zhang Xueliang de ziyou wenti* (The Problem of Zhang Xueliang's Freedom), advertised in the League of Chinese Democratic Political Groups' *Guangming bao* (Hong Kong), 10 October 1941, 1.

37. NA, R.G. 226 (OSS), document no. 7724, Addison E. Southard, Hong Kong, to State, dispatch no. 1035, 23 October 1941, 4, 6.

38. Chang, *Third Force*, 98, 102. *Dagongbao* was one of two newspapers Chiang read daily, according to Zhang Junmai. Ibid., 102.

39. Chiang himself ordered the National Military Council to provide funds to Zhang's school. GS 4, no. 5, 73. The NSP also received a subsidy, paid to Zhang as party chairman. "Transmitting a Memorandum of a Conversation with the Representative in Hong Kong of the 'National Socialist Party,'" pp. 4-5 of the memorandum.

40. *Zhongguo ge xiao dangpai*, 74. This publication was stamped "secret."

41. Zhou Xiangguang, "Ji Minzu wenhua shuyuan," 13.

42. "Zhongguo minzhu shehui dang jianyao shigao," 19.

43. Zhou Xiangguang, "Ji Minzu wenhua shuyuan," 13; Zhou Xiangguang, "Zhanshi chansheng," 3.

44. Ibid. Zhang Dongsun returned to Beijing early in the war to resume teaching at Yenching University, while Luo and Pan took up appointments at the Southwest Associated University (*Xinan lianda*) in Kunming. BDRC, 1: 132; 2: 436; 3: 62.

45. "Chinese National Socialist Party's Cultural Institute," 2.

46. Zhou Xiangguang, "Ji Minzu wenhua shuyuan," 36.

47. Anthony J. Shaheen, "The China Democratic League and Chinese Politics, 1939-1947" (Ph.D. diss., University of Michigan, 1977), 39.

48. Van Slyke, *Enemies and Friends*, 174; YX, 32.

49. Zuo Shunsheng, "Reminiscences," 181.

50. Shaheen, "The China Democratic League," 59.

51. "Transmitting a Memorandum of a Conversation with the Representative in Hong Kong of the 'Chinese National Socialist Party,'" 7.

52. Van Slyke, *Enemies and Friends,* 174-75.

53. Ibid., 176.

54. Chang, *Third Force*, 114.

55. Van Slyke, *Enemies and Friends*, 176.

56. Alitto, *The Last Confucian*, 310; Van Slyke, *Enemies and Friends*, 176.

57. Ibid.; Epstein, *The Unfinished Revolution in China*, 152-53.

58. Zuo Shunsheng, "Reminiscences," 183-84.

59. Li Huang, "Reminiscences," 752.

60. Zuo Shunsheng, "Reminiscences," 182-83.

61. Chang, *Third Force*, 114.

62. Epstein, *The Unfinished Revolution in China*, 153.

63. Shaheen, "The China Democratic League," 76.

64. Zuo Shunsheng, "Reminiscences," 190-91.

65. Zuo Shunsheng, "Reminiscences," 191-92.

66. Van Slyke, *Enemies and Friends*, 176.

67. Zuo Shunsheng, "Reminiscences," 187.

68. *Zhongguo minzhu tongmeng gaikuang* (The General Condition of the China Democratic League) (Nanjing: Tongyi chubanshe, 1947), 29, cited in Van Slyke, *Enemies and Friends*, 177. Since this is a GMD source and that party regularly charged the League's successor, the China Democratic League, with being "in cahoots" with the Communists, it is difficult to tell whether the assertion concerning CCP aid to the League is true. According to Van Slyke, the book is marked "top secret."

69. Zuo Shunsheng, "Reminiscences," 195.

70. Chang, *Third Force*, 115; Alitto, *The Last Confucian*, 310-16; Van Slyke, *Enemies and Friends*, 177.

71. Zuo Shunsheng, "Reminiscences," 184, 189.

Epilogue

Although it may have appeared that way at the end of 1941, Zhang's political career was by no means over following Chiang Kai-shek's crackdown. Unlike fellow NSP member, Luo Longji,[1] Zhang was not dropped from the People's Political Council (PPC) and remained a member in good standing right up to its termination in 1948. Moreover, in 1941, prior to the crackdown on him, Zhang was one of the founding members, along with other minority-party leaders and intellectuals, of the third-force organization, the League of Chinese Democratic Political Groups.[2] Despite the fact that he was confined to Chongqing and under surveillance by the secret police,[3] he also played an important role in the league's successor, the China Democratic League (DL), formed in October 1944.[4] When not occupied with the PPC or league business, he also did a good deal of writing during these years of restricted movement.

At the end of 1944, the Generalissimo relented and permitted Zhang to travel to the United States to attend a conference of the Institute of Pacific Relations.[5] In addition, Chiang appointed him a DL member of the Chinese delegation to the founding meeting of the United Nations in San Francisco in the spring of 1945.[6] While in the United States, Zhang spent much of his time studying the American constitution, which was to help him when it came time to draft a constitution for China the following year.[7]

After his return to China, Zhang served as a DL member of the Political Consultative Conference, called in January 1946 to resolve the fast-blossoming dispute between the Guomindang (GMD) and the Chinese Communist Party (CCP).[8] His unique contribution was to prepare the draft constitution that, with some changes, became the constitution of the Republic of China on Taiwan.

In that sense, what one Chinese intellectual refers to as Zhang's "dream" came true.[9] His draft was carefully reviewed by his fellow members of the PPC Committee for Review of the Draft Constitution, which included representatives from the CCP, GMD, and minority parties.[10] It was then adopted on 25 December 1946 by the Constituent National Assembly (CNA).[11]

Unfortunately, constitutionmaking did not solve the real problem in China, namely, armed struggle between the two major political parties. When Chiang

Kai-shek convened the CNA in November 1946 to consider the constitution, the CCP refused to participate, and by early 1947 the final split between the two warring parties had occurred. More to the point for our study, Chiang Kai-shek's invitation to Zhang's group—renamed the Chinese Democratic Socialist Party (DSP) in the summer of 1946, following the merger of the NSP with the Democratic Constitutionalist Party—to participate in the CNA led to bitter intraparty wrangling over whether to accept. When Zhang, on behalf of the DSP, agreed to take part, the result was a split in his party when some DSP members bolted and formed the Reform Faction of the DSP. This schism largely destroyed any chance his group might have had to serve as a meaningful "third force."[12] The segment of the DSP led by Zhang then participated in the last-ditch GMD regime and in the end accompanied that government into exile in Taiwan (where the DSP still exists in these postdictatorship days of the mid-1990s). In November 1948, near the end of the Republic of China's tenure on the mainland, Zhang may have rued his earlier decision to cooperate with Chiang Kai-shek, for he advised the latter to resign his post as president.[13]

Unlike some of his fellow minor-party colleagues—such as Luo Longji, Zhang Bojun, and Zhang Dongsun[14]—Zhang chose not to remain in China and serve the communist dictatorship, whose future treatment of intellectuals he could easily envision, thanks to his earlier studies of Soviet Russia. As we have seen, as early as 1927, he had realized that under communism one's fate was settled by the class to which one belonged. Hence, on 25 April 1949, two days after the People's Liberation Army took Nanjing, the GMD capital, he left his Shanghai home for Macao.[15]

His decision to depart could only have been confirmed when his name appeared on a list of "war criminals" announced by the Communists on Christmas Eve, 1948. According to the broadcast, the forty-two figures on the list (including Chinese Youth Party leader Zeng Qi) were "war criminals well-known for their heinous crimes, who, all Chinese agree, should receive the just penalty." Zhang could not have missed the news, for the list was picked up by the Associated Press and published in the Shanghai English-language press.[16]

Hence, he did not have to suffer through the Campaign against Counter-Revolutionaries, the Anti-Rightist Movement, or the decade-long Cultural Revolution, which convulsed his homeland during the final two decades of his life. Following a two-day visit in mid-October 1949,[17] he also declined to take up residence in Taiwan, preferring instead to emigrate to the United States in 1952 (after two years in India).

During the early years of his exile, he participated in a last-gasp effort of the third force, joining such notables as former GMD general, Zhang Fakui, and former GMD official, Gu Mengyu, to establish the Fighting League for Chinese Freedom and Democracy (*Zhongguo ziyou minzhu zhandou tongmeng*) in Hong Kong. Although it stimulated some interest during the years 1952 through 1954, it quietly folded after the United States decided, as a result of the Korean War, to throw its support to the Chiang Kai-shek government on Taiwan.[18]

From 1954 until his death in 1969, Zhang continued to write on politics in the PRC and Taiwan, publish books and articles on philosophy, dabble in emigre politics, and travel to Europe and Asia.[19] In the 1960s, he also was associated with the operation of one last journal, *Ziyou zhong* (Liberty Bell), in whose pages one may find his final thoughts about the fate of modern China.[20] He never relinquished his belief in democracy and socialism, formed nearly a half-century earlier.

His death contained more than a little of the ironies of the passage of time, for this man who had kowtowed to the last Qing emperor in 1911 as a *Yang Hanlin* died in Berkeley during the height of the counterculture and anti-Vietnam War protests. He had come a long way from Qing-era Jiading and experienced more than most. Throughout it all, he continued to participate in the intellectual and political life of his beloved China, never missing an opportunity to participate in a scholarly or political debate. The voluminous written record of his thought and politics that resulted makes it but a matter of time before the full biography he so richly deserves appears.

Notes

1. Luo was dismissed in 1941, after the Second Council. Fredric J. Spar, "Human Rights and Political Engagement: Luo Longji in the 1930s," in Jeans, *Roads Not Taken*, 77.

2. BDRC, 1: 33-34. Other charter members included Zhang Lan, Huang Yanpei, Liang Shuming, and Zuo Shunsheng. Ibid., 33.

3. For a description of a search of Zhang's home by GMD Special Services personnel, see Yang Yongqian, *Zhonghua minguo xianfa zhi fu*, 123-24.

4. BDRC, 1: 34. For a brief description of this organization, see Roger B. Jeans, "China Democratic League," in Haruhiro Fukui, ed., *Political Parties of Asia and the Pacific*, 2 vols. (Westport, CT: Greenwood, 1985), 1: 168-71.

5. YX, 33.

6. BDRC, 1: 34. Officially, the meeting was called the United Nations Conference on International Organization.

7. Zhang Junmai, *Bianzheng weiwuzhuyi*, 194.

8. YX, 33; BDRC, 1:34. The other DL delegates were Zhang Lan, Luo Longji, and Zhang Dongsun. Ibid., 1:34.

9. As a noted Chinese political scientist concluded, "The Constitution as passed by the National Assembly . . . was very much the same as the one handed to it by the government" [i.e., Zhang's draft as approved by the Committee for Review of the Draft Constitution]. Ch'ien Tuan-sheng, *The Government and Politics of China*, 324. More precisely, it has been suggested that 90 percent of the contents of Zhang's draft were retained in the final version. Wen-shun Chi, *Ideological Conflicts in Modern China*, 138.

10. For the complete text of the PPC resolution setting up the committee, see *The China White Paper*, 2 vols. (Stanford: Stanford University Press, 1967), 2: 619-21.

11. Wen-shun Chi, *Ideological Conflicts in Modern China*, 138. For a succinct but lucid analysis of the process of adoption of the constitution, see Ch'ien Tuan-sheng, *The Government and Politics of China*, chap. 21.

12. Ibid., 354-55. For a more detailed account of the split, see Lloyd E. Eastman, "China's Democratic Parties and the Temptations of Political Power, 1946-1947," in Jeans, *Roads Not Taken*, 192-94.

13. Chang, *Third Force*, 240-43. On 21 January, Chiang resigned as president and left Nanjing for his home town of Fenghua. Ibid., 243.

14. During the years 1949-1954, a number of non-CCP "democratic personages" were appointed by the PRC government to important positions. Zhengyuan Fu, *Autocratic Tradition and Chinese Politics* (Cambridge: Cambridge University Press, 1993), 215. Among these were former NSP member Luo Longji and Third Party leader Zhang Bojun, both stalwarts of the DL who elected to remain in the "new China." As a result of the Anti-Rightist Movement launched in 1957, they were persecuted and, in 1958, removed from all their posts. For biographical sketches of the two, see BDRC, 1: 98-100; 2: 433-38. Zhang Dongsun, Zhang's lifelong friend up to their parting of ways during the civil war of the late 1940s, chose to remain at Beijing University, where he was chairman of the philosophy department. In 1951-52, he was accused of being an American spy and stripped of all his posts. He later died in prison. BDRC, 1: 133; Wu Ningkun, *A Single Tear: A Family's Persecution, Love, and Endurance in Communist China* (New York: Atlantic Monthly Press, 1993), 18, 358.

15. YX, 45. The stream of memoirs by Chinese intellectuals who have suffered decades of persecution by the Communists have amply confirmed Zhang's pessimism. See, e.g., Wu Ningkun's *A Single Tear*.

16. USDS, *Foreign Relations of the United States, 1948, the Far East, China*, vol. 7 (Washington, D.C.: U.S. Government Printing Office, 1973), 718-19.

17. YX, 45.

18. For a brief history of this organization and Zhang's involvement with it, see Yang Tianshi, "The Third Force in Hong Kong and North America During the 1950s," in Jeans, *Roads Not Taken*, chap. 12. For brief descriptions of Zhang Fakui's and Gu Mengyu's involvement, see BDRC, 1: 61; 2: 254-55.

19. He took brief trips to Switzerland, England, and Germany, as well as Japan, Korea, and other countries in Asia. Wen-shun Chi, *Ideological Conflicts in Modern China*, 138. His best-known work on philosophy was the two-volume, *The Develop-*

ment of Neo-Confucian Thought (1957, 1962).

20. *Ziyou zhong* began publication in Hong Kong in 1965 and published many of Zhang's writings during the last four years of his life.

Bibliography

The following list, which includes all sources mentioned in chapter notes, is divided into works by Zhang Junmai (listed chronologically), writings by other authors, and letters and interviews.

Works by Zhang Junmai

Zhang Junmai. "Mule Yuehan yiyuan zhengzhi lun" (John [Stuart] Mill's *Considerations on Representative Government*). *Xinmin congbao* (Journal of the New Citizen), no. 90 (1906): 35-70.

———. "Yefangsi shi *lunlixue* ([William S.] Jevons' *Logic*). Translated by Li Zhai [Zhang Junmai]. *Xuebao* (Academic Journal) 1, nos. 1-7 (1907).

———. "Lun jinhou mindang zhi jinxing" (On the Advancement of the People's Party Henceforth). *Xinmin congbao*, no. 95 (1907): 1-17.

———. "Waiguo bannian jishi" (A Record of Events Abroad [During the Past] Six Months). *Zhenglun* (Political Discussion) 1, no. 1 (1907): 89-109.

———. "Zhanshi Ouzhou waijiao zhi xin mishi" (A New Secret History of Europe's Wartime Diplomacy). *Da Zhonghua* (The Great Zhonghua Journal), 1, no. 7 (1915): 3d article; no. 8 (1915): 4th article.

———. "Oudong xin zhanqu zhi waijiao chaoliu" (Diplomatic Currents in the New War Zone in Eastern Europe). *Dongfang zazhi* (Eastern Miscellany) 13, no. 2 (1916): 8 pp.

———. "Ying junxu dachen Lude Qiaoqi shi zhi junhuo yu zhanzheng guan" (The Views of England's Secretary of War, Lord Kitchener, on Munitions and War). *Dongfang zazhi* 13, no. 4 (1916): 13 pp.

———. *Shengzhi tiao yi* (A Discussion of Provincial System Regulations). 2d ed. Shanghai: Shangwu yinshuguan, 1916.

———. "Eluosi suweiai lianbang gongheguo xianfa quanwen" (The Complete Text of the Constitution of the Russian Soviet Federated [Socialist] Republic). *Jiefang yu gaizao* (Emancipation and Reconstruction) 1, no. 6 (1919): 25-39.

———. "Deyizhiguo xianfa quanwen" (The Complete Text of the German Constitution). *Jiefang yu gaizao* 2, no. 8 (1920): 39-84.

———. "Ji Faguo zongxuanju ji zongtong xuanju" (Notes on the French General and Presidential Elections). *Jiefang yu gaizao* 2, no. 9 (1920): 44-68.

———. "Deguo xin gonghe xianfa ping" (A Critique of the Constitution of the New German Republic). *Jiefang yu gaizao* 2, nos. 9-12 (1920). Reprinted in *Xin*

Deguo shehui minzhu zhengxiang ji (see later entry).
Zhang Junmai, and Zhang Dongsun. "Zhongguo qiantu: Deguo hu, Eguo hu?" (China's Future: Germany or Russia?). *Jiefang yu gaizao* 2, no. 14 (1920): 18 pp. Reprint of two letters from Zhang Junmai to Zhang Dongsun in April, and the latter's reply in July.
———. "Du *Liu xingqi zhi Eguo* (On *Six Weeks in Russia*). *Gaizao* 3, no. 1 (1920): 61-71; no. 2 (1920): 51-63.
———. "Zhengzhi huodong guo zuyi jiu Zhongguo ye?" (Are Political Activities Really Sufficient to Save China?). *Gaizao* 3, no. 6 (1921): 1-6.
———. "Guomin zhengzhi pinge zhi tigao" (The Elevation of the Character of National Politics). *Gaizao* 4, no. 2 (1921): 1st article.
———. "Xuanni zhi shehui gaizao tongzhi hui yijianshu," (Presentation of a Proposal by the Association of Comrades for Social Reform). *Gaizao* 4, no. 3 (1921): 1st article.
———. "Xueshu fangfa shang zhi guanjian" (My Humble View of Scholarly Methods). *Gaizao* 4, no. 5 (1922): 9 pp.
———. "Ying De Mei sanguo shizhi ji Guangzhou shizhi shang zhi guancha" (The Municipal Systems of England, Germany, and the United States, and Observations of the Municipal System of Canton). *Gaizao* 4, no. 7 (1922): 2d article.
———. *Guo xian yi* (Suggestions on the National Constitution). Shanghai: *Shishi xinbao* guan, 1922; reprint (with deletions), Taipei: Shangwu yinshuguan, 1970.
——— [Zhang Jiasen]. *Xin Deguo shehui minzhu zhengxiang ji* (Notes on Political Aspects of the New German Social Democracy). Shanghai: Shangwu yinshuguan, 1922.
———. "Zailun renshengguan yu kexue bing da Ding Zaijun" (A Further Discussion of Science and a Philosophy of Life, with a Reply to Ding Wenjiang). In *Kexue yu renshengguan* (Science and a Philosophy of Life), 2 vols., 1: 3d article. Shanghai: Yadong shuju, 1923.
———. "Zhengzhixue zhi gaizao" (The Transformation of Political Science). *Dongfang zazhi* 21, no. 1 (1924): 9 pp.
———. *Guonei zhanzheng Liujiang* (Six Lectures on Civil War). Wusong: Guoli zhengzhi daxue, 1924.
——— [Chang, Carsun]. *Bulletin of the National Institute of Political Science: Its Purpose and Its Work*. Wusong: [The National Institute of Political Science], 1926.
——— [Zhang Jiasen]. *Wuhan jianwen* (Observations in Wuhan). Wusong: Guoli zhengzhi daxue, 1926.
——— [Shijie shi zhuren]. *SuE pinglun* (A Critique of Soviet Russia). Shanghai: Xinyue shudian, 1927.
———. "*Renshengguan zhi lunzhan* xu" (Introduction to *The Polemic Over a Philosophy of Life*). In *Renshengguan zhi lunzhan*, 2 vols., 1: 17 pp. 3d ed. Shanghai: Taidong tushuju, 1928 (first published in 1923).
——— [Zhang Junmai?]. "Fakanci" (Introduction). *Xinlu* (The New Way), 1, no. 1 (1928): 1-19.

———. "Yijiuyijiu zhi yijiueryi nian lu Ouzhong zhi zhengzhi yinxiang ji wuren suo de zhi jiaoxun" (Political Impressions during My Stay in Europe, 1919-1921, and Lessons I Learned). *Xinlu* 1, no. 5 (1928): 19-27.
———. "Pi xunzheng shuo" (A Refutation of the Theory of Tutelage). *Xinlu*, 1, no. 7 (1928): 1-14.
——— [Chang, Carsun]. "Richard Wilhelm, der Weltburger." *Sinica* 5, no. 2 (1930): 71-73.
——— [Chang, Carsun]. "Der Idealismus in der chinesischen Philosophie zur Zeit der Sung-Dynastie." *Forschungen und Fortschritte* 6, no. 17 (1930): 224-25.
——— [Chang, Carsun]. "Philosophisches Ringen im heutigen China." *Die Tatwelt* 6, no. 1 (1930): 25-33.
Laski, Harold. *Zhengzhi dianfan* (A Grammar of Politics). Translated, with an introduction, by Zhang Shilin [Zhang Junmai]. Shanghai: Shangwu yinshuguan, 1930; reprint, Taipei: Shangwu yinshuguan, 1970.
Zhang Junmai [Chang, Carsun]. "Die Hauptfragen in der Konfuzianischen Philosophie." *Sinica* 5, nos. 5/6 (1930): 213-26.
——— [Chang, Carsun]. "Die staatsrechtliche Krisis der chinesischen Republik," *Jahrbuch des offent lichen Rechte der Gegenwart* 19 (1931): 316-55.
——— [Chang, Carsun]. "Die Stellung der Kanonischen Literatur im modernen Geistesleben Chinas." *Sinica* 6, no. 1 (1931): 13-26; no. 3 (1931), 97-108.
———. "Wo zhi Eguo guan" (My View of Russia). *Zaisheng* (National Renaissance) 1, nos. 1, 5-7 (1932).
———. *Shitailin zhixia zhi SuE* (Soviet Russia under the Rule of Stalin). Peiping: Zaisheng zazhi she, 1933; reprint, Taipei: Shangwu yinshuguan, 1971.
———. "Shanxi duiyu weilai shijie dazhan de zeren" (The Responsibility of Shanxi in Regard to the Future World War). In *Minzu fuxing zhi xueshu jichu* (The Academic Basis for National Revival). 2 vols. Peiping: Zaisheng she, 1935.
———. "Minzhu ducai yiwai zhi disanzhong zhengzhi" (The Third Type of Government Besides Democracy and Dictatorship). *Yuzhou xunkan* (The Universe) 1, no. 6 (1935): 1-12.
———. "Yanci" (Speech). *Xinmin yuekan* (New People Monthly) 1, no. 2 (1935): 2 pp.
———. "Zhonghua minzu zhi zili anzai?" (Wherein Lies the Chinese Nation's Own Strength?). *Yuzhou xunkan* 3, no. 3 (1935): 1-4.
———. "Guangxi jianshe yu Zhonghua minzu zhi gaizao" (Guangxi Reconstruction and the Reform of the Chinese Nation). *Yuzhou xunkan* 3, no. 4 (1935): 5-8.
———. "Jiaoyujia yu guomin qizhi de bianhua" (Educators and Changes in National Character). *Yuzhou xunkan* 3, no. 10 (1935): 1-4.
———. "Wo cong shehui kexue tiaodao zhexue zhi jingguo" (My Leap from the Social Sciences to Philosophy). *Yuzhou xunkan* 3, no. 11 (1935): 9-15.
———. "Shuyuan zhidu zhi jingsheng yu Xuehai shuyuan zhi zongzhi" (The Spirit of the Academy System and the Aims of the Xuehai Institute." *Yuzhou xunkan* 4, no. 7 (1936): 13-18.
———. "Ruijin shi jingshenshang fanGong de diyixian" (Ruijin Is the Front Line in the Spiritual Defense against Communism). *Zaisheng* 4, no. 4 (1937): 6-10.

———. "Hanxue Songxue duiyu wu guo wenhua shishang zhi gongxian" (The Contributions of Han and Song Learning to Our Country's Cultural History). *Yuzhou xunkan* 5, no. 3 (1936): 2-6.

——— [Li Zhai]. "Gongchandang biangeng fangxiang yu renlei dexing zhi juewu" (The Communist Party's Change of Course and the Realization of Humanity's Moral Character). *Zaisheng* 4, no. 9 (1937): 1-11.

———, trans. with an introduction and short biography of Ludendorff. *Quan minzu zhanzheng lun* (Der Totale Krieg). By Erich Ludendorff. Shanghai: Zhongguo guomin jingji yanjiusuo (Institute for Research on the Chinese National Economy), 1938; reprint, Chongqing: Shangwu yinshuguan, 1943.

———. *Liguo zhi dao* (The Way to Found the State). Guilin: n.p., 1938; reprint, Taipei: Chinese Democratic Socialist Party Central Headquarters, 1969.

———. "Zhi Mao Zedong yifeng gongkaixin" (An Open Letter to Mao Zedong). *Zaisheng*, no. 10 (1938): 1-2.

———. "Da Chen Shaoyu Yan'an yanci zhong fudai zhiwen" (A Reply to the Questions Appended to Chen Shaoyu's Speech in Yan'an). *Zaisheng*, no. 16 (1939): 1-2.

———. "Nan you suo jian" (Observations during [My] Travels in the South). *Zaisheng*, no. 28 (August 1939): 1-3.

———. "Zhongguo zhanshi xianzheng shishi ji qi buzhou" (The Implementation of Constitutional Government in Wartime China and Its Steps). *Zaisheng*, no. 32 (November 1939): 3-5.

———. "Minzu wenhua shuyuan yuanqi" (Prospectus of the Institute of National Culture). *Zaisheng* (Taiwan series), no. 14 (1972): 26-31. Originally published in 1939.

———. "Wuren chu kangzhan shidai zhong zhi taidu" (The Attitude of Those of Us Living in the Era of the War of Resistance). *Dongfang zazhi* 37, no. 13 (1940): 59-62.

———. "Dian you zagan" (Miscellaneous Impressions of a Trip to Yunnan). *Guojia shehui bao* (National Socialist), 26 July 1940, 3; 27 July 1940, 4.

———. "Hu Shi sixiangjie luxian pinglun" (A Critique of the Hu Shi Ideological Line). *Zaisheng*, no. 51 (1940); reprint, *Zaisheng* (Taiwan series), no. 37 (1974): 22-32.

———, trans. with an introduction by Zhang Junmai. *Yunnan ge yizu ji qi yuyan yanjiu* (Studies of the Tribes of Yunnan and Their Languages). By Henry R. Davies. Changsha: Shangwu yinshuguan, 1941.

———. "Nianyunian lai shijie zhengchao jitang zhong women di lichang" (Our Position in the Turmoil of the World's Political Trends during the Past Twenty-Odd Years). *Zaisheng*, no. 108 (1946): 3-6.

———. "Wu guo zhengdang fazhan zhi huigu yu wu dang zhi jianglai" (Retrospect on the Development of Our Nation's Political Parties and the Future of Our Party). *Zaisheng*, no. 109 (1946): 3-4.

———. *Zhonghua minguo minzhu xianfa shijiang* (Ten Lectures on the Democratic Constitution of the Republic of China). Shanghai: Shangwu yinshuguan, 1947.

———. "Women tuiju Xu Fulin xiansheng jingxuan fuzongtong" (We Nominate Mr.

Xu Fulin to Run for Vice-President). *Zaisheng*, nos. 210/211 (1948): 4.
———. "Wode xuesheng shidai" (My Student Era). *Zaisheng*, no. 239 (1948): 7-8.
———. "Tan zuijin zhengju" (On the Recent Political Situation). *Zaisheng*, no. 244 (1948): 2-3.
———. "Dongnan Ya, Aozhou yu Malai ji Zhongguo zhengju ganxiang dawen" (Answers to Questions on My Impressions of Southeast Asia, Australia, Malaya, and China's Political Situation). *Zaisheng*, no. 314 (1952): 2-6.
——— [Chang, Carsun]. *The Third Force in China*. New York: Bookman, 1952.
———. "Yu Chen Yuan shi lun Li Zhizao yi *Ming-li tan* zhi yuanben" (A Discussion with Mr. Chen Yuan on the [Western] Original for Li Zhizao's translation of *An Investigation of Logic*). *Zaisheng* 5, no. 1 (1954): 5-6.
———. *Zhonghua minguo duli zizhu yu Yazhou qiantu* (The Republic of China's Independence and the Future of Asia). Hong Kong: Ziyou chubanshe, 1955.
——— [Chang, Carsun]. *China and Gandhian India* (Calcutta: Brahmo, 1956).
———. "Liang Rengong zhuan xu" (An Introduction to a Biography of Liang Qichao). In Mao Yiheng, *Liang Qichao*. Hong Kong: Yazhou chubanshe, 1957.
———. "Chongyin *Wuxu zhengbian ji* xu" (An Introduction to the Reprint of *A Record of the 1898 Coup d'Etat*). In Liang Qichao, *Wuxu zhengbian ji*. Taipei: Wenhai chubanshe, 1957.
——— [Chang, Carsun]. *The Development of Neo-Confucian Thought*. New York: Bookman, 1957.
———. *Bianzheng weiwuzhuyi bolun* (A Refutation of Dialectical Materialism). Hong Kong: Youlian chubanshe, 1958.
———. "Zhang Junmai xiansheng fangRi jiangyan jiyao" (Extracts from Mr. Zhang Junmai's Lectures While Visiting Japan). *Minzhu Zhongguo* (Democratic China) 2, no. 5 (1959): 3-9.
———. "Zhuiyi [Zeng] Muhan" (Recollections of Zeng Qi). *Minzhu chao* (Current Democracy) 2, no. 18 (1961): 3.
———. "Zhi Liang Hancao xiansheng lun wushi nianlai zhengzhi wenhua han" (A Letter to Mr. Liang Hancao Discussing the Politics and Culture of the Past Fifty Years). *Minzhu Zhongguo* 5, no. 16 (1962): 3.
———. "Ping Liang Rengong xiansheng *Qingdai xueshu gailun* qizhong guanyu Ouzhou wenyi fuxing Song-Ming lixue Dai Dongyuan zhexue san dian" (A Critique of Mr. Liang Qichao's [Treatment of] the European Renaissance, Sung-Ming Neo-Confucianism, and the Philosophy of Dai Zhen in [His Book], *Intellectual Trends in the Qing Period*). *Minzhu pinglun* (Democratic Critic) 15, no. 2 (1964): 26-29.
———. "Zhang Dongsun xiansheng bashi shouxu" (Wishing Mr. Zhang Dongsun Longevity on His Eightieth Birthday). *Ziyou zhong* (Liberty Bell) 1, no. 3 (1965): 22.
———. "Mao chao yu Qin zheng, Xin Mang, Sui Yang" ([A Comparison of] Mao [Zedong's] Dynasty with the Qin Government, [Wang] Mang [of the] Xin [Dynasty], and [the Emperor] Yang [of the] Sui [Dynasty]). *Ziyou zhong* 3, no. 9 (1967): 2-5, 8.

———. *Shehuizhuyi sixiang yundong gaiguan* (A General Survey of Socialist Thought and Movements). Taipei: Zhang Junmai xiansheng jiangxuejin jijinhui (Mr. Zhang Junmai Scholarship Foundation), 1978.

Works by Other Authors

Alitto, Guy S. *The Last Confucian: Liang Shu-ming and the Chinese Dilemma of Modernity*. Berkeley: University of California Press, 1979.

"Benzhi disannian zhi yunming yu shiming" (The Fate and Mission of This Journal in Its Third Year). *Zaisheng* 3, no. 1 (1935): 20 pp.

Bernal, Martin. "The Triumph of Anarchism Over Marxism." In *China in Revolution: The First Phase, 1900-1913*, ed. Mary C. Wright, 97-142. New Haven: Yale University Press, 1968.

Biggerstaff, Knight. *The Earliest Modern Government Schools in China*. Ithaca: Cornell University Press, 1961.

Bo Yang. "The Ugly Chinaman." In *Seeds of Fire: Chinese Voices of Conscience*, ed. Geremie Barme and John Minford, 168-76. New York: Farrar, Straus & Giroux, 1988.

Boorman, Howard L., and Richard C. Howard, eds. *Biographical Dictionary of Republican China.* 5 vols. New York: Columbia University Press, 1967-79. Vol. 5 is a personal name index by Janet Krompart.

Borkenau, Franz. *World Communism: A History of the Third International.* Ann Arbor: University of Michigan Press, 1962.

Boyle, John H. *China and Japan at War, 1937-1945: The Politics of Collaboration*. Stanford: Stanford University Press, 1972.

Brandt, Conrad, Benjamin Schwartz, and John K. Fairbank. *A Documentary History of Chinese Communism*. Cambridge: Harvard University Press, 1952; New York: Atheneum, 1966.

Braunthal, Julius. *History of the International*. Vol. 2, *1914-1943*. New York: Praeger, 1967.

Brunet, Rene. *The New German Constitution*. Translated by Joseph Gollomb. New York: Knopf, 1922.

Buck, David D. Review of *The Dewey Experiment in China: Educational Reform and Political Power in the Early Republic*, by Barry Keenan. In *The American Historical Review* 83, no. 3 (1978): 783-84.

Bunker, Gerald E. *The Peace Conspiracy: Wang Ching-wei and the China War, 1937-1941*. Cambridge: Harvard University Press, 1972.

Busche, Helen E. "Minor Parties and Political Groups and Their Efforts to Expand Democracy in China, 1927-1947." M.A. thesis, University of Chicago, 1948.

Bush, J. D., ed. *The National Sun Yat-sen University: A Short History*. Guangzhou: The National Sun Yat-sen University, 1937.

Chamberlain, William Henry. *Soviet Russia: A Living Record and a History*. Boston: Little, Brown, 1930.

Chan, Lau Kit-ching. *The Chinese Youth Party, 1923-1945*. Hong Kong: Centre for Asian Studies, University of Hong Kong, 1972.

Chan, Wing-tsit, trans. and comp. *A Source Book in Chinese Philosophy*. Princeton: Princeton University Press, 1963; Princeton Paperback, 1969.

Chang Hao. *Liang Ch'i-ch'ao and Intellectual Transition in China, 1890-1907*. Cambridge: Harvard University Press, 1971.

Chang Kia-ngau. "Chang Chia-ao Autobiography" (English translation), ca. 1960. Chinese Oral History Project, Special Collections Library, Butler Library, Columbia University.

———. "Wo yu jiaxiong junmai" (My Brother, Junmai, and I). In Wang Yunwu et al., *Zhang Junmai xiansheng qishi shouqing jinian lunwen ji*, 102-05.

Chang P'eng-yuan. "The Constitutionalists." In *China in Revolution: The First Phase, 1900-1913*, ed. Mary C. Wright, 143-83. New Haven: Yale University Press, 1968.

———. *Liang Qichao yu minguo zhengzhi* (Liang Qichao and Republican Politics). Taipei: Shihuo chubanshe, 1978.

Chen Guangfu. "The Reminiscences of Ch'en Kuang-fu." As told to Julie Lien-ying How, 1963. Chinese Oral History Project, Special Collections Library, Butler Library, Columbia University.

Chen, Jerome. *China and the West: Society and Culture, 1815-1937*. Bloomington: Indiana University Press, 1980.

———. *Yuan Shih-k'ai, 1859-1916*. 2d ed. Stanford: Stanford University Press, 1961.

Chen Jitang. *Chen Jitang zizhuan gao* (Draft Autobiography of Chen Jitang). Taipei: Zhuanji wenxue chubanshe, 1974.

Chen Shaoyu [Wang Ming]. *Old Intrigues in New Clothing*. Bulletin no. 7, 1-19. Chungking: New China Information Committee, 1939.

Cheng Bijin. *Chen Bonan xiansheng nianpu* (A Chronological Biography of Chen Jitang). Taipei: Sili Deming Xingzheng Guanli Zhuanke Xuexiao, 1972.

Cheng Cangpo. "Zhuiyi Zhang Junmai xiansheng" (Recollections of Mr. Zhang Junmai). *Zhuanji wenxue* 48, no. 1 (1986): 27-28.

Cheng Wenxi. "Junmai xiansheng zhi yanxing" (The Words and Deeds of Mr. [Zhang] Junmai). In Wang Yunwu et al., *Zhang Junmai xiansheng qishi shouqing jinian lunwen ji*.

———. "Junmai xiansheng nianbiao changbian" (A Chronological Biography of Mr. [Zhang] Junmai). *Minzhu chao* 20, no. 11 (1970)-21, no. 8 (1971).

Chi Wen-shun. *Ideological Conflicts in Modern China: Democracy and Authoritarianism*. New Brunswick, NJ: Transaction Books, 1985.

Chiang Kai-shek. *Resistance and Reconstruction*. New York: Harper & Row, 1943; reprint, Freeport, NY: Books for Libraries Press, 1970.

Ch'ien Tuan-sheng. *The Government and Politics of China, 1912-1949*. Cambridge: Harvard University Press, 1950; Stanford: Stanford University Press, 1970.

The China White Paper (originally issued as *U.S. Relations with China with Special Reference to the Period, 1944-1949*). 2 vols. Stanford: Stanford University Press, 1967.

Chinese Ministry of Information, comp. *China Handbook, 1937-1943*. New York: Macmillan, 1943.

Chou Hsiang-kuang [Zhou Xiangguang]. "Ji Minzu wenhua shuyuan zhi chuangli yu fengbi" (Recollections of the Founding and Closing of the Institute of National Culture). *Zaisheng*, no. 346 (January 1954): 12-14.

———. *Modern History of China*. Delhi: Metropolitan, 1952.

———. *Political Thought of China*. Delhi: Chand, 1954.

———. "Zhanshi chansheng de Minzu wenhua shuyuan" (The Institute of National Culture that Emerged during Wartime). *Guojia shehui bao*, no. 264, 6 April 1941: 3; no. 265, 7 April 1941: 3.

Chou Min-chih. *Hu Shih and Intellectual Choice in Modern China*. Ann Arbor: University of Michigan Press, 1984.

Chow Tse-tsung. *The May Fourth Movement: Intellectual Revolution in Modern China*. Cambridge: Harvard University Press, 1960.

Chu, Samuel C. *Reformer in Modern China: Chang Chien, 1853-1926*. New York: Columbia University Press, 1965.

Chu Wen-lin et al. *China's Struggle with the Red Peril*. Taipei: China Chapter, Asian People's Anti-Communist League, World Anti-Communist League, 1978.

Clarkson, Jesse D. *A History of Russia*. New York: Random House, 1962.

Coble, Parks M. "The National Salvation Association as a Political Party." in *Roads Not Taken*, ed. Roger B. Jeans, 135-47.

———. *The Shanghai Capitalists and the Nationalist Government, 1927-1937*. Cambridge: Harvard University Press, 1980.

Council of International Affairs. *Chinese Yearbook, 1938-1939*. Chungking: The Commercial Press, 1939.

Craig, Gordon. *Germany, 1866-1945*. New York: Oxford University Press, 1978; Oxford University Press paperback, 1980.

Crowley, James B. "A Reconsideration of the Marco Polo Bridge Incident." *Journal of Asian Studies* 22 (May 1963): 277-91.

"Dabian liangze" (Two Responses). *Zaisheng*, no. 32 (1939): 1-2.

De Bary, William T., Wing-tsit Chan, and Chester Tan, comps. *Sources of Chinese Tradition*. New York: Columbia University Press, 1960; paperback in 2 vols., Columbia University, 1964.

"Deguo de Guoshedang" (The National Socialist Party of Germany). *Zaisheng*, no. 9 (1938): 2.

"Democracy versus One-Party Rule in Kuomintang China: The 'Little Parties' Organize." *Amerasia* 7, no. 3 (1943): 97-120.

Ding Wenjiang, ed. *Liang Rengong xiansheng changbian nianpu chugao* (First Draft of a Chronological Biography of Liang Qichao). 2 vols. Taipei: Shijie shuju, 1958.

Dirlik, Arif. *The Origins of Chinese Communism*. New York: Oxford University Press, 1989.

Durant, Will. *The Story of Philosophy*. New York: Washington Square Press, 1952.

Eastman, Lloyd E. *The Abortive Revolution: China Under Nationalist Rule, 1927-1937*. Cambridge: Harvard University Press, 1974.

———. "China's Democratic Parties and the Temptations of Political Power." In *Roads Not Taken*, ed. Roger B. Jeans, 189-99.

———. "Nationalist China during the Sino-Japanese War, 1937-1945," In *The Cambridge History of China*, vol. 13, part 2: *Republican China, 1912-1949*, ed. John K. Fairbank and Albert Feuerwerker, 547-608. Cambridge: Cambridge University Press, 1986.

———. "The Rise and Fall of the 'Blue Shirts': A Review Article." *Republican China* 13, no. 1 (1987): 25-48.

———. *Seeds of Destruction: Nationalist China in War and Revolution, 1937-1949.* Stanford: Stanford University Press, 1984.

Eastman, Lloyd E., Jerome Ch'en, Suzanne Pepper, and Lyman P. Van Slyke. *The Nationalist Era in China, 1927-1949*. Cambridge: Cambridge University Press, 1991.

Edwards, Paul, ed. *The Encyclopedia of Philosophy*. 4 vols. New York: Macmillan and Free Press, 1967.

Epstein, Israel. *The People's War*. London: Gollancz, 1939.

———. *The Unfinished Revolution in China*. Boston: Little, Brown, 1947.

Fairbank, John K. *The Great Chinese Revolution: 1800-1985*. New York: Harper & Row, 1986.

———. *Trade and Diplomacy on the China Coast: The Opening of the Treaty Ports, 1842-1854*. Cambridge: Harvard University Press, 1953; Stanford: Stanford University Press, 1969.

———. *The United States and China*. 4th ed. Cambridge: Harvard University Press, 1983.

Fairbank, John K., Joseph Esherick, and Marilyn B. Young. "Imperialism in China: An Exchange." *Bulletin of Concerned Asian Scholars* 5, no. 2 (1973): 32-35.

Fairbank, John K., and Liu Kwang-ching, eds. *Modern China: A Bibliographical Guide to Chinese Works, 1898-1937*. Cambridge: Harvard University Press, 1961.

Fairbank, John K., and Edwin O. Reischauer. *China: Tradition and Transformation*, rev. ed. Cambridge: Houghton Mifflin, 1989.

Fairbank, John K., Edwin O. Reischauer, and Albert M. Craig. *A History of East Asian Civilization*. Vol. 2: *East Asia: The Modern Transformation*. Boston: Houghton Mifflin, 1965.

Feuerwerker, Albert. *China's Industrialization: Sheng Hsuan-huai (1844-1916) and Mandarin Enterprise*. Cambridge: Harvard University Press, 1958.

Forbes, Andrew D.W. *Warlords and Muslims in Chinese Central Asia: A Political History of Republican Sinkiang, 1911-1949*. Cambridge: Cambridge University Press, 1986.

Fraser, John. *The Chinese*. New York: Summit Books, 1980.

Fu, Zhengyuan. *Autocratic Tradition and Chinese Politics*. Cambridge: Cambridge University Press, 1993.

Fung Yu-lan. *A Short History of Chinese Philosophy*. Ed. Derk Bodde. New York: Macmillan, 1948; reprint, New York: Free Press, 1966.

Furth, Charlotte. "May Fourth in History." In *Reflections on the May Fourth Movement: A Symposium*, ed. Benjamin I. Schwartz, 59-68. Cambridge: Harvard University Press, 1972.

———. *Ting Wen-chiang: Science and China's New Culture*. Cambridge: Harvard University Press, 1970.

"General Chiang Kai-shek Returns to Nanking; Leaders Discuss Nation's Problems at Kuling." *China Weekly Review* 81 (July 1937): 270.

Gillin, Donald G. *Warlord: Yen Hsi-shan in Shansi province, 1911-1949*. Princeton: Princeton University Press, 1967.

Goldstein, Carl. "Innocents Abroad." *Far Eastern Economic Review*, 15 September 1994, 22-27.

Gould, Randall. *China in the Sun*. New York: Doubleday, 1946.

Great Britain. Foreign Office. FO 371 (general correspondence series).

Grieder, Jerome B. *Hu Shih and the Chinese Renaissance: Liberalism in the Chinese Revolution, 1917-1937*. Cambridge: Harvard University Press, 1970.

———. *Intellectuals and the State in Modern China: A Narrative History*. New York: Free Press, 1981.

Gunther, John. *Inside Asia*. New York: Harper, 1939.

"Guojia shehui dang xuanyan" (An Announcement of the National Socialist Party). *Zaisheng*, no. 43 (1940): n.p. (inside front cover).

"Guomin canzheng hui lijie canzhengyuan xingming suoyin" (Name Index of Councilors in the Various People's Political Councils). *Zhuanji wenxue* 35, no. 2 (1979), 21-24.

Han Guojun. *Zhisou nianpu* (My Chronological Biography upon Arrival at Old Age). Taipei: Wenhai chubanshe, 1966.

Harrison, James P. *The Long March to Power: A History of the Chinese Communist Party, 1921-1972*. New York: Praeger, 1972.

Hay, Stephen N. *Asian Ideas of East and West: Tagore and His Critics in Japan, China, and India*. Cambridge: Harvard University Press, 1970.

Ho, Franklin L. "The Reminiscences of Ho Lien (Franklin Ho)." As told to Crystal Lorch Seidman, 1967. Chinese Oral History Project, Special Collections Library, Butler Library, Columbia University.

Hollander, Paul. *Political Pilgrims: Travels of Western Intellectuals to the Soviet Union, China, and Cuba*. New York: Oxford University Press, 1981; reprint, Harper Colophon, 1983.

Hoover, Calvin B. *The Economic Life of the Soviet Union*. New York: Macmillan, 1931.

Horne, Alistair. Review of *War by Timetable: How the First World War Began*, by A.J.P. Taylor. In *The Washington Post Book World*, 30 November 1969.

Hsu, Immanuel C.Y. *The Rise of Modern China*. 5th ed. New York: Oxford University Press, 1983.

Hsueh, Chun-tu. *Huang Hsing and the Chinese Revolution*. Stanford: Stanford University Press, 1961.

Hu Yinghan. *Wu Xianzi xiansheng zhuanji* (A Biography of Mr. Wu Xianzi). Hong Kong: Author, 1953.

Hu Ziping, ed. *Zhongguo zhengzhi renwu* (Chinese Political Personalities). Fuzhou: Dada tushu gongsi, 1948.

Huang Jilu. "Huiyi yu Junmai xiansheng yiduan tanhua" (Recollections of a Conversation with Mr. [Zhang] Junmai). *Zhuanji wenxue* 28, no. 3, (1976): 22-24.

Huang, Philip C. *Liang Ch'i-ch'ao and Modern Chinese Liberalism*. Seattle: University of Washington Press, 1972.

Huang Shen Yi-yun (Madame Huang Fu). "My Husband and I: Personal Reminiscences of an Eminent Chinese Woman." Ed. and trans. by Te-kong Tong, 1960. Chinese Oral History Project, Special Collections Library, Butler Library, Columbia University.

Huang Yanpei. *Huang Yanpei riji zhailu* (Extracts from Huang Yanpei's Diary). Compiled by the Center for Research on Republican China, Chinese Academy of Social Sciences. Beijing: Zhonghua shuju, 1979.

Huang Yizhou. "Huang Xing yu Mingde xuetang" (Huang Xing and the Mingde School). In Zuo Shunsheng, *Huang Xing pingzhuan* (A Critical Biography of Huang Xing), 169-73. Taipei: Zhuanji wenxue chubanshe, 1968.

Hummel, Arthur W., ed. *Eminent Chinese of the Ch'ing Period (1644-1912).* Washington, D.C.: Government Printing Office, 1943; reprint, Taipei: Cheng-wen, 1970.

Hung Mao-hsiung. *Carsun Chang (1887-1969) und seine Vorstellungen vom Sozialismus in China* (Carsun Chang and His Introduction of Socialism to China). Inaugural-Dissertation zur Erlangung des Doktorgrades des Fachbereichs 12, Ludwig-Maximilians-Universität München, 1980.

Hutchings, Graham. "A Province at War: Guangxi during the Sino-Japanese Conflict, 1937-1945." *China Quarterly*, no. 108 (1986): 652-79.

Ienaga, Saburo. *The Pacific War: World War II and the Japanese, 1931-1945*. New York: Pantheon, 1978.

Isaacs, Harold R. *The Tragedy of the Chinese Revolution*. 2d ed. New York: Atheneum, 1966.

Israel, John. *Student Nationalism in China, 1927-1937*. Stanford: Stanford University Press, 1966.

Israel, John, and Donald W. Klein. *Rebels and Bureaucrats: China's December 9ers*. Berkeley: University of California Press, 1976.

Jeans, Roger B. "China Democratic League." In *Political Parties of Asia and the Pacific*. ed. Haruhiro Fukui. 2 vols., 1: 168-71. Westport, CT: Greenwood, 1985.

———, ed. *Roads Not Taken: The Struggle of Opposition Parties in Twentieth-Century China*. Boulder, CO: Westview, 1992.

———. "Syncretism in Defense of Confucianism: An Intellectual and Political Biography of the Early Years of Chang Chün-mai, 1887-1923." Ph.D. diss., George Washington University, 1974.

Jiang Yuntian. "Jiang xu" (Introduction by Jiang [Yuntian]). In Wang Yunwu et al., *Zhang Junmai xiansheng qishi shouqing jinian lunwen ji*, 2-4.

———. "Zhang Junmai xiansheng yisheng dashi ji" (A Record of Major Events in the Life of Mr. Zhang Junmai). *Minzhu shehui* 5, no. 2 (1969), 24-26.

Jinbudang xuanyanshu (Manifesto of the Progressive Party). n.p., n.d.

Johnson, Chalmers A. *Peasant Nationalism and Communist Power: The Emergence of Revolutionary China, 1937-1945*. Stanford: Stanford University Press, 1961.

Jones, F. C. *Japan's New Order in East Asia: Its Rise and Fall, 1937-1945*. London: Oxford University Press, 1954.

Jordan, Donald A. *The Northern Expedition: China's National Revolution of 1926-1928*. Honolulu: University Press of Hawaii, 1976.

Kirby, William C. *Germany and Republican China*. Stanford: Stanford University Press, 1984.

Kolakowski, Leszek. *Main Currents of Marxism*. 3 vols. New York: Oxford University Press, 1981.

Koo, Wellington V.K. "The Memoirs of Dr. Wellington V. K. Koo." Done with Julie Lien-ying How, et al., 1958-67. Chinese Oral History Project, Special Collections, Butler Library, Columbia University.

Kuo, Warren. *Analytical History of the Chinese Communist Party*. 4 vols. Taipei: Institute of International Relations, 1970.

Kwok, D.W.Y. *Scientism in Chinese Thought*. New Haven: Yale University Press, 1965; New York: Biblo & Tannen, 1971.

Langer, William L., comp. and ed. *Encyclopedia of World History*. Boston: Houghton Mifflin, 1952.

Lary, Diana. *Region and Nation: The Kwangsi Clique in Chinese Politics, 1925-1937*. Cambridge: Cambridge University Press, 1974.

Lazitch, Branko, and Milorad M. Drachkovitch. *Lenin and the Comintern*. Stanford: Hoover Institution Press, 1972.

Legge, James. *The Four Books*. Taipei: Yishi chubanshe, 1971.

Levenson, Joseph R. *Liang Ch'i-ch'ao and the Mind of Modern China*. Cambridge: Harvard University Press, 1953.

Li, Chien-nung. *The Political History of China, 1840-1928*. Princeton: Van Nostrand, 1956.

Li Daming. *Bei you yinxiang* (Impressions from a Northern Journey). Shanghai: Dongfang wenhua chubanshe, 1937.

Li Dasheng. "Guoshi: Zhang Junmai xiansheng" (National Scholar: Mr. Zhang Junmai). *Mingbao yuekan* 4, nos. 4-6 (1969).

Li Huang. "Jingdao Zhang Junmai xiansheng" (Solemnly Mourn for Mr. Zhang Junmai). *Minzhu shehui* 5, no. 2 (1969):17-20.

———. "The Reminiscences of Li Huang." Translated by Lillian Chu Chin, 1971. Chinese Oral History Project, Special Collections Library, Butler Library, Columbia University.

Li Zongren. "The Reminiscences of General Li Tsung-jen." As told to Te-kong Tong, 1964. Chinese Oral History Project, Special Collections Library, Butler Library, Columbia University.

Lilley, Charles R. "Tsiang T'ing-fu: Between Two Worlds, 1895-1935." Ph.D. diss.,

University of Maryland, College Park, 1979.

Lin Beili. "Qingjiao Zhang Junmai xiansheng" (A Request for Advice from Mr. Zhang Junmai). *Xinhua ribao*, 14 January 1939, 4.

Linebarger, Paul M.A. *The China of Chiang Kai-shek: A Political Study*. Boston: World Peace Foundation, 1941.

Liu, James T.C. "German Mediation in the Sino-Japanese War, 1937-1938." *Far Eastern Quarterly* 8 (February 1949): 157-71.

Liu Jingyuan. "Yifeng gongkaixin de fanying: da Lin Beili nushi" (A Response to an Open Letter: A Reply to Madame Lin Beili). *Zaisheng*, no. 13 (1939): 1-2.

Lo Jung-pang. *K'ang Yu-wei: A Biography and a Symposium*. Tucson: University of Arizona Press, 1967.

Luo Fu [Zhang Wentian]. "Common Defense against Communism Means China's Downfall." *Jiefang*, nos. 63 and 64 (1939).

Luo Wengan. *Yuzhongren yu* (Words from a Prisoner). Taipei: Wenhai chubanshe, 1971.

MacKerras, Colin, and Robert Chan, comps. *Modern China: A Chronology from 1842 to the Present*. London: Thames & Hudson, 1982.

Mao Tse-tung. *Selected Works of Mao Tse-tung*. 5 vols. Beijing: Foreign Languages Press, 1961-1977.

Mao Yi-heng. *Emeng huiyilu*. Taipei: Wenhai chubanshe, 1974 [1954].

Mei, Y.P. "Thus We Live in Chungking." *Asia*, July 1941: 349-51.

Meisner, Maurice. *Li Dazhao and the Origins of Chinese Marxism*. New York: Atheneum, 1970.

Michael, Franz H., and George E. Taylor. *The Far East in the Modern World*. 3d ed. Hinsdale, IL: Dryden, 1975.

Mitarevsky, N. *World-Wide Soviet Plots, as Disclosed by Hitherto Unpublished Documents Seized at the USSR Embassy in Peking*. Tientsin: Tientsin Press, [1927].

Morgan, David W. *The Socialist Left and the German Revolution: A History of the German Independent Social Democratic Party, 1917-1922*. Ithaca: Cornell University Press, 1975.

Moseley, Leonard. *Hirohito: Emperor of Japan*. Englewood Cliffs, NJ: Prentice-Hall, 1966.

Nathan, Andrew J.. *Chinese Democracy*. New York: Knopf, 1985.

———. "Constitution Research Society." In Political Parties of Asia and the Pacific, ed. Haruhiro Fukui, 2 vols., 1: 236-37. Westport, CT: Greenwood, 1985.

Norins, Martin R. *Gateway to Asia: Sinkiang, Frontier of the Chinese Far West*. New York: Day, 1944.

North, Robert C. *Moscow and [the] Chinese Communists*. 2d ed. Stanford: Stanford University Press, 1963.

North, Robert C., and Xenia J. Eudin. *M.N. Roy's Mission to China: The Communist-Kuomintang Split of 1927*. Berkeley: University of California Press, 1963.

Office of Strategic Services (OSS). Research and Analysis Reports. Record Group

226. National Archives, Washington, D.C.
"Outstanding Events in the Sino-Japanese War: A Day-to-Day Summary." *China Weekly Review* 92, no. 8 (1940): 278.
P'an Wei-tung. *The Chinese Constitution: A Study of Forty Years of Constitution-Making in China*. Washington, D.C.: Catholic University Press, 1945.
Peck, Graham. *Two Kinds of Time*. 2d ed., revised and abridged. Boston: Houghton Mifflin, 1967.
Perleberg, Max. *Who's Who in Modern China*. Hong Kong: Ye Olde Printerie, 1954.
Pinson, Koppel S. *Modern Germany: Its History and Civilization*. New York: Macmillan, 1954.
Qu Qiubai. "Xiandai wenming di wenti yu shehuizhuyi" (The Problem of Modern Civilization and Socialism). *Dongfang zazhi* 21, no. 1 (1924): 11 pp.
Ramm, Agatha. *Germany, 1789-1919: A Political History*. London: Methuen, 1967.
Roden, Donald. *Schooldays in Imperial Japan: A Study in the Culture of a Student Elite*. Berkeley: University of California Press, 1980.
Rosenberg, Arthur. *Geschichte des Bolschevismus von Marx bis zur Gegenwart*. Berlin, 1932.
Rosinger, Lawrence K. *China's Crisis*. New York: Knopf, 1945.
———. *China's Wartime Politics, 1937-1944*. Princeton: Princeton University Press, 1944.
Scalapino, Robert A., and Harold Schiffrin. "Early Socialist Currents in the Chinese Revolutionary Movement: Sun Yat-sen versus Liang Ch'i-ch'ao." *Journal of Asian Studies* 18, no. 3 (1959): 321-42.
Scalapino, Robert A., and George T. Yu. *Modern China and Its Revolutionary Process: Recurrent Challenges to the Traditional Order, 1850-1920*. Berkeley: University of California, 1985.
Scanlan, James P. "Lenin, V.I." In *The Encyclopedia of Philosophy*, ed. Paul Edwards, 8 vols., 3-4: 434-35.
Schaller, Michael. *The U.S. Crusade in China, 1938-1945*. New York: Columbia University Press, 1979.
Schiffrin, Harold Z. *Sun Yat-sen and the Origins of the Chinese Revolution*. Berkeley: University of California Press, 1968.
Schwarcz, Vera. *The Chinese Enlightenment: Intellectuals and the Legacy of the May Fourth Movement of 1919*. Berkeley: University of California Press, 1986.
Selle, Earl Albert. *Donald of China*. New York: Harper & Brothers, 1948.
Shaheen, Anthony J. "The China Democratic League and Chinese Politics, 1939-1947." Ph.D. diss., University of Michigan, 1977.
"Shelun" (Editorial). *Yuzhou* 14, no. 8 (1984): 2.
Sheng, Yueh. *Sun Yat-sen University in Moscow and the Chinese Revolution*. Lawrence: Center for Asian Studies, University of Kansas, 1971.
Sheridan, James E. *China in Disintegration: The Republican Era in Chinese History, 1912-1949*. New York: Free Press, 1975.
Shewmaker, Kenneth E. *Americans and Chinese Communists, 1927-1945: A*

Persuading Encounter. Ithaca: Cornell University Press, 1971.

Shi Yi. "Wo suo zhidao Zhang Junmai xiansheng shengping" (What I Know about Mr. Zhang Junmai's Life). *Zaisheng*, no. 345 (1953): 11-16; no. 346 (1954): 15-19.

Shih, Vincent Y. C. [Shi Youzhong]. "Wo suo renshi de Zhang Junmai xiansheng" (The Mr. Zhang Junmai I knew). *Zhuanji wenxue* 28, no. 3 (1976): 20-22.

Shyu, Lawrence N.L. "China's 'Wartime Parliament': The People's Political Council, 1938-1945." In *Nationalist China During the Sino-Japanese War, 1937-1945*, ed. Paul K.T. Sih, 273-313. Hicksville, NY: Exposition, 1977.

———. "The People's Political Council and China's Wartime Problems, 1937-1945." Ph.D. diss., Columbia University, 1972.

Sima Qian. *Historical Records*. Trans. Raymond Dawson. Oxford: Oxford University Press, 1994.

Snow, Edgar. *People on Our Side*. New York: Random House, 1944.

Spar, Fredric J. "Human Rights and Political Engagement: Luo Longji in the 1930s." In *Roads Not Taken*, ed. Roger B. Jeans, 61-81.

———. "Liberal Political Opposition in Kuomintang and Communist China, 1928-1958." Ph.D. diss., Brown University, 1980.

Spaulding, Robert M. "Detour through a Dark Valley." In *Japan Examined: Perspectives on Modern Japanese History*, ed. Harry Wray and Hilary Conroy, 252-57. Honolulu: University of Hawaii Press, 1983.

Spence, Jonathan D. *The Gate of Heavenly Peace: The Chinese and Their Revolution, 1895-1980*. New York: Viking, 1981.

———. *To Change China: Western Advisers in China, 1620-1960*. With new introduction and conclusion. New York: Penguin, 1980.

Storry, Richard. *A History of Modern Japan*. Baltimore: Penguin, 1972.

Sun Baoyi. "Junmai xiansheng jinhou de zhengzhi dongxiang" (Mr. [Zhang] Junmai's Future Political Course). *Zaisheng*, no. 269 (1950): 4-5.

———. "Junmai xiansheng yu minzhu shehuizhuyi (Mr. [Zhang] Junmai and Democratic Socialism). *Ziyou zhong* 4, no. 2 (1970): 23-24.

——— (Sun Chengzhai). "Du Wang [Housheng] zhu 'Zhang Junmai sixiang' hou de ganxiang" (Reflections After Reading "Zhang Junmai's Thought" by Wang Housheng). *Zaisheng* 4, no. 20 (1953): 51-55.

Tan, Chester. *Chinese Political Thought in the Twentieth Century*. New York: Anchor, 1971.

Tang Zhijun, ed. *Zhang Taiyan nianpu changbian* (A Chronological Biography of Zhang Taiyan). 2 vols. Beijing: Zhonghua shuju, 1979.

Tao, Menghe [L.K. Tao, Tao Lu-kung], and Leong Yew Koh [Liang Yu-kao]. *Village and Town Life in China*. London: Allen & Unwin, 1915; reprint, Westport, CT: Hyperion, 1973.

Teng, Ssu-yu, and John K. Fairbank. *China's Response to the West: A Documentary Survey, 1839-1923*. Cambridge: Harvard University Press, 1954; reprint, 1979.

Thomas, John N. *The Institute of Pacific Relations: Asian Scholars and American Politics*. Seattle: University of Washington Press, 1974.

Thomson, David. *Europe since Napoleon*. 2d ed. New York: Knopf, 1962.

Thomson, James C. Jr. *While China Faced West: American Reformers in Nationalist China, 1928-1937*. Cambridge: Harvard University Press, 1969.

Ting Hsu Lee-hsia. *Government Control of the Press in Modern China, 1900-1949*. Cambridge: Harvard University Press, 1974.

Tongyi wenti lunzhan (The Polemic over the Problem of Unification). Chongqing: Duli chubanshe, 1939.

Treadgold, Donald W. *Twentieth Century Russia*. 8th ed. Boulder, CO: Westview, 1995.

Tseng Yuhao [Zeng Youhao]. "Minzhu zhengzhi de jingshen shi rongxu yidang shanyi piping de quanli—taolun Chen Shaoyu xiansheng dui Zhang Junmai xiansheng de zhiwen" (The Spirit of Democracy is the Right of Toleration for Well-Intentioned Criticism by Other Parties: A Discussion of Mr. Chen Shaoyu's Questioning of Zhang Junmai). *Zaisheng*, no. 17 (1939): 8.

———. *Modern Chinese Legal and Political Philosophy*. Shanghai: Commercial Press, 1930.

Tung, William. *Revolutionary China: A Personal Account, 1926-1949*. New York: St. Martin's, 1973.

United States Department of State. *Foreign Relations of the United States, 1948, The Far East, China*. Washington, D.C.: U.S. Government Printing Office, 1973.

———. General Files and Decimal Files. Record Group 59. National Archives, Washington, D.C.

———. Canton, Hong Kong, Kunming, Peiping, and Tientsin Post Files. Record Group 84. 800 decimal series. National Archives. Washington, D.C.

Van Slyke, Lyman P., ed. *The Chinese Communist Movement: A Report of the United States War Department, July 1945*. Stanford: Stanford University Press, 1968.

———. *Enemies and Friends: The United Front in Chinese Communist History*. Stanford: Stanford University Press, 1967.

Wakeman, Frederic, Jr. *Policing Shanghai, 1927-1937*. Berkeley: University of California Press, 1995.

Waldersee, Alfred Graf von. *A Field Marshal's Memoirs*. London: Hutchinson, 1924.

Waldman, Phyliss. "Chang Kia-ngau and the Bank of China: The Politics of Money." Ph.D. diss., University of Virginia, 1984.

"Wang Ching-wei's First Statement." *Oriental Affairs* 11, no. 2 (1939): 99-100.

Wang Fan-hsi. *Memoirs of a Chinese Revolutionary*. New York: Columbia University Press, 1991.

Wang Peihuai. *Geming de baojian* (The Sword of Revolution). n.p.: Weihuang she, 1936.

Wang, Y. C. *Chinese Intellectuals and the West*. Chapel Hill: University of North Carolina Press, 1966.

Wang Yanjin. "Xiang qianbei Zhang Junmai xiansheng yishi" (Anecdotes about a Member of the Previous Generation from My Native Place, Mr. Zhang Junmai). *Minzhu shehui* 5, no. 3 (1969): 7-11.

Wang Yunwu et al. *Zhang Junmai xiansheng qishi shouqing jinian lunwen ji* (A Collection of Essays Commemorating Mr. Zhang Junmai's Seventieth Birthday). Taipei: Editorial Committee for the above work, 1956.

Warner, Marina. *The Dragon Empress: Life and Times of Tz'u-hsi, 1835-1908, Empress Dowager of China*. New York: Atheneum, 1986.

Wei, William. *Counterrevolution in China: The Nationalists in Jiangxi during the Soviet Period*. Ann Arbor: University of Michigan Press, 1985.

Wenhua gongying she, comp. *Minguo sanian shiyong guomin nianjian* (1941 Citizens' Yearbook for Practical Usc). Guilin: Wenhua gongying she, 1941.

West, Philip. *Yenching University and Sino-Western Relations, 1916-1952*. Cambridge: Harvard University Press, 1976.

White, Theodore H., and Annalee Jacoby. *Thunder Out of China*. New York: Sloan Associates, 1946; repr., Da Capo, 1980.

Whiting, Allen S. *Soviet Policies in China, 1917-1924*. New York: Columbia University Press, 1954; reprint, Stanford: Stanford University Press, 1968.

Who's Who in China: Biographies of Chinese Leaders. 5th ed. Shanghai: *China Weekly Review*, 1936; 6th ed. Shanghai, 1950.

Wilbur, C. Martin. *Sun Yat-sen: Frustrated Patriot*. New York: Columbia University Press, 1976.

Wilbur, C. Martin, and Julie Lien-ying How. *Missionaries of Revolution: Soviet Advisors and Nationalist China, 1920-1927*. Cambridge: Harvard University Press, 1989.

Woodhead, H. G. W. ed. *The China Year Book*. Shanghai: The North China Daily News & Herald, 1939.

Wright, Mary C., ed. *China in Revolution: The First Phase, 1900-1913*. New Haven: Yale University Press, 1968.

———. *The Last Stand of Chinese Conservatism: The T'ung-chih Restoration, 1862-1874*. Stanford: Stanford University Press, 1957; reprint, New York: Atheneum, 1967.

Wu, Ningkun. *A Single Tear: A Family's Persecution, Love, and Endurance in Communist China*. New York: Atlantic Monthly Press, 1993.

Wu Xianzi. *Zhongguo minzhu xianzheng dang dangshi* (A Party History of the Chinese Democratic Constitutionalist Party). San Francisco: *Shijie ribao* (World Daily News), 1952.

Wu, Xiangxiang. "Liang Qichao Xu Zhimo lun SuE" (Liang Qichao [and] Xu Zhimo on Soviet Russia). In Wu Xiangxiang, *Jindai shishi luncong* (Collected Essays on Events in Modern History), 2: 303-12. Taipei: Wenxing shudian, 1964.

———. "Zhang Gongquan xiansheng de qinglian dianfan" (Mr. Chang Kia-ngau's Honest and Upright Example). *Zhuanji wenxue* 36, no. 4 (1980): 87-89.

———. "Zhang Junmai laohe wanlixin" (Zhang Junmai: Old Crane with the Ten-Thousand *li* Heart). In Wu Xiangxiang, *Minguo bai ren zhuan* (Biographies of One Hundred Men of the Republic), 3: 1-35.

Xiang Goufu. "Minchu xianzheng jianwen lu" (A Record of My Experiences with

Constitutional Government During the Early Republic). *Koushu lishi* (Oral History), no. 1 (1989): 77-104.

Xiao Wenzhe, comp. and ed. *Xiandai Zhongguo zhengdang yu zhengzhi* (Modern Chinese Political Parties and Politics). Nanjing: Zhongwai wenhua she, 1946.

Xie Fuya. "Zhang Junmai xiansheng er san shi" (Two or Three Matters about Mr. Zhang Junmai). *Minzhu shehui* 5, no. 2 (1969): 22-23.

Xie Youwei. "Wo yu Zhang Junmai xiansheng" (Mr. Zhang Junmai and I). *Wenyi fuxing*, no. 14 (1971): 10-12.

Xiong Fuguang. "Ma Fu xiansheng yu Fuxing shuyuan" (Mr. Ma Fu and the Fuxing Academy). *Zhuanji wenxue* 24, no. 3 (1974): 24-31.

Xiong Shihui. "Xiong xu" (Introduction by Xiong [Shihui]). In Erich Ludendorff, *Quan minzu zhanzheng lun*, 5-6.

Xu Fulin. "Guojia shehui dang zhi chengli shi" (History of the Founding of the National Socialist Party). *Guojia shehui bao*, 7 July 1940, 4.

Xu Zhimo. *Xu Zhimo Yingwen shuxin* (English Letters of Xu Zhimo). Ed. Liang Xihua. Taipei, 1979.

Xuehai shuyuan tushuguan shumu (Catalogue of the Xuehai Institute). Guangzhou: Xuehai Institute, 1936.

Xue Huayuan. *Minzhu xianfa yu minzuzhuyi de bianzheng fazhan* (The Dialectical Development of Constitutional Democracy and Nationalism). Taipei: Daohe chubanshe, 1993.

Yang Hanhui. *Xiandai Zhongguo zhengzhi jiaoyu* (Modern Chinese Political Education). Peiping: Renwu shudian, 1932.

Yang Jialuo. *Minguo mingren tujian* (Illustrated Biographies of Famous Men of the Republic). 2 vols. Nanjing: Zhongguo cidian guan, 1937.

Yang Mingwei. "Guanyu Zhang Junmai xiansheng de gongkaixin" (Concerning Mr. Zhang Junmai's Open Letter). *Zaisheng*, no. 14 (1939): 11-12.

Yang Tianshi. "The Third Force in Hong Kong and North America During the 1950s." In *Roads Not Taken*, ed. Roger B. Jeans, 269-73.

Yang Yongqian. *Zhonghua minguo xianfa zhi fu: Zhang Junmai zhuan* (The Father of the Constitution of the Republic of China: A Biography of Zhang Junmai). Taipei: Tangshan chubanshe, 1993.

Yao Songling, ed. *Zhang Gongquan xiansheng nianpu chugao* (First Draft of a Chronological Biography of Mr. Chang Kia-ngau). 2 vols. Taipei: Zhuanji wenxue she, 1981.

Yokota Minoru Newspaper Collection. Seminar on Modern China, Toyo Bunkyo, Tokyo.

Young, Ernest P. *The Presidency of Yuan Shih-k'ai: Liberalism and Dictatorship in Early Republican China.* Ann Arbor: University of Michigan Press, 1977.

Yu, P.K. *Research Materials on Twentieth-Century China: An Annotated List of CCRM Publications*. Washington, D.C.: Center for Chinese Research Materials, Association for Research Libraries, 1975.

Zeng Youhao. See Tseng Yu-hao.

Zhang Dongsun. "Shi de shiming yu lixue" (The Mission of Scholars and Song-Ming Neo-Confucianism). *Guancha* 1, no. 13 (1946): 3-8.

Zhang Shiming. "Zhang Junmai xiansheng yu Guangxi" (Mr. Zhang Junmai and Guangxi). *Ziyou Zhong* 1, no. 2 (1970): 28-29.

Zhang Zhiben. "Some Personal Reminiscences of Zhang Zhiben." Condensed, edited, and transcribed by Zao Gaifu. Taipei: Institute of Modern History, Academia Sinica, 1960.

———. "Zhang Zhiben tanhua bilu" (A Record of Conversations With Zhang Zhiben). Taipei: Academia Sinica, Institute of Modern History, 1960. (A Chinese version of the preceding entry.)

Zhang Zhiyi, comp. *Kangzhan zhong di zhengdang he paibie* (Political Parties and Groups in the War of Resistance). Chongqing: Dushu shenghuo chubanshe, 1939.

Zheng Xiaoyuan. "Tianmo liangfeng huai Zhang Junmai xiansheng" (At the end of the Day When a Cold Wind Arises, I Think of Mr. Zhang Junmai). *Minzhu Zhongguo* 4, no. 23 (1961): 8.

Zhongguo ge xiao dangpai xiankuang (The Present State of Affairs of Minority Parties in China). n.p., 1946.

Zhongguo guojia shehui dang xuanyan (Manifesto of the National Socialist Party of China). n.p., 1938.

"Zhongguo minzhu shehui dang jianyao shigao" (A Brief Draft History of the Chinese Democratic Socialist Party). *Minzhu Zhongguo* 1, no. 10 (1951): 19-23.

Zhongguo minzhu tongmeng gaikuang (The General Condition of the China Democratic League). Nanjing: Tongyi chubanshe, 1947.

Zhou Xiangguang. See Chou Hsiang-kuang.

Zuo Hongyu. *Kangzhan jianguo zhong zhi Zhongguo qingnian dang* (The Chinese Youth Party during the War of Resistance and National Reconstruction). n.p.: Guohun shudian, 1939.

Zuo Shunsheng. *Huang Xing pingzhuan* (A Critical Biography of Huang Xing). Taipei: Zhuanji wenxue chubanshe, 1968.

———. "The Reminiscences of Tso Shun-sheng." As told to Julie Lien-ying How, 1965. Chinese Oral History Project, Special Collections Library, Butler Library, Columbia University.

———. "Zhuidaohui zhici" (Memorial-Service Speech). *Ziyou zhong* (H.K. ed.) 1, no. 1 (1970): 30-31.

Letters

Chan Wing-tsit. Letter to author, 28 July 1977.

Machemer, Corona, Harper & Row. Letter to author, 10 March 1980.

Nishikatsu Rihei, Head of the Office of Academic Records, Waseda University, Tokyo. Letter to author, 6 October 1972.

Richard Wilhelm Papers. Privately held by Hellmut Wilhelm, Seattle, Washington. Includes several letters from Zhang Junmai to Richard Wilhelm.

Interviews

Carsun Chang. Interview with Lawrence N. L. Shyu. Berkeley, 7 June 1966.
Cheng Wenxi. Interview with author. Taipei, Taiwan, 24 June 1976.
Vincent Y. C. Shih. Interview with author. Taipei, Taiwan, 29 June 1976.
Zhang Jiazhu. Interview with author, San Francisco, California, 28 July 1976.

Glossary

Ariga Nagao 有賀長雄
Bai Chongxi 白崇禧
Bailudong shuyuan 白鹿洞書院
Baohuang hui 保皇會
Baokelan 鮑克蘭
Baoshan xian 寶山縣
Beipei 北培
Beiyang Army 北洋軍
biyaner 碧眼兒
bizhan 筆戰
bianfa 變法
Bokyo 防共
Bolaote 勃勞特
Bo Yang 柏楊
budui 不對
bugeming 不革命
Cai Songpo (Cai E) 蔡松坡 (蔡鍔)
canmouzhangzhe 參謀長者
canyi 參議
Cao Kun 曹錕
Chan Wing-tsit 陳榮捷
Changde 常德
Chang Kia-ngau 張嘉敖
chaodai de guojia 朝代的國家
chexiang 車箱
Chenbao 晨報
Chen Bulei 陳布雷
Chen Duxiu 陳獨秀
Chen Guofu 陳果夫
Chen Jitang 陳濟堂
Chen Jiongming 陳炯明
Chen Lifu 陳立夫
Chen Shaoyu 陳紹禹
Chen Sheng 陳勝
Chen Yukun 陳玉崑
Chen Zhimai 陳之邁
cheng 誠
Cheng Wenxi 程文熙
Chiang Ching-kuo 蔣經國
Chiang Kai-shek 蔣介石
chulu 出路
Chun Mu 春木
Citefusike 刺特甫司克
Dagongbao 大公報
daguanjian 大關鍵
Dali 大理
dashi 大師
Datong 大同
Daxue 大學
Dai Zhen 戴震
dandaozhiru 單刀直入
danghua 黨化
dangjun 黨軍
Dangshi yanjiuhui 黨史研究會
Dangyi xuexiao 黨義學校
daoshi 導師
daotai 道台
degao wangzhong 德高望重
dexing 德性
Deng Xiaoping 鄧小平
diguozhuyi 帝國主義
disan shili 第三勢力
Ding Wenjiang 丁文江
Dongbei jun 東北軍
Dongfang jiefang hui 東方解放會
Dongfang zazhi 東方雜誌
dongYa zhurenweng 東亞主人翁

dujing 讀經
dujun 督軍
Duli pinglun 獨立評論
duliang 度量
Du Yuesheng 杜月笙
Duan Qirui 段祺瑞
Duiwai maoyi ju 對外貿易局
Eguo zhenxiang 俄國眞相
er you heyu jinshi minguo liguo zhi dayi 而有合於近世民族立國之大義
fandong 反動
fandongpai renwu 反動派人物
fangeming 反革命
Feng Jinbai 馮今白
fengshui 風水
Feng Youlan 馮友蘭
Feng Yuxiang 馮御香
fucong 服從
fugu 復古
fuli 富力
Fuxing shuyuan 復性書院
fuzongcai 副總裁
gailiangzhuyi 改良主義
Gan Jiehou 甘介侯
gaoshi 高師
gezhi chengzheng 格致誠正
genben dafa 根本大法
Gongchan yanjiuyuan 共產研究院
gongren huiyi 工人會議
Gu Mengyu 顧孟餘
Gu Yanwu 顧炎武
guandu shangban 官督商辦
guanshang hegu 官商合股
guanxi 關係
Guang fangyan guan 廣方言館
Guangming bao 光明報
Guang Xu 光緒
Guofang canyi hui 國防參議會
guojia jihua 國家計劃
guojia minzu 國家民族
Guojia shehui bao 國家社會報
Guojia shehuizhuyi 國家社會主義
Guojiazhuyi pai 國家主義派
guojia zibenzhuyi 國家資本主義
guojia zuzhi 國家組織
Guoli zhengzhi daxue 國立政治大學
Guoli zizhi xueyuan 國立自治學院
Guomin jun 國民軍
Guomin ribao 國民日報
Guomin shengji huiyi 國民生計會議
guopo jiawang 國破家亡
guoti 國體
Guo xian yi 國憲議
Han Guojun 韓國鈞
Hang Liwu 杭立武
Han Wudi 漢武帝
heyu renxing 合於人性
hezhong gongji 和衷共濟
heian shidai 黑暗時代
Hou Xuefang 侯雪舫
Huguang 湖廣
Hu Hanmin 胡漢民
Hu Shi 胡適
Hu Shiqing 胡石青
Huaxing hui 華興會
Huang Bocheng 黃伯誠
Huang Fu 黃郛
Huang Shaohong 黃紹竑
Huang Xing 黃興
Huang Zongxi 黃宗羲
ji 集
jisi guangyi tuanjie liliang 集思廣益團結力量
jituan jilu 集團紀律
Jixieguan zhi shizailun 機械觀之實在論
jianku 堅苦
Jiangnan gaodeng xuexiao 江南高等學校
Jinan 濟南
Jiyutō 自由黨

Jiading xian 嘉定縣
Jiang Baili 蔣百里
Jiang Tingfu 蔣廷黻
Jiang Yong 江庸
Jiang Yuntian 蔣勻田
jiaorang 交讓
jiaota shidi 腳踏實地
Jiaozhou Bay 膠洲灣
Jiefang yu gaizao 解放與改造
jin 斤
Jinbu dang 進步黨
Jing'ansi 靜安寺
jingxue 經學
jingying gongchang fa 經營工廠法
jinshi 進士
Jinsilu 近思錄
jiushi minzhu 舊式民主
juren 舉人
Junshi zu 軍事組
junzi 君子
junzi anran er rizhang zhi li 君子暗然而日彰之理
Kaishintō 改進黨
Kang Youwei 康有爲
Kangzhan daodi 抗戰到底
kanji 漢字
Keluomina 克羅米那
Kong Xiangxi 孔祥熙
Koo, Wellington V. K. 顧維鈞
kouhan tianxian 口含天憲
laocheng zhi lie 老成之列
Laodong yuan 勞動院
laoye 老爺
Lei Binnan 雷賓南
li 里
Li Daming 李大明
Li Dazhao 李大釗
liguo 立國
Liguo zhi dao 立國之道
Li Hongzhang 李鴻章
Li Huang 李璜
Lixing she 力行社
Li Yuanhong 黎元洪
Li Zhai 立齋
Li Zhizao 李之藻
Lizhou 澧州
Li Zongren 李宗仁
lianbangguo 聯邦國
LianE rongGong 聯俄容共
Liang Qichao 梁啓超
Liang Shiqiu 梁實秋
Liang Shuming 梁漱溟
Liaodong 遼東
lingxiu 領袖
Liu Jingren 劉鏡人
Liu yi 六藝
Longhua 龍華
Long Yun 龍雲
Lu Dingkui 陸鼎揆
Lu Xiangshan 陸象山
Lu Xiufu 陸秀夫
luxing guomin yiwu 履行國民義務
Lu Zuofu 盧作孚
Luo Fu 洛甫
Luo Jialun 羅家倫
Luo Longji 羅隆基
Luo Wengan 羅文幹
Ma Fu 馬浮
Ma Liang (Xiangbo) 馬良（相伯）
Mao Zedong 毛澤東
Mianren shuyuan 勉仁書院
Minbao 民報
minyi 民意
minzhu dangpai 民主黨派
Minzu wenhua shuyuan 民族文化書院
minzu zhongxin sixiang 民族中心思想
Mingde she 明德社
Mingde xuetang 明德學堂
Ming li tan 名理探
Ming Taizu 明太祖
Mo Dehui 莫德惠
Mou Zongsan 牟宗三
mu 畝

neiyou waihuan 内憂外患
Niu Yongjian 鈕永建
nuoruo nongmin yu wuzhi zhi qingnian 懦弱農民與無智之青年
Okuma Shigenobu 大限重信
Pan Guangda 潘光旦
peiyu renge 培育人格
pinxing 品行
Prince Su (Shanqi) 肅親王（善耆）
qianggan chu zhengquan 鎗杆出政權
Qiangxue hui 強學會
Qin Dechun 秦德純
Qin Shihuang 秦始皇
Qing 清
Qingbang 青幫
qinggan 情感
qing quanxian ming zeren 清權限明責任
qiu weimiao weixiao yu yewu 求惟妙惟肖於野鶩
Qu Qiubai 瞿秋白
Qu Shiying 瞿世英
quanli 權力
renge jiaoyu 人格教育
Rengong 任公
renqing wuli zhi chang 人情物理之常
Ren Zhuoxuan 任卓宣
rongGong 容共
Ruan Yuan 阮元
Shao Lizi 邵力子
Shehui suoyou weiyuanhui 社會所有委員會
sheji jiaofa 設計教法
she jiaji qiu yewu 舍家雞求野鶩
Shenbao 申報
Shen Junru 沈鈞儒
shenyi 審議
shengyu guangxun 聖諭廣訓
shengyuan 生員
shi 史
shidaifu 士大夫
Shijie shi zhuren 世界室主人
Shi Liangcai 史量才
Shishi xinbao 時事新報
Shitailin mingyixia zhi dongfang daxue 史泰林名義下之東方大學
Shitailin zhixia zhi SuE 史泰林之下之蘇俄
shiyansuo 試驗所
shi you zhijian 師友之間
Shi Youzhong 施友忠
shuben shenghuo 書本生活
shuyuan 書院
si da zhengce 四大政策
shujishi 庶吉士
Sima Guang 司馬光
Song Jiaoren 宋教仁
Song she 松社
SuE pinglun 蘇俄評論
sui 歲
Sui Yangdi 隋煬帝
Sun Chuanfang 孫傳芳
Sun Fo 孫科
Sun Yatsen 孫逸仙
suweiai 蘇維埃
Tan Yankai 譚延闓
Tang Taizong 唐太宗
Tao Menghe 陶孟和
Tongmeng hui 同盟會
tuibi xianlu 退避賢路
Ukita Kazutami 浮田和民
Wang Fuzhi 王夫之
Wang Jingwei 汪精衛
Wang Ming 王明
Wang Shijie 王世杰
Wang Yangming 王陽明
Wang Youqiao 王幼僑
Waseda University 早稲田大學
wei gongchanzhuyi xianyu gangluozhe 爲共產主義陷於綱羅者

Wei Jingsheng 魏京生
weiyi zhi zhongxin sixiang 惟一之中心思想
wenhua fuxing 文化復興
wenjian 穩健
Wen Tianxiang 文天祥
wenzhang laoshou 文章老手
wobei 我輩
Wu Guang 吳廣
Wu Jingxiong 吳經熊
Wu Leichuan 吳雷川
Wu Luzhen 吳祿貞
Wu Peifu 吳佩孚
wushangdi 無上帝
Wu Tiecheng 吳鐵城
Wu Yifang 吳貽芳
xian 縣
Xianfa yanjiu hui 憲法研究會
Xianzheng dang 憲政黨
Xianzheng xinzhi 憲政新誌
Xiangdao zhoubao 嚮道週報
xiaoju shanlin zhi tufei 嘯聚山林之土匪
xiezuo chengwen 寫作成文
Xinhua ribao 新華日報
Xinhua xinbao 新華新報
xinli 心力
Xinlu 新路
Xinmin congbao 新民叢報
xinshen zhi kezhi 心身之克治
xingzheng dagang 行政大綱
xingzheng gangyao 行政綱要
Xiong Shihui 熊式輝
Xiong Xiling 熊希齡
xiucai 秀才
xiuyang tuanti 修養團體
xiuzheng de minzhu zhengzhi 修正的民主政治
xiuzhengpai 修正派
Xu Fulin 徐傅霖
Xu Junmian (Xu Qin) 徐君勉（徐勤）
Xu Zhimo 徐志摩
Xuantong Emperor 宣統
xuefeng 學風
Xuehai shuyuan 學海書院
Xuehai tang 學海堂
xuetian zhidu 學田制度
xuezhang 學長
Yan Huiqing 顏惠慶
yanmi zhi dang 嚴密之黨
Yan Xishan 嚴錫山
yangcheng fazhi jingshen 養成法治精神
yang Hanlin 洋翰林
Yang Yuzi 楊毓滋
Yanjiu hui 研究會
Ye Qing 葉青
yi 意
yiji 異己
yili zhi xue 義理之學
yiti xuexiao shuo 一體學校說
yizhi 意志
yizhi benfu 一致奔赴
youjiaowulei 有教無類
Yu Songhua 俞頌華
Yuzhou xunkan 宇宙旬刊
yuanzhang 院長
Yuan Shikai 袁世凱
Zaisheng 再生
Zaisheng she 再生社
Zeng Guofan 曾國藩
Zeng Qi 曾琦
Zeng Youhao 曾友豪
Zhang Bojun 章伯鈞
Zhang Daofan 張道藩
Zhang Dongsun 張東蓀
Zhang Fakui 張發奎
Zhang Ji 張繼
Zhang Jiluan 張季鸞
Zhang Jiaao 張嘉敖
Zhang Jiasen 張嘉森
Zhang Jiazhu 張嘉鑄
Zhang Jian 張謇
Zhang Junmai 張君勱
Zhang Qun 張群
Zhang Shilin 張士林

Zhang Taiyan(Binglin) 章太炎（炳麟)
Zhang Wentian 張聞天
Zhang Xueliang 張學良
Zhang Zhiben 張知本
Zhang Zhidong 張之洞
Zhang Zuolin 張作霖
zhezhong 折衷
zhencao 貞操
Zhendan xueyuan 震旦學院
zhengfu pai 政府派
Zhenglun 政論
Zhengwen she 政聞社
Zhengwu te weihui 政務特委會
zheng xianyu yizhong wenzibing 正陷於一種文字病
zhi 知
zhigui 指歸
Zhili Clique 直隸派
zhiqi shuangzhi 稚氣爽直
zhiren siming 制人死命
zhishi 智識
zhishi laodongzhe 智識勞動者
Zhixing Institute 知行學院
Zhongguo guojia shehui dang 中國國家社會黨
Zhongguo minzhu shehui dang 中國民主社會黨
Zhongguo minzhu zhengtuan datongmeng 中國民主政團大同盟
Zhongguo qingnian dang 中國青年黨
Zhongguo zhi jiating yu nongcun 中國之家庭與農村
Zhongguo ziyou minzhu zhandou tongmeng 中國自由民主戰鬥同盟
Zhongshan 中山
Zhongxue wei ti Xixue wei yong 中學爲体西學爲用
Zhongyang ribao 中央日報
Zhongyang xingzheng yuan 中央行政院
zhongyong 中庸
zhongyong zhi dao 中庸之道
zhou 州
Zhou Enlai 周恩來
Zhou Zhongyue 周鍾嶽
Zhu Jiahua 朱家華
zhunao 主腦
Zhu Qinglai 諸青來
Zhu Xi 朱熹
zhuyi 主義
zhuanzheng adou 專政阿斗
zidong jingshen 自動精神
zixue 子學
ziyou 自由
Ziyou zhong 自由鍾
Ziyiju shiwu diaocha hui 諮議局事務調查會
zongmishu 總秘書
Zou Lu 鄒魯
zun Kong 尊孔
zuoren 做人
Zuo Shunsheng 左舜生

Index

About the Author

Roger B. Jeans, Elizabeth Lewis Otey Professor of East Asian History, has taught at Washington and Lee University in Lexington, Virginia, since 1974. He is editor of *Roads Not Taken: The Struggle of Opposition Parties in Twentieth-Century China* (Westview Press, 1992), coeditor of *Goodby to Old Peking: The Wartime Letters of U.S. Marine Captain John Seymour Letcher, 1937-1939* (Ohio University Press, forthcoming), and author of numerous articles and conference papers on Zhang Junmai and his political parties.

Jeans received his Ph.D. in modern Chinese history from George Washington University. He has studied, researched, and traveled in East Asia. In the early 1970s, he attended the Inter-University Program for Chinese Language Studies in Taiwan, and in the early 1980s he carried out research in the PRC. He has been a visiting research scholar at the University of Washington and University College and the Institute for Chinese Studies at the University of Oxford.

He has served as chairman of Washington and Lee's East Asian Studies Program, editor of *Republican China*, president of the Southeast Conference of the Association of Asian Studies (AAS), and chairman of the AAS's Council of Conferences.